Husband. Fat...

Praise for Ilario Pantano's

WARLORD

"Now and then from the battlefront come tales which . . . see through the pall of smoke to provide insights which count in the strategic view. . . . *Warlord* is such a dispatch. . . . Unvarnished and personal. . . . A human drama, gritty and often self-effacing."

—Defense & Foreign Affairs Strategic Policy

"Inspiring. . . . A great story."

—The Washington Times

"In the search for a window into what daily life is like for our troops in Iraq, *Warlord* provides one Marine's very vivid account."

—The Weekly Standard

"Demonstrate to the world there is 'No Better Friend, No Worse Enemy' than a U.S. Marine."

—J.N. Mattis, Major General, U.S. Marines
Commanding General's Message to All Hands, March 2003

Warlord is also available as an eBook

WARLORD

No Better Friend, No Worse Enemy

By Ilario Pantano

With Malcolm McConnell

THRESHOLD
EDITIONS

New York   London   Toronto   Sydney

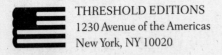

THRESHOLD EDITIONS
1230 Avenue of the Americas
New York, NY 10020

ISBN-13: 978-1-4165-2427-4
ISBN-10:   1-4165-2427-4

This Threshold Editions trade paperback edition May 2007

10   9   8   7   6   5   4   3   2   1

THRESHOLD EDITIONS and colophon are trademarks of
Simon & Schuster, Inc.

Manufactured in the United States of America

For information regarding special discounts for bulk purchases,
please contact Simon & Schuster Special Sales at 1-800-456-6798
or business@simonandschuster.com.

Let us raise a glass,
To us and those like us.
There aren't many,
And the good ones are dead.

Corporal Michael Speer	Killed in Action April 9, 2004
Gunnery Sergeant Ronald Baum	Killed in Action May 3, 2004
Lance Corporal Andrew Zabierek	Killed in Action May 21, 2004
Lance Corporal Brian Kelly	Killed in Action July 16, 2004
Lance Corporal Nicholas Morrison	Killed in Action August 11, 2004
Corporal Christopher Belchik	Killed in Action August 22, 2004

* * *

2nd Lieutenant James J. Cathey	Killed in Action August 22, 2005
Private First Class Shane M. Cabino	Killed in Action October 6, 2005
Corporal Nicholas O. Cherava	Killed in Action October 6, 2005
Lance Corporal Jason L. Frye	Killed in Action October 6, 2005
Lance Corporal Patrick B. Kenny	Killed in Action October 6, 2005
Staff Sergeant Richard T. Pummil	Killed in Action October 20, 2005
Lance Corporal Andrew D. Russoli	Killed in Action October 20, 2005
Lance Corporal Steven W. Szwydek	Killed in Action October 20, 2005
Lance Corporal Kenneth J. Butler	Killed in Action October 21, 2005
Corporal Benny G. Cockerham III	Killed in Action October 21, 2005
Hospitalman 3rd Chris "Doc" Thompson	Killed in Action October 21, 2005
Captain Tyler B. Swisher	Killed in Action October 21, 2005
Sergeant Michael P. Hodshire	Killed in Action October 30, 2005
Lance Corporal Nicholas D. Schiavoni	Killed in Action November 15, 2005
Lance Corporal Tyler J. Troyer	Killed in Action November 19, 2005
Sergeant Sean H. Miles	Killed in Action January 24, 2006

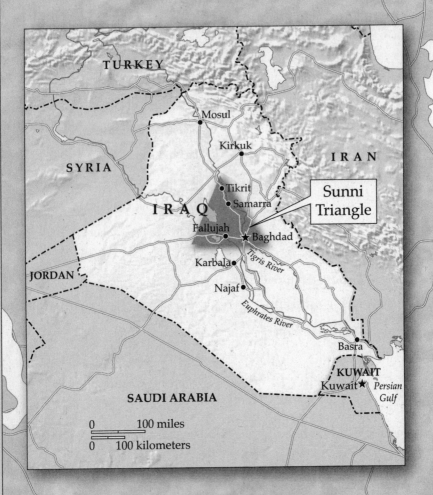

Iraq, 2004

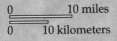

0	10 miles
0	10 kilometers

N
W E
S

TURKEY

SYRIA

△ Mosul

● Kirkuk

● Tikrit
● Samarra

I R A N

IRAQ

● Fallujah

Sunni
Triangle

★ Baghdad

● Karbala

Tigris River

JORDAN

Najaf ●

Euphrates River

Basra ●

KUWAIT
Kuwait ★ *Persian Gulf*

SAUDI ARABIA

0	100 miles
0	100 kilometers

● Ramadi

Lake Habbaniyah

Lake Razzaz

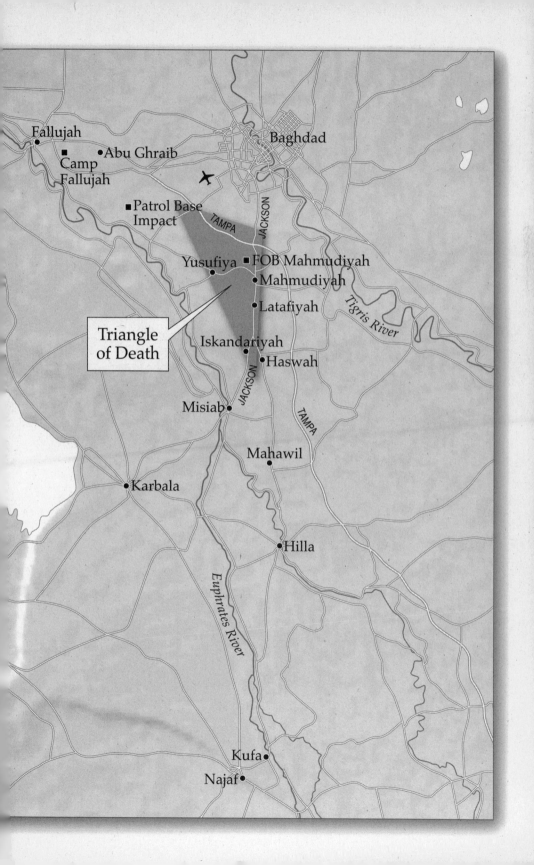

AUTHOR'S NOTE

The dates and times of events occurring in the Area of Operations of 2nd Battalion, 2nd Marine Regiment in 2004 have been verified using that unit's communications and operational logs.

The sworn testimony and other legal exchanges quoted in this book came directly from the hearing transcript: "Verbatim record of a hearing held in accordance with Article 32, Uniform Code of Military Justice, Conducted at Camp Lejeune, North Carolina, on 26 through 30 April 2005."

A glossary of military terms appears on p. 395.

PROLOGUE

Area of Operations: Warlord

**38S MB 394 663 Military Grid Reference System
(33° 08' N. Lat. 44° 21' E. Lon.)
15 April 2004, 1703 Hours**

"*Kuff!* Stop!"

Can the others see this? Ten meters down the broken gravel road in each direction, Doc Gobles and Coburn are guarding a narrow defensive perimeter.

A beat of time . . . one second, half that . . . a microsecond. Freezing hot adrenaline. A rifle is firing.

The butt of the M-16 is snugged against a shoulder stiffened by dried sweat and fear. The salt stains on the flak jacket trace a history like the tree rings of war. A new ring is forming.

The selector switch is on burst. Each press of the trigger sends three metal-jacketed 5.56 mm bullets slashing into flesh. They are close. Real close. The bullets go right through the men into the car, into the trees. Into Iraq.

More a continuous blast than a drumbeat as the rifle pounds. A shower of brass shell casings glints in the fading daylight.

The butt thuds, hollow now against the stained flak jacket. Empty mag.

Fuck.

The index finger, the only bare skin on the gloved right hand, hits the button to drop the empty magazine while the left deftly snatches a new one from a pouch on the web gear. The fresh magazine with twenty-eight more rounds slams home. The bolt releases, driving a round into the chamber. More three-round bursts.

Seconds later, the weapon is empty, quickly reloaded, and the muzzle begins to sweep for new threats. The men are twisted, their bodies finally still. Blood from their wounds smears down the car's white doors and soaks into the dry mud.

Mosquitoes whine. Dogs bark. An Apache attack helo banks over Main Supply Route Tampa, baiting someone to challenge it, but no one does. America owns the skies. The challenge comes on the shitty little roads to nowhere that only a few will ever remember. Off to the left, the faint tap and crack of a firefight: M-16s and AK-47s. The white noise of Iraq.

A radio squawks, static, words and numbers . . . another IED on Tampa. Another bomb. How many today?

"Doc. Coburn. Mount up. IED."

As the squads re-form and climb onto the seven-ton trucks, night vision goggles are pulled out of pouches and mounted to helmets. Beside the stinking irrigation canal, the brush and reeds are dense. A good ambush site is getting better as the sun sets. Overhead, the cloudless spring sky retains light. But down here, darkness does not fall. It *rises*.

The trucks jolt into the swelling night. The world has shrunk to the shimmering green circle of NVGs.

And we have another job to do.

ONE

Article 32 Hearing
CLOSING ARGUMENTS

Camp Lejeune, North Carolina
30 April 2005

"Premeditated murder."

Major Stephen Keane, the lead government prosecutor, was using his most persuasive courtroom voice. Even though this was the fifth and final day of the Article 32 hearing—the military equivalent of a grand jury—Keane might have been pressing his case to a general court-martial's panel of senior officers.

". . . The elements are that these two people are dead," he said, striding between the prosecution's table to the left and the dais in the right corner where the investigating officer, Major Mark Winn, presided. "That the death resulted from Second Lieutenant Pantano shooting them. His own confession and the witness statements established that . . ."

My civilian defense counsel, Charlie Gittins, seated beside me to the left, tensed in his chair, about to rise and object. With close-cropped hair and reading glasses on the tip of his nose, Charlie looked benign, maybe an accountant or a State Farm agent. Big mistake. Charlie was a pit bull, a meat eater. He'd graduated from the U.S. Naval Academy and practiced law as a Marine officer, ultimately becoming a lieutenant colonel in the reserves. And during years in private practice, he had earned a reputation as the most effective defense attorney practicing at the military bar.

Keane was taunting us with the word "confession." In the twelve months since that sunset encounter with the insurgents near Mahmudiyah, I had been debriefed by my intel guys and made one official statement to the executive officer of Regimental Combat Team 1. Sure, I killed people, and I commanded my men to kill even more of them, but I had never *confessed* to any crime.

". . . The killing of these two people by the accused was unlawful." Keane let his words register. There was a closed-circuit television camera mounted in the right rear corner of the courtroom, feeding the proceedings to the press in another building. ". . . At the time and place of the killing the accused had a premeditated design to kill these people . . ."

Now Charlie did rise to object. But Major Winn overruled him, noting he would not permit objections to the closing arguments, whether the government's or ours.

Keane rocked confidently on the soles of his tan boots. He was lanky in pressed cammies, seemingly a combat-hardened Marine. But he had no combat experience. None. Still, he was dangerous. His mission was to see me executed or sitting in federal prison for the rest of my life.

In combat you learn to focus intently on the noises and movements that could kill or wound you or your men. An unnaturally straight line in the sand beside a road that might mark the buried det cord of an IED. Men changing a tire up on an overpass. A freshly cut palm trunk floating down a canal.

You also learn to filter out the nonessential sensory input . . . the stink of a dead donkey covered with flies, the "Mista! Mista!" of ragged kids begging for MRE candy . . . a mortar hitting too far away to be dangerous. That's how you survive war; it's an adaptation a good officer makes to bring his men home alive.

For the five days of the hearing, and even the months leading up to it, I'd been in this type of survival mode. Some days it seemed like I had never come off that patrol. I wondered if I ever would.

Part of my mind scanned the windowless courtroom, the overhead fluorescent tubes so much brighter than that April afternoon south of Baghdad. My eye glided once more across my defense table. Charlie was still hunched, ready to object if Keane pressed his luck, despite Major Winn's admonition. To my right, the Marine Corps defense counsel, Major Phil Stackhouse, listened intently to his opponent's argument, jotting an occasional note on a legal pad. His short white hair marked him as the cool water balancing Charlie's molten heat. Farther right, Captains Courtney Trombly and Brandon Bolling filled out my defense team.

But they were not my only support. My wife, Jill, and my mother, Merry, sat in the gallery just behind me. Mike Gregorio, a Marine Vietnam vet and commander of American Legion Post 10 in nearby Wilmington, was with them.

". . . It is patently obvious," Keane continued, "that he intended to kill these two Iraqis . . ."

I looked back at Jill's and my mother's faces. A mix of anger and sadness. Jill was a classic, dark-eyed beauty, a former international model and executive, now the mother of our two small children. Merry, like Jill, was dark-haired, with deep, intense eyes and a widow's peak just like mine. She glared at Keane in contempt.

Overhead, a fluorescent tube was flickering with a dry buzz. This courtroom was part of an H-shaped redbrick block that dated back to World War II. The carpet was fraying, lowest-bidder industrial gray. The jury box and witness stand, both empty now, were the same municipal blond wood.

Keane was moving toward the core of his argument. ". . . He knew he would shoot them prior to taking them back to the car. The searching of this vehicle was a subterfuge. . . . You don't use two Iraqis to search at the same time. We all know that is wrong. We all know that is ridiculous. . . . *This* lieutenant would never make such a mistake."

This lieutenant.

Keane was trying to use a classic martial arts strategy to turn my strengths, the unique circumstances of my background, against me. *This* lieutenant wanted to smash his fucking skull.

Jill's face was clenched in a scowl as Keane focused his attack on me as an officer, a Marine, a person.

I understood her anguish. In fact, I felt responsible for it. Sitting on the candlelit deck of our apartment on West Forty-third Street in the summer of 2001, drinking Sauvignon Blanc and planning our October wedding, there was no way we could have foreseen the events that had led us to this courtroom.

But in retrospect, the trail was brutally direct.

The downtown N train was slow that Tuesday morning. I was going to be late for my nine o'clock meeting. I hated being late; it was a sign of poor discipline, of disrespect. As the subway crawled through the tunnel south of Penn Station, stopping, only to jerk ahead and then stop again, I gnawed on my impatience.

The meeting with our boutique publicist on Twenty-eighth Street was important to Filter Media, the consulting company I had launched a year earlier with several partners. J.R., an old friend and my chief operating officer, was to meet me there so we could plan publicity around a series of conferences that Filter would be rolling out that fall. As an Interactive Television (iTV) think tank, we helped to formulate strategies for cable companies, major brands, and their advertising agencies. After a year of hustling and scrapping, as the rest of the dot-com economy seemed to implode all around us, we had built our brand as subject matter experts and the market was coming our way.

The train's brakes squeaked, and the lights blinked once. The sweep of the minute hand on my Rolex dive watch revealed 0903. The black face and dial worked with a tuxedo, but the watch was rugged enough to meet military specs.

Not that anybody in the crowded car would mistake me for a soldier. Certainly not a Marine. My curly hair spilled down to the collar of my pewter Armani shirt. The khakis were creaseless, but the buckles on my suede Gucci loafers gleamed, an old habit. Instead of a briefcase, I carried a trendy nylon messenger's bag with a rubber rain flap. They'd started calling people that looked like me metrosexuals. That was cool. I kind of liked a game of wolf in sheep's clothing. No one saw the anchor-globe-and-eagle U.S. Marine Corps tattoo on my chest just below my "meat tag." Or the words "Semper Fidelis."

The train lurched ahead. 0905. I was halfway out the door, flipping open my cell phone as we pulled into the Twenty-eighth Street station. I took the stairs three at a time and was almost across Fifth Avenue before I noticed that the traffic was stalled in all directions. Hitting the redial button, I got another busy signal at the publicist. Couldn't these cell phone companies even keep their comm channels open? We were paying them enough.

Sirens, lots of sirens. Had to be a big fire somewhere. Manhattan. Sirens day and night. I'd been born and raised here. I jabbed the redial again. Still busy. Now I was really pissed off. I had business . . . this little start-up is gonna die on the vine if we don't close a deal.

But something weird was happening. A car stopped along Twenty-eighth Street had all four doors open and people were grouped around, listening to the driver's radio.

"Another plane just hit the World Trade Center." The voice sounded like Howard Stern. Even *he* wouldn't try a sick joke like that. What was this, some kind of H. G. Wells *War of the Worlds* hoax?

For the first time, I looked down Fifth Avenue and saw the smoke, gray and black in the bright September morning. We were about two miles from the Twin Towers, but even at this distance I could see the glitter of shredded insulation—or maybe paper—floating in the sunlight. Tinsel. From the planes? From the towers?

Down the block, J.R. and the middle-aged publicist were jogging toward me. Their faces were tight with fear and outrage. We met on the sidewalk, more a collision than a business encounter. The crowd flowed onto Fifth Avenue, and we stood with thousands of others, staring south at the smoke and floating debris engulfing the two towers.

I spoke. J.R. replied. The publicist managed a brittle sentence. None of our words stayed in my memory.

A woman beside me in the intersection kept asking, "What happened? Oh, my god! What's happening?" She repeated her question louder and shriller five times. Ten.

Finally I turned. "They have attacked our country. They've killed our people. We're at war."

I spoke again to J.R. and the publicist. But again the words had no impact. The phrase *We're at war* bounced silently in my mind. It had been almost eleven years since I had fought as a young Marine grunt in Kuwait during Desert Storm. That war had been short, but brutal. The flaming oil wells, the charred Iraqi armor with the stench of burnt flesh. Four days and it was over.

This war, I realized, would last much longer.

My cell phone rang. "Honey," Jill said, her voice tight. "You have to come home right away."

I had been walking north with the crowds for twenty minutes. "No, Jill," I said. "There's something I have to do."

"Ilario," she said, the strain breaking through now. "They just hit the Pentagon."

"Goddammit!" I was venting at the only place I could. "Who the hell . . ."

Before we met in 1999, Jill had never known anyone who'd served in the military. I'd had to patiently explain that the Marines were in fact a separate, elite corps of warriors. Now she would know war. The crowds streamed north, thickening as people poured out of each crosstown street onto the wider avenues. A gasp swept over the thousands of New Yorkers around me in the street. Far to the south, the first of the World Trade Center towers had collapsed. The pillar of gray-black smoke and ash was massive, a man-made volcano.

I worked through the packed streets toward the West Side and turned into a familiar doorway on Ninth Avenue. It had been over a year since I'd been to this barbershop. The Hungarian woman cutting hair this morning stood rooted before the television set, flipping back and forth from Peter Jennings to Tom Brokaw—trying to make sense of this nightmare.

I sat in the chair and used my hand to show her what I wanted. "The sides right down to the skin. Leave just a little piece of hair on top. But short, really short."

She looked at me doubtfully, but took the electric clipper and did as I asked. *High and tight.* As the hair fell, the years peeled back. I was no longer an aspiring metrosexual master of the universe. I was once more what I had always been, a Marine.

I was leaving the barbershop when Peter Jennings announced that a United Airlines jet had crashed in Pennsylvania, undoubtedly the fourth hijacking of the morning.

Jill opened the dead bolt on the door after my first ring. She saw my hair and instantly realized what was happening. "You can't go," she gasped, then hugged me close and spoke in a softer tone. "Ilario, don't go. You don't *have* to."

That was obvious. I had already served my country in war. I was now thirty, and the Corps might not even want me back. But they'd spent a lot of time and money training me as a Scout Sniper after Desert Storm. If America was going to go after the people who'd hit us—and I knew we would this time—trained snipers would be valuable assets. And I was in better shape now, both mentally and physically, than I'd been when the DIs had shouted the teenage recruits off the bus at Parris Island in August 1989. In 2001, I regularly raced in biathlons and had run the New York and Marine Corps marathons four times, but I was experienced enough to know bullets, land mines, and shrapnel could kill even the fittest swinging dicks. It wasn't about fitness, it was about toughness. Mental toughness. In war, it is about "who has the biggest teeth."

The TV was showing endless tape loops of the North Tower collapsing. The smoke pillar was twice as thick, drifting up the Hudson.

"Jill," I reasoned, "our country's under attack. For Christ's sake! We're at war whether we want it or not."

"But . . ."

"We've got to go downstairs. I need your help, Jill." There'd be plenty of time to talk later. Now there were practical considerations. If terrorists poisoned the water supply, the city would die. We had to prepare.

But before leaving the apartment, I called my mother at her apartment on the East Side near the U.N. "I'll come and get you."

"No," she said. "Stay with Jill. I'm okay here. Ilario, I can hear the jets, Air Force fighters. I saw one."

F-15s were circling Manhattan, ready to shoot down any hijacked airliners. This was surreal.

Back down on the street, Jill and I trotted past the firehouse toward the corner deli. I slowed, and then stopped. The cars of the Rescue 1 firefighters were parked at odd angles, some with their front wheels up on the sidewalk where the guys had abandoned them, hurrying to join their crews that morning. Three of the vehicles had the red-and-gold decal of Marine Corps veterans. I recognized the car of Ken Marino. He had a wife and two young daughters. Marines go toward the sound of the guns.

A TV in the deli blared out news updates. ". . . As many as ten thousand dead. . . ."

The doors of the Rescue 1 truck bay were open. NYFD radio channels squawked unanswered inside, the noise more chaotic than any comm traffic I'd ever heard on a combat net. I realized the guys from Rescue 1 were gone, swallowed by that volcano.

Jill and I lugged as many plastic bottles of water and cans of food as we could carry back to the apartment.

While she was stacking them in the kitchen, I turned to leave.

"Ilario, where the hell are you going?" Her face was pale, frightened.

"To the storage locker," I explained. "I need my gear."

"*What* gear?"

"My cammies, my ammo pouches . . . my war gear."

Jill frowned, not fully understanding. I was speaking a foreign language. All that equipment was from another life.

Jill had graduated from New York's High School of Music and Art and had quickly been discovered by Robert Mapplethorpe, the master of edgy black-and-white photography. After posing for him in studio work and magazine shoots, she had spent much of the next seven years modeling in Tokyo, Paris, and Milan. Then Jill had gone into furniture and home design, becoming a vice president for merchandising at an exclusive Manhattan retailer. When we'd met two years earlier at a "Spin" exercise class, she saw a recently divorced guy approaching thirty who had an ambitious plan to get rich with a new-media start-up. She'd found my background unusual and attractive: Growing up in a rough Manhattan neighborhood, a scholarship to a fancy prep school, and military service—all of which gave a tough edge to my artsy appeal.

I could mingle with socialites at gallery openings, hair down to my shoulders, sipping a cosmo from a frosted glass, and appear perfectly in place. But if I described my four years of service as a Marine enlisted man, these people seemed confused. *They* didn't know any Marines. Going to NYU and then becoming a commodity trader at an investment bank like Goldman Sachs was the more traditional and highly coveted New York trajectory for a young guy on the move. I had done that too, but then chose to give up my seat at the last freestanding investment bank on Wall Street to jump into media. Launching my own business showed a cowboy streak, and it made for great conversations at smoky parties.

That was who I'd been when we'd met. Up until 9:05 this Tuesday morning, when I looked down Fifth Avenue at the rising smoke, that was who I was. Now the world had changed. I was different. I was a Marine again.

"The country's going to need people like me, Jill. I've got to be ready to go."

"Go where? What about your family?"

"This *is* for my family!"

She turned away, eyes glistening in a mix of fear, sadness, and anger.

I'd have time to explain it all later. Now I had to prep for combat.

Camp Lejeune
30 April 2005

Major Keane was summarizing his arguments well. He was a skilled prosecutor. But we hoped he wasn't as skillful as he himself seemed to believe.

". . . The way many people feel about this case is understandable. No American would like to believe that a Marine officer could execute two prisoners or detainees. Some people may say, 'So what if he did? They were probably bad guys anyway.' "

Keane let those harsh words resonate before continuing.

". . . That is not how the Marine Corps does or should operate. We do not look the other way at law of war violations . . ."

Law of war. What about the law of bring-your-guys-home-so-you-don't-write-letters-to-their-grieving-moms? I kept my face blank. I understood both the law of war and war itself. I also understood that if I had ended up dead on that gravel road there would have been no trial. There would have been a lot of Marines standing around talking about that stupid fucking dead lieutenant. But no trial. If one of my men had ended up dead there would have been no trial. That was the cost of doing business. There are losses that we can accept and there are the ones that we can't. Well, that's not good enough for me.

". . . Remember," Major Keane went on, "it does not matter one bit if they were or were not insurgents. Under the law of war, they are protected as detainees."

Keane was pacing again, but careful not to turn his back to Major Winn.

"The Marine Corps operates within the bounds of the law of war," he emphasized. Then he turned and stared at me. "On April 15th the accused did not. The question now is: What should be done?"

TWO

Article 32 Hearing
DAY ONE

Camp Lejeune
26 April 2005

We had a plan to enter the building. My mother, my wife, and I walked silently past the press gauntlet outside the redbrick Legal Services Support Section, while Charlie Gittins peeled off to take questions at a microphone stand. Reporters shouted from behind the orange barricades as we entered the courthouse for the first time. I tried to keep my back straight and shoulders square. I had seen perp walks on TV, and I knew people around the world were judging me from the way my arms swung or my head tilted. I could sense the anguish of my family as they trailed behind me.

Gittins had worked high-profile cases before and understood the importance of managing the message. Setting the right tone on day one of the hearing was vital. The entire U.S. Marine Corps, hell, the entire DoD, would be watching the coverage, and if we didn't dominate it, the prosecution would.

The charges against me were the most serious to be leveled at a commissioned officer in combat since the My Lai massacre in Vietnam. Two counts of premeditated murder, destruction of civilian property, dereliction of duty, and conduct unbecoming an officer. When the prosecutors wrote up their charge sheets, they spared no opportunity to paint me as a monster. In effect they took their best shot because according to military protocol, they wouldn't be able to tell their story again until the hearing.

When Gittins stopped at the microphones, his manner was calm but resolute. He looked like a sober, competent lawyer: well-cut dark blue suit with muted rep tie and matching blue shirt. The enamel American flag lapel pin was small, understated. His hair was short and his chunky Naval Academy ring meant that even now he was still part of the military mafia.

He briefly discussed our view of the case and concluded, "It was a combat-justified killing."

"Then why do you think the military's pursuing these charges?" a reporter called as Gittins turned to enter the building.

"You'd have to ask the Marine Corps that," he said flatly. Gittins stepped back to the mike, and then faced it again to continue in a more emotional tone. ". . . I think it sends a bad message to the young heroes who are fighting in Iraq right now that they'd have to worry about armchair quarterbacks second-guessing their decisions made in a very dangerous place."

The networks were rolling and ABC's *Nightline* would broadcast a special report on my case that night. By dawn, Charlie's remarks would appear in the *Earlybird,* the Pentagon's morning news summary, and it wouldn't be the first time news of my case reached the E-Ring. The commandant's office would read the piece; so would the staff of the Joint Chiefs.

There were rumors of Marine snipers on nearby rooftops, and guards patrolled the grounds with rifles and radios. Inside, we had to pass through a metal detector flanked by two Marine MPs before entering the courtroom. I wondered if anyone had bothered to think of the consequences before the government had set this process in motion. The latest death threat came from Muslim extremists on a web site out of Pakistan.

I saw the irony that the institution was trying to protect me even as it tried to destroy me. No, that was too dramatic. They were doing their job, and their job was to protect the Corps at all costs. Somewhere in

D.C., a general was shaking his head in anger and disgust. Somewhere else, in a fighting hole or in the bar at a VFW, Marines were shaking their heads in shock and disbelief—but for different reasons. Ahh, the beloved Corps. Even as I tried to get my head around that, though, I couldn't stop worrying about the threat to my two children while I myself was in a secure courtroom.

Media presence in the room itself was held to a three-person pool with rotating print, television, and radio reporters. There wouldn't have been any press at all had it not been for John Desantis, a local reporter with the *Wilmington Star News.* John had broken the story back in February, and when he discovered the hearing was to be closed, he lobbied his parent company, the *New York Times,* which in turn applied pressure. A closed-circuit TV camera relayed the proceedings to the much larger press contingent in another building.

My family and a few symbolic supporters—including Linda Anderson, the mother of one of my men—sat in the right-hand gallery behind the defense team. Some of my Marines had tried to get in but were turned away at the door. Major Keane and his prosecution team were at a table to our left. The jury box on the far left side of the room was empty except for Major Winn's legal advisor, Colonel David Wunder (a senior JAG officer), and the sketch artist.

Although it was technically a hearing to determine if the prosecution's charges had merit, I was convinced this was just a dress rehearsal for a general court-martial. There was too much institutional investment behind the charges for this not to go all the way.

If Keane did manage to build a persuasive body of evidence against me during the Article 32—including convincing witness testimony and forensic exhibits—his success would start momentum rolling and lay a solid foundation for a conviction at trial. And since the press was following the hearing so closely, Keane also would have gained the psychological edge, making our already difficult job that much harder.

As the saying goes, it was his game to lose. But as I took my seat between Gittins and Stackhouse and waited for the investigating officer, Major Winn, to open the proceedings, the tired metaphor "game" seemed especially trite. This hearing was rooted in a war that was still being fought and the stakes were much bigger than just my fate. Men might live or die half a world away based on what would happen in this room.

Major Winn kicked off the pre-testimony voir dire process by carefully
requesting that the prosecution and defense counsel state their legal
qualifications, attest that they were properly sworn, and note the authority that had "detailed" (assigned) them to this case. In this regard,
an Article 32 hearing differed from civil legal proceedings. Next, the
process would reverse and the attorneys would have the opportunity to
assess the investigating officer to determine his impartiality. It was like
selecting a jury of one. Winn spoke slowly, feeling his way on this unfa-
miliar terrain. He was an infantry officer who had served in combat
twice, first as a young platoon commander in Desert Storm, and later
as a battalion executive officer (XO) in Iraq in 2004 during the second
and decisive fight for Fallujah.

As Major Winn questioned Keane about his prosecution team, the
first dramatic outburst of the hearing erupted. Keane noted that he
himself had detailed his assistant counsels, Captains Lee Kindlon and
John Reh, "to this court-martial."

My throat tightened.

Gittins sprang up. "Objection. It's not a court-martial."

Keane was trying to seize the initiative, hoping to seed the false information with the media reps watching the closed circuit that this
was in fact a formal military trial so that they'd shape their reporting
accordingly. But Gittins parried.

". . . They have been detailed to this *Article 32 hearing* by myself,"
Keane continued, jutting his chin defiantly. Even standing at his table,
Keane had a theatrically aggressive, swaggering appearance. This was
heightened by the green, digital-pattern camouflage utility uniforms
we all wore.

The week before, our defense team had requested that I be allowed to wear "alphas," the Marine Class "A" uniform with dark green
trousers, a belted jacket, and a khaki shirt and tie. Alphas, made so familiar by Jack Nicholson and Oliver North, were much more dignified
than these digital cammies, and had the additional benefit of road-
mapping one's career with colorful ribbons and badges.

Cammies were our real business suit, and I ate, slept, and shit in
them for a good part of my adult life. But the battlefield pedigree
seemed out of place behind the desks surrounded not by sandbags but
by carpet. This was an administrative action thousands of miles re-

moved from the context that was to be scrutinized, and yet seemingly arbitrarily, we were wearing a uniform for killing an enemy in a jungle or training to kill in Lejeune's piney forests.

"Then why not desert cammies?" I had asked my team incredulously. Even the ones that didn't have holes and stains had enough sun fade to make the point that over here was different from over there.

"No. It will be greens," Stackhouse had explained with the strained patience of a twenty-year veteran accustomed to telling clients things they don't want to hear. "Keane doesn't want your fruit salad decorations in front of the cameras. Desert cammies would tie all *this* to reality, to a real shooting war that a lot of people are conflicted about. You need to be removed and painted as a rogue. They are lifting you out of Iraq and dropping you on I-95."

While I was being isolated, Keane was endearing himself. We knew he wouldn't be able to resist, but it still surprised us, when only ten minutes into the initial background screening of Major Winn, Keane let slip that *he* had originally served "as an infantry officer," and had commanded a rifle company earlier in his career.

"He broke out the grunt credentials early," I scrawled on my notepad and slid it to Gittins and Stackhouse. Gittins smiled silently, waiting.

As the initial legal bricklaying proceeded, I thought about uniforms and the warrior's profession, a preoccupation that had dominated so much of my life. And which once again might lead to my death, or worse, my dishonor.

During the weeks before the hearing, I'd often wake before dawn, slip out of bed without disturbing Jill, and go to the kids' room. If my case went to hell and I ended up serving years in the brig, I didn't want to miss a minute with Domenico and Pino, even while they slept. Chests rising and falling. A cough. A cry. I had already missed so much during the long months of training and the long months of war.

I had wanted so desperately to be an example to them. To teach them. To show them. But what would they think of talking to their father through a visitor window? What would the drive home be like? How long before Jill would remarry and I wouldn't even be their dad anymore? What would they remember about that pale man in the orange jumpsuit?

Metropolitan Museum of Art, New York
August 1979

My mother, Merry, was an art student in Italy when she met my father, Benito. They married at the U.N. chapel in New York in 1968. Mom worked in the couture department of Bergdorf Goodman before I was born. Fashion and art were her passions. Soon after my birth she started a handbag company, "WeTwo," with her sister, Lynda. The girls from Salina, Kansas, who grew up riding horses, had great critical success. Their handbags appeared in magazines like *Vogue* and *Elle,* but they were soon put out of business by department store knockoffs. Using her bilingual skill, Mom then took a job as an office assistant for an Italian engineering company and eventually built a career as a marketing manager.

My father was twenty-nine when he and my mother came to New York. In Italy he had been a soldier, a rail engineer, and a writer, but his options narrowed when he arrived in Manhattan, speaking no English. For the first ten years of my life, Papa worked multiple jobs, even as he went to Pace University to learn the language. In the beginning, he stood long minimum-wage hours in the assembly line of a Queens comb factory. Once, picking up an extra night shift as a clerk in a liquor store, he was robbed at gunpoint. That was New York in the seventies, but he never complained.

When I was a boy, my favorite place to visit was the Metropolitan Museum of Art. This Saturday morning, it was Papa's turn to take me.

I held his hand as we crossed Fifth Avenue. He was a *Milanese* (via Calabria), and thought poorly of his only child dashing wildly ahead in an undignified way, no matter how eager I was to pound up the wide steps and enter the Hall of Arms and Armor. I stepped off the curb as the yellow "Walk" sign flashed a warning. Papa tugged my hand. "Ilario . . ."

Even at age eight I realized that Italian was as much a language of gestures and facial expressions, separated by subtle head tilting and random words like *"bene,"* as it was made up of precise vocabulary. I never really learned to speak Italian, although I could understand it, but more importantly I could understand *my* father. I felt like I could read his mind. "Ilario . . ." Papa commanded, his voice rising slightly as he scanned the lanes of cars revving to jump the light. In his belted

raincoat and trademark Ray-Ban aviator's glasses he looked imperi-
ously European.

"I know, Papa, 'Wait for the light.' "

"*Bravo.*"

I begged my parents to take me to the museum's Hall of Arms and
Armor so many times that they joked it was the only place I ever
wanted to go.

That wasn't quite true. I liked it when Mom and I went to
Jan's Hobby Shop up in the Eighties on York Avenue or to the model
store down on Mott Street, next to my elementary school in China-
town. She would help me pick out paints and brushes and we would
work quietly together, I on a plastic kit and she on a carved piece of
jewelry. We listened to Johnny Cash records while I built F-4 Phantom
jets, Spitfires, and Panzer Mark IVs. She'd help me wrap cardboard
swords with tinfoil and we would sketch pictures of knights from my
books.

But when it came to arms and armor, I didn't have to make do with
models. The museum had a huge collection of the real thing. On this
August Saturday, I stopped just inside the entrance of the central hall,
the best place to feel the magic. The main display of this hall held
three pairs of mounted, fully armored knights—visors closed for
battle—on equally well-armored horses. The knights had long lances
pointing straight up, butts braced at the right stirrup. Plumes of colorful feathers adorned some helmets. Others had horns.

In display cases around the sides of the hall, polished suits of
chain mail and plate stood on pedestals. Nearby rooms held case after
case of swords, daggers, and crossbows. Most were etched and gilded,
inscribed in curving letters that Papa tried to translate. But to me the
words were perfectly clear. Noblemen, "*nobile,*" wore this armor and
fought with these weapons.

To a boy of eight, the concept of centuries past was difficult. All I
really knew was that good and brave men had pulled on these actual
breastplates and helmets and defended their castles beneath the colorful banners hanging from the ceiling.

My father was always patient with me during these Saturday pilgrimages. Sharing the quiet aura of idealized European culture with
his son was a gift to a man denied youth by an aching, empty belly.

Benito almost starved to death as a child during World War II. His
family had huddled in their shell-blasted houses in Calabria, existing

on a few olives and crusts of bread smeared with grease from the British soldiers' Bully Beef tins they'd retrieved from garbage dumps.

Somehow, Papa had found the strength each day to jump up and hang from the branch of an old olive tree, hoping to stretch his stunted body. He didn't grow on the outside, but inside he became strong.

On our soccer trips to Central Park, he'd join pickup games, often with younger South Americans showing off for their girlfriends. Some of them were real bulls with wide shoulders and thick necks. But my father had almost been selected by a professional Italian team as a teenager in Milan. He had legs like chiseled stone and could dribble and pass the ball in a dazzling blur that left the hefty Colombians and Argentineans sprawled panting on the grass. We would walk home as the sun was setting. With a cigarette dangling from his lips, he'd tell me stories about my family in Italy. I was the last Pantano male in our family, and here I was in America. I needed to know.

When I was four, my parents moved from a small flat off Ninth Avenue to an apartment on the thirty-sixth floor of a subsidized housing project on Eleventh Avenue, in the heart of old Hell's Kitchen. This was a tough neighborhood under the control of the Westies, a brutal Irish-American gang that Rudy Giuliani once called "the most savage organization in the long history of New York City gangs."

The Westies bragged about their don't-give-a-shit killers who included lots of cokeheads and drunks. Most mornings there'd be little plastic crack vials with red and yellow caps strewn beside piles of cigarette butts among the slides and swings of the building's playground. One of the toughest Westie shot-callers, Jimmy McElroy, lived in our building, as did lots of low-level soldiers. Sometimes my mom and I would get stuck in the elevator with these pillars of the community, smelling their stale booze stink, seeing their jumpy coke eyes. I felt defenseless to protect my mother, but knew I would die trying.

Mom was a beautiful woman who wore her long hair piled on top of her head in a bun, which accentuated her slender, graceful neck. They'd openly look her up and down, but never made comments. Maybe they knew we were different. Maybe they thought my dad was connected because of his heavy accent, sharp dress, and the terrible scar on his forehead. Nobody except Mom and I knew this came from crashing down a stone staircase as a kid, running away from his cousin with a bowl of pilfered cherries.

My father railed at any comparison to "wise guys." He had seen plenty of the real thing up close in the instep of the Italian boot, rocky, inhospitable country, dominated by the *'Ndrangheta,* the local Mafia. He taught me that honor and dignity couldn't be stolen, they had to be earned. Hard work. Minimum-wage work if need be, but not shortcuts. Not *Mafiosi,* regardless of the temptations of power and money. The Pantanos had once known both. They had owned an olive-growing estate in Tripolitania (western Libya), which Mussolini's fascists nationalized in the 1930s. Papa was born in Calabria in 1938 to a family of landowners on the verge of losing it all. Hitler just sped up the process.

My father, like most people who have tasted war, did not want to talk about it. But as I grew older, he realized that my fascination was growing. Maybe it was the territorial violence of my neighborhood. Maybe it was the nobility of the chivalric ideal, the warrior's code. Or the appreciation of a country that had granted my father citizenship in 1976, a year of lofty celebration. Maybe I didn't want to stand by and let happen to my family what had happened to his. Maybe I was just a freak. But from a very young age, I was on a collision course with war.

Benito taught me the reality he had lived as a small boy. He told me stories of hiding beneath his mother with his brother and sisters in a muddy hole beside their ruined house as bombers roared overhead. His agonized memories of crying for his mama when she would leave to search for food. He was sure she would never come back . . . and he is haunted by those memories to this day.

After spring storms, if they were lucky, the village kids would find dead baby octopuses in the surf, turn them inside out, and bring the precious protein home to their mothers. But there were other, less wholesome objects in the surf . . . impossibly huge sea mines, studded with detonator spikes. He and the other boys played with these mines. The prongs of the rusty spheres were tangled with seaweed, like ocean monsters with tousled hair, sleeping on the beach. They slept until his friends climbed over them and hit the steel with rocks to hear the clanging sound.

"Ilario . . . the *mostro marino,* it explodes." He shook his head for a long moment. Then he silently held his thumb and index finger about an inch apart to demonstrate the pieces left of his friends.

He taught me that wearing a uniform wasn't the same thing as having honor. During the Allied invasion of Italy in 1943, some British soldiers passing through my father's village were throwing biscuits to a starving dog. My great-grandfather, Nonno Giuseppe, asked for a biscuit for his grandchild. The soldier threw it in the mud next to Benito's scrambling feet. My great-grandfather yelled, "Don't touch that!" as he grabbed his shotgun off his shoulder to shoot the offender. He was quickly overpowered and beaten by the other soldiers.

"Ilario . . . family. At all costs."

Two summers later, my parents bought me a beautiful black Ross dirt bike with padded handlebars for my tenth birthday. I tied red-and-yellow yarn in a bow to the handgrips, further making it mine. I wheeled it across Eleventh Avenue to ride in Clinton Park. But I made only a couple of laps before three older kids blocked my way.

"Nice bike," one of them said. And that was all the talking.

They circled and they pounced. It was predatory. Very natural, really. I wasn't from their tribe. They started to beat on me when I didn't let go, but they didn't get to finish the job.

My father pounded into the park in his shorts and sandals with black socks, swinging a wooden game bat from Yankee Stadium. He'd seen the whole confrontation from our balcony on the thirty-sixth floor, and had grabbed his friend John along the way. Even with kids, around here you had to watch the odds and the angles. The three punks took off toward the rubble of the half-demolished West Side Highway along the river. From then on, every step out of my house held the possibility of conflict or a rematch.

In seventh grade I was accepted, with a lot of financial aid, at the Horace Mann School, way up in Riverdale—a two-hour round-trip on the subway. But I didn't mind the ride; it transported me to a whole different world than Hell's Kitchen. The shaded, grassy campus was palatial and the walls of the Victorian stone buildings were free of graffiti. The kids were beautiful and rich and smelled good. That one was the son of Rupert Murdoch. This one talking to Lizzie Grubman was a Calvin Klein model.

Hearing about a dozen kids being flown to the Super Bowl for a birthday party made me realize that my parents had opened a doorway to a new life. The classes were small, and we were challenged to think. I studied as much military history as I could and read my way through the school's library shelves, from *The Killer Angels* to Philip Caputo's *A Rumor of War*.

I read Eric Hammel's *The Root,* and I was done.

I knew I had to be a Marine officer. The book covers the Marines' deployment to Beirut ("the Root") from 1982 to 1984. Although the disastrous suicide truck bombing of the Marine barracks is the emotional core of the narrative, there was another story that ignited my imagination. In 1983, as the invading Israeli Defense Forces armor pushed deeper into Beirut's outskirts and threatened to thrust aside the Marines' token perimeter, Captain Chuck Johnson faced down three Israeli Centurion tanks, armed only with his .45 caliber handgun. When the tanks refused an order to turn around and instead began to roll their way into the Marine position, Captain Johnson jumped onto the lead tank and ordered it to turn around or he'd blow the Israeli colonel's head off. For his bravery and audacity, he was lauded by then–Secretary of Defense Caspar Weinberger, for what today would have been considered a court-martial offense. That was the "old Corps," where the buck stopped with the officers of the line. Captain Johnson was the kind of warrior I wanted to be.

But first I had to finish high school. And that education cost my parents dearly. I was too young to realize that my financial aid to Horace Mann was generous, but not a free ride. Mom was still an office worker, and my dad had just started working as a tour guide, showing visiting Italians the sights, sounds, and tastes of New York. We didn't go out much, but on Friday nights we'd order pizza from a joint called Corbo's on Ninth Avenue and Fifty-fourth. After dinner, Papa and I would wrestle on the floor of the living room while we watched TV shows. Friday meant *Miami Vice*. Mom would curl up on the couch behind us reading a book while my dad and I sprawled out on pillows. He would start snoring as it got later, but commercials would signal the end of the cease-fire. Once the melee started, even moms were fair game for tickling.

One afternoon, after buying my books for eighth grade, I was on my way to get a baloney and Muenster cheese sandwich at the corner deli. There were three junior Westies bullshitting on the curbside bench reserved for elderly and disabled. One kid jumped up and rushed me like a maniac, grabbing at my neck.

"Got any gold?" he shouted, his dirty hands searching my throat and collar for chains. I was a deer in the headlights. "Gimme yer gold!" His eyes were like pinballs and he seemed wired.

Before I could react, he was strangling me. I knew what to do, but I was stunned by his sheer audacity. No ritual dance. No posturing. Pure ambush. Why would someone attack me for no reason? I'd fought box cutter–wielding monkeys before, but now I couldn't get past my own shock. Finally, I broke the kid's grip on my throat, flipped him onto his back, and drove my fists into his face, over and over.

Then his two buddies grabbed my neck and shoulders and dragged me to the ground so the first one could kick and smash my gut. Again I broke the grip and ran into the nearby deli. But before I made the door, I was sucker-punched to the side of my head and almost crumpled.

The sound of the fight was like a chow bell ringing. An excited crowd began to gather both inside the deli and out. Taunts and jeers were flying. A minute later, two big women in sooty work clothes came to my rescue. I knew the twin sisters who lived in my building and worked as welders nearby. They formed a human shield with the strength of their arms and shoulders as they hustled me out of the deli and safely into an elevator.

Once I was inside, they returned to the sidewalk. They grabbed the punk who'd attacked me, dragged him into a nearby pizzeria, beat him, and then repeatedly smashed a chair across him, breaking his arm in several places. The message was clear: You fucked with the wrong kid. Our building is *our* turf.

My dad got home just as the sisters returned. "Don't worry, Mr. Pantano. We took care of the problem."

Finally, a little breathing room.

**Camp Lejeune
26 April 2005**

The interrogation roles shifted, and the attorneys began vetting the investigating officer. The prosecution must have liked Major Winn for the job because Major Keane asked him only a few questions.

KEANE: There's been various versions of events presented in the media and this case is widely publicized. Have you seen any of this media coverage?

WINN: No, I have not.

KEANE: Do you agree not to consider anything you may or
may not have heard or seen about this case?

WINN: Yes, I do agree.

KEANE: Do you agree to only consider the evidence presented in this investigation and to completely dis-
regard any outside comments on the evidence?

WINN: Yes, I do.

KEANE: No further questions.

I turned a Diet Coke can in my hand and wondered why that had
been so brief. The prosecution wanted him, so by deduction, the defense, my defense, did not.

WINN: Mr. Gittins?

GITTINS: Actually, it's Captain Bolling who is going to conduct the voir dire, sir.

Exhale. I knew that. I knew that Gittins and Stackhouse couldn't
do it all, but it still pained me that our first round was going to be conducted by our most junior attorney. These were deep waters for someone six years my junior, even if he did outrank me. It was very nice that
Brandon Bolling went to University of Detroit Mercy Law School and
had served stints overseas. I was happy for him and his family, but I
didn't need *very nice*.

Major Keane and the prosecution were throwing a lot of weight
around the room. They had come in with boxes of files, notebooks, and
legal pads. They looked like they literally had all the facts. All of them.
Well, if they did, they weren't sharing.

Captain Bolling went about showing Major Winn that the defense
had made numerous requests for notes, service records of witnesses,
intelligence reports, activity reports, and even the Rules of Engagement that applied at that time in April 2004. Finally, after Captain
Bolling rattled off a list of fourteen pieces of evidence the prosecution
had failed to provide, Major Winn inquired softly:

WINN: Major Keane, have you made everything that
you've got available to—you know—reasonably
available—to the defense?

KEANE: I have, sir.

WINN: Thank you.

What the hell? I felt a sharp jolt of panic. The defense needed Winn to fully meet the responsibilities of his role and be confident enough in his knowledge of the law to stand up to the prosecution. It was a tall order to ask a grunt officer to act like a judge, but that is what the situation required. We had been waiting for some of this evidence since the charges were filed, almost three months before.

BOLLING: Well, sir, I'm going to object to that because that's not the standard. You can go and you can have produced anything that you think is relevant and important . . . It's very easy just to say, "Look, I don't want that right now," and then the trial counsel doesn't have it and then we can't have it, but it doesn't mean that it's not relevant or that it's not important to the determination of this case, and I would think that certainly you can see by the nature of the items I requested, it probably is not an outlandish request to ask for the Rules of Engagement that covered somebody's conduct who's being charged with violating those Rules of Engagement and murdering somebody.

The words "murdering somebody" seemed to hang in the silent courtroom.

Hell's Kitchen, New York
August 1982

My parents' concern that despite my schooling at Horace Mann, I remained stubbornly preoccupied with all things military only worsened in the early 1980s.

One afternoon after school I stood on our balcony looking down the Hudson River and watched straining tugboats push and pull the long gray slab of the decommissioned aircraft carrier USS *Intrepid* up to the old Pier 86 on Twelfth Avenue. Commissioned in 1943, *Intrepid* had fought in bloody Pacific battles in World War II, recovered spacecraft during the Apollo moon landings, and then launched strike planes against North Vietnam. A patriotic entrepreneur named Zachary Fisher had saved the ship from a scrap yard in Asia and intended to turn it into a living memorial and museum, dedicated to the American military and achievements in aviation.

Intrepid needed volunteers to accomplish this dream. I lived less than ten blocks away and was more than ready to help. Somehow, I knew working on the ship would change my life. It did.

I was among the first group of young volunteers. Veterans from World War II, Korea, and Vietnam, both from the original crew and from sister services, mentored me for hundreds of hours as I learned to wield a rust-picking hammer and to paint the corridors and hangar deck. I stooped and sweated in compartments where Japanese kamikazes had killed scores of sailors, first off the Philippines and later near Okinawa.

I was really happy to work alongside the veterans on the *Intrepid*. Many of them proudly wore faded old tattoos, the names of ships . . . and the tattoo I found most intriguing, the anchor-globe-and-eagle of the United States Marine Corps.

When I was fifteen, I joined the Young Marines branch of the Sea Explorer program. A Marine Vietnam vet named Jim ran the unit on the *Intrepid*. His day job was constructing the museum's exhibits. But the Marine Corps remained his true love. Riding in on his Harley with square-toe engineer boots and a red USMC baseball hat, he was the archetype of a Marine.

Kids took the train from all the boroughs to come be a part of the *Intrepid* program. Our first challenge was a weekend "Boot Camp," during which Jim, Anthony, and Rene taught us close-order drill, military customs, and courtesy—"Sir, Yes, Sir!"—and physical fitness. We would stand at attention during uniform inspections and rattle off past victories at strange-sounding places: Belleau Wood, Guadalcanal . . . Tarawa, Okinawa, the "Frozen" Chosin Reservoir in Korea . . .

I learned every verse of the "Marines' Hymn."

"The hymn belongs to *every* individual Marine," Jim taught us. "And those individuals make up the Corps."

Just to make sure we learned quickly, our Young Marine instructors reinforced their lessons with push-ups. We ran along the pier, chanting cadence. Jim yelled at us. We yelled at each other. We learned that there was dignity in polishing a pair of boots well. We found discipline, which for many of the kids was their first taste of it.

Before the Young Marines, my dad and I used to "camp out" on our balcony when the apartment got too hot in the summer. Now I went on actual camping trips to the Adirondacks, where we stayed in lean-tos and learned to eat "survival rations": worms and dandelion greens. We did land navigation with a map and compass and patrolled the woods wearing combat utilities, our faces smeared with camouflage paint. It felt very *Lord of the Flies.*

There had been plenty of girls at Horace Mann that I lusted for, but despite my gifts of flowers or hand-drawn pictures, I got no "satisfaction," as Mick Jagger put it. The whole Marine thing was a little too square for most of the urban hipsters. Then, the summer before my senior year, lightning struck. I was introduced to "Dee" through a friend, and in her urgency to exact revenge on an ex, she decided to use me like a prop for her Mrs. Robinson fantasy. A sixteen-year-old boy doesn't say no to a beautiful twenty-two-year-old. Instead, he says thank you and pinches himself to make sure he isn't dreaming.

She taught me a lifetime of sensual lessons in hotel rooms, at friends' apartments, and in Central Park. One night a bunch of the Young Marine staff headed to the Copacabana, off of Fifth Avenue, in their dress uniforms (Alphas). Dee and I joined them, and I got in for free wearing my cadet uniform. The cigar I was chomping didn't hurt. We drank and danced and grinded the night away.

Caught up as I was with school, the Young Marines, and Dee, I'd been too self-centered to realize that my parents' marriage was in trouble. Or maybe I had noticed subconsciously and that is what drove me to seek the surrogate family of the *Intrepid* and later the warrior tribe of the Corps.

I didn't know all the reasons they got divorced, but I certainly felt a measure of guilt over the cost of my education. I was entering the adult world. And by my senior year at Horace Mann, while other kids were sweating over their college applications, I had already decided that I would enlist in the Marines. My goal, as I proudly declared to my parents, was eventually to become the commandant of the Marine Corps. I would follow in the footsteps of all of the best officers: I would join and then get a university degree after doing time as an enlisted man. Coming up through the ranks as a "mustang" is what Chesty Puller did, and it was what General Alfred Gray, the commandant at the time, and arguably our best ever, had done when he enlisted in 1950. I wanted to see the world as a private. Then, my logic went, I would know what my men had gone through and would be better suited to lead them.

"College," I assured my troubled parents, "isn't off the table, it's just being delayed." So before twelfth grade even began, I had a Delayed Entry Program contract in hand. I had officially enlisted.

Both my parents had to sign, since I was only seventeen. Reluctantly, they did, knowing that I would do it with or without their support as soon as I turned eighteen. This program is typically reserved for recruits seeking a specialty vocational assignment like aircraft mechanic or meteorologist. But I wanted to be a grunt, and I was determined to lock in the Infantry Military Occupational Specialty (MOS). My biggest fear was that the needs of the Marine Corps would dash my hopes for glory on the battlefield and they'd turn me into some kind of intelligence analyst non-combatant pogue instead of the fabled "0311."

My recruiter, Sergeant Baez, shrugged and smiled as he did the paperwork. I was the easiest sale he'd ever made. Others wouldn't be so lucky. One of the sergeants at the Times Square station had "Fuck Off" written on the soles of his patent leather shoes. If a candidate walked in who wasn't worthy, the shoes went up on the desk. I thought that was so cool. That was the Corps' ploy, of course.

Camp Lejeune
26 April 2005

I was initially skeptical of Captain Bolling's ability and worried that he might cave in to pressure from senior prosecutors in the JAG office. I had even considered having him moved off my case. The military practice of alternating tours between defense and prosecution meant that almost all the lawyers had worked with each other on both sides of the fence. The incestuous environment lent itself to a free flow of communication that was not what I had in mind as I battled for my life. But as Bolling continued to dig at Major Winn's impartiality, I began to see that I had badly underestimated his abilities. He was doing an excellent job of putting all of the defense's concerns into the record. And because he was our junior attorney, it wouldn't damage the professional relationship that Gittins and Stackhouse would need with Winn once the hearing was actually under way. Brandon was taking one for the team.

BOLLING: Did you consult with your legal advisor about your decision not to allow the defense to make an opening statement at this hearing?

WINN: I informed him of my decision, but that is a decision I made.

BOLLING: Based upon what?

WINN: Based upon the fact that I didn't need—I felt that I could fairly judge the evidence presented to me without hearing someone else's point of view before it's presented to me.

BOLLING: I think you would agree with me, sir, that Lieutenant Pantano should be afforded every reasonable opportunity to present any evidence in this case, correct?

WINN: Yes.

BOLLING: So what's unreasonable about the defense's request to make an opening statement?

WINN: Opening statement isn't evidence. So—I don't consider that evidence. I consider if it's presented as fact as evidence, so I don't consider opening statements from either side as evidence.

Winn was starting to get irritated, but Bolling remained adamant.

BOLLING: Well, what facts are you aware of that would allow you to draw the conclusion that you don't need to listen to a road map of the evidence that's going to be presented in the case?

WINN: I don't know any facts of the case yet.

BOLLING: So then how can you say that the *request* for an opening statement is not a necessary thing?

WINN: Because I believe it's not.

BOLLING: Just because that's how you feel about it?

WINN: Because I believe that I can fairly evaluate the evidence that's presented to me, and I don't believe an opening statement is evidence nor is it required under Rule of Court-Martial 405.

BOLLING: So how do you know then what to be in tune to as to what is and what isn't relevant?

WINN: Evidence that's presented to me is going to be what I decide as the investigating officer's role whether it's relevant or irrelevant. That's part of my duties as the investigating officer.

BOLLING: What's your definition of "relevant," sir?

WINN: Something that pertains to the case.

BOLLING: In what way?

WINN: Something that I deem is relevant to the case. For example, if you presented somebody's report card from the third grade and he got a C in penmanship, I wouldn't consider that pertinent to the case.

Parris Island, South Carolina
23 August 1989

Every Marine's got boot camp stories. Some of them are even true.

It was well after midnight when I stepped off the bus into the humid heat and onto the famous yellow footprints painted on the asphalt. It was hard to think with the drill instructors screaming at us. Half of it was real terror and half of it was a macro out-of-body understanding that I was *really* here, this was *really* happening, and I was *not* going home for thirteen weeks. Jim had yelled at his Young Marines aboard *Intrepid*. But these no-shit drill instructors, the DIs, roared and bellowed like wild animals.

"Listen up, recruits, the first and last words out of your filthy sewers will be 'sir'! Do you understand that?"

And so it began.

That long night continued. At some point between getting my head shaved, being issued uniforms, and filling out all the confusing paperwork, I realized that it was my birthday. I wouldn't have known if a DI hadn't yelled it out. I was so punch-drunk.

Everything I did was wrong. I was not fast enough. I was not loud enough. I was not strong enough. In the hour or so that the DIs gave us to sleep that night before reveille at dawn, I felt like I was going to cry. This wasn't like the books or the movies. This wasn't heroic. This sucked, and I wanted to go home.

A few nights later, the senior drill instructor, Staff Sergeant Fisher, dumped out the carefully folded and aligned contents of our lockers for the *third* time. Everything I owned in the world was now comingled with everyone else's shit. A huge pile of our personal belongings stood in the middle of the squad bay. Then sheets and blankets came off of our racks and joined the heap. Now we had to climb it like Mount Suribachi. We had to get our stuff. Any stuff.

We had "10 . . . 9 . . . 7 . . . 5 . . . 2 . . . *You're fucking done!*" Again. Faster. Get back. Just a big pile of soap dishes, socks, and shoe polish. A blur of shower shoes and white underwear. Thirteen weeks of this?

That night, I did cry. I missed my girlfriend, Haley, and I tried to imagine what she might have had for dinner. I couldn't remember mine. I tucked her perfumed letters into my pillow hoping that if our racks were dumped someone would be kind enough to return them to me. I missed my life. I missed my childhood image of the Marine Corps. My fantasy of polish and idealism was being violently overthrown by a rough group of sweaty men. The men remembered, so the organization remembered. The men had flaws, so the organization had flaws. In fact it wasn't an organization at all, it was a living, breathing 213-year-old organism.

Slowly, we began to change. Every event we survived made us tougher. Every march we completed drew us together tighter. The shared suffering and triumphs were all part of a carefully choreographed schedule of rituals. We became proud members of Platoon 1102, Charlie Company, 1st Recruit Training Battalion. If we weren't shouting "Kill!" we were definitely shouting "Senior Drill Instructor Staff Sergeant Fisher! Best on the Island! Best in the Corps!" And we'd chant as we ran, beating our chests or beating our weapons in a primal ritual preparation for war, just as men have done for thousands of years.

We learned to strip down and reassemble all the initially baffling bits of steel and springs that made up our M-16A2 rifles. Handling the weapon became automatic. It became instinct. It was a month before the DIs allowed us anywhere near live ammunition on the firing range. Shooting was an exercise in humility for many guys, a source of pride for others. The standards were exacting, but even without the hunting pedigree of many of my peers, I excelled. One reason was the inspiration I took from one of our marksmanship instructors. He was a Marine Sniper doing a turn of duty at recruit training, and I idolized him as if he were the legendary Carlos Hathcock incarnate.

One day I got the courage to ask the sergeant how a Marine became a Sniper. Getting the question from a "boot" so early in his training pipeline was a constant source of eye-rolling tedium. "*You* want to be a Sniper? How about you start by qualifying!" Ahh, that everpresent disdain, but beneath it there was a lesson.

I'd spent my youth absorbed with distant dreams: When I'm older . . . When I'm a Marine . . . It was a distraction that allowed me to not focus on my reality, to bypass my here and now.

Those days were over. In the crucible of Parris Island, I learned the things I always knew, but had not connected: There is no "deep" fight, no big picture, if you don't survive the "close" fight first. My inattention to the smallest detail could get me—or worse, one of my buddies—killed. It was fine to dream, when there was time, but now it was time to perform.

In those hot, exhausting weeks, 1102 tried hard to please our DIs. Rage-fueled perfection inspired us and scared the shit out of us. Bodies and minds broke, sometimes spectacularly, and our numbers shrank from sixty to forty. We were in a race to find physical toughness, the warrior ethos, and discipline: "the instant obedience to orders." We learned about primal human motivations and triggers.

We learned the lessons of pain and pain avoidance. You spend a lot of time in the Marines threatening pain, practicing pain, inflicting pain, or avoiding pain.

Group punishment taught us to take our new profession seriously. If the group failed, you failed. If you failed, the group failed. To up the stakes, we learned the history and traditions of those who had gone before. Standing on the shoulders of giants, like two-time Medal of Honor–winner Sergeant Major "Dan" Daly, prepared us to fight hard when our day would come.

On November 18, 1989, the men of 1102, like the dozens or perhaps hundreds of 1102s that had graduated before them, inherited a legacy, real or mythical. I became a meritorious Private First Class, which meant I'd earned a single, red-bordered chevron to wear on each sleeve of my alphas. I wasn't a kid sneaking past the doorman of a nightclub anymore. I was a United States Marine.

Family and friends came to the graduation. Bands played. We marched. Everybody stayed in step. It took my family a long time to spot me in the formation.

The week before graduation, we'd watched the Berlin Wall fall on CNN. "Shit," a glum recruit whispered. "The fucking *commies* are going belly-up. Now who the hell we going to fight?"

Camp Lejeune
26 April 2005

Toward the end of the voir dire, Captain Bolling had Major Winn state for the record that he was scheduled for promotion to lieutenant colonel and would serve on the staff of Major General Richard Huck when the 2nd Marine Division returned to Iraq. General Huck was the commander of the 2nd Marine Division. All the grunts at Camp Lejeune were his. He also had the dubious privilege of approving the charges against me.

It was the general's staff that read the Naval Criminal Investigative Service (NCIS) report and started the legal process moving. It was his staff that had charged me with two counts of premeditated murder, destruction of civilian property, dereliction of duty, and conduct unbecoming an officer. It was his staff that didn't think the matter warranted more research, more interviews, or more information before they drafted charges. It was his staff that concluded sufficient cause to go after a Marine lieutenant, perhaps to make an example, in order to preserve the good order and discipline of the service. It was his legal advisor that felt confident to charge the max, and it was his legal advisor whose balls would be in a sling if this didn't go the way he wanted. If this didn't proceed at least to a court-martial, whoever had put this together would be hating life. Oh, and General Huck happened to be the guy who was going to review Winn's fitness reports, in effect, controlling his future career. Great.

My team had heard enough. Notes were passed. Bolling nodded and then executed.

BOLLING: Sir, at this point in time, the defense team would like to challenge you based upon an implied bias, as well as an appearance of partiality, based upon what just came out in the voir dire.

WINN: Okay . . .

Winn was caught flat-footed, although I don't know how he hadn't seen this coming.

> WINN: . . . I don't believe that I have an implied bias . . . The point of this hearing is for me to determine the facts of the case as they pertain to Second Lieutenant Pantano. And I believe that I have the ability to fairly and impartially judge the facts of the case and the merits of the case against Second Lieutenant Pantano. So I would deny the challenge.

We knew it was a long shot, but we'd hoped Bolling laying out our concerns would give Winn a chance to step aside so we could get an actual military judge to preside over the case. The request had clearly irritated Winn, but the anger was focused squarely on Brandon, so in that regard he had accomplished the mission. But in the process we had pissed off the very officer who held my cards. The next hour did nothing to ease the dull throb that was becoming a headache.

The prosecution began presenting and labeling their various evidentiary exhibits. Gittins objected to Keane's description of the two dead Iraqis in the big blow-up photos mounted on an easel—and conveniently facing the closed-circuit TV camera. Keane had just called the two men I had killed "victims."

"Objection." Gittins was on his feet, facing Major Winn. "Sir, I would ask that we not refer to these people as victims until we've made an actual determination as to whether or not there's been a crime. If it's a justified killing, they're not victims . . ."

Major Winn upheld the objection and instructed the attorneys to refer to the dead men as "alleged victims."

Saudi–Kuwait Border
January 1991

The young Marines with whom I'd gone through boot camp needn't have worried about running out of wars to fight. Only fourteen months after we proudly marched before our families on the Parris Island parade ground, most of us were sleeping in the gravelly sand of the Saudi desert a few klicks from the berm marking the border with Kuwait.

And we never forgot that there were a couple hundred thousand Iraqi troops on the other side of that berm—most of them combat veterans of the long war with Iran—armed with tanks, artillery, and chemical weapons.

I'd gotten my wish and become a grunt, but not just a rifleman. I was assigned to the 6th Marine Regiment as an Anti-Armor Assault man (TOW missile gunner). Part of my job included learning to drive a Humvee, identifying both friendly and enemy tanks, and firing our missiles—all on top of the other basic Marine skills of killing with a rifle, machine gun, grenade, knife—or fists if we had to.

TOW gunners tended to be misfits by virtue of our rarity. In the early nineties there was only one TOW platoon in a regiment (comprised of three infantry battalions). So, out of about three thousand men there were only sixty of us, which fomented a sort of Bad News Bears/Badass Bears mentality. It didn't hurt our egos that we were "tank killers" and this was going to be a tank war in the open desert.

One of the more colorful guys in my platoon was a lance corporal named Tommy, a tattooed thug from New Jersey or New York or whatever he felt like telling you. He was a salty old bastard in his mid-twenties who never let us new guys forget that he had been demoted more times than we had whacked off. He was a bar fighter who would take out male or female arresting officers with the same indifference, and all of us young Marines thought he was "the shit"—a grunt superhero. Back at Camp Lejeune, Tommy would wake up late for formations lying naked on the floor in the middle of the squad bay uncertain of how he got there or even where he was. His insolence and aggression were tolerated, so the rumor went, because he smoked pot with the platoon sergeant's wife out in town.

Wow. That was the old Corps. Today his ass would have been bounced so fast that his neck would snap, but not then. The Corps still had a bad heart and clogged arteries from feasting on a lot of greasy seventies rejects . . . it would take time for the machine to clean itself out.

One of the advantages of the TOW platoon billet was that we got Humvees and radios that actually worked. The M-220 tube-launched, optically-tracked, wire-guided missile worked too, and at 2.5 miles, it had the longest range on the battlefield. Our officers and sergeants assured us that the Soviet-built Iraqi T-55 and T-62 tanks on the other side of the berm couldn't hope to hit us. We were untouchable.

As a boy, looking at six-hundred-year-old knights or samurai behind glass, I might have considered that kind of lopsided advantage unsporting or even dishonorable. But in a museum I also saw them from another perspective. They had been killed off. Made extinct by the rigidity of their own codes. Inflexible in the face of an enemy that used new or different weapons or tactics, the honorable warriors of old were now relegated to our museums and our imaginations.

Instead, we had bombarded an enemy that lacked an air force for forty-five days and nights.

We used cruise missiles launched from ships hundreds of miles away. And I was glad. Glad that our B-52s could carry eighty five-hundred-pound bombs. Glad that our M-1 tanks could shoot through the berms that the Iraqis would hide behind. I rejoiced in the 3,750 meters' worth of advantage that my TOW provided. That gave us 3,750 chances to get home that the other guy didn't have. And all of a sudden, I began to see war, and the world, for what it was, not what I wanted it to be. I thought I had escaped the street, but it was all street. I thought I had escaped the jungle, but it was all jungle. It was all the same. Savage and unfair. But familiar.

Our platoon and the whole 6th Marines were at the far left end of the 2nd Marine Division, which was left of the 1st Marine Division anchored in the Persian Gulf. To our left there was the Army's Tiger Brigade and about four hundred thousand Coalition troops formed up in-depth along the border berm, waiting to see if President George H. W. Bush, Secretary of State James Baker, the Frogs, the Russians, and all the assorted Arab cronies of Saddam Hussein could convince the Iraqi dictator to pull his army out of Kuwait.

We waited, getting into nervous fistfights in the beginning, and then bullshitting each other that we weren't scared, but trying not to think about Iraqi nerve gas or the multiple minefields they'd laid in front of us. The worst threat seemed to be these ten million (mostly Italian—*Viva Italia!*) land mines. Scarier even than the invisible gas. Land mines were sudden and undeniable. At least for gas we had the bullshit antidotes that nobody trusted, clumsy "anti-chem" MOPP suits, test kits, and even masks . . . but nothing for mines.

"A cloud of red-paint mist," we were told: that was what mines could make out of a Marine. Mines could keep you awake at night, as you pictured your severed legs smoking on the sand. Even more terri-

WARLORD   37

fying was the image of your crotch shredded from a Bouncing Betty that popped up to explode right at scrotum level. The seemingly imminent death of myself and my friends filled my dreams.

I'd gotten my first tattoo before we'd flown to Saudi from the Marine Corps Air Station Cherry Point in North Carolina. I rationalized that it was for my parents, even as I sought the approval of my platoon mates. The "meat tag" was as much about bravado as it was about making your body identifiable. Several tight printed lines near our hearts spelled out name, Social Security number, blood type, and the letters "USMC," in case our heads and limbs got blown off and the only thing left was the torso inside our flak jackets. The tattoo artist was a redneck named Jessie. He had a makeshift chicken-wire pen for his python. His greasy hair and ugly face were covered by a hockey mask (like in the *Friday the 13th* movies)—to protect him from hepatitis spatter, I guess.

Precombat nerves also appeared in less permanent ways. A bunch of us chopped our hair into Mohawks, which was immediately met with punishment and a remedial head-shaving. Tommy cut "FTS" into his chest hair: "Fuck the Suck." In the 1990s, we called the Marine Corps "the Suck" just as grunts in Vietnam had called it "the Crotch." That was our boyish response to going to war. We wanted combat more than anything and we feared it more than anything. And we rebelled against the very institution that was giving us what we wanted.

Following one of the traditions of war, I covered every reflective surface on my Humvee with tan masking tape, then with black marker I drew menacing eyes and scowling teeth, like the VW Beetle, "Herbie" on crack. I got in trouble for that and had to repaint my vehicle. I also stenciled drivers' and gunners' call signs on the Humvee's flimsy door panels: there was the "Godfather," "Swing," and "the Great White Hunter." I was "GQ" because I was always trying to escape from this flat, dusty void through magazines. With their perfumed pullouts and clean, glossy pages of models, they were a tunnel to the other side. To the world.

As the ground war grew closer, we formed tighter bonds. We stopped lying about all the girls we'd fucked and talked about what "it" was really going to be like. I was closest to two Marines who had joined the platoon about the same time I did. Jeff Dejessie came from Bellville, a shit suburb of Newark, New Jersey, which I mercilessly teased him was really just a shit suburb of New York. The teasing would stop when he'd get off the cot and make like he was going to stomp my scrawny ass.

We'd often driven back to Lejeune together and he would regale me with tales of fights, strippers, and tattoos. We'd share his home-made wine, provolone, and salami and he'd tell me fresh stories of fights, strippers, and tattoos.

Hans Heinz was from rural Culpepper, Virginia. His father was a highly decorated Marine infantry officer in Vietnam and had been wounded several times. We looked to Hans for clues about what to ex-pect, since his dad's stories were as close as any of us had been to war. But Hans, with his surfer-boy looks and laid-back approach, wasn't much help. No secondhand story ever would be.

We would get our news from the one kid who'd had the presence of mind to bring a transistor shortwave radio. He'd stand on the roof of his dug-in Humvee at night, holding his radio up to snare the BBC, and we would wait for him to come down off the mountain with "word." The most valuable commodity in the Marine Corps was word. It was straight information about you and what you were supposedly doing. Grunts *never* know what's really happening, so we were always seeking elusive reliable information. "What's the word?" "Shut the fuck up! He's got word!" "Did you hear the word?"

On January 29, word came down that at least one Iraqi armor brigade had invaded the Saudi border town of Kafji. Our platoon com-mander gave a simple order: "Mount up. We've got a mission."

Holy shit.

I had just taken my boots off for the first time in a week and had been in a deep sleep. Instinct and training took over getting me dressed and my rocket launcher zeroed and op-checked. I was so frightened that my lips were smacking together spasmodically, making it hard to draw a breath, but I was still able to do what was required on autopilot. I would never be that scared again in my life, but I was able to function. My cherry had been broken. The irony is that we didn't even go into the fight. But like the young heroes we thought we were, Jeff, Hans, and I had exchanged letters to be given to our parents just in case we got killed.

On February 23, just before we crossed through the breach into Kuwait that the engineers had cut through the berm, my gunner, Sergeant Ocasio, a veteran of the bloody Marine occupation of the

Root, got a "Dear John" letter. I was nervous that this would mess with his head. And there could be no doubt that it was head-fuck time with a couple of thousand oil wells burning out ahead of us. That had to be the biggest smoke screen in the history of warfare.

But the sameness and the staleness of war blended my fear into dull fatigue. I would drive through minefields, staying on the tail of the vehicle in front of me with my hands casually woven through the steering wheel, balancing MRE cheese on a big square cracker while simultaneously trying to only get the "right" amount of hot sauce on it. Sergeant Ocasio would kick me in the head from the missile turret whenever he wanted to change direction. And, the more dense the unexploded American bomblets or the Iraqi mines became, the more often we had to turn.

Fatigue killed sensation. One day passed. A night, another day. The oil fields blazed on our right front. When the wind shifted toward us, the smoke rolled in like a choking curtain, a solid black wall.

Sometimes the Marines' Vietnam-vintage M-60A3 main battle tanks clanked past us in the smoke. They were so decked out in bolted-on reactive armor—which exploded enemy rounds—and jagged mine plows that they looked like apocalyptic raiders from the *Mad Max* movies. But we were always glad to have them near.

We were shelled continuously, most of the Iraqi 155 mm rounds overshooting us or landing wide. Jeff snapped a picture as an Iraqi 155 shell exploded to the left of my Humvee. A rare, shit-your-pants snapshot. But fortunately, the Marine artillery and its counter-battery radar were able to silence the Iraqi guns every time before they fired off a more accurate second salvo. That incredibly fast high-tech response saved us several times.

As we pushed north through the smoke and blowing sand, my platoon scored several dozen tank kills, but I personally did not fire a missile. My position in the formation was at the rear left of a triangular wedge, and all the contact was occurring on the right side of our platoon. We drove past the smoldering hulks of Iraqi armor as the ammunition inside was cooking off, showering sparks and debris everywhere. Through the smoke, you could smell the barbecue stench of burnt flesh.

ZIIINNNNG . . . snap. ZIIINNNNG . . . snap. Snap . . . ZII-INNNNG. ZIIINNNNG. ZIIINNNNG. The sound was like a drill buzzing by my ears. I could hear the rounds whipping through the smoke, an obscene whoopee-whistle. I spun the launcher to the rear, but I couldn't see anything, even through the thermals. This Humvee had about enough armor to stop a BB gun. I assumed, from the flat trajectory of the incoming rounds, that they were fired from an elevated position, but far away . . . like the 25 mm chain gun on a Marine Light Armored Vehicle (LAV-25).

Friendly fucking fire.

The firing didn't last long and I don't remember the radio chatter and I don't recall what happened next: I just remember feeling very alone in the smoke, even as my brothers were all around me. That night we slept in shifts and couldn't see our hands in front of our faces. We were smothered by the stinking smoke, which permeated everything. The assault held up until daylight to minimize the risk of more "blue-on-blue" friendly-fire incidents—always a concern when you have lots of hopped-up young men with guns, particularly when they can't see.

Four months later in New York, men and women stood on windowsills and screamed. Shredded paper hung in the air, shimmering against the blue spring sky. Fire engines and police cars ran their sirens and blasted their horns.

"When you spend more time marching in parades than you do in actual combat," Jeff Dejessie joked, "you get PTPD, Post-Traumatic Parade Disorder."

I grinned as we marched up Broadway to City Hall. Later we got wasted at the USO Victory party on the *Intrepid*. I was home.

Camp Lejeune
26 April 2005

The legal bullshit was over and we were getting down to business. Major Winn looked up from his dais and began to read aloud.

> WINN: Okay. Second Lieutenant Pantano, the purpose
> of this investigation is threefold: to inquire into
> the truth of the matters set forth in the charges,
> to examine the form of the charges, and to secure

information in order to determine the appropriate disposition of the charges in this case.

Winn glanced down at me. I was sitting erect in my black office
chair. My starched cover—Marine jargon for hat—was sitting on the
table in front of me next to my soda and a pack of gum.

Stackhouse had warned me against chewing gum in the courtroom, but I assured him it was what I did when I was in combat. He
shook his head at my arrogance, no doubt wondering if I was trying to
lose the case for him. I had a legal pad, but the pages were blank. Our
sleeves were rolled up because of the heat outside on the base, and my
bare arms rested on the table. I tried to control my shivering, which I
assured myself was from the AC.

In Iraq we kept our sleeves rolled down all year long, regardless of
the heat. To do otherwise was considered a sign of weakness, they'd
told us.

WINN: Second Lieutenant Pantano, at the outset, I will
         explain your rights under Article 31, UCMJ.
         They are as follows: No person subject to the
         UCMJ may force you to incriminate yourself or
         answer any questions if the answer may tend to
         incriminate you. In a few moments I will advise
         you of the nature of the charges against you. You
         have the right to remain silent regarding these
         charges. If you choose to make a statement in
         any form, or answer any questions about the
         charges, your statement or answer may be used
         against you in a trial by court-martial.

A long pause.

WINN: Do you understand these rights under Article 31,
          UCMJ?
PANTANO: Yes, sir, I do.

And so it began.

Camp Lejeune
December 1991

As a freshly minted corporal and salty twenty-year-old combat vet, I finagled a coveted slot to Scout Sniper school that fall. In the Marine infantry, becoming a Scout Sniper is like graduating from the JV grunts to the varsity.

I had been training to get into the best possible shape. I skipped the stuffing on Thanksgiving and then went out and ran eight miles in the snow while my family feasted. Sniper school would grind down muscle and fat with equal ruthlessness. It's the cycle of the Marine Corps: you're constantly preparing for something, you accomplish it, and then you must begin preparing again. War. School. Boot Camp. Officer Candidate School. Anything. Like a knife, the edge has to be constantly honed, renewed.

Being accepted to one of the most prestigious programs in the military had been particularly tough for me. Most of the other Marines in the course were either from elite reconnaissance units or were currently serving with Scout Sniper platoons in the regiments and learning on the job. I was almost denied access because of my lack of background as a "rifleman." (TOW gunners were often looked down upon by traditional infantry because of the constant reliance on the Humvee to transport us, our weapons systems, and all of the junk food we threw into our vehicles. The rifleman, on the other hand, had nothing but his boots and what he could carry on his back.) But because of my high rifle and fitness scores and my attitude, I made it through the screening.

"What the living fuck does a New York City boy know about sniping?" a staff sergeant asked with a scowl.

"Staff Sergeant, where did you think sniping was invented?" I shot back, hoping guts would make up for inexperience.

He almost broke a grin, and I knew I was in.

Almost half the class didn't graduate, but those who did learned some solid skills, or as we called them, the "skills to kill." For eight weeks we slithered like snakes and we lay still like logs—in sleet and rain. We shot our heavily modified .308 caliber hunting rifle, the M-40A1, until our fingers hurt, and then kept shooting. We shot moving targets at night and had to qualify on targets a thousand yards away—more than thirteen city blocks. That's like hitting someone in

Times Square from the top of the Empire State Building. We hid while groups of men equipped with binoculars and radios searched for us, even as we fired blanks at them. There was no need to confirm a hit because, with our skill, that was considered a given.

We built our own ghillie suits, reinforcing the bellies and legs of our cammies with canvas so the fabric wouldn't rip apart as we low-crawled across rocks and rough ground. The term "ghillie" came from Scottish Highland gamekeepers lying in ambush to catch poachers. We had other quarry in mind.

We covered nets with torn strips of colored burlap, and wove, stitched, and glued them to the limbs and torsos of our uniforms to mimic the grass and leaves around us. The durability of the ghillie suit wasn't a bragging right of fine craftsmanship, it was critical for survival. The enemy hunts snipers and any little trace you leave behind is a "target indicator," which could mean your mission is compromised and you die—probably a very bad death over a long period of time. We accepted that harsh reality just as we all accepted learning the skill to kill—that uncanny ability of a sniper to reach out and snatch away someone's life without that person or anyone else ever knowing that we were there. It was a deal with the devil that we all made readily, if not gladly.

We learned that in the right terrain, a Scout Sniper team could hold off a thousand-man battalion, by shooting them one at a time to maximize painful screams and to spread fear and dissent in the ranks. We mastered a weapon even more lethal than the rifle: the radio. A well-timed artillery barrage or air strike from an unseen observer was devastating.

"Imagine," we were taught by serious men of purpose, whose students included SEALs and FBI SWAT teams, "the psychological value of your enemy writing letters to his family complaining about how unseen killers had struck at the time and place of their choosing and once again had killed a comrade."

We trained in the psychological power of fear as a weapon.

"This isn't about playing fair, gents," another instructor taught us. "This is about breaking the enemy's will to fight. Say the point element of a larger force is moving on a ridgeline below you. First shot is to the hip of the point man. Crack his pelvis and the pain is so intense, he can't stop screaming as he crumples." Some of us adjusted in our chairs, others took notes. The fatigue of forty-eight-hour patrols and pack runs was washing away as we realized we were hitting the mother lode, the *word* of the sniper's world.

"As the point man is screaming, the enemy unit goes to cover. Next guy up will be the medic. Drop him. Now what do you think happens to that platoon or squad? They know you're out there, but if you've paid attention and done your job right they don't know where. The unit leader orders the next guy up and you know what he says? He says, 'Fuck you, I ain't going.' "

Some of us chuckled, but most were rapt as the instructor continued. "What have you done? Well, after two shots, it's probably time to move before they dump a ton of arty on your ass, but what have you done to that unit? At worst, you bagged two bad guys. But at best—at best, you broke them down and caused a mutiny. They are stalled and the units behind them have to wait as they unfuck. You got into the enemy's heads and made them combat-ineffective with two bullets."

I had not needed to take notes, and could have recited that burly sergeant's words back to him verbatim if required. In a single fifty-minute class, he had taught me an enduring secret of war: chivalry was for museums. My job was to kill or cripple the enemy, and then to escape unseen.

Like a lethal ghost.

THREE

Article 32 Hearing
DAY ONE

Camp Lejeune
26 April 2005

First Lieutenant Samuel Cunningham was the prosecution's lead witness. We'd served together in combat around Mahmudiyah and Fallujah, and I knew him well. Sam was a good guy, a strong leader and the senior lieutenant in the battalion. As I watched him swear his oath and take the witness stand, he radiated discomfort. Sam wasn't very happy about having been ordered here to testify against me. He tried to avoid making eye contact with me, and over my shoulder, I saw my family glaring at him. So I snuck Sam a little wink to indicate everything would be cool. I wanted to reassure him, "Do what you've got to do, Sam. It's okay. We're all men here." I never got the chance to say that, but he didn't need me to tell him.

Our unit, 2nd Battalion, 2nd Marine Regiment (known as 2/2 or the Warlords), had grown to a task force of over one thousand troops when we took over the area of operations (AO) around Mahmudiyah and Latafiyah south of Baghdad in the spring of 2004. The infantry battalion was the hub of the task force. At its core were the rifle companies: Easy, Fox, and Golf—each comprising four platoons. The battalion also had Weapons Company made up of three CAAT (Combined Anti-Armor Team) platoons and an 81 mm mortar platoon. CAATs had six to eight Humvees with heavy machine guns, grenade launchers, and TOW missiles. The combination of heavy weaponry and high mobility ideally suited them for rapid strikes. The 81 mm mortar platoon was considered the battalion's hip-pocket artillery.

In March and early April, Sam and his men were working hard to mentor the Iraqi National Guard (ING) battalion stationed across Alternate Supply Route Jackson (Highway 8) a few klicks southeast of our battalion's Forward Operating Base (FOB). The Combined Action Platoon (CAP), of which Sam was the commander, was responsible for training, equipping, supplying, and often fighting beside the Iraqis. It hadn't been an easy mission, either for Sam's Marines or for their Iraqi "allies." In April 2004, the insurgency caught fire: IEDs ("improvised explosive devices," or roadside bombs), suicide car and truck bombs, sniping, and company-size ambushes. The news media had taken to calling our AO the "Triangle of Death." For the Iraqi troops whom Sam's platoon advised, the area was especially dangerous. The region was dominated by a couple of badass, pro-Saddam Sunni Arab tribes who were blood enemies of the predominantly Shiite ING troops. If the insurgents captured an ING soldier, he faced hours or days of torture, followed by execution. But the guard troops had cast their lot with us, most just to keep their families alive by earning the few bucks a month the new Iraqi government authorized us to pay them.

Without Sam's CAP present, most of his Iraqi troops wouldn't venture out of their walled compound. If they did leave the barbed wire and guard towers, they covered their faces so they wouldn't be recognized. That was to protect them and their families. We would learn that there were no Rules of Engagement in the intimidation game. Kids and women ended up dead as easily as anyone.

Soon after we arrived in country, word spread of Iraqi police discovering headless bodies with bound hands dumped in a school soccer field. That was enough to keep people indoors. But unless the ING patrolled the area, the insurgents—to the Marines either "Ali Babas," "Hajjis," or just "Cunts" (an epithet we'd learn while training with Royal British Marines), depending on our mood—would shut down supply routes Jackson and Tampa.

By mid-April 2004, the insurgents had already blown big holes out of the highway bridges, almost cutting the supply route into Baghdad and Fallujah. The sudden and aggressive attacks were so effective that they prompted an irate senior Marine commander to remind his battalions: "If we could take goddamn Mount Suribachi, we sure as hell better hold a fucking highway!" Sure we could. It just meant everything else would stop.

Sam was tasked to move out to Main Supply Route Tampa, which intersected Jackson, and hold several bridges and overpasses due south of Baghdad with the *help* of the Iraqis. The ING was so heavily infiltrated with "Muj" (mujahideen fighters) and so corrupt that mass dismissals occurred almost weekly at every level of the command. The turnover only added to the flow of hijacked weapons, radios, and intelligence to the terrorists. But we had our orders and our determination. Sam and I and our fellow platoon commanders would never give up and concede defeat. Even though the mission had suddenly become harder than we'd ever imagined, our Marines were indomitable.

Major Keane began by taking his witness through the events of that Thursday afternoon north of Mahmudiyah.

> KEANE: Did anything significant happen on April 15th?
>
> CUNNINGHAM: Third Platoon, Easy Company, had come out to conduct a cordon and knock, [surround and search a house] approximately about one thousand meters from our position. At which, the day prior, CAAT Black, which was just off to our northeast, had taken fire from that vicinity.
>
> KEANE: So Third Platoon, E Company, had to pass through your lines to conduct this cordon and knock?
>
> CUNNINGHAM: Yes, sir.
>
> KEANE: What time did they arrive at your position?
>
> CUNNINGHAM: Sometime in the late afternoon, sir . . .
>
> KEANE: Who was the commander of this QRF [Quick Reaction Force]?

CUNNINGHAM: Lieutenant Pantano, sir.
    KEANE: Did you see Lieutenant Pantano as his unit
           passed through your lines?
CUNNINGHAM: Yes, sir, I did.

Sam continued to describe the tricky maneuver of one heavily armed unit moving through another's fighting positions—Cunningham had a squad of nervous, ill-trained Iraqi National Guard dug in near the bridge.

CUNNINGHAM: We had had radio trouble in that area, sir,
            during the day. So I had no prior knowledge
            of them coming up there.

We'd appeared unannounced in the slanting twilight, the distinctive squatness of the Humvees and our helmeted silhouettes the only visual clue preventing a friendly-fire disaster.

The 1990s

After I graduated from Scout Sniper school, my battalion sent me to Infantry Squad Leader school in an effort to bolster my traditional grunt skills. The course was open to almost anyone with an "03" infantry specialty above the rank of corporal and it wasn't nearly as rigorous or challenging as sniper school. I already knew the curriculum material cold, especially subjects like writing patrol orders and tactical communications that were so difficult for a lot of the other noncommissioned officers.

So I focused on helping some of the good guys who were struggling. And I was gratified to do so. One sergeant had just come from several years training recruits on Parris Island and I felt honored to be able to help a former drill instructor. My own boot camp memories were still painfully fresh, but his infantry skills had atrophied, especially land navigation, so I became his personal guide through map reading, compass orientation, and all the other bits and pieces I'd taken for granted as a Scout Sniper moving "tactically" in enemy territory.

In the process of not taking the course as seriously as I should have, I went overboard with my wiseass attitude. One of the instructors, a staff sergeant who struck me as a tad soft, smoked a pipe and carried it around during our classes. So I bought pipes for every member of our squad.

One morning as we marched to a tactical-problem sandbox, the instructor ordered us to halt. He strode up and down our ranks and verified that every one of us had a pipe in the breast pocket of his woodland-pattern cammie utilities. And then he stopped to glare at me. My classroom commentary had established me as the instigator.

"Pantano, you think I'm fucking funny?"

"No, Staff Sergeant."

"Well, I think *you* are funny. I think you're so fucking funny that I'm gonna bounce your sorry ass outta this course."

I wasn't bounced, but after graduating number two at Scout Sniper school, I managed to graduate from the Squad Leader school dead last.

I learned some important lessons in the course, though. The infantry squad, made up of three four-man fire teams, was the basic building block of the Marine Corps. The squad leader, usually an experienced corporal or a sergeant, had to have sound judgment and be accountable to his platoon commander for his troops' actions. He needed initiative, judgment, decisiveness, and many more leadership traits and tools that the Marines tried to instill in its NCOs. Squad leaders got the men trained, got them fit and kept them in shape for combat, made sure their weapons and equipment were well maintained, and, more importantly, made sure that the Marines who used them were proficient.

You didn't need ammunition or a range to practice bringing your rifle to your shoulder and aiming—in response to an ambush. Snap that eight-pound M-16 up a hundred times in an afternoon and you've built some muscle memory. Practice clearing a malfunction a hundred times and you've learned a skill. Practice changing magazines to keep up the "mad-minute" high volume of fire to break an ambush, and you've become dangerous to the enemy.

It didn't take money and fancy simulators. The Spartans didn't have such luxuries, and the Corps doesn't need them. All that's required are basic skills and the force of will. It takes hard men willing to do hard things in order to set an example that others can and will follow. It takes squad leaders, probably one of the most essential assignments in the Marine Corps.

The "fighter-leader" concept means that if you want your Marines to charge in the confusion and fear of combat, you don't yell "Charge" from the bleachers and look for the score on the morning sports page. You jam in a fresh magazine, grab the guy next to you, and charge. You lead.

There are plenty of leadership challenges in peacetime, too. If a Marine is extra fond of cheeseburgers and he can't close his flak jacket over his belly, you fix it. If he can't run a hundred yards without falling down, you fix it. If a weapon is rusty after being out in the field for a week, you better fix it fast. If one of your men is insubordinate, you don't go running to complain to the platoon sergeant or the lieutenant. You take the guy out behind the barracks and settle things.

In the old days we called it "wall-to-wall" counseling; now it is technically hazing and it's illegal. That's a damn shame. Violence isn't the only tool and it certainly shouldn't be the first out of the box, but to take physical domination off the table is unnecessarily limiting. Being a warrior is a tough business, and even in peacetime, a good NCO has to earn the respect of his men. If you accomplish that, they'll follow you as their leader in combat.

Twelve years later, that lesson would become a critical factor in my life.

From Squad Leader school, I returned to my Scout Sniper platoon with the 1st Battalion, 6th Marines (1/6). We began training for a Mediterranean "float" (deployment) with the 22nd Marine Expeditionary Unit (MEU). A MEU teamed an infantry battalion (eight hundred men) with light armor, artillery, and aircraft aboard a naval task force of transport ships and an assault aircraft carrier. As America's emergency-response force, we could swoop down on and destroy just about any target in the world, from a drug lab to an air base; we could rescue hostages from a besieged embassy or provide relief to victims of a natural disaster. The very presence of a MEU off the coast was a tool of our national power projection.

We did work-ups for six solid months—two or three exhausting missions a week—sneaking onto a beach by Zodiac rubber boats or fast-roping out of big CH-53 Sea Stallion helicopters. As a sniper team we would clandestinely insert prior to a larger raid force coming in behind us. We would send back intelligence on the targets and guide the raiders onto the objective. Then just prior to the raid we would "reduce" threats like air-defense equipment operators or key leadership.

Preemptive decapitation. Finally, we would extract with the raid force by boat, bird, or black Cadillacs (a road march in combat boots).

The rubber boat ops were my favorite. When we pulled off the beach Corporal Howard, my assistant team leader, and I would trail our legs over the inflated sausage-link gunnels of the Zodiacs. Watching out over our sectors of fire we'd start critiquing the performance of our team, "Head Hunter 2," in hushed voices. My mind would wander down to the cold green fire of the phosphorescence churned up in the wake. It was beautiful.

By fall 1992, the 22nd MEU was cruising up and down the Adriatic as war was breaking out among the fragments of the former Yugoslavia. One of the missions we trained for was recovering NATO aircrew downed during relief flights over Bosnia, the same type of mission that saved Air Force Captain Scott O'Grady's life three years later.

As we waited for a call that never came, we continued to train, both on ship and off. The LPH-9 *Guam* was a huge rusty shitbucket that had taken my company first sergeant to Vietnam more than twenty years before. The amphibious assault ship reminded me of a smaller cousin of *Intrepid*. We ran on the hangar deck, shot our weapons off the sides of the "boat," and taught one another classes.

Occasionally, even in the marginal winter weather, the Navy would get the helos up so we could practice fast-roping down onto the heaving deck, a great way to break a leg. In fast-roping, our only equipment was a pair of hardware store leather gloves and our boots. The idea was to "grip" the thick braided rope with the edges of the boot soles and let it whiz through your gloved hands on the way down. It was always a fast ride. And the only way to stop safely was to judge your distance right and squeeze your boots harder while you tightened the pressure on the rope—without the friction burning through your gloves.

The first guy to fast-rope out of a helicopter at sea needed to have really big balls because without the weight of a body on the rope, the rotor wash blew it out at an obscene angle from the helo. That was disconcerting when you were sitting in the troop compartment looking out the "hell hole" and fifty feet below, the rope might be whipping like a snake over the water instead of the deck.

"Listen up," our instructor taught us. "You just gotta trust your fellow Marines, and let gravity do its magic."

The first time I fast-roped onto the flight deck with both the big helo and the huge ship corkscrewing, I tasted the same sour metallic fear that I'd known in the Gulf. Hot engine exhaust forced its way up my nostrils and rotor wash buffeted my cheeks.

I didn't puke then, I thought. *Don't let me puke now.* I seized the rope, clamped my boots onto it, and slid off the ramp.

On that deployment, I spent three weeks in Israel, working with IDF snipers.

I went to the top of Masada—the sheer, tan limestone butte above the Judean wilderness where about a thousand Jewish rebels held off the besieging Romans in 72 A.D. In the end, of course, the Romans captured the fortress by building a ramp up the side for their catapults and battering rams. But when the legionnaires broke through the walls, they found that all the Jewish holdouts had committed suicide—fathers killing wives and children before falling on their own swords—rather than surrender into slavery.

The story that made my cheeks flush with emotion was learning that elite Israeli paratroopers ran up to the top to swear their oath of service. "Masada shall never fall again!"

One of the Israeli snipers asked me some provocative questions.

"Did you fight in Kuwait?"

I thought it was cool that this Gaza vet was asking me about the "big" war and I'm sure I said something arrogant about Desert Storm.

"But why? What are you doing here? Are you mercenaries? We fight for our home, but you are volunteering to fight thousands of miles from *your* home."

As a smug, newly hatched twenty-one-year-old sergeant, I replied, "I'd rather fight the enemy in your backyard than in mine."

Back on the ship on February 26, 1993, I had just finished working out and was mixing some protein powder in the steamy berthing area that fifty of us shared, when Corporal Howard burst in and grabbed me.

"Hey, P," he gasped. "Terrorists exploded a bomb in the parking garage of the World Trade Center's North Tower. Six people KIA and over one thousand wounded."

I wouldn't see pictures until our next port, but the thought of choking office workers, their faces stained with soot, streaming out of the building drove me to a furious outburst.

"Mother*fuckers,*" I said. "That's my *home.*" Guys who had never even seen Manhattan were looking up from their card games, not fully comprehending.

And then I thought about the cocky response I'd given the Israeli sniper.

I thought of my father the tour guide who went to the towers once a week. I dreamt of my mother in her Midtown office trying frantically to find a staircase as smoke and fire consumed her. But I shrugged off the terrorist attack as an isolated incident. An anomaly.

I got good news aboard ship during the final months of my four-year enlistment: I'd been accepted at New York University. I wanted a liberal education in the heart of the city to balance my deep-seated predisposition for the military. If I later gravitated back to the Corps, perhaps I would become an officer. As a child of the Cold War, it seemed like big war had become obsolete. There was no one left to fight. Meanwhile all my peers from Horace Mann were finishing college and starting careers, and I needed to catch up. I had mapped out a number of different paths, from senator to astronaut, but my first choice was a career in the FBI as a sniper with their hostage rescue team.

As a twenty-two-year-old freshman in the fall of 1993, I struggled, adjusting to all of the freedom, the women, and the ignorance. I stormed out of one of my first classes when a kid didn't know the significance of December 7, 1941—and then said indignantly that the date "wasn't important." I'd thought it would be good to have my hawkish views challenged, but this was a little overwhelming.

To augment my paltry GI Bill checks, I got a job at the Outback, an Aussie-style bar on 93rd Street. The place had boomerangs and buffalo horns on the walls, blaring music, and sawdust on the floors. Typical of any successful New York nightspot, most of the staff were models, actors, or both and there was no shortage of drama. The female bartenders dressed in Daisy Dukes and cut their tank tops into little more than bras. All of us wore heavy boots to protect our feet from the slosh of spilled drinks and broken glass. I started out lugging five-gallon buckets of bar ice, changing the empty Foster's kegs, dumping ashtrays, and swabbing up puke in the toilets. But I was soon promoted to bartender. By 4:00 A.M. each day, we were all slick with sweat from dancing on the bar and had just enough energy to clean up and count our sizable tips.

One night while digging bottles of Bud Light out of a cooler, I caught sight of a beautiful young woman with jet-black hair making her way along the bar. It wasn't long before Courtney and I had fallen in love and were living together. Her compassion made her a wonderful social worker and role model for the kids that she was determined to help. I respected her sense of service and she respected mine, but she was glad mine was behind me. Her family graciously welcomed me even though Courtney was already a professional woman and I was a bartender just starting college. They knew I loved their daughter and they took to me like a son.

I got it into my head that I could work as an actor to help pay my way through college. Friends convinced me that I had a look, and I thought it was worth a shot. But there was no sense pretending I was any good, so after one acting class I never went back. Too macho to be a meat puppet. Too self-conscious to learn the craft.

Despite these flaws, I did land parts on two CBS "School Break Specials" working with some real young actors on the rise. In *My Summer as a Girl,* I played a dumb-jock boyfriend to one of the girls Zach Braff tried to attract while he was disguised as a chambermaid at a resort. In *Same Difference,* a Romeo and Juliet–type show, I was Dominic, the stereotypical "Guido" who thought it would be funny to hang bagels on a Jewish girl's house and run away. After lots of goofy drama the couple, their families, and the whole neighborhood were brought together through a miracle and the spirit of Passover and Easter.

During production, my buddy Jeff would swing by the set and raid the free food at the craft services table. We would laugh that only three years before we'd been sitting in the desert waiting to die. Now I teased him that he was the inspiration for my part.

And I couldn't miss the irony of my taking a role that initially disparaged my Italian ancestry—after all the cultural pride my father had instilled in me. But Italians in America had learned to go beyond negative images in the media and popular entertainment. Later, of course, it became obvious that there were millions of people in the world so lacking in cultural confidence that the smallest perceived slight would send mobs into the street, burning embassies, flags, and effigies of their professed enemies.

Acting was fun, but I couldn't commit to the long apprenticeship, and I definitely wasn't inspired by the myopic worldview shared by much of the talent. I was more interested in graphic design and pithy advertising copy. As a teenager, I had cut out the Absolut ads from magazines and put them on my wall. In the Marines, I designed

T-shirts for my buddies. So, while I was at NYU studying economics, I took classes at the School of Visual Arts.

One afternoon I went shopping for suits with my friend and mentor, Bruce, a successful thirtysomething Wall Street trader. We were at his personal tailor where the salesmen tossed bolts of the finest Loro Piana fabrics around haphazardly, trying to satisfy their rich and finicky young customers.

Almost in passing, Bruce mentioned another friend, Michael, who was a highly respected magazine professional. "Ilario, what I do with money is just as creative as what Michael does with words," Bruce said sardonically. "The only real difference is that I make *six times* more than he does."

Holy shit. That closed the door on the creative universe for this son of an immigrant.

Camp Lejeune
26 April 2005

KEANE: At that point, did you encounter the accused?

CUNNINGHAM: Yes, sir.

KEANE: And did you have a conversation with him?

CUNNINGHAM: Yes, sir.

KEANE: What did that conversation consist of?

CUNNINGHAM: He said that two Iraqis were killed. He had left a sign out on the vehicles by the bodies.

KEANE: Did he say what was on the sign?

CUNNINGHAM: Yes, sir.

KEANE: What?

CUNNINGHAM: "No better friend, no worse enemy."

KEANE: What was your reaction to hearing that he had left a sign on the bodies?

CUNNINGHAM: I was surprised. I said, I told him it was inappropriate. He should go back and pick it up.

KEANE: Why was it inappropriate?

CUNNINGHAM: It's just unprofessional. It shouldn't be left out on the bodies.

KEANE: Why not?

CUNNINGHAM: It's like letting someone know who is responsible for doing it, like a death card almost, if you will.

KEANE: So did you tell him to do anything with regards to that sign?

CUNNINGHAM: Just to go back and take it off the car, sir.

KEANE: What did he do after you told him to do that?

CUNNINGHAM: He ran back in that direction to grab the sign.

KEANE: Did you see him again?

CUNNINGHAM: Yes, sir, I did.

KEANE: Did you have another conversation with him?

CUNNINGHAM: Yes, sir. They were mounting up to move out. I asked him if he called in any type of transportation for the bodies to make it back to the morgue. He did not.

KEANE: Why were you concerned about transporting the bodies back to the morgue?

CUNNINGHAM: We just didn't want to leave them out just north of my position, sir.

KEANE: Why?

CUNNINGHAM: Just proper procedure, you know, call in a medevac for any casualties and have them taken to the morgue.

KEANE: Is there any reason why you wouldn't want to leave the bodies of the people that Marines had killed out in the open?

CUNNINGHAM: It's just not right, sir.

KEANE: Okay. Had he made any arrangements to have the bodies retrieved?

CUNNINGHAM: No, sir. They got a call to go. Easy 3 got a call to go on an IED escort. They had to escort EOD [Explosive Ordnance Disposal] down to an IED. And knowing—yes, sir, knowing that they had to get up and move down to the IED site, they weren't able to call anybody yet.

KEANE: Did he ask you to do anything with regards to these bodies?

CUNNINGHAM: He asked if I could call to take care, to call in a medevac for it.

KEANE: What was your reaction to that?

CUNNINGHAM: I wasn't too happy about it, just that they were left there. However, I knew he had to go because when the battalion calls, you go, especially with IEDs. So I arranged for transportation for the two bodies.

New York
1995

Twenty credits a semester was crushing me, but I had to catch up. Engaged to be married to Courtney, I was now feeling heavy pressure to perform financially. I wanted to build a life for a new family and make sure that I could take care of my parents when the time came. I transferred into the Stern School of Business undergraduate program and began analyzing the institutions that made up the financial services industry on Wall Street, just blocks south of my campus. I was fortunate in that I had no shortage of friends and family who wanted to present me with professional opportunities. But I needed the right cultural fit. Reading Michael Lewis's *Liar's Poker* whet my appetite to return to the run-and-gun locker room mentality that I had come from, but I needed something more than unprincipled, undisciplined gambling. I needed the warrior ethos, an elite band of brothers working together to perform a mission.

I needed to work at Goldman Sachs.

They had a dark-suit-and-white-shirt reputation, tough, very smart, but basically honest traders. I saw Goldman as my new Marine Corps, my new family. As the last private investment bank on Wall Street, Goldman didn't reward with stock, they rewarded with partnership, but only for the best of the best. Just the idea of "partner" at a private bank that was widely considered one of the city's most profitable held mysterious and powerful implications. A secret society, but one that everyone in the money business longed to be part of.

But if you didn't have people inside the firm pulling, you couldn't even hope for an interview. I got lucky.

My day of interviews was as rigorous and grueling as reputed. I reported to the energy trading team at the commodities group, and over the course of eight hours I met with nine different partners, traders, and floor brokers.

There was one Young Turk of a floor broker named John who could hardly fit a tie around his thick neck or be heard through the raspy voice that he'd ruined screaming out bids on the trading floor of the New York Mercantile Exchange.

He studied my resume a moment and then tossed it on his desk. "I can see here that you're pretty tough, huh?" he said. "Maybe we should go outside . . ." and he leaned forward.

I leaned forward. "We don't have to go outside. We can *go* right now."

He grinned, and I got the green light from him. That had been a gut check, a reminder that smart people—usually brash, macho guys who didn't flinch from risk—stood to make fortunes. Where I was going to be starting, as a clerk on the floor, it was all teeth and elbows, but if I could survive, maybe I would become an actual trader. Another trader reminded me of the stakes involved and that the business rewarded profitability over character. He slid back in his chair with a smug expression. "Ilario, do you have *any* idea how much money I made four years ago while you were over there fighting in the Gulf?"

With the Kuwaiti oil fields blazing, Scud missiles striking Israeli and Saudi cities, and the four-day ground war unfolding under a screen of media censorship, it had been a good time for a gutsy oil trader.

And then I thought of the exhausted Marines humping through the minefields in the smoke of burning oil and flesh. Flag-draped coffins from enemy and friendly fire. I also pictured the blackened husks of the Iraqi draftees roasted alive when my platoon's TOWs had zapped their tanks.

I was in shock, and I think the evil of that guy's comment didn't register until years later. In that moment, though, as I heard those words, I was fascinated. I was looking at the wizard, the man behind the curtain. Later it would make me sick to think about what that man had said, but sitting there sweating and hungry I was awed. This was the oil trading *business* after all. And who knew the price of oil better than me?

On my way home, I called my parents and my fiancée from a pay phone and breathlessly reported, "I think they liked me."

That night, Courtney and I went to a new bistro on Second Avenue and splurged. My mother's eyes lit up the first time I walked into her apartment with my single-breasted dark suit, white shirt, and Hermès tie. My dad bought me a briefcase and thanked God that I had traded in one uniform for another of finer cloth.

This was a hell of an opportunity, but now I had to prove myself. The trading desk at 85 Broad Street seemed as weirdly futuristic as the bridge of the Battlestar Galactica. Stations of monitors and Bloomberg machines showed jagged-line EKGs of price history. There were dozens of stations, with each trader often working two, and hundreds of flashing speed dials and direct lines to brokerage houses all over the world—Tokyo, Hong Kong, Frankfurt, London. In a business where seconds count, the pressure is always intense. Wall Street evolution. You adapt or you die. I had mastered the ability to survive before, and I was determined to do it again.

But the symbols of those little flickering screens were bewildering. "H" for March, "J" for April. Collars, swaps, straddles, EFPs, bid, ask . . . The glowing EXIT signs above the doors seemed to be the only comprehensible words in the room. Yet the firm expected me to memorize hundreds of trading symbols and terms instantly. If I didn't learn it all fast, there was no shortage of hungry candidates to take my place.

Once more in my life, I began as a recruit, at the bottom. At 6:00 A.M. each day I printed all the risk reports and laid them out on the traders' desks so they'd be ready to manage their complex positions. Then my real day would begin with a walk down to the trading floor of the mercantile exchange at 4 World Trade Center, a low black building at the foot of the Twin Towers.

As a phone clerk, my job was to communicate a picture of what was actually going on in the trading pit. I stood on a wooden crate, so I could see over everyone else's shoulders, and gave color commentary on the market. I yammered like the announcer at a racetrack or an auctioneer, in an effort to paint a picture of who was buying and selling in real time. Then, when a trader was ready to buy or sell, I would get the job done using a Goldman broker—or I'd outsource if they wanted me to be sneaky. The ability to follow the shouts, the hand signals, and the winks was what made a good phone clerk. I was trying to ride a bull, but hadn't yet become an urban cowboy.

I made blunders that cost tens of thousands of dollars. The first time that happened, I actually found an empty cardboard box to pack up my personal stuff, sure that I'd be fired. But the hammer never fell. My mistake had equaled a minor rounding error when weighed against the tens of millions of dollars that were made or lost every day in energy commodity training. And I was honest. A few months before I started at Goldman, a rogue trader in Singapore had cost his bank 1.3 billion dollars by stuffing bad trades into his desk. Nick Leeson's cover-up caused the collapse of Britain's Barings Bank, an institution that had financed the Napoleonic wars and the Louisiana Purchase. Risk. Reward. Some of the traders who successfully managed hundreds of millions of dollars of futures contracts or "physical" oil and gas deliveries could find themselves with annual bonuses of double-digit millions, year after year. These were the guys Tom Wolfe had accurately dubbed "Masters of the Universe."

Camp Lejeune
26 April 2005

Major Stackhouse was taking his time now that the prosecution had completed their questioning. The reporters in the gallery behind me were making notes and trying to gauge the reactions of my family and the investigating officer. My mother and wife forced quick smiles when I turned to check on them. No healthy person wants a loved one to relive a trauma. Most war memories stay buried or trapped in a bottle for a reason.

> STACKHOUSE: You have no firsthand knowledge of what happened down in the area that this raid or cordon and knock took place; correct?
>
> CUNNINGHAM: No, sir.
>
> STACKHOUSE: Except for what you heard with respect to gunshots?
>
> CUNNINGHAM: Yes, sir.
>
> STACKHOUSE: And your memory of what you heard was

gunshots coming so rapid they sounded like a SAW [Squad Automatic Weapon, a belt-fed light machine gun], is that correct?

CUNNINGHAM: Yes, sir.

STACKHOUSE: Was there a long gap in the shooting or did it sound like a pretty consistent string of fire?

CUNNINGHAM: Pretty consistent, sir.

STACKHOUSE: Do you recall how heavy of a unit Lieutenant Pantano brought in with him?

CUNNINGHAM: It was pretty sizable. I remember I believe he had his entire platoon with support from Human [Intelligence] Exploitation Team. And I believe he had a .50 cal on one of the seven-tons. He had some heavy guns with him as well.

STACKHOUSE: And a machine-gun section? Do you remember seeing there being M-240s on HMMWVs [Humvees] and things like that as well?

CUNNINGHAM: Yes, sir.

STACKHOUSE: That is [a] pretty heavy unit rolling in to do a cordon and knock; wouldn't you say?

CUNNINGHAM: Yes, sir.

Baltimore, Maryland
1997

I wanted to be one of the Masters. Working to learn all aspects of the business, I put in twelve-hour days and then headed off to school at night. My employers were generous, even paying for part of my undergraduate education. I was one of the few people actually working at the firm who had not yet completed his degree. It took me three years at NYU to graduate. And I was ready for my first big assignment.

In 1997, electricity markets had recently been deregulated. I had the honor to be recruited for a start-up effort that Goldman was creating in partnership with the big utility company Baltimore Gas & Electric, to be called Constellation Power. The intent was to marry

Goldman Sachs's risk management culture with the utility's knowledge of power generation and transmission infrastructure.

The long days on the trading floor and the nights in the NYU classrooms had finally paid off. After two years I had earned my place on the team. Stu, our brilliant operations manager, was a rabid UMass fan who took me under his wing and taught me how to build a business. Scott, the guy across the desk, was a no-shit rocket scientist who had designed avionics for F-14 missile-avoidance systems, and to my right was Dan, who had graduated from law school at twenty-four. Raj was a Princeton grad student and virtual tennis pro, but not the only athlete. Our boss, Rich, was a Columbia grad and longtime trader who just happened to have played football for the Dallas Cowboys. Most of the guys picked up their families—Courtney's job kept her in New York—and left Wall Street with cardboard boxes of office supplies, headed for a backroom in Baltimore. Before long we had built a profitable business. In 2005 it would be sold for billions.

But trying to meld financial services and power generation produced a monumental clash of cultures. Our biggest hurdle was that the utility business had remained basically unchanged for over a century. It was fundamentally a business whose ethos was keeping the lights on, or more to the point, not letting them go *out*. Talk about risk-averse . . . belt-and-suspenders all the way.

The mechanics of trading electrical power as a commodity were similar to buying and selling crude oil or natural gas futures, but with less liquidity since the industry was so new. I woke at 4:30 A.M. to watch the latest forecast updates on the Weather Channel for an hour. I looked at weather maps and the big utilities' generation schedules and tried to anticipate what power demand would develop in the coming hours, days, and even months. A heat wave or a snowstorm was like a lottery ticket, just not for the ratepayers.

I'd sit and listen as the brokers might announce that the anticipated market was "twenty-three bid at twenty-five for next-day megawatt hours." Taking a position on a couple of thousand next-day contracts could earn you and the firm big bucks—*if* a megawatt hour that you'd bought for $23 actually sold for two dollars more.

The first time I actually put on a position (made a trade) of my own, I felt like I was leaning out into the rotor wash of a helo, about to grab the fast rope.

From our Baltimore office, I watched as the big fish like Enron tried to move the market up or down, literally throwing money away with erratically priced trades in order to maintain influence and control. (Later, we would all learn that they were secretly subsidizing the liquidity of the energy market with shareholder dollars.) At the time we only knew they were bullying the field by buying high in order to escalate the price or selling at a loss in order to drive a price into the ground.

Early on, I realized that commodity trading was like war. Markets were about fear and pain—just like war. They were about manipulation and psyching out your opponents—just like war. They were about imposing your will—just like war. And just like war, "the only unfair fight is the one you lose."

I'll never forget an early lesson I learned about how traders viewed the world. When I'd arrived at 85 Broad at dawn on July 18, 1996, a guy ran into the office shouting, "Holy shit. A jumbo jet crashed off Long Island. It might have been shot down!" In the same breath he was yelling, "Buy oil!" which triggered a frantic dash to the phones. That might have seemed disgusting or even heartless, but the guys who reached their phones minutes or even seconds faster than their colleagues made millions more. The unsuspecting sellers in the Far East or Europe who hadn't yet gotten the news of the TWA Flight 800 crash and who were happy to sell into excited demand soon lost their shirts as the price screamed up. And, in turn, those sellers had to come back into the market to cover their short selling—driving prices up even higher.

Profitability was the single most important factor driving everything we did, and I enjoyed its many benefits, but I was getting tired. In electricity trading, the perpetual "fucking the ratepayer," as I called it, was one of the factors beginning to turn me off to the whole financial services industry. I understood the importance of wealth creation, but when I watched Enron, I was uncomfortable. It was too early for it to be obviously criminal, but it didn't feel right. Fortunately, I was on a team that was significantly more principled.

I was making good money, but honestly wasn't happy. The strain of separation from my wife had become unbearable for us both. We'd rented a beautiful apartment in a gentrified old brick cannery on the Baltimore Harbor, but I lived alone. Courtney stayed in New York because she had a large caseload of clients to whom she was devoted. I was commuting home on the weekends, usually by train. I felt that I was on a fast track to financial success: after all, I had the dream job, the dream apartment, and a dream car—a silver BMW convertible—and my inky black Kawasaki Ninja 750 with dual headlights, custom exhaust pipe, and a rear tire so fat it looked like it fell off of a dragster.

Despite—or because of—all that, our marriage was disintegrating. We would spend the weekends trying to get to know each other after a week apart and then come Sunday night rip off the Band-Aid again as I trudged to the train station or straddled my bike for the high-speed 180-mile run down the interstate to Baltimore. Back to an empty apartment.

Lots of people could have made that arrangement work, I guess. But I felt like I was busting my hump to provide a certain lifestyle, and it wasn't being appreciated. Perhaps if I'd listened better, I would have recognized the things that were not as important to her as I'd thought. Perhaps if I had been a better partner, more attentive and communicative, I could have convinced her to stay with me in Baltimore. But I couldn't. I didn't. I failed, and our marriage failed.

As the bond between us tore, my ambivalent motivation for continuing the job ebbed away. For a year, I'd sacrificed to expand one of the first electricity trading ventures to originate from Wall Street, helping to quickly grow the business from the eighty-fifth to the fourth largest American power marketer. But this no longer mattered to me, nor did the fact that the company was going public and I'd be abandoning a six-figure salary and a stack of cash from stock options.

After three years I had reached a psychological critical mass where the money was no longer more important than happiness. Still, quitting Constellation Power and the people who had invested so much faith in me was a wrenching decision for a first-generation American whose job had made his parents so proud. I left my prestigious position, my fancy apartment, and my fancy car in Baltimore and headed back to New York on my motorcycle to find a new life.

Camp Lejeune
26 April 2005

Sam described the Iraqi response after the bodies had been collected.

> STACKHOUSE: You said the ING squad that was guarding
> that bridge or working that bridge with you

was nervous. Why were they nervous, again?

CUNNINGHAM: Just that evening, sir, there was an unusual amount of chatter. They were standing in a group. I believe they were nervous—from what they had told me, they were nervous from these two individuals [who] came from a large tribe within the area.

STACKHOUSE: A "dangerous tribe," I think you said?

CUNNINGHAM: Yes, sir.

STACKHOUSE: The kind of tribe that is involved in the insurgency?

CUNNINGHAM: I am not sure, sir. I know they were really scared of this tribe. But I am not sure if they were insurgents or not, sir, the tribe.

STACKHOUSE: Well, these are members of the Iraqi National Guard that are concerned of it though; right?

CUNNINGHAM: Yes, sir.

STACKHOUSE: And the Iraqi National Guard, you'd agree, is often a target of the insurgency; right?

CUNNINGHAM: Yes, sir.

New York
1998

The guy on the other end of the desk had gelled silver hair that made his black suit darker. The director of marketing at Oktober Films was a serious man who had taken the time to see me because a friend had begged. Other than the obscure movie posters and a window that looked out onto Astor Place, my blue shirt and blazer were the only color in the room. I wondered where all the sexy shit that I'd read about in *Entertainment Weekly* actually happened because it sure wasn't here.

He scanned my face, my wire-rim glasses and short hair. Then he flipped through my resume again, noting my Goldman Sachs experience, my NYU economics degree, the years spent in the Marines, and of course, Horace Mann. It was my first media interview and I called it way wrong. I looked like I should be behind the counter at Blockbuster instead of closing deals on a cell phone while sipping a soy latte. To him I was just another zero-creativity Upper East Side yuppie trying to sneak into the New York independent film party.

"Look, Ilario," he said in a friendly but condescending tone, "film and television are the coolest deals in town, and everyone wants in. People, even lawyers, are willing to work for free, starting right at the bottom."

"Sure," I answered. "I understand."

"Good." He was on his feet, giving me a dismissive handshake. "We'll call you if we have anything."

He never called. Neither did Miramax. Neither did several other leads. Coming off the Wall Street fix with time on my hands, I needed some adventure and decided to spend a couple of weeks in Russia. Although I didn't speak the language and knew no one in Moscow, Vlad, a tall, red-haired, chain-smoking buddy of mine from NYU who'd been a Russian firefighter, had charmed me with tales of intrigue and spectacular lawlessness and corruption. Grudges, he said, were settled with AKs. Underemployed Chechnya vets made great mafia hit men. It was the Wild West—East?—and I had to see it for myself.

The trip freed me from the frustration I'd encountered in Manhattan. The first afternoon in Moscow, I sat in a little café at the G.U.M. department store, drinking a beer and smoking a Cuban cigar, watching the lines of tourists file into Lenin's Tomb across Red Square. The gilded onion domes of the Kremlin were even gaudier than the familiar TV images.

I could almost see rows of tanks and huge missile launchers, and the divisions of Red Army infantry parading through the square in synchronized lockstep. As a kid, those pictures had both fascinated and scared me. But on this warm afternoon, Red Square had become a parade ground for prostitutes. The center of the Russian capital was overrun with them. At night, my hotel phone would ring, and whores with cigarette-raw voices would ask in broken English, "Are you interested in Erotic Massage Program?" Only the Russians can take the sex out of sex. Given Moscow's violence, past and present, I decided to avoid anything called a program.

Passing through the city's ornate Metro stations, I was almost overwhelmed by ironic sights. In every subway car there were veterans of the Great Patriotic War, as they call World War II, their musty, threadbare suit jackets still plastered with campaign ribbons. I knew from reading history that the Soviet Union had suffered horribly in that war, losing more than twenty million soldiers and civilians. But actually riding on the subway with these old vets—survivors of so much combat—it was easier to understand how a militarized Soviet culture had evolved into the Cold War. It had been the absolute duty of all Russians to ensure that their beloved Motherland, the *Rodina,* would never be invaded again. Experiencing this for myself, I better understood the motivations of what had once been our most bitter and fearsome enemy. An enemy must be understood if it is to be defeated.

But, just as Metro passengers my age and older got up to offer those survivors of Stalingrad or Kursk their seats in crowded cars, the young Muscovites hardly seemed to notice them. They were too busy swapping Metallica and Michael Jackson CDs.

When I got off the escalator at the Arbat station, the first thing I saw was a billboard of Michael Jordan, seemingly suspended above an NBA court, like a superhero about to slam dunk. The red Nike swoosh on his shoes glowed in the twilight. *He was one of our tools,* I realized. Western entertainment—from sports to MTV—had been a lot more appealing than the Young Pioneers or Komsomol. The Russian kids I saw wanted to be like us, not to be our enemies. I was witnessing firsthand the effects of America's ultimate weapon, the strength of our free economy and institutions, what my professors at NYU had called soft power.

Back in New York, I kept on interviewing, and a funny thing happened as my hair grew longer: I got a job on a sitcom news satire, *Lateline*. John Markus, the executive producer, and Al Franken, the show's other exec and the star, sat down with me because a friend had begged. But unlike the others who had looked me over and passed, they were impressed by my resume. Most striking to them was my wartime service, which prompted them to thank me and shake my hand.

Wow, I'm going to work in television.

As I soon learned, production assistants are the lowest-paid rung on the television ladder, and they certainly have to be prepared to do anything. I helped assemble sets, photocopied scripts, ordered pizza, seated the studio audience, or maybe pushed a camera into position. Some nights I did all of those things.

The comedic premise of *Lateline* was to expose what "really happens" behind the scenes on network news magazine shows like *Night-*

line. Al Franken played a klutzy correspondent who took himself far too seriously. Franken brought a lot of his old *Saturday Night Live* wackiness to the show to bounce off guest stars like G. Gordon Liddy, William F. Buckley, and Dana Carvey.

One night, Liddy did a Watergate spoof, where he rappelled through the ceiling in a black jumpsuit, insisting of course, on doing his own stunts, only to be accidentally "shot" by a bumbling Franken.

I was having fun and growing my knowledge base, but being a PA could be unpleasant when snotty teenage celebrities dismissed me as a flunky after I brought their coffee. Some nights it was hard to remember that I'd fought in a war and traded multimillion-dollar commodity positions. If I wanted to work in entertainment, however, I'd have to pay my dues.

Sadly, we produced only thirteen episodes of *Lateline,* in part because NBC couldn't find the right time slot for political satire. Given the success today of faux news like *The Daily Show* and *The Colbert Report,* we were probably ahead of the times.

Having learned about the stratified world of traditional TV production on the set of *Lateline,* I started developing my own projects to capture some of the dot-com bubble. In the fall of 1999, an old friend and financier who knew about a web-based business I was developing thought I would be a perfect fit for a film company called the Shooting Gallery. The independent studio had produced films like the Academy Award winner *Sling Blade,* which was made in 1996 for $1 million and sold to Miramax for $10 million. That had put them and the film's star, Billy Bob Thornton, on the map.

Now they were expanding into the Internet. After some negotiations—protracted because nobody knew the value of entertainment company options packages in this new medium—I signed on. But I didn't stay long. The Shooting Gallery sold me on its model of integrated media and the economies of scale it could achieve by leveraging its production assets across traditional film, television, commercials, and the Internet. In late 1999, the market was going in their direction. Mark Cuban had become a billionaire when he sold his Broadcast.com business to Yahoo. The Shooting Gallery was hustling to play catch-up and I wanted to be a part of it. But after seven months, I realized that the industry was changing, the market was cooling, and many of my assumptions about the management were wrong. I left and took one of my team members with me.

We started our boutique consulting company in the summer of 2000 looking to capitalize on a specific niche that was both underserviced and protected by high barriers to entry. We had tried to convince the management at the Shooting Gallery to focus resources on the field of interactive television, and when they wouldn't, we'd decided to do it on our own. In the midst of trying to rent an office for my new start-up, I got a cryptic cell phone call in Times Square from a burly voice in Amsterdam. As I stood still in the traffic noise, not far from the Armed Forces recruiting station, the caller informed me, "The guns will be here Friday."

A producer-friend back at the Shooting Gallery had alerted me to a one-month gig as a consultant on a horror-action flick called *The Shaft*. The film's fictional setting was a landmark Manhattan skyscraper where the demonic express elevator had suddenly started killing people in rather gruesome ways. Much of the movie was filmed in Amsterdam, with some exteriors shot in New York. My intriguing phone call had come from the executive producer, Bill Gilmore, who was producing movies before I was born, including one of my favorites, the Marine Corps courtroom drama *A Few Good Men*. He had assembled a crew of action-actor regulars, including Dan Hedaya and Michael Ironside, as well as relative newcomer Naomi Watts.

One premise of the script was that Americans would react to homicidal technology with an equally murderous paramilitary response. I suggested they replace the National Guard tanks with heavily armed New York police SWAT units. The only trouble was that none of the Dutch or New York extras knew how to hold an MP-5 submachine gun, let alone give a believable impression of shooting one.

That was why I was needed. The project was probably the most fun I'd ever had. I was flown around, driven in Mercedes limos, and treated like a rock star in fine hotels, all because I knew about guns and tactics but could also talk film to a director—with my ponytail flopping all the while.

I taught both actors and extras, mainly in Amsterdam, which provided the interiors for the Manhattan building. Then the production moved to New York to shoot exteriors. The union-wage savvy New York extras were even more jaded than the pot-smoking slackers I'd worked with in Amsterdam. I put the New York crew through half a day of weapons training, which most of them mastered. Due to budget and time constraints, I was forced to keep them near the set, the Alliance

Capital Building on Sixth Avenue. I had the twenty-five SWAT bubbas line up and face their reflections in the window glass to practice "presenting" their weapons to imaginary targets. As I was strutting back and forth on this virtual firing line, nostalgically barking commands and adjusting body positions, a bored young cop looked on, sneering at what he saw as impostors playing with guns.

When that assignment ended, I went back to launching Filter Media with my partners. Chief among them was my Shooting Gallery friend, Vlad, yet another chain-smoking Russian of the same name, who by twenty-five had pioneered interactive media at companies like Time Warner and later at Fox Interactive, where I had cherry-picked him. Our crew of gutsy entrepreneurs included Vlad's wife, Emily, another innovator who'd managed all of MSNBC's interactive properties and web content. There was Az, a former Coast Guard hot-dog engineer who could build anything from nothing and had literally helped get MSNBC off the ground. Finally, there was my dear friend J.R., who left the financial security of a top-tier law firm to take a risk on our vision and become Filter's chief operating officer.

Our goal was to be the fastest and most nimble, multitalented evolving-media consultancy in the city. We did production work for Sony Pictures Television and strategic planning for Mattel's Barbie division. We chaired conferences at Columbia University and won awards for our designs. All we had to do was hang tight, keep our faith, and land the right contracts.

We worked the kind of hours you'd expect when it's all yours to lose, but we found time to enjoy our lives too. We grilled steaks on the deck of my apartment overlooking the Manhattan skyline. We ate spanakopita from the Greek bakery on Ninth Avenue. We drank sangria and toasted one another, and I toasted Jill, the woman beside me whom I would marry one day.

In the midst of my biathlon training, I had seen Jill at the New York Sports Club in Midtown. Covered in sweat, there were no pretenses, and in skimpy gym clothes there were no illusions. She was hot. A trainer who worked at the gym introduced us twice before I finally got the nerve up to give her my card and ask her to coffee "sometime." She asked me what I was doing that night, and we became inseparable.

Jill and I sat in Central Park and shared sandwiches after we had biked the six-mile loop. I would look at her as she pulled the Sunday *Times* out of her backpack and she would blush. And we would kiss and giggle on our little blanket. Our little island. We drove up to her friends' place in Connecticut and played futuristic masquerade to ring in Y2K. All the revelers strutted their finest millennium masks, but Jill and her girlfriend Claudia took it to another level in slinky silver "space" dresses and metallic makeup.

Our love grew more intense in 2000 and, somehow, even stronger in 2001. When I asked Jill to marry me, I gave her an antique ring, the diamond shaped like a timpani drum surrounded with blue sapphires. We drank frozen mojitos that we made in the blender as we'd watch the sun set over the city. I was fascinated by her grace and elegance, which extended to everything she did, even landscaping our deck with plants, flowers, and herbs, transforming a sterile concrete slab into an oasis.

Jill would sometimes talk about her years modeling on the international fashion circuit. On our first date at an Italian restaurant on Lexington Avenue I confessed, "I've had *some* experience traveling, too. But I was only a tourist once. Most of the time, I traveled on Navy ships, helicopters, or rubber boats. Then there was a little outing into Kuwait in a Humvee."

Jill listened politely, but had no frame of reference with which to absorb what I was describing. As trite as it sounds, we really did come from different worlds.

To her, I was a creative "downtown" guy, which made falling in love that much easier. Jill also understood and supported my ambitious dreams for Filter Media. We were engaged in May 2000, and set our wedding date for October 20, 2001.

In fact, I was thinking about wedding arrangements on September 11, 2001, as I stood in the slowly moving car of the N train, heading down to 28th Street to meet J.R. at the publicist's office.

That meeting, of course, was cancelled. But our wedding was not.

Camp Lejeune
26 April 2005

The prosecution was tying up its second round of questions.

> KEANE: How long had your unit been in Iraq on April 15th?

CUNNINGHAM: Just over a month, sir.

KEANE: And during this time period, was this the time period where the contractors had been strung up on the bridge in Fallujah?

CUNNINGHAM: Yes, sir.

KEANE: How soon before April 15th, if you can recall?

CUNNINGHAM: I believe it was at the end of March, sir, around the 30th of March.

KEANE: Thank you. No further questions.

STACKHOUSE: I have a few more. Just one second, sir.

I passed Stackhouse a note. He studied it and then started in on Sam.

STACKHOUSE: You had said that April, thus far, had been a pretty hectic month?

CUNNINGHAM: Yes, sir.

STACKHOUSE: Can you tell us what you recall of it being a hectic month?

CUNNINGHAM: Basically, the country exploded across the board, Fallujah, Ramadi, around our area. On 7 April, we got into our first contact, which was in Rasheed, which is just south of the mixing bowl, by a large amount of [Shiite cleric Moqtada] al-Sadr's militia. Also on the 9th of April, there was a substantial firefight in Latafiyah, which is just to the south of Mahmudiyah. We sustained our first KIA there and several wounded Marines as well. 11 April, we had that—actually, that was 11 April. Also, we also had— that is when the insurgents were blowing up the bridges on MSR Tampa. We had a Special Forces unit within our area sustain a KIA, several wounded in action. And we had to rescue them as well.

STACKHOUSE: Ambushes and IEDs?

CUNNINGHAM: Yes, sir.

STACKHOUSE: Most of the ambushes coming [at] dusk, sundown time frame? Do you recall?

CUNNINGHAM: Yes, sir.

STACKHOUSE: Anything else you remember about it? I mean, that paints a pretty hectic month, but do you recall anything else?

CUNNINGHAM: Golf Company was in a—one platoon from Golf Company, I believe it was a QRF. They were ambushed out towards Yusufiyah as well.

STACKHOUSE: Is it fair to say that everybody in the battalion, from what you know, was on high alert?

CUNNINGHAM: Yes, sir.

FOUR

Article 32 Hearing
DAY ONE

Camp Lejeune
26 April 2005

The Naval Criminal Investigative Service agent smiled at me while he washed his hands. Probably carrying under his sport coat, but I didn't see a holster bulge when I squeezed past him into the tiny bathroom. He threw his wet paper towels in the trash and nodded politely, leaving me alone for the first time that day. After making sure not to get water on my uniform as I splashed my face, I gave myself a long minute just to stare in the mirror.

Back at the table with my four lawyers, I turned a fresh Diet Coke can, reading every last word of the ingredients . . . carbonated water . . . citric acid . . . Captain Courtney Trombly shot me a grin. She was trim, athletic, with short blond hair and a wide smile. The next prosecution witness would be her responsibility. Across the aisle, Captain John Reh, assistant government counsel, was on his feet waiting for his witness to arrive. Perhaps a foot shorter than Keane, Reh was the one I had been warned about. He had worked cases as a defense lawyer and knew how to argue both sides. Reh's witness, an Arabic-speaking Marine who was an Algerian national, was sworn in. Duct tape covered his nametag and Major Winn had asked the media to refer to him only as Corporal "O," so his work with the Counterintelligence Marines was not compromised.

REH: Corporal O, what is your current billet?
  O: Field messman, sir, and I have a secondary MOS, which is 8611, linguist. I am a Marine linguist, sir.

The corporal spoke with a slight accent that could have been French or North African Arabic. His complexion was light, and he looked southern European.

REH: Would you give a description, again, about your actual job, how it worked?
  O: My actual job was just to translate to my senior sergeant, staff sergeant. And my job was just, basically, translating, sir, word by word.

Captain Reh positioned several wide photographic blow-ups of two dead Iraqi males on the easel next to the witness.

REH: Do you recognize these photographs?
  O: Yes, sir. That's the two bodies, sir.
REH: What do they depict?
  O: Excuse me, sir?
REH: What do they—what are they showing you?
  O: The two detainees that were shot, sir.

The poster-size photos were gruesome, shocking, an image of combat that people rarely saw on television. Each dead man was slumped against the inside panels of the open driver's side and rear doors of the small white car. There were wide blood smears starting higher on the door panels, leading down to the bodies. The prosecution had made sure to place the enlarged photos so that they faced the closed-circuit television camera and the media watching the hearing from another building.

REH: Okay. Do you remember where—where they were in the car?

O: They were [in] the same position, sir, basically.

REH: Okay. It didn't appear to you that anybody had been moved or anything like that?

O: No, sir. No, sir.

REH: Okay. And you said that you had believed that they had been shot in [the] back. Why do you say that?

O: Because you can tell between an exit wound and an entrance wound, sir.

REH: Explain what you mean by that.

O: Well . . .

TROMBLY: Objection, sir. There is no foundation been laid that he is an expert on entry or exit wounds.

REH: Just asking his general impression, sir.

WINN: Okay. I am going to go ahead and sustain the objection.

REH: Very well, sir. [to Corporal O:] Where did—well, let me ask you this question: Where, to you, did it appear they had been shot? [to Major Winn:] That's—that is a general question I think that he can answer, sir.

WINN: I will let him answer. But I am not going to let him voice his opinion on his determination of entry and exit wounds.

REH: Very well, sir. [to the witness:] Where did it appear to you they had been shot?

O: On their back, sir.

REH: And why—what do you base that knowledge on?

O: On their position, sir.

REH: And where was that?

O: They were on their knees. And they were basically laying down. Their stomach was laying down against the vehicle means they got shot in the back, sir.

Officer Candidate School
Marine Base Quantico, Virginia
18 January to 28 March 2003

The infiltration course this February morning led us, panting with strain, along the steep trails through the pine trees and down to a long barbed-wire entanglement in a hollow. The trails under the criss-crossed barbed wire were well worn by decades of crawling candidates. That meant this year's record cold and snowfall had left a three-inch sheet of ice on the six inches of near-freezing water above the nine inches of chilled mud.

The double-timing column of candidates paused at the edge of the obstacle to consider their unfortunate fates while instructors cracked the ice with axes and sledgehammers.

On command, we dove in, slid under the barbed wire, and began smashing ice with our elbows and knees. I sank into the cold water. The pain was blinding and I gasped—only to swallow a mouthful of gritty frozen mud.

Pain, I reminded myself, was only a thought, a flicker of mini-amperage in the wiring of your brain. Pretend this mud is just a frozen frappuccino from Starbucks. I repeated my mantra, *Pain does not exist*. That bullshit lasted maybe fifteen seconds, and then pure survival instinct took over. But I was at a standstill because candidates ahead of me were literally freezing up trying to negotiate the underwater obstacles. My limbs would also seize before I made it out. I was going to die, and I wished death would hurry up. But I kept thrashing, elbows and knees, gasping air when I could, spitting out mud when I couldn't.

But all the candidates weren't so lucky. Guys around me started to succumb to hypothermia. We were in our boots, cammie trousers, and sweatshirts, but soaked to the bone, just as generation after generation of Marines that came through Quantico had been and others to come would be.

By our common suffering, we were forging a bond, not only with our fellow candidates, but with history.

During each dawn PT (physical training) session, our company officers were out there with us. But while we wore cammie trousers and plain olive sweatshirts, they wore forest green with four stark white letters printed on their chests: USMC. Across their backs was a title that reminded us that we weren't actually in hell: OFFICER CANDIDATE SCHOOL.

The motto of OCS was *Ductus exemplo,* "Lead by Example." And this morning, Major Castelli, our rhino of a company commander, who'd been a football star at Annapolis, showed us what leadership by example meant. Without hesitation, he dived into the frozen mud and water to haul out candidates who'd gone limp with hypothermia. A lot of us stood on the bank, shivering violently in our own struggle to survive the cold, not fully aware of what was happening.

That night, as we basked in the warmth of the squad bay, we talked about the men who had fought before us. And we felt like pussies.

War in winter is always cruel: Washington's troops starving and shoeless at Valley Forge, Napoleon's Grande Armée retreating from Moscow through the snow . . .

But for us, there was one place and one battle like no other, Frozen Chosin, the Marine breakout from the Chosin Reservoir in North Korea in the winter of 1950. It had been so cold that gasoline froze. C-rations froze in the cans. The limbs of the dead froze at grotesque angles and their bodies were used to stop bullets. The 1st Marine Division and a few courageous Army troops had fought a Chinese force that outnumbered them ten to one for weeks in those conditions and had finally escaped the encirclement.

And here we were, whimpering after crawling through some freezing mud for a few minutes.

Maybe I was too old for this. Maybe my duty as an American was to stay home and bring a loving, healthy productive child into the world. I'm sorry, my son. This isn't someone else's fight.

I missed Jill and our baby, Domenico, desperately as I thought back to the fall of 2001. Confident that I'd be recalled to the Corps as a Scout Sniper, I had wanted to leave behind a survivor to carry on the Pantano name in case I was killed in combat.

On September 16, 2001, I'd gone out to the Marine Corps Reserve center in Garden City on Long Island to apply for reenlistment. The NCOs I'd met were friendly but overwhelmed. The problem seemed to be that I'd been out of the Corps "a long damn time," and that in this interval, service records had gone from paper to computerized files.

The gunnery sergeant in charge of recruiting Marines with prior service confirmed what I'd feared: the Corps was gripped in a confused spin-up, mobilizing reservists and trying to sort through the deluge of applications from prior-service Marines like me hoping to get back in to fight the terrorists who'd attacked us.

Back in Manhattan, I got off the subway as close to Ground Zero as I could. There were National Guard Humvees blocking the streets. Troops had dust filters hanging from their necks. The ruins of the Twin Towers and the surrounding buildings were still covered in soot and ash and in some places still smoldering. It looked like fucking Pompeii in 79 A.D. The air smelled of burnt plastic and death. Fire engines and emergency vehicles were crushed under a hundred floors of graves. My friend Kevin Cleary was in there. He worked for Euro Brokers, but had given me one of my first bartending jobs at a place that he owned. I had other friends at Euro, at Cantor . . . These were the guys I was on the phone with every day when I was a trader. I recognized the jagged heap of rubble that had been the old mercantile exchange at 4 World Trade Center. That was where I'd broken into commodities trading as a clerk.

Masada shall never fall again.

There was a trendy tattoo parlor on East Houston Street. The kid was busy tattooing a colorful memorial for an EMT who had lost a dozen brothers.

God bless them. God bless us all.

I waited my turn. It took him about a half hour to tattoo "USMC" in heavy Celtic letters inside my right forearm. The fine print underneath read "Scout Sniper." Despite the vague warning of the recruiter in Garden City, I was certain that I'd soon be able to reenter the Corps as a sergeant in my old MOS.

"Give me corporal. I don't care," I'd told him.

Very few Scout Snipers branded their flesh in this manner. If a Marine was captured with such a tattoo, it was an invitation to die badly. But watching the blood bubble up as the artist's buzzing needle injected the ink beneath my skin only strengthened my resolve never to be captured.

That primal desire to fight my country's enemies became much stronger after Jill's pregnancy was confirmed and the new Bush administration struck back at al-Qaeda and the Taliban in Afghanistan. It was becoming increasingly difficult for me to focus on "digital subscriber growth," "DVRs," or "video on demand." Somehow, I had to become part of Operation Enduring Freedom, and I needed to be honest with my partners at Filter Media about my shift of commitment and my new intent. They were both partners and my friends, and they understood. Commerce had been eclipsed by national security, by national survival. Az, my fortysomething engineer, took a long drag on a cigarette as he pledged, "I'd be right there with ya if I was fifteen years younger."

While I prepared to return to duty I took a freelance assignment planning and managing "high-risk" productions for a small independent television producer in New York. After launching a project in Afghanistan, I was quickly promoted to the director of operations. As their name implied, CameraPlanet sent film and video crews almost anywhere, including Third World hot spots and war zones—which were often the same places.

A lot of creative documentary filmmakers and adventurous TV journalists wanted to do high-risk production in Afghanistan, so CameraPlanet needed someone who understood both the military and the media. The first time you do something is always the hardest, and this was the first time anyone had taken a high-definition TV camera into a war zone. Mark Cuban's HDNet hired us to produce a series of documentaries on Pakistan and Afghanistan. The talent was former CNN correspondent Peter Arnett—who'd gotten fired from that network for lending his name to a badly flawed Vietnam War documentary. I didn't give a shit who he was, I was excited to build the plan, hire the security professionals to execute it, and to put teams in country. Arnett and I didn't get along, and he once complained to my boss, Steve, that he wanted me fired because I had to be with the "fucking CIA"!

I wasn't fired, but I did run projects for the State Department, National Geographic, and one for Nickelodeon on the children of Afghanistan, which won an Emmy. I couldn't have done any of it without my former British Commando partner, Chris, and his unflappable sense of humor. Twenty years in the forces and a ton of unconventional experience (he had been a United Nations WMD inspector in Iraq with Scott Ritter) were the perfect tools for what would be our toughest but most rewarding mission: to shoot a documentary and simultaneously facilitate a relief mission to help the beleaguered women of Afghanistan free themselves from Taliban oppression. Willa Shallit, the executive director of V-Day, hired me to get Eve Ensler, the creator of the *Vagina Monologues*, safely into Kabul for the first celebration of

International Woman's Day in that country's history. But even as I was helping women who were half a world away, my own woman was suffering beside me.

At sunset on a warm summer evening in 2002, Jill had her first sips of wine after giving birth to our son. This had been a tough nine months for everyone, but now at least we had some relief. Domenico had finished nursing and was playing sleepily in his crib just inside the door.

I, too, sipped some wine and glanced at the dark blue tattoo on my forearm.

I looked down at Domenico's crib. He'd stopped fighting sleep and was curled up, cuddling the blanket my mother had knit him. My throat tightened and I almost broke into tears. His face, his head of thickening dark hair, his heavy eyelashes, were so much like Jill's that a wave of protective love for both of them swept over me.

If defending my wife and child wasn't worth fighting for, what was?

Jill knew how I felt. And slowly since the shock of 9/11, we'd reached a tense truce on my reentering the Corps. I had failed in one marriage already and was determined not to repeat my mistakes. We talked endlessly as I tried to assuage her fears. I was as relentless as she was reluctant, but in the end she understood.

"I have to do this. It's who I am. To deny it is to deny my own existence."

We reached a compromise and I promised to delay reentry in the Corps until she'd had the baby and the support of our nearby families was well established. Every day of 2002 I trained my body and my mind for the rigors that would follow. I cut out an article on Pat Tillman and his heroic decision to leave the NFL for Army basic training and pinned it to my board at work.

I'll be joining you soon.

And now that Domenico was born, it was my turn to make good on a pledge. But as each day had passed, I knew that Jill's secret hope that our family would escape this war quietly grew stronger.

"Jill," I said after a long silence. "It's time. I've got to put my paperwork in now. I'm going to request an age waiver and apply for OCS. I can't wait much longer." I would be thirty-one in a few days, and the official application cutoff was twenty-eight. There'd be other waivers needed, as well, for my dependents, even for having tattoos (to assure no candidate carried a gang tag). The machine wanted young, unblemished, unattached clay to mold.

Jill sighed, looked away and wouldn't take my hand. "Ilario, you know how I feel. You've got to think about your family."

"I *am* thinking about my family."

And that was more or less the way things stood between us in 2002.

My officer recruiter, Captain Diorio, worked hard to pull all the requisite forms together. Unlike my first enlistment, I was exactly the kind of prospect a recruiter avoids. Lots of time and paperwork up front with a high probability of failure in training due to my age-weakened body. When I went in to pick up my acceptance letter, I enjoyed the irony that Captain Diorio's office was aboard the *Intrepid*.

And they say you can't go home again.

Camp Lejeune
26 April 2005

REH: When you first saw this scene, what was your feeling?

  O: It looked weird to me, sir. That was the only thing.

REH: Why did it look weird to you?

  O: It was two dead bodies, sir. I mean, I don't know, I guess. There was two detainees dead, sir.

REH: What happened next?

  O: After that, sir, we had a call that there was another vehicle approaching from the north, it was a black vehicle. Me and Sergeant "M," we walked down there, sir. That is when we saw, like—as soon as I got on the scene, sir, I seen a Marine slashing the tire of a vehicle and some Marines basically pushing—taking the detainees and dragging them all the way—like, fifteen, twenty feet away from the dead bodies.

REH: Who was in that vehicle?

  O: I remember, sir, I think it was, like five or six bodies [men] inside the vehicle; it was labor workers, sir.

REH: Okay. And how did you determine that?

o: Because we talked to them, sir.

REH: All right. And what happened to these individuals?

o: They were dragged like fifteen, twenty feet away from the [dead] bodies, sir, and face down on the ground.

REH: Could they see them from where they were?

o: Yes, sir.

REH: What was their demeanor?

o: They were mad that they were [pause]. They were mad at us. And they were mad and scared, sir, both mad and scared.

REH: Okay. Did [you] have a conversation with Lieutenant Pantano after that?

o: No. We were just told to translate a word for him—a phrase for him, sir.

REH: Okay. And what did he tell you to translate?

o: He told me to tell them like, basically, if any of them want to decide to join the insurgency, that something was going to happen to them [the same] as those bodies, sir.

REH: Did you see a sign over the bodies?

o: Yes, sir.

REH: What did that sign say?

o: "No better friend, no worse enemy," sir.

Officer Candidate School
Marine Base Quantico, Virginia
18 January to 28 March 2003

In boot camp, the DIs count push-ups. In Officer Candidate School, the instructors count the words in an essay. The exercise could either be a punishment from a sergeant instructor or a regular class assignment. Either way, the assignment deprives you of valuable sleep. No one among us thought the instructors actually read the things, but we knew they counted every single word we scribbled.

First Lieutenant Jones, our platoon commander, had just finished a class on the "Fourteen Leadership Traits," and we were tasked to write about one of them. I chose *Integrity,* and that choice almost got me kicked out of the Marine Corps.

I cited an "ironic inconsistency" at work in the Corps: Marines wore white gloves with their dress blues—literally clean hands—yet we idealized profane, hard-drinking gunnery sergeants who'd punch a lieutenant's lights out and steal a general's Humvee to fetch beer for their men coming out of the field. We idealized the guy who broke the rules and would do anything for his troops, yet violators were court-martialed. Clearly, I added, Americans as a people were conflicted about their sense of integrity because they were able to vote out of office a man like President George H. W. Bush and vote twice for a man like Bill Clinton, despite his record as a draft dodger and his personal failings.

Where was our integrity when we fought in camouflage, which by its nature was designed to "deceive" the eye? We talked about honor and yet we studied and mastered the art of the ambush, learning to exploit whatever advantage of terrain, darkness, or explosive device that we could to surprise and kill an enemy that was stunned by our violence. Exactly as we should. In the gunfighter community, I stressed, if you ever find yourself in a "fair" fight, your tactics suck. Mothers of America didn't want you bringing their sons into fair fights with 50/50 odds; they wanted you to bring their sons home alive. Period.

A few days later, the platoon was busy writing letters, clipping toenails, and studying for tests when the squad bay went pin-drop silent. Sergeant Instructor Staff Sergeant Cusamano stood with his arms crossed and a cruel smirk directed right at me.

What now? Our sergeant instructors had made breaking my balls their life's mission. I was a goddamn "prior," a former enlisted man aspiring to become an officer. In their minds, Candidate Pantano figured he was better than them, thought his shit didn't stink. Torment was their method of trying to break me.

Part of their resentment stemmed from priors sharing what they'd learned about the Corps as enlisted men. Our instructors, like the DIs at Parris Island, wanted to control that knowledge—we weren't even allowed to wear watches—and with it our lives. Most of the candidates were college seniors or recent grads in their early twenties who knew little of the military and less of the Marine Corps. The *USMC: Scout Sniper* tattoo on my forearm made me a magnet for instructor wrath. This particular ass-chewing was about my essay.

"The platoon commander wants your ass in his office immediately,

Candidate Pantano!" Thirty sets of eyes watched me scramble to the hatch and bang three times.

"Good evening, sir. Candidate Pantano reporting as ordered, sir!" I bellowed, almost knocking myself over backward.

"Get in here."

I snapped to attention at his desk.

I was suddenly aware of my near nudity, dressed in flip-flops and green nylon running shorts that we called man-panties.

First Lieutenant Jones's desk was bare of the usual memorabilia from deployments or war. He might have been a supply officer and was probably watching Fred Flintstone when I was in the desert. My disdain hadn't been lost on him during our previous weeks of training. His disdain hadn't been lost on me during the half dozen times I'd been called into his office for an ass-chewing.

He was gripping the pages of my essay so hard that his knuckles were bloodless.

"Is there any reason why I shouldn't eject you from OCS right now?" he demanded, trying to control his outrage. "You've clearly got a character flaw."

"Sir, I believe in what I wrote."

"Do you have a fucking problem with integrity?"

"No, sir, I was merely trying . . ."

Staff Sergeant Cusamano was leaning into my ear, wasting no time feasting on my ass. "OH. YOUWANNATALKBACKTOTHEPLA-TOONCOMMANDER! HAVE YOU LOST YOUR FUCKING MIND?"

Jones tossed me the essay. "Write it again, Candidate. And if I see any more of that bullshit, you *will* be standing in front of Major Castelli, on your way out the door.

"YOUUNDASTANDDAT?" Cusamano's forehead veins were pulsing as he slammed the door behind me. "GOAWAY! MOVE-NASTY, MOVE!"

That night, while the rest of my platoon was sleeping, I sat on a toilet in the head, rewriting the essay. And the next night. And the night after that.

Camp Lejeune
26 April 2005

REH: You said you found AK-47s in the house; is that correct?

O: Inside the house. Yes, sir.

REH: Is that uncommon?

O: It is common, sir. Every Iraqi house has, like, one or two AKs.

REH: No further questions at this time, sir.

WINN: Defense?

TROMBLY: Corporal "O," at the beginning of your testimony, you said that you were a field messman; correct?

O: Yes, ma'am.

TROMBLY: Could you explain what the duties of a field messman are, please?

O: Basically, support the troops and bringing—I mean, which is like basically cooking, field cooking, ma'am, just basically supporting the troops by providing food and nutrition to the troops, ma'am.

Courtney Trombly smiled to put the corporal at ease. Her manner was relaxed.

TROMBLY: You testified that you showed up on the scene and there were three men under the bridge, being detained; correct?

O: They weren't under the bridge. They were on the side of the road, ma'am.

TROMBLY: On the side of the road?

O: Yes, ma'am.

TROMBLY: And who were these men?

O: The old man was the owner of the house. And the two other[s] were his sons, ma'am.

TROMBLY: And who had detained them?

O: I believe it was the platoon that were there.

TROMBLY: But you are not sure?

O: I am not sure, ma'am.

TROMBLY: And were you the only ones to interrogate these—these Iraqis?

O: I don't interrogate, ma'am, I translate. Sergeant "M" was interrogating. I was translating for him, ma'am.

TROMBLY: Was Sergeant "M" the first Marine who had interrogated these Iraqis?

O: I don't know that, ma'am.

TROMBLY: You don't know?

O: No, ma'am.

TROMBLY: So, you didn't know at the time that these Iraqis had complained that their house had been overrun by insurgents; right?

O: No, ma'am. I didn't know that.

TROMBLY: And you didn't know that these Iraqis had actually provided a map to the unit, asking the Marine Corps for help; did you know that?

O: No, ma'am.

TROMBLY: So you only knew that you were supposed to show up to support the raid with Lieutenant Pantano, right?

O: Yes, ma'am.

TROMBLY: Okay. What did you know about that area? Did you know that a lot of attacks had been coming from the area of the target house?

O: We heard that, ma'am. We got briefed about it.

TROMBLY: And you heard that mortars had been coming from that area—

O: Yes, ma'am.

TROMBLY: —knocking down bridges, right?

O: Yes, ma'am.

TROMBLY: And you heard that attacks, small-arms fire, had been coming from this area as well?

O: Yes, ma'am.

TROMBLY: And going in there, you felt, and the unit felt, that it was, very likely, a "bad house," right?

O: Yes, ma'am.

TROMBLY: And that is why it was raided, right?

O: Yes, ma'am.

TROMBLY: And the unit you were supporting, Lieutenant
Pantano's platoon, they were going in hard,
weren't they?

O: Yes, ma'am.

Officer Candidate School
Marine Base Quantico, Virginia
18 January to 28 March 2003

After the first weeks of OCS, when the weakest candidates had been cut, our platoon sergeant took it on himself to teach us what it meant to be *real* Marines.

Sergeant Instructor Gunnery Sergeant Legé (Le-jay) was one of the most singularly impressive men I'd ever met, the quintessential warrior, well over six feet with a hard, muscled frame and a face like a cyborg.

"Listen the fuck up," he'd whisper, knowing we were so afraid we dared not make him raise his voice. He had staff sergeant subordinates who would toss our bunks and make our life hell. His job was to teach, and he did much of it while striding around the squad bay after lights-out. Gunny Legé had done the usual tour as a "Hat" [drill instructor] at Parris Island, only there were rumors that his assignment had been cut short due to some sort of mysterious and violent infractions, which only added to his mystique.

"I would rather rip out my best friend's throat, and then try to save him, than lose a fight."

Gunny Legé described monumental brawls . . . with sailors at Subic Bay, with Italian cops in Naples, with outlaw bikers outside Pendleton. The thrust of his stories was that you never gave your opponent a chance: if you, as a United States Marine, were going to get in a fight, the only outcome would be your opponent's face exploding into a bloody mess between your fists. Take any bruise or injury. The only thing that mattered was victory.

His favorite text was *The Book of Five Rings* by the Samurai Miyamoto Musashi, which taught warriors to overcome fear and become one with their fighting spirits. To demonstrate his message, the Gunny would have us drag out the pugil sticks and "fight, goddammit, fight like you mean it."

Marine pugil sticks were five feet long and had two padded ends about as hard as a boxing glove. Wielded with both hands, you could rough up your opponent pretty bad. That was what Gunny Legé wanted, for us to accept pain and to return it in an overwhelming fashion unacceptable in civil society.

"When I fight at a bar or in a bare-knuckle event, I don't dance around and trade love taps for twelve rounds," he explained. "I find the opening, smash my opponent's fucking face, let him pick up his teeth with broken fingers, then go have a beer. I ain't got time for anything less." If he thought anyone was holding back, that unfortunate candidate got the chance to fight him in the center of the squad bay.

We didn't hold back.

After a month, we received the occasional twenty-four-hour weekend liberty, but were forbidden from leaving the immediate area. It was a clever policy that gave young officer candidates just enough rope to hang themselves. A weekend didn't go by without at least a few candidates deserting. Good riddance. We were looking for future leaders, not privates. If you didn't want to be here, then get the fuck out. We had our share of guys who raised their hands and requested to drop while in the midst of training, too. But the great thing about the liberty was the chance to return to your family and then leave the Corps from the safety of your girlfriend's arms instead of before the harsh stares of thirty other candidates who were all suffering just as bad as you.

The draw of sweet civilian life could be especially powerful while you were in the blast furnace of OCS. I certainly thought hard about what I was doing, what I was risking, and what I was leaving behind. There were definitely days when even Wall Street seemed better than enduring another moment under a sergeant instructor's prodding, remorseless thumb.

Twenty-four hours was also enough time to get into a drunken brawl if you were so inclined. Another weakness best discovered before you were in command of forty young Americans—Gunny Legé's ethos notwithstanding.

I knew what the rules were, and I chose to break them. I took the train to New York every weekend so I could see Jill and our seven-month-old son. Mostly I got in so late it was just a chance to slide into bed with her and then play with our baby for an hour after Sunday morning breakfast. He'd touch the stubble on my head and laugh. Jill would look at my bald head and grimace. My haircut represented a choice that required her to accept sacrifices, for which she had not bargained. Returning to Quantico was always wrenching, kissing my wife and Domenico goodbye after only a few hours together to catch the early-morning train. This was a violation of the OCS honor code and could have resulted in my immediate discharge, had I been caught. It was a calculated risk and nothing was going to stop me from seeing them. Nothing.

Even in the profane monastery of OCS, we all knew America and a handful of its allies were about to invade Iraq. On March 20, 2003—a week before our scheduled graduation—our superiors allowed the candidates to watch President Bush address the nation. "On my orders, Coalition forces have begun striking selected targets of military importance to undermine Saddam Hussein's ability to wage war. These are opening stages of what will be a broad and concerted campaign."

Iraq, I thought. That bright Tuesday, September 11, 2001, striding up Broadway among the crowds of shocked people, I'd known that America would counterattack. But I had not known when or how.

Marines had fought in Afghanistan during Operation Enduring Freedom that fall, helping overcome al-Qaeda. But I had missed that battle. Now I would miss the invasion that would topple Saddam Hussein. But I suspected there would be plenty of work for me in Iraq after I earned my commission as a lieutenant in the Marine Corps. I had chosen the path of the professional warrior, pledged to defend his country. And I intended to honor that pledge wherever it took me.

On the morning of Friday, March 28, 2003, my mother and two close buddies from the Gulf, Hans Heinz and Jeff Dejessie, pinned the gold bars of a Marine second lieutenant onto the epaulettes of my dress-green alpha blouse. A ring formed around us that included Chuck, Carlos, James, and Mike. They were vets and friends from our service together in Desert Storm who had come from across the country to show their support. It was difficult to celebrate. Just that week twenty-two Marines had been killed and 150 injured in the battle for Nasiriyah.

By tradition, the first salute rendered to a newly commissioned lieutenant is rewarded by a silver dollar, signaling the loss of your virginity. You always remember your first. I had rehearsed a little speech and I eagerly searched for Gunnery Sergeant Legé.

I couldn't find him.

Camp Lejeune
26 April 2005

TROMBLY: You said that Lieutenant Pantano briefed you at the start of the mission, correct?

O: Yes, ma'am.

TROMBLY: And you witnessed him giving orders and explaining his plan?

O: Yes, ma'am.

TROMBLY: And you saw him at the vehicle near where the insurgents were detained?

O: Yes, ma'am.

TROMBLY: And you saw him after the shooting?

O: Yes, ma'am.

TROMBLY: And then you saw him as he was moving his platoon out to move on to the next mission; right?

O: Yes, ma'am.

TROMBLY: You saw him getting accountability for [accounting for] his Marines and moving everybody out?

O: Yes, ma'am.

TROMBLY: And his demeanor—did his demeanor ever change during this entire mission?

O: It was the same, ma'am.

TROMBLY: Same all the way through?

O: Yes, ma'am.

TROMBLY: Even after the shooting?

O: Yes, ma'am.

TROMBLY: And you have worked with him on a few missions; right?

O: Two or three, ma'am, or more.

TROMBLY: Two or three?

O: Yes, ma'am.

TROMBLY: Was his demeanor on those other missions any
　　　　different than his demeanor this day?

O: No, ma'am.

The Basic School
Marine Base Quantico, Virginia
11 April to 9 October 2003

I was afraid that I was in trouble a little over halfway into the four-mile endurance course. It was hot and humid; the sun was beating on my Kevlar like a fist. We ran the E-course in full gear: boots and cammies, ammo pouches with magazines, two full canteens, field pack with extra water, Kevlar helmet, and of course the eight pounds of the M-16 rifle. We literally had our hands full, and if you made it to the finish line with any mud in the barrel of your weapon, you automatically failed.

The starting line was at the "regular" obstacle course, where we had to negotiate the usual iron bars and phone poles. Even if you tried to pace yourself, the O-course was a demanding test of upper- and lower-body strength and endurance. The moves were explosive heaves of your entire body weight, and they stole oxygen and energy from your muscles. We threw ourselves blindly over walls and balanced on steeply angled beams, all the while trying not to fall and break a leg, a pelvis, or a neck. After the three-story rope climb, the average Marine was spent, assuming he even reached the top. But as young lieutenants we had to lead, and physical toughness was a priority, so the O-course was just the beginning of our fun.

From there, the E-course was a murderous sequence of muddy trails up and down hills, across log bridges, and more ropes to be climbed. Often you found yourself running through lonely stretches of woods, away from the jeering instructors or the support of your fellow lieutenants. It was just you, and that was when you had to dig deepest. No one was looking. No one would call you out if you slowed to a walk. Alone in the woods, you had to find hidden personal reserves of will to keep your body moving. If you staggered along, walking too much of the course, you would fail, and as a result not graduate from The Basic School, or TBS, the next step in becoming an officer after completion of OCS. Your career as an officer would be over. If you took shortcuts, other officers would notice and you could expect that your leadership scores would reflect your lack of spine. Just about everyone tried their best.

There was plenty of lumpy puke splashed along the course today to prove our desire. On this morning, the heat made it tough going even without all the combat gear. Hell, the FBI ran it "slick" and felt like heroes. But here we were burdened under a total of over thirty pounds of muddy, awkwardly swinging, waterlogged weight.

And I was too hardheaded for my own good. Staff Sergeant Williams, the enlisted advisor who always looked out for his guys in Charlie Company, had warned us that morning. "Look. You still got months of training ahead of you. Don't do anything stupid."

Fuck that. Some British Royal Marines had been at the TBS pub talking shit about how fast and tough they were. I was on a mission, and given my strong showing on our earlier practice run, I wanted to beat the Brits. I pulled out ahead of the pack once we cleared the obstacles and started humping up the hills. I was well hydrated and the heat wouldn't get me. I tried to push the pain in my legs and back out of my mind, to forget the raw gasps as I sucked for wind. Pain was just a state of mind. This E-course was only the mirror image of breaking ice in that muddy February swamp. Think of what the Marines on Guadalcanal and Tarawa had gone through . . .

Thinking didn't work. The pine trees around me got very bright, and then very dim. "Pantano . . ." someone was yelling. The dumb guys were running in the *wrong* direction. Weren't they? Why was I blowing my little orange "rescue me" whistle?

There were faces above me. I was on the ground, and hands were tearing off my gear. They dragged me back to the company area and covered me in ice and wet towels. The ambulance was en route to take me to the aid station. I had stopped sweating and felt neither heat nor cold. But I did hear the words "Silver Bullet." *No.* That was the dreaded rectal thermometer whose threat alone was enough to compel good behavior from Marines. By the time I reached the corpsmen half an hour later, my rectal temperature was still 104 degrees: major heat stroke. My muscles had been secreting so many toxins that the temperature regulation built into my metabolism had shut down.

Luckily the incident had come late in the week, so I had the weekend to regain my strength. The one thing I did *not* want to happen would be ending up with a permanent light-duty assignment due to a medical condition. I'd get dropped. I wanted to be selected for the infantry and the grunts don't need "broke dicks."

Idiot.

I was doing so well and I almost threw it away.

In TBS, newly commissioned Marine lieutenants are subjected to mental and physical challenges several degrees more severe than those encountered in OCS. Here, the officer instructors didn't mock and taunt us as sergeant instructors like Legé and Cusamano had. This was professional development. The purpose of TBS was to form solid junior officers, not to weed out civilian wannabes who'd watched too many recruiting commercials on TV and hoped to become part of "The Few, the Proud . . ." OCS had been like initiation to a fraternity. A constant string of physical and mental challenges, not designed to train as much as they were designed to cull the weak. TBS was where the institution made the investment of time and money, and they were jamming four years of undergrad school into six months.

These 180 days of intense instruction combined the classroom with the practical every day. We did get liberty for part of almost every weekend, but usually had take-home class assignments. This led to several pejorative epithets for TBS: "Time Between Sundays" and "The Big Suck." For me, home had become a neat little apartment in nearby Fredericksburg. Jill was still a long way from adjusting to life as a Marine Corps wife. She hadn't made many friends among the wives who were often ten years her junior. She had been an executive, and many of the lovely young brides hadn't finished college yet. But at least our having weekends together more frequently helped.

I tried hard to be a good dad and husband, and I think my success came from my genuine peace and contentment at work. I brought my joy home at the end of my day because I was so thrilled to be doing what I loved. Yes, we had traded an elitist lifestyle, but the *quality* of our lives was enriched by the purity and peace that came when you felt you were accomplishing your true vocation. I brought no frustration home from the office, and I loved, respected, and admired my colleagues and my instructors. They were truly the best of America. A smart, talented, driven team fueled not by money or glamour, but by love. Love of their families, love of their country, love of the Corps and the values that it represented to them.

We lived by a code of Honor, Courage, and Commitment. Our word truly was our bond. People died if you didn't fulfill your obligation. In the business world, you just went to court or paid the fine if you fucked up. In this job, you went to a funeral, if you came home at all. The most telling example in the differences between my old and new life came in the form of accepted social behaviors. In my media life, it was widely considered cool to do drugs or cheat on your wife. In the Corps, those behaviors were criminal and would result not just in the traditional punishments, but in the loss of your career as a professional Marine. The stakes involved were obvious every day as America fought in Iraq.

Leadership wasn't just taught, it was demonstrated. On our first day of TBS training, all the young lieutenants of the company had to endure the pain, terror, and humiliation of being subjected to tear gas. The gas chamber taught students to trust the reliability of their chemical warfare equipment, and when we removed our masks, to learn how to survive cloaked under the asphyxiating fear of the gas. As students were finally allowed to escape the chamber into the fresh air outside, we gasped, coughed, choked, and loosed yard-long streams of mucus. But we were soon slapping each other's backs and howling with laughter.

Each incoming platoon immediately shared a tough bonding experience when we looked around the gas chamber and saw that our staff platoon commanders and instructors were suffering right there beside us. The biggest lesson came from the littlest guy, our company XO. Captain Hasseltine actually went through the tear gas chamber with every platoon in his company—six times in one day. What a fucking motivator. *Ductus exemplo.*

To further instill leadership, students passed through rotating billets, holding every position in a rifle platoon. For a given week, one student was the platoon commander, one the platoon sergeant, one the guide, three were squad leaders, and nine were fire team leaders. We all wrote weekly evaluations, both up and down the food chain, which combined to form one's leadership score. Periodically throughout the course, students evaluated and ranked every member of their platoon in what were officially called "peer evaluations," but which we often described as "spear evaluations." All contributed to your final class standing, which in turn would affect your assignment selection.

One of the greatest professional achievements of my life was being voted by my peers to represent and speak for them as the "Mess President" during our formal dining-in ceremony. The dinner was attended by a host of VIPs. But as much fun as it was to play dress-up in our blues, it was just another in a series of well-conceived training evolutions. That night, as we chose the right spoon or the proper glass with which to toast, we were discovering the "gentleman" half of our profession. I addressed my peers with a deeply personal reflection:

> *I'd like to bring you back for a moment to the heated emotion and uncertainty that followed in the wake of 9/11. Specifically, the chatter that we all generated as we reached out to friends and family, far and wide, in a desperate effort to reconnect and demonstrate our resolve. E-mails depicting prophesies, "I told you so's," and doctored photos were just a small part of the collective emotional groan as our nation recoiled from the blow.*
>
> *There was solace to be found in the words and experiences of those great generations that had gone before us. And I suspect you will remember, as do I, the litany of courageous quotes rescued from oblivion by our friends and family that clogged your in-boxes. In that particular state of vulnerability, one of those quotes struck me with the impact of its power and brevity, two things to which I am unaccustomed. Winston Churchill reminded us that:*
>
> > *Sometimes it is not enough to do your best.*
> > *Sometimes, you must do what is required . . .*

After all the long hours in the classrooms, and all the longer days and nights in the field, we finally reached the last week. Everybody was jumpy, hoping he'd get his choice of MOS. All I wanted was infantry. The trouble was, so did most of my class. Infantry was literally where the action was; that was where you could lead Marines at the tip of the spear in combat. I felt good about my chances. Even though the doctors had warned me that I'd always be prone to heat stroke after that close call in August, I ran the E-course again on a warm day in late September and came in second—beating 190 Marine officers almost ten years younger.

On that Wednesday, forty-one second lieutenants were summoned across the street to the mysterious and infamous "Little Red School House," headquarters of the Infantry Officer Course (IOC), which we aspiring grunts had dubbed the "Little House of Manhood." This was the mythical place I had been praying I would end up after the nine harsh months of training.

A thick-necked captain with a white raccoon-eyed racing stripe from too many days spent shooting on the range in sunglasses looked us over skeptically.

"Congratulations, bitches, you get Monday off for Mr. Columbus. Spend it with your family. That's not a threat, it's a warning. We've got you for sixty days and you *will* be in the field for forty-five of 'em." Captain Gehris smiled as our eyes rolled and we groaned, twisting wedding rings nervously on our fingers. He and his team would be right there with us as we earned our Ph.D.s in infantry leadership.

"You will be here at 0700 the Tuesday after you graduate from TBS. You better start hydrating now; at 0330 the following morning there's going to be a little indoc."

This was Corps jargon for a ballbuster, a brutal gut-check test that would combine physical, psychological, and tactical challenges to be completed under rigid time limits. Hell of a way to say hello.

At home in Fredericksburg with Jill and Domenico that weekend, I flipped through the TV news channels, trying to get caught up on the situation in Iraq. Less than six months before, President Bush had proudly announced "Mission accomplished," the end of "major combat operations" in Operation Iraqi Freedom.

But now fighting was flaring up again, with sniper and rocket-propelled grenade (RPG) attacks on Coalition troops. Improvised roadside bombs—IEDs in military parlance—exploded daily. The Pentagon dismissed these attacks as the work of "dead-enders" from the Baath Party and Saddam Hussein's defeated army. Most of the country welcomed the Coalition as liberators.

Maybe, I thought, watching the CNN footage of a smoldering Humvee near Tikrit.

A shadow crossed the living room: Jill, in her bathrobe, cradling Domenico.

"Was the volume up too high?" I asked. "Did I wake you up?"

"I wasn't sleeping," she said, taking a final look at the harsh images on the screen before leaving the room.

Camp Lejeune
26 April 2005

TROMBLY: The house still hadn't been searched; right?

O: It was getting searched, ma'am.

TROMBLY: So it was all going on at the same time?

O: Yes, ma'am.

TROMBLY: And intel from the house hadn't come back to that area near the car; had it?

O: Not yet, ma'am.

TROMBLY: And you said that these two individuals denied being insurgents?

O: Yes, ma'am.

TROMBLY: Was that rare for Iraqis to deny being insurgents?

O: Every time, ma'am, they will deny.

TROMBLY: How often did Iraqis deny being insurgents with you?

O: Every time, ma'am.

TROMBLY: So you weren't surprised that they didn't confess to being insurgents, were you?

O: No, ma'am.

TROMBLY: So you hadn't asked these individuals about what was in their house?

O: No. We asked—we asked if they knew any insurgents, if there was any weapons cache around the area, basic questions, ma'am.

TROMBLY: Right. But you weren't able, at that time, to ask them about what the Marines had found in their house because you didn't know about it yet?

O: Yes, ma'am.

Infantry Officer Course
Marine Base Quantico, Virginia
13 October to 19 December 2003

We were in the fortieth hour of the exercise. Two sunsets, two dawns. A few minutes' sleep. In that time, we'd navigated a swamp, silently infiltrating on a rainy fall night, dug into three separate fighting positions miles apart, and completed a twenty-mile "road" march—actually an ankle-twisting slog with a full rucksack and ammo load along the steep, rutted trails.

I had a raw sore throat and felt like a zombie. But the rest of my platoon was just as bad. I'd been elected class commander, so I couldn't puss out. We were halfway through the two months of IOC, and the instructors intended to test our limits.

Marines rarely had the luxury of shooting after a long night's sleep, but rather after days of movement and patrols. Panting through the trees as I scanned for targets, I realized again that such realistic training has saved countless lives, even as it has cost a few. In combat there are no good or easy decisions, only the lesser evil. As in training.

The Israelis I'd met as a Scout Sniper had distilled this philosophy down to "Sweat lots in peace. Bleed little in war." That concept had been rendered by many military leaders, from Russian Generalissimo Aleksandr Vasilyevich Suvorov in the 18th century to Major Evans Carlson, leader of the Marine Raiders in World War II.

The approach worked. But it could be dangerous. Safety had previously been a priority in our training as Marines. Not anymore. IOC was designed to push the traditional envelope. Realistic training meant loaded weapons in the hands of exhausted Marines. That was good: only by having our lives in our own hands were we able to experience the intensity of combat. A student had been killed on a live-fire range a few classes before ours. The accident did not launch the automatic ass-puckering responses that you would expect from military bureaucrats. In fact, our training became even more dangerous and intense.

That morning at the tactical range, we moved through the trees, hardly able to see one another over the rolling hills. Yellow balloons stapled to trees *menacingly* represented al-Qaeda and gave the instant feedback pop-of-death when hit with a single well-aimed shot. That wasn't how it worked in the real world, but it made for decent low-budget training. After several run-throughs of the live-fire course at different speeds and angles with different students in charge each time, we were finally done for the week.

"Umm, does someone want to tell those drivers they forgot something," Nick deadpanned as we watched our support Humvees drive off the range, leaving us five miles from our barracks and the weekend. His humor flared into hot indignation. A few of the captains stayed behind to taunt us and to ensure that the four-man fire teams ran back together.

"Hell! I *want* to be here tomorrow when you do this again, so take your fucking time, pigs!" Gehris shouted, double-timing backward. No sleep. One chow a day. Constant movement. The adrenaline suck of shooting "high-speed" ranges and blowing claymores and demo all day and night. And now this.

Dada. Dada. Daaadaaaa. I heard my son's voice, but it was hard for me to picture his face. He was changing so fast and I was always training.

I'll make it. I will be home with my family. Or I will die trying.

Ryan, John, and Brian were just as determined as I was, so our fire team started off in the drizzling gloom. "If it ain't rain'n, we ain't train'n," John cheered with the popular refrain from his time as prior enlisted grunt. I wasn't the only one dumb enough to get out, go to school, and come back in to lead Marines as an officer. I was surrounded by *my* people. I was home again. We ran and cursed and fumed and panted. But soon we had made it back to our families. To our other families.

IOC was known for its varied and secretive curriculum. We visited Aberdeen Proving Ground in Maryland to check out all sorts of foreign weapons, including the AK-47s, AK-74s, and the RPGs that the enemy emerging in Iraq—they were now officially called "insurgents"—used against us. We flew out to the vast high desert of the Marine base at Twentynine Palms, California, and joined live-fire exercises day and night with tanks and LAVs, helos and jets. We went to the emergency room of Washington, D.C.'s busy hospitals to experience spurting arteries and sucking chest wounds, the product of stabbings and gunshots.

Most of us hoped never to witness such gore. But we knew we would.

Camp Lejeune
26 April 2005

TROMBLY: Okay. Corporal "O," let's talk about the second vehicle stop, the labor workers?

O: Yes. Yes, ma'am.

TROMBLY: You said there were five to six men in that vehicle?

O: I believe six, ma'am.

TROMBLY: And you said that Lieutenant Pantano had you translate for you—

O: Yes, ma'am.

TROMBLY: —for him? And what did he translate?

O: He just told me to tell them, like, if they joined the insurgency or, you know, if they decide in the future to join the insurgency, the same thing is going to happen to them as the two dead bodies, ma'am.

TROMBLY: Was that the first time you had been asked to translate a message like that?

O: No, ma'am.

TROMBLY: How often did you translate a message like that to Iraqi civilians?

O: Approximately every time we do a raid or something like that, ma'am.

TROMBLY: So other platoon commanders besides Lieutenant Pantano had given you the same message to translate?

O: Something like that. Yes, ma'am.

TROMBLY: And why was that being done?

O: Well, just to scare the people, to keep our Marines safe, ma'am.

TROMBLY: To scare them; right?

O: Yes, ma'am.

TROMBLY: In your mind, was that statement, "If you join the insurgency, the same thing is going to happen to you," that was fact; wasn't it?

O: Yes, ma'am.

TROMBLY: So it wasn't really a threat?

O: It wasn't a threat, ma'am.

TROMBLY: Approximately how many times, over your extended duty in Iraq, did you translate something like that for the Marine Corps?

O: I don't count. Many, many, ma'am, many times.

TROMBLY: So again, it wasn't unusual?

o: No, ma'am.

TROMBLY: And you said, that you knew—you had heard the phrase, "no better friend, no worse enemy," before?

o: Yes, ma'am.

TROMBLY: So was that like the motto of the Marine Corps over there?

o: Something like that, ma'am, yes, during a combat environment. Yes, ma'am.

TROMBLY: And had you ever been asked to translate that to Iraqi civilians before?

o: Yes, ma'am.

TROMBLY: How many times were you told to translate that to the Iraqis?

o: Many times, ma'am.

TROMBLY: Hundreds, like the other message?

o: Yes, ma'am.

TROMBLY: And again, what was the point of translating that to the populace?

o: Every time we go to a bad neighborhood, ma'am, we have to do that because a lot of people join the insurgency for money. So basically we would, kind of like, not threaten them but warn them. We can be their best friend. And if they choose to join the insurgency, we can be their worst enemy.

TROMBLY: So you are trying to weigh in on their decision of whether or not they are going to join the insurgency for money or—

o: To think about it. Yes, ma'am.

Infantry Officer Course
Marine Base Quantico, Virginia
13 October to 19 December 2003

The IOC training that probably impressed us most was Class IO801–807 Killology. On the afternoon of Thursday, October 23, the class instructors, Captains Gehris and Reid, handed out prep sheets for the next morning's class.

"Pay attention to this," Gehris said. "It's important."

Pivotal to the training was the question of how best to break through the normal civilized inhibitions against taking human life. And until we overcame that inhibition in ourselves and in the Marines we'd lead, we would never be effective infantry officers.

That night at home, I studied the prep sheet:

> *Introduction: Combat involves killing; however, even within the armed forces it is rarely discussed, let alone studied . . . Prior to and during this class, the students should think about and be prepared to discuss the following:*

> - *Is killing a foreign act?*
> - *What are the resistances to killing?*
> - *What are the body's physiological responses to killing?*
> - *How can resistance to killing be lowered?*

The list continued, forcing us to face the true nature of our chosen profession.

Early the next morning, the class discussion centered on a 1987 *Washington Post* article, "Death and the Dark Side of Command," by Fred Downs, a decorated Army Infantry officer who'd lost an arm in Vietnam.

"If I were in charge of training officers," Downs wrote, "I would start by establishing a class called: 'The Dark Side of Command.' It would be about the basic realities of combat: Killing the enemy and taking ground. This is a side of command that is rarely discussed within the military. It's hard to talk about because it involves subjects that are taboo in our society—subjects like death, fear, ego, destruction, and mental illness."

That statement got our attention.

> *The "Dark Side" assumes that in war, there are no universal truths except the will to survive and the need to live with yourself afterward. . . .*
> *An infantry lieutenant is unique because the infantrymen he*

leads participate in the most personal killing that is done in wartime. Only a few men in his platoon will be natural killers, men who accept killing as part of the job and think very little about it other than that it must be done in the most effective way. There may be the occasional psychopathic killer in a platoon, but they are dangerous, unstable and unreliable. Their need for killing is not derived from survival or as a wish to serve their country or God, but from craziness.

The majority of men in the platoon will kill out of necessity and in the heat of battle. But they will go through a number of psychological questions and challenges afterward because they are bothered by what they have done.

A combat platoon is composed of young men who have been raised with a moral belief that killing is wrong. Parents, religious leaders, teachers and government officials have all taught us that it's wrong to kill. The sixth commandment, "Thou shalt not kill," is basic to our society. It is not easy to break that command, nor is it easy to live with the results afterwards unless the man is reassured that the killing was okay. The guilt may still be there years later and may be a burden that is carried to the grave. . . .

This was the straight word, and we all recognized it. The class was unusually silent and somber at the end.

To make sure we hadn't lost our edge, the instructors then ordered us behind the barracks, where we were issued boxing gloves and proceeded to beat the crap out of each other in three-minute rounds.

The Infantry Officer Course graduation was on Friday, December 19, 2003. The morning began with the traditional steak-and-eggs breakfast served on tables covered with camouflaged ponchos rather than linen. This was a day for warriors only. Mothers, sisters, and wives were not invited. This was not their place and it was understood among the graduates in the room that there were many aspects of our profession that could never and should never be shared.

My friend, Ryan, the honor graduate of our class—a prior enlisted Force Recon Marine—was awarded a custom .45 pistol, Model 1911, from an officers' association in recognition of his excellent performance.

We all gave a short address to our classmates before we went on to our next assignments. John quoted Kublai Khan's captain of the guard: "We seek neither glory in combat nor the spoils of victory, only death to our enemy." That was John. Short, tough, and to the point, the way an officer should be.

I, of course, was more loquacious, but with good intentions. I quoted from Bob Woodward's book *Bush at War,* which described a ceremony that Special Operations forces in Afghanistan conducted in the bitterly cold mountains on February 5, 2003, after the defeat of al-Qaeda and the Taliban.

> *There was a pile of rocks arranged as a tombstone over a buried piece of the demolished World Trade Center . . .*
>
> *One of the men read a prayer. Then he said, "We consecrate this spot as an everlasting memorial to the brave Americans who died on September 11, so that all who would seek to do her harm will know that America will not stand by and watch terror prevail.*
>
> *"We will export death and violence to the four corners of the earth in defense of our great nation."*

Camp Lejeune
26 April 2005

TROMBLY: Did you actually search the car?

O: No. I didn't search the car, ma'am.

TROMBLY: So you never really looked closely at the vehicle or looked into it?

O: I just walked by it, ma'am.

TROMBLY: So you just walked by it?

O: Yes, ma'am.

TROMBLY: Kind of a passing glance?

O: Yes, ma'am.

TROMBLY: Okay. And after the shooting, it was the same thing; wasn't it? You were walking by it to get to the second vehicle that had been stopped—

O: Yes, ma'am.

TROMBLY: —and it was a passing glance?

o: Yes, ma'am.

TROMBLY: So you didn't examine the bodies?

o: No, ma'am.

TROMBLY: And you didn't stop to inspect them?

o: No, ma'am.

TROMBLY: And you really just kept on walking because you had another mission to do—

o: Yes, ma'am.

TROMBLY: So you didn't get a real close look at what was in the car?

o: Just walking by, ma'am.

TROMBLY: Just walking by . . .

TROMBLY: Thank you, Corporal "O," I appreciate your time. [to Winn] Nothing further, sir.

Mom handled calls from reporters as we drove home that night. I fished through the glove box for some peanuts. Jill slept in the back, exhausted from a day that had started before dawn with a hair and makeup session, preparing for an appearance on *Good Morning America* shot live at a nearby hotel room the network used as a studio. She and my mother were terrific. Merry had become quite experienced in the three months since she began speaking out about my case. She had created the web site DefendTheDefenders.org to raise money and awareness for my defense, and it had proven a tremendous success. Letters, checks, and e-mails were pouring in from all over the country, as well as from Canada, Japan, England, and Australia. I would be able to pay for the best lawyers and forensic consultants with something more than my second lieutenant's salary.

Mom flipped her phone closed and announced, "Tonight it's *Nightline,*" as she settled back in her seat and closed her eyes. She had done the on-camera interview for them weeks before. With the energy remaining from the intense day in the courtroom, I was curious what angle the show would take. Dinner was as quiet and pensive as the car ride. Thankfully, the kids were already asleep when we got home.

At 11:30 P.M., George Stephanopoulos introduced the evening's program as the camera zoomed in. "Tonight, on the battlefields of Iraq, when does killing become murder? And who's to say where to draw the line? A U.S. Marine is charged. Today . . . his first official hearing, but the story of Lieutenant Pantano has already sparked a fiery debate . . . Tonight: rules of war, justice, and survival in the combat zone . . ." Stephanopoulos went on to open a ten-minute pretaped segment that gave an overview of my case, my background, and my support.

In one scene, G. Gordon Liddy declared, "In World War II, if we had applied these kinds of rules, about seventy-five percent of the troops would have been in jail."

Twelve minutes into the segment, reporter Mike Cerre gave an up-date from the Camp Lejeune courthouse: "Well, the prosecution wasted no time in addressing the self-defense claim that Pantano's lawyers have been claiming all along. They produced a witness who had been one of the interpreters on the interrogation team that talked to the suspects prior to the shooting. They spoke to them for about fif-teen minutes and they had determined that they were unarmed and they were probably not suspects or insurgents and were just visiting family in the area and were to be released. So that goes right to the heart of the fact: was Lieutenant Pantano endangered by these two men . . ."

I turned off the television.

FIVE

Forward Operating Base
Mahmudiyah, Iraq
20 March 2004

The bullet-shredded Chevy Suburban was one of the first things I saw when our long convoy from Baghdad International Airport dismounted inside the berm of the Forward Operating Base (FOB). It was only minutes after sunrise, but the morning was already getting hot. With the heat came the flies and the taint of sewage and smoldering trash from the town of Mahmudiyah three klicks to the south of the FOB along Highway 8—Route Jackson.

As the Marines tossed down their gear from the trucks, my platoon sergeant, Staff Sergeant Jason Glew, and I stepped over to check out the Suburban. Every surface of the big brown SUV was pocked with fat, round bullet holes, the rear and driver side windows blown out. It sat crippled on three flat tires.

"Gotta be AKs," Glew said as he studied the holes.

"They got jumped right near here." I checked my compass.

I'd heard the story on TV: On January 27, two CNN vehicles were driving on Jackson, just south of here, when a rust-colored Opel sped up behind them with a guy standing in the open sunroof, aiming a Kalashnikov assault rifle. He fired at close range, hitting both Suburbans. A security guard in the lead vehicle shot back and that Suburban managed to get away. The two Iraqi employees in the trailing SUV weren't as lucky. They were hit from behind. And then, like a jackal finishing off crippled prey, the Opel pulled alongside and the gunman emptied a magazine through the shattered window. The bursts of metal-jacketed 7.62 mm rounds ripped the driver, Yasser Khatab, and producer, Duraid Isa Mohammed, into bloody chunks.

It had been an execution, not an act of war.

Glew and I bent and looked inside. The front seat was heaped with shards of safety glass. But there was something curved, like dirty white plastic, lying on the center console. Pieces of skull. I looked at the Suburban's overhead liner: brown bloodstains, another white splinter of skull, which had imbedded in the roof panel, sticking out like an arrow tip. I tried to envision the forces that had blown a man's head apart so violently that the fragments had become shrapnel.

"Welcome to Iraq," I said.

Our unit, 2/2, was taking over the AO from the Army's 3rd Battalion, 505th Parachute Infantry Regiment of the 82nd Airborne Division. They were the Panthers. We were the Warlords, the only Camp Lejeune battalion augmenting the 1st Marine Division from Camp Pendleton near San Diego.

In North Carolina, there had been a bar-fighting tradition among the Fort Bragg Airborne and Camp Lejeune Marines—before 9/11. But as I looked around the rows of desert-tan General Purpose tents and plywood buildings, I sensed no animosity between the Army troops and Marines. I figured that we were all in this fight together and that there were enough bad guys to go around outside the concrete-block blast wall along the highway and the steep sand berm bulldozed up on the other three sides of the FOB.

The 2/2 battalion commander, Lieutenant Colonel Giles Kyser, gave us our welcome-aboard brief. Inside the berm, we could go "slick"—no flak jacket or Kevlar helmet, much more comfortable than I'd expected. The camp had some other pleasant features: showers, a hot chow hall with CNN television, an Internet café/phone center, and a gym. There had even been a laundry service until the week before. That was when the Muj had gunned down the women who'd had the courage to try earning a little money by washing the Americans' skivvies. Another service was set to begin, and I wished them better luck.

This base was scheduled to be the battalion's home for the seven-month deployment during the phase of the war that the Pentagon was now calling Operation Iraqi Freedom II (OIF II). The rest of the world called it the insurgency.

But I was hopeful that the remaining "dead-enders" from Saddam Hussein's regime really were losing support, and that the Warlords would prove stronger in peacekeeping than in warfighting. Kyser had described our mission this way before deployment: "We want the people of Mahmudiyah to think of us as *their* Marines."

We'd be tough, but fair. If someone threw a stone at us, we'd twist his arm, not flatten his house with a two-thousand-pound bomb. What Colonel Kyser did not have to articulate was the general assumption among the Marines that the Army troops we were replacing had been too heavy-handed, that they sometimes overreacted to threats, calling in helicopter gunships to suppress a lone sniper or a counter-battery artillery barrage in response to a single mortar round or rocket. That just drove more Iraqis into the insurgent camp.

Marines had been taught to fight "smarter" than that.

I almost stumbled humping my hundred pounds of gear down the row of tents toward the GP-Large that I'd share with Easy Company's junior officers and senior NCOs. It had been nearly forty hours since I'd slept. The 3rd Platoon that I commanded had been ordered to provide convoy security for the two-hundred-odd cats and dogs of the battalion's Headquarters and Support Company (H&S, the "Hiders and Sliders") who'd flown with us on Air National Guard C-130s from Kuwait to Baghdad International.

That assignment had been something of an honor, I'd told the men to beef up their morale. I was one of about fifty combat vets in Easy Company, and some of my young Marines were obviously scared—just as I'd been during Desert Storm, waiting to cross the berm into Kuwait and drive the Humvee into the Iraqi minefields hidden in the smoke.

So I'd worked them hard during the week we'd staged at Camp Udari in Kuwait: squad tactics, Immediate Action Drills for near and far ambush, PT, and Arabic language classes. This training had been on top of our final predeployment edge-honing. Those days and nights had been tense and hectic. None of us had really known what to expect in Iraq. We ate every meal at the big chow hall like it would be our last.

Before the 1st Marine Expeditionary Force deployed to Iraq, our commander, Lieutenant General James Mattis, reminded us of the watchwords he had given his division when they had invaded Iraq in March 2003: "Demonstrate to the world there is 'No Better Friend, No Worse Enemy' than a U.S. Marine." Addressing us a year later, General Mattis had prefaced that maxim: "First, do no harm."

So, I'd told my guys, we had to be ready to make friends or to kill people. And we better be damn good at both.

"Hey, sir," Lance Corporal Faleris, one of the burly, meat-eating young machine-gunners, had asked on our last day in Kuwait. "What's the real deal gonna be up there, peacekeeping or ass-kicking?"

We'd just finished the last exercises with the Arabic language CDs and *Islam for Dummies* books I'd bought with my own money to supplement the third-grade-level crap the Corps had issued. Knowing some of the language and something about the culture might help save the lives of my platoon—mine included. I'd even started growing a mustache because Iraqi men were generally not considered mature or serious without one.

"Let's hope it's peacekeeping, Faleris," I answered. A dandelion in the bud vase of a Volkswagen Beetle came to mind and I grinned. "We're professionals. You gotta kill, ya kill, and then go back to kissing babies with a smile on your face. Cool like a cucumber."

"Roger that, sir," he said, smiling at my theatrics but struggling with the duality.

It was a tall order to just flip on and off such an extreme level of violence. But that was what the job required. During our Security and Stability Operations (SASO) training in California, the instructors had told us that ensuring stability "might" sometimes mean dominating the Iraqi population with overwhelming force. No shit, Dick Tracy. If insurgents saw us react weakly to IEDs, ambushes, or sniper attacks, I knew, they'd just step up the violence, hoping that we *would* overreact and kill innocent civilians, whose families and fellow tribesmen would then flock to the insurgency. But if we didn't let the Muj pull any shit on us from the get-go, we might successfully manage to convince the people in our AO that their best interests lay in cooperating with us to revive the economy and rebuild schools, roads, and hospitals. The problem with that approach, I saw, was that those same Iraqis might then become targets for insurgent assassins. Just like the CNN crew and those poor laundry women.

And there was another problem in our AO. Mahmudiyah was Sunni Arab turf. Under Saddam Hussein, the ruling Baathists had rewarded the loyalty of the local sheiks and party leaders with farms, businesses, and villas.

But in 2003, the situation had flipped. America and its allies had toppled Saddam and installed an interim government led by Shia—which most Sunni Arabs boycotted—that was working on a "democratic" constitution and national elections.

The Shia now also dominated the Iraqi security forces, which included the police, the Iraqi Civil Defense Corps (soon to be renamed the Iraqi National Guard—ING), the Facilities Protection Service (assigned to guard government buildings and businesses), and the new Iraqi army battalions slowly being trained north of Baghdad. Most Sunni Arabs refused to serve in these peacekeeping forces. The net result of this arrangement was that Shiite Arabs (60 percent of the population), whom the Sunnis had subjugated for centuries and brutalized for decades under Baathist rule, were now the local armed force responsible—with the Coalition—for maintaining order.

I'd had the chance to think about those complex problems the night before, perched in the turret cupola of a seven-ton truck in the thirty-five-vehicle convoy. Through the phosphorescent green shimmer of my night-vision goggles, the Airport Road had seemed spooky as we passed through blacked-out districts. The NVGs worked fine, but there were bright security lights on occasional houses that maxed out the optics, blinding me.

Once we left the Airport Road and turned south on Highway 1—Main Supply Route Tampa—there were fewer lights, but more obvious potential IED hazards along the shoulder: wrecked cars, piles of garbage, road-killed dogs, and the odd dead donkey stinking like an open grave, all good places to hide a bomb. From my training as a sniper, I was especially concerned about the overpasses, which provided excellent positions for ambushes.

Every good leader thinks, *If I were an insurgent, what would I do . . .* Of course the Marine Corps considered this warrior's skill worthy of an acronym, EMPCOA (Enemy's Most Probable Course of Action). In this instance, I'd place charges or use a car bomb to drop a fucking overpass on the Marines' trucks. Kill two birds with one twenty-ton stone. A bridge was also a great place for a little kid to crouch and drop a grenade on a passing truck. Just a little something to be remembered by.

But if we did take the odd sniper round, I didn't want my riflemen who were spread throughout the convoy to swing away from their assigned sectors and burn up a thousand rounds of badly aimed fire. Fifty miles an hour on a dark night didn't add up to good hits for anybody.

"Overpass, one klick ahead," I said into the pager-sized short-range Icom radio. Each of my squad leaders acknowledged. We passed safely under the bridge and then another.

There were also vehicle checkpoints (VCPs), which had to be approached slowly and cautiously to make sure the armed men blocking the road really were American soldiers.

At one VCP, I noticed a nervous-looking Iraqi interpreter (a "terp"). He'd probably never seen our new and distinctive digital pattern cammies and wondered who the fuck we were, rolling up in the middle of the night. To put the terp at ease, I raised my NVGs and greeted him with the Muslim salutation I'd had my guys practice in Kuwait, *"As-salaam alaikum"* (Peace be unto you). This showed more respect than the simple *"Marhaba"* (Hello) that the Corps phrase book taught, and went beyond "No Better Friend" cultural sensitivities. The more formal greeting required a polite response: *"Wa alaikum salaam"* (And unto you, peace). I was eager to try it out because I planned to use the greeting in our AO, figuring that a really hard-core, American-hating insurgent would have a hard time with the respectful answer.

Those VCPs and overpasses had kept my adrenaline spiking during the slow drive south. Now, safely inside the FOB, I headed for the tent, tiredly shifting the weight of my bulging rucksack and sea bag. All I could think about was grabbing some sleep.

Camp Lejeune
27 April 2005

On the second day of the hearing, the prosecution called a Marine judge advocate, Captain William J. Schrantz, as a government witness. He had been the JAG officer with 2/2 in Iraq.

The assistant government counsel, Captain Reh, started the direct examination of Schrantz by handing him a card that had been marked as evidence.

REH: Captain Schrantz, what is that?
SCHRANTZ: This is the ROE card that was distributed from

1st Marine Division that was given to all the Marines.

Schrantz explained that he had taught the 2/2 Marines a "class" in the Rules of Engagement.

REH: Was this actually the ROE card that you used in your presentation?

SCHRANTZ: It is.

REH: Tell me a little bit about the class itself, with respect to the Rules of Engagement.

SCHRANTZ: I broke the class down for Rules of Engagement into two separate sections. They had already received one period of instruction previously from someone. I'm not sure who gave the class. I didn't know if they had actually gotten the card broken down or scenarios. So I broke the class down into two sections. The first section was, I took sentence by sentence, and I went down the ROE card. And I explained the card that they would have. And then later, there were some scenarios—some—I guess you could call them just vignettes, where they would be hypotheticals that were provided by One MEF [1st Marine Expeditionary Force]. And that was the second part of the class. It was a practical application with multiple-choice answers.

REH: Describe some of these vignettes.

SCHRANTZ: It covered a host of things. I can't remember what they are. An example would be you're on a patrol and you see a crowd of angry people gathering, and they pick up sticks and rocks. What do you do? And it would give you four choices to choose from.

After Schrantz finished describing our ROE class, Assistant Defense Counsel Bolling cross-examined the witness.

BOLLING: Did you have any opportunity to interact with many of the Iraqi civilians or citizens while you were over there?

SCHRANTZ: I did a great deal, as a matter of fact.

BOLLING: That was throughout the course of your duties, correct?

SCHRANTZ: It was.

BOLLING: Okay. Why don't you just tell us what your duties were and how that got you to interact with the civilians?

REH: Object, sir. Relevance.

WINN: Note the objection on the record. Go ahead and continue.

SCHRANTZ: I was responsible for the claims and investigations and payments for damages that could potentially have been done to their homes, to their streets, to their families, injuries. I was responsible for that as well. And then also, once we moved around so many times, it became necessary for me to become a part of the civil affairs team. So I integrated with the community that way as well.

BOLLING: Were you ever approached in any manner concerning ROE violations, by the citizens?

SCHRANTZ: Not in that term, but I would be approached all the time. I'd work out of a trailer, so I would have someone escort the person in one by one. And there were many instances where they would say their homes got shot by Coalition forces and that they weren't doing anything. So if they came to ask for money or for us to help them or to compensate them, it was always that—their statement was always that we shot them without cause.

I kept my expression neutral. Brandon Bolling was careful in the courtroom. I wanted to listen as intently as possible without betraying anxiety.

BOLLING: Were families who filed claims inclined to claim essentially innocence, asking for damages and injuries just to get money?

SCHRANTZ: That was my sense a lot of times. Yes. There were many legitimate claims, but there were many claims that I couldn't substantiate. I don't remember—they knew if they came in and they were at fault or they were terrorists, that their claim would not be paid. So no one would ever come in and not profess their innocence. They were always innocent and, "You damaged me in some way, and I deserve compensation because of that. I'm innocent."

BOLLING: Did anyone file a claim for some kind of compensation based upon the wrongful killing of any of the two Iraqis at any point in time?

SCHRANTZ: I paid quite a few claims for death cases, unfortunately.

BOLLING: Did anyone ever come seeking a claim for you from the 15 April 2004 incident involving Lieutenant Pantano?

SCHRANTZ: No.

FOB Mahmudiyah, Iraq
20 March 2004

I didn't get much sleep that first morning at the base. Just before noon, Staff Sergeant Glew and I left on our first patrol, joining a four-Humvee convoy from the 505th that was releasing three men back to the Iraqi police station next to the city council compound in Mahmudiyah. I didn't know why the men had been picked up, but after a screening it was determined that there wasn't enough to hold them. The Panthers decided to get some mileage out of releasing them to their families with a little ceremony. Were they apologizing? I didn't really understand what was going on, but I was excited to see the sights.

Our Humvees didn't look like tour buses, though. They were protected by slabs of rusty "Hajji" armor that had been stuck on with jagged welds at shops in town. The floors were layered with sandbags and water cans. This little convoy could have come right out of *The Road Warrior,* a forbidden R-rated movie I'd seen as a kid, which had impressed me with the ingenuity of its scavengers.

The image was enhanced by the dust bandanas two of the M-249 SAW gunners wore across their faces, standing up in their turrets. One soldier's bandana even had a printed skull in the middle, like something you'd pick up at a Goth head shop on St. Marks Place. All the Airborne guys had obsidian-dark ballistic eye-protection glasses, giving them the bug-eyed look of aliens. My set was still in a box somewhere in my sea bag.

"You people ready to roll?" Lieutenant Asher casually asked his drivers and SAW gunners. "Okay. Let's do it. Oh, yeah . . . keep your intervals."

Glew and I looked at each other. That was probably the shittiest patrol brief I'd ever heard, nothing about specific tasking and rally or medevac plans in the event of ambush. But as I climbed into the backseat of Asher's Humvee—my load-bearing vest hanging up on every protrusion—I realized that these paratroopers probably knew this stretch of Iraq as well as the local people. The 505th had been patrolling the AO for eight months, and Asher recognized that his soldiers did not need another detailed brief. Besides, the Airborne guys were practically on the plane: in a week they'd be flying back to Fort Bragg. The Army had a traditional term for this, FIGMO: "Fuck it. I got my orders."

Our Humvees turned right outside the FOB entrance and rolled south on Jackson toward Mahmudiyah. Highway 8 was a wide, surprisingly smooth four-lane blacktop road. The night before, I'd seen the blurred images of palm groves and tall reeds along canal banks through my NVGs. In the glaring heat of the day, this vegetation seemed cool and inviting, especially after the sand-and-gravel flats of Kuwait. But the dense trees and thick stands of reeds could hide mortar and RPG firing positions. Maybe I was just being paranoid. So far, Asher certainly didn't seem nervous.

A tan concrete water tower appeared ahead, and then the northern edge of Mahmudiyah—a sprawl of one- and two-story buildings taking shape out of the rippling sun glare on the asphalt. There was a blue-tipped minaret off to the right, and several more large concrete water tanks on the left. Then we were in the town itself. The storefronts facing the road had overhanging concrete sunshades and doorways protected by folding steel grates, some painted bright yellow or green. Racks of soda cans and candy stood beside new satellite dishes piled like potato chips. There were donkey carts rolling on recycled car axles and wheels. But most of the traffic was much more modern: Kia minivans, Opel sedans, and a few orange-and-white Toyota Land Cruiser taxis.

"Anybody making money around here?" I asked.

Asher nodded wryly. "Not to hear them talk about it. There's plenty of cash in Mahmudiyah, most of it in U.S. green. We've been financing the shit out of this place. Whenever we bruise a watermelon, they want *salatia*. That's either compensation or a bribe."

I thought about the private Blackwater security guards we'd met at Baghdad International the previous afternoon. Several of them were former Marines lugging AKs, which they preferred over M-16s for the stopping power. They were waiting for a batch of Ecuadorian mercenaries, about as weird a deal as I could imagine. But then one of the former Marines upped the ante, hoping to barter some intel word for one of our new digi-boonie covers.

"You guys heard about the Republican Guard general standing up his own security firm?" he'd asked. "The sonofabitch wants his piece of the pie, so he has his guys shoot up a likely customer once a week just to create demand. If he's already got the job he shoots it up once a month just to remind you how much you need him. Fucking Al Capone–smart."

I remembered the Egyptian soldiers looting refrigerators and car seats out on battered Kuwait city streets, but I never realized that war and crime could be this intertwined.

Our Humvee rolled up behind another cart in central Mahmudiyah, but the oncoming traffic prevented us from passing. So we had to settle for the clop-clop pace of the donkey.

"Not too close," Asher ordered his driver. "I don't like the look of that dude in the man-dress on the back."

The Airborne guys called the *dishdasha,* the traditional one-piece robe, a "man dress," which I found belittling. Among the Iraqis, I intended to use the proper Arabic word, even when speaking through a terp. It was just one more sign of respect, which I hoped would be reciprocated.

The cart clomped left into a side alley near the *souk,* the open market, wide as a city block. Now we were directly behind a big rusty dump truck spewing sooty diesel exhaust.

"Stay the hell back from that one," Asher told the driver.

Was he finally giving in to end-of-tour nerves? I didn't want to ask him what was so menacing about a dump truck. Then I saw. The deep load bed could both hide and protect twenty Muj with AKs or RPGs.

The 505th were pros. After serving a tour in Afghanistan, they'd done a great job damping down violence in this AO for the past eight months. In that time, Asher's battalion had suffered one Killed in Action (KIA) and around twenty Wounded in Action (WIA)—not too bad, I thought, for a four-hundred-man infantry outfit spread very thin on the ground, and which patrolled day and night.

I hoped we'd be that lucky.

The 505th had also built an efficient and comfortable base. But already I got the sense that the Airborne had developed an "inside the wire," "outside the wire" outlook about the area of operations. Their aggressive patrolling was a protracted show of force, meant to dominate the local Iraqis first and win them over as friends second. So far it was working. February was a quiet month theater-wide. March was looking that way too.

Now I swallowed in the dusty heat, brushing a fly off the drinking tube of the camelback water pouch hanging on the back of my vest before taking a sip of warm water. Achieving that goal would be a lot more complicated than I'd thought. We would need dump trucks like that one to repair roads and rebuild schools and clinics, but could we be certain every truck was legitimate? The night before, our convoy had passed flatbeds stacked with white ten-kilo liquid propane tanks, any one of which could have been an IED. Yet keeping the cooking gas moving along Route Jackson up to Baghdad was a priority. And we didn't have time to have our gutsy Explosive Ordnance Disposal teams carefully search every potentially dangerous truck.

Our Humvees swung past a lone sentry in a light blue uniform shirt and darker blue pants who dragged open a single strand of concertina wire. With that, we were through the flimsy gates of the Iraqi police compound. Looking at the cops inside, I saw that a few had been issued Glock 9 mm pistols and others had AK-47s with short, cut-down stocks. The compound itself seemed well maintained, with a paved courtyard, reasonably clean white walls, and dark-framed windows. It was obvious where the Baathist government had invested its money.

While the Iraqi police (IP) signed for the prisoners, Asher took me over to meet the IP watch officer. I felt a little awkward with so much combat gear hanging off me, while all these guys had were slacks and 9 mms.

"*Marhaba,*" Asher said to the man.

The officer shook Asher's hand and then mine. "*As-salaam alaikum,*" I said.

He placed his hand over his heart, another sign of respect. "*Wa alaikum salaam.*"

I was on a roll.

Heading toward the Humvees, Asher glanced over his shoulder at the prisoners we'd "repatriated."

"Wonder when *you'll* see them again."

Family members hugged the men and snapped happy reunion pictures.

I looked dubious as I realized this was one of his last patrols.

"Under current Coalition policy," Asher said, "we can't hold them long. But it gets better: Once we let them go, we can't just reach out and snag them again. We gotta treat them like cops would in a civilized environment, but we have none of the tools. There's no centralized ID system. No phone listings or address books that we can reference. No driver's licenses or water bills. And, everybody goes by at least three names, none of which can be verified." He shook his head. "We tried to make an ID system for some of the police and security guys, but we're not the only ones with color printers and laminating machines."

"So we're releasing those suspects?"

"There's nothing we can do. The Iraqi police are just starting to get their shit together. What the fuck do they care about some suspicious dudes we pick up? They're probably neighbors. Hell, they're probably cousins!"

We both laughed at the futility.

I looked out at the mix of vehicles rolling by on the dusty blacktop road. Donkey carts, BMWs, trucks, and vans. For a moment, I tried to remember the Arabic words for "car," "truck," or "van." Nothing. The heat, fatigue, and the toxic hangover of too much adrenaline in the night.

A man in a *dishdasha* approached us before we reached the Humvees and whispered something to Asher's terp.

"This man says there are rockets . . . *Katyusha* [Russian-made 122 mm Katyushas] . . . in his farm," the interpreter announced.

Asher nodded. "Let's check it out."

The Mahmudiyah city council building was right next to the Iraqi police compound. Before we left the area, Asher introduced Staff Sergeant Glew and me to a couple of the notables standing in the crowd of men outside the council. Some old-timers wore well-cut *dishdashas,* traditional checked *kaffiyehs,* and plastic sandals. Several younger men had on Western pants and shirts.

The introductions were a mixed success. I took off my helmet and sunglasses so they could clearly see my eyes. I even took off my flame-resistant Nomex gloves and extended my right hand, leaving my weapon dangling from my neck. I knew the value of a first impression and wanted them to recognize we were serious about helping them to rebuild. Two of the councilmen returned my formal greetings, smiled warmly, and went through the heart-touching routine. Others dropped my hand almost as soon as they'd touched it and mumbled a curt response.

We rolled south on the crowded main drag and then took a side road past the souk. "You should look at the market as long as we're here," Asher said.

I dismounted, again getting hung up on the fucking clumsy, newly issued load-bearing gear I wore over my Kevlar vest. A few men under the sunshades above the stalls were watching my klutzy performance with scorn.

The market had pushcarts and concrete stalls heaped with onions and sacks of dried beans, piles of withered eggplants, ropes of garlic, cloth in bolts . . . aluminum and plastic kitchen gear, including toy guns. Naturally, the butchers lacked refrigeration, so the flies were thick on the hacked-up sheep and goat carcasses.

Passing between the stalls, I stopped to greet some of the men crowding the aisles. Many seemed friendly and politely returned my handshakes. But others walked away, only then to spin around and examine Glew and me with contempt. Again, our digital-pattern cammies and dark mud-brown flak jackets set us apart from the 505th. We were the new guys on the block.

I had to assume that every Iraqi in the AO over age three had heard by now that the Airborne was swapping out for the Marines. But who were these Marines? A couple of the young men in Western clothes standing near a date stall looked me over closely. *I'm* the fresh meat here, I thought. This was how the experienced cons at Rikers Island inspected the busloads of new bitches.

Our M-16s hanging across our chests on patrol slings, our bulging ammo pouches, flak jackets, radios, and helmets didn't intimidate hard cases like this.

"*As-salaam alaikum,*" I said.

They scowled. I smiled extra wide and cursed silently as they cursed me. Fuck 'em. Enough hearts and minds for today. I had another job. This market could be a very dangerous place, with plenty of room to plant IEDs and nice crowds to attract suicide bombers. The flat roofs of buildings surrounding the souk could hide a dozen snipers. Any time we were called to the market in the future, we'd have to respond with cautious tactical discipline.

While I was looking over the setup, Asher and his platoon sergeant, a Ranger named Britt, were pacing among the stalls. Their interpreter, a pleasant young guy with mirrored sunglasses whom they called "Lee," had disappeared. *Shit,* I thought, striding over to Asher. While I'd been playing tourist, somebody had snatched the Army terp. It took Asher about four seconds to issue a string of brief commands into his radio, dispatching the four Humvees to block the surrounding streets.

"Did you see those two black Kia minivans circling the block when we were pulling in here?" he asked.

"No," I said, shaking my head. How could I have been so dumb? This wasn't something they taught at IOC, but any kid in Hell's Kitchen learned to spot an unmarked Caprice Classic. That knowledge came with the turf. Now I was on somebody else's turf.

As the Army guys were stopping the two Kias, Lee came out of the market. He shrugged when Asher asked him where the hell he'd been. Maybe he'd been buying green peppers. Maybe he'd been tipping off Muj ambushers where we were headed to check on the rocket cache. I got even more suspicious when Lee casually announced he was staying in town and would see us back at the FOB.

This duty was going to be a lot harder than the straightforward riot control and civic action they'd taught us in SASO training.

As we climbed into the vehicles, the *muezzin* at a nearby mosque started the call to the noon prayer, the *Dhuhr.* The scratchy voice on the loudspeaker made me jump. *Allahu akbar* . . . God is great. Right. That ancient phrase drew the faithful. It was also the jihadists' invocation to martyrdom.

About a kilometer to the south, our Humvees bumped off the

pavement and onto a narrow lane of dry, rutted mud that wound between plowed fields and the high stands of reeds along irrigation canals. Jolting in the Humvee, I had to fight down a wave of claustrophobia. The reeds would provide snipers plenty of concealment, while the hard mud of the canal banks would offer them cover against our weapons. On this leg of the patrol, a tobacco-chewing corporal had joined me in the back of the vehicle.

"You guys get many snipers out here?" I asked him.

"No, sir," he said, grinning. "The Iraqis don't have much of a hunting culture, not like back home. They sort of go by the *Inshallah* school of marksmanship . . . you know, 'spray and pray.' "

We finally found the plowed field where the informant had reported seeing the 122 mm rockets. There was some freshly turned earth, a few sandal prints, but nothing else.

"We having fun yet?" the corporal asked.

That first afternoon, after stuffing myself with hot chow—meat loaf, mashed potatoes, and gravy—I drank two quarts of orange Gatorade.

Then I set to work on my gear. These load-bearing vests we'd been issued were less than worthless, snagging whenever we climbed in and out of vehicles. We all knew they sucked, but our command had mandated that our gear be standard, "uniform," no civilian hunting knives or bandanas for the Marines. Now that we were finally in-country, the rules were changing. We were adapting. Even the battalion commander was walking around with a "high-speed" uniform rig. So much for uniformity. I took my three M-16 ammo pouches, my compass case, Icom radio, first-aid kit, and camelback water bag and mounted them directly on the straps of my Kevlar vest. Now they were snug against my body and didn't flop around whenever I moved.

Then I pulled on the fully modified Kevlar vest, loaded with my ammo and gear. Heavy. It would be hard to run far wearing all this. Even with the insulated roof, the GP tent was hot and I was sweating from the effort. And this was only the end of March. What would July and August be like?

Lying back on my rack, I tried to sleep, but kept thinking of the months ahead, both in Iraq and in the States. Two days before leaving Kuwait, I'd received an e-mail with the good news that Jill was expecting our second child. Now Domenico would get the chance to be a big brother. It wasn't going to be easy for Jill, waiting for the new baby and being mother to an energetic two-year-old. And worrying about a husband in the combat zone.

But maybe the dead-enders actually would get the message that their best interests lay in the political process. And peace, *salaam,* would take root and spread. Maybe the dump trucks would be used on construction projects and not as homegrown Armored Personnel Carriers.

Trying to doze off, I hoped that a little combat nap would pump me up. But I couldn't sleep long.

I had to work on the company vehicle plan for Captain Weston. Having fought one war in a truck, I volunteered to help organize our fledgling vehicle fleet. At Camp Lejeune we had rarely gotten to work with vehicles, but now we were inheriting the Army's trucks. Examining the large- and small-scale maps of our AO, it was clear that choke points—especially bridges—along Tampa and Jackson would be vulnerable spots for both the Muj and us. Our vehicle checkpoints could cut off traffic on Highways 1 and 8 and their feeder roads, preventing insurgents from massing. But the checkpoints that we and Iraqi security forces manned also made good targets for suicide bombers.

And we had a larger mission than simply keeping the highways open. We had to be able to respond to insurgent activity in towns and on the surrounding farms and to the attacks on our outposts. The biggest problem was that none of the little canal roads were on our maps. Hopefully we'd get some of that near-mythical satellite imagery—"You can see a Muj squatting to take a shit"—but for now, we were pretty much blind.

We planned to augment our low-slung Humvees with big seven-ton trucks. They had titanium armor plates bolted around the open troop bays, which gave the Marines riding there some cover from small-arms and shrapnel. Just as important was the height of the seven-ton, which rode on tall wheels. This meant the force of an IED blast was dissipated below. And the height of the truck also gave the machine-gunner in the cupola and the riflemen behind commanding fields of fire. But maneuvering the big vehicles through the back alleys of towns like Mahmudiyah and Latafiyah would be tough.

When I dropped off my draft plan at the Easy Company office, Gunny Naylor offered his crazy snaggle-toothed grin.

"Thanks, Lieutenant." He wasn't overly fond of saying "sir" to second lieutenants. That was okay by me. He was a salty bastard who had served in the Gulf and OIF I. Now he was back for a third helping. He could call me anything he wanted. "Oh, yeah," he added. "You're on alert for an ambush patrol tonight. Check with the CO for the details."

Captain Weston was in his room next door, working on an order. "This is the biscuit factory," he explained, tapping the detailed map of Mahmudiyah. "It's a good overwatch of Jackson south of town. You'll be joining the Army as an observer tonight. They swear by it."

That was what I was afraid of. The Airborne had used the place so often for ambush patrols that either the Muj would bypass it or booby-trap the roof before we got there. But I sucked it up. There was no complaining about "I," "me," or "my." There was the mission and the men, and nothing else.

Out in the hallway, one of my buddies from TBS and IOC stopped me. There were six of us here with 2/2 who had trained together from the beginning, and were tight, even though we were split into the separate companies. Lieutenant Stibb, a Goliath of a college wrestler, informed me that one of our brothers had taken shrapnel in the face.

"I think McDaniel is gonna be okay," Stibb told me through a big wad of tobacco in his cheek. They were both in Fox Company, but we all felt the near miss collectively.

Lieutenant Brandon McDaniel had been patrolling Jackson north of the FOB when the small triggering device of a huge IED exploded near his vehicle. By a miracle, the main charge—four 155 mm artillery rounds—had not blown. But he'd been hit in the face with shrapnel. Brandon's ballistic glasses protected his eyes, and he'd requested an immediate return to duty. The IED had employed redundant radio-operated detonators. When the EOD team reached the device buried at the side of the road, the second detonator had started vibrating. Someone had them under close observation, sending a cell phone signal to activate the remaining charge. The EOD guys were able to snip the wires before they got blown into tiny pieces.

The roof of the biscuit factory had not been booby-trapped. But after sunset it had gotten cold. I was with an Airborne rifle squad that included an M-240 machine gun. We lay behind sandbags, which both concealed us and blocked the gritty wind. Another fire team had a security post on the ground floor. They were lucky to be out of the chill night. Shit, here I was, less than two days in-country, and already whining about the weather.

The Iraqi Facilities Protection Service had set up a half-assed checkpoint on the highway. But there wasn't much traffic. And the Iraqis were hardly rigorous. They searched two beat-up hatchbacks crowded with women and kids. But they just waved through a couple of newer minivans and sedans carrying men of military age. And the Iraqis allowed a rumbling truck loaded with barrels and bales under tarps to roll slowly through the checkpoint without stopping.

We had no way of knowing what they were saying down there. The agents might have been telling any Muj they encountered, "Cool it, Muhammed. There're Americans watching us from the roof of the factory." And watch was all we could do.

After midnight, a loud firefight broke out at another Facilities Protection post south of us. There were AKs blasting on auto and semi-auto, back and forth, snap-tap-tap . . . tap-tap-tap-tap-snap-snap. Red tracers sailed and bounced in both directions. Then I heard the chug of the mortars up at the FOB, and 81 mm illumination rounds popped, hanging little parachute flares that cast a stark glare and deep shadows across the road and buildings. Whenever one of the flares went out, the tracers started flying again. Night in Iraq.

Around sunrise, the workers showed up at the factory and started baking their trays of flat tea biscuits. The air smelled of peacetime, flour, and sugar. It was daylight when we loaded up all our weapons and gear and got ready to head back to the FOB. A timid, smiling old baker with a gap between two gold teeth came out and gave us a pile of warm biscuits neatly folded in a sheet of newspaper. *"Shukran,"* he said. "Thank you."

I was feeling pretty good, biting a sweet, warm biscuit as we neared the base. Maybe our ambush had kept bad guys from moving on the road. Maybe the firefight and illumination rounds had been part of a normal night.

But back at the Easy Company office, I learned that a Warlord had just been medevaced with a sucking chest wound after being hit by another IED on Jackson. Some of us got warm tea biscuits, while others were hit by red-hot shrapnel.

In the afternoon, word flashed around the FOB that "a bunch" of guys from the 7th Marines had been killed in some shit-burg farther up in Al Anbar Province to the northwest. That rumor turned out to be bad scoop. But the possibility that it could have been true was pretty grim. As was the sense of isolation and confusion in which we were operating. There were over 25 million people in Iraq, but fewer than 150,000 Coalition forces. It was entirely possible that a convoy or patrol caught alone could be overrun and just disappear.

Camp Lejeune
27 April 2005

Major Winn was taking notes, listening as closely as I was. Now Bolling moved ahead with his recross-examination of Schrantz.

BOLLING: I want to shift focus on the flexi-cuffing, okay? Essentially the Iraqis were flexi-cuffed when they were determined to be a threat, right?

SCHRANTZ: When? Just in general?

BOLLING: Right.

SCHRANTZ: You know, I think it would probably depend. The only time that the SOP [standard operating procedure] actually required it would have been during transportation. The rest of it would have been up to the on-scene commander to decide. They were to decide that.

BOLLING: And removing flexi-cuffs also would be a subjective decision that the on-scene commander can make, right?

SCHRANTZ: It would have depended on that situation. There were a lot of times the commander could choose—even if he knew that that person was a really bad person, he could decide not to for— not to detain him, for several reasons. Maybe he didn't think he was a threat, maybe he wanted to try to befriend him, maybe he wanted to try to get some information out of him prior to flex-cuffing him. Once you flex-cuff them, you could imagine they wouldn't be as cooperative.

BOLLING: Did you, yourself, ever have anybody unflex-cuffed in order to get information from them?

SCHRANTZ: Unflex-cuffed, yes, not to get information from them, but just to have a dialogue with them, yes.

A few minutes later, Bolling changed direction.

BOLLING: I'm showing you, Captain Schrantz, some slides from the brief that General Mattis gave to the Marines of 2/2. What does that slide say at the top?

SCHRANTZ: Self-defense.

BOLLING: What's the definition it provides for self-defense?

SCHRANTZ: I wasn't at this brief. Do you want me to read it anyway?

BOLLING: Yes.

SCHRANTZ: "Nothing in the ROE limits your right and obligation to use force necessary to defend yourself, your unit, and coalition forces."

BOLLING: Is that definition applicable to Lieutenant Pantano on the 15th of April 2004?

SCHRANTZ: It would have been, and I actually think that's on the card as well.

BOLLING: Now, this slide, what's that slide say at the top?

SCHRANTZ: "Escalation of force."

BOLLING: It says you're supposed to shout a verbal warning, show your weapon and your intent to use it, shove, get physical, and then shoot, aim center mass and shoot to kill. Was the information contained on this slide applicable to Lieutenant Pantano on the 15th of April 2004?

SCHRANTZ: This was General Mattis's predeployment brief?

BOLLING: Yes.

SCHRANTZ: Yes, then it would have been.

BOLLING: Okay. Please read for me the very last words down there at the bottom.

SCHRANTZ: Okay. "Just shoot if you don't have time to go through the steps, 'shout, shove,' " et cetera.

BOLLING: Okay. So if Lieutenant Pantano didn't have time to go through the steps, he could just shoot and he's in compliance with the instructions that were provided to him, correct?

SCHRANTZ: In accordance with that slide.

FOB Mahmudiyah, Iraq
21 March 2004

Just after dawn on our second day in-country, the 82nd let us watch a raid on the compound of a suspected Muj leader, Said Adnan, who was supposed to have been a Baathist hotshot before the war. His villa was palatial, with a dome and green-tiled archways. But it was basically empty. He and his family were living in a smaller, air-conditioned guesthouse, but were *mysteriously* absent when we arrived.

"You are welcome to look where you wish," a cousin said through our terp. "You will find nothing."

Maybe. We went from room to room, while a barefoot old Shiite servant unlocked doors. One opened on what could only be described as a hidden sanctuary to the cult of Saddam Hussein. There were dozens of vintage silver-framed photographs of Said and his family posing with the dictator, which Saddam had signed. "Thanks for the memories, Adnan old buddy . . ." I guessed. Ornate swords and some long-barreled muskets hung on the walls. Heaps of beautiful carpets were piled in the corners. I jotted an inventory in my notebook and told the old servant to make sure to keep the door locked.

But we'd found no modern weapons. Nostalgia for Saddam Hussein was not a crime. He was locked up in an American cell in Baghdad and was never coming back, no matter what happened to the rest of the country.

As we left the estate in the full light of morning, I got a chance to look over the surrounding plots and houses of the tenant farmers. The usual mud-and-straw hovels, a few with rusty metal roofing. This wasn't even Third World, more like Fourth or Fifth . . . India-level poverty. The fields stank of human shit—you could actually see turds glistening in the sun—no doubt the only fertilizer the tenants could afford.

From that day on, we called Adnan's estate the "Shit Farm."

Over the next week, the Warlords patrolled and set up random checkpoints and ambushes throughout our area of operations. We expanded our ink spot, with Fox Company operating around Latafiyah, the town that straddled Jackson fifteen klicks south of the FOB. With the Airborne now gone, we were on our own.

I led my first platoon raid late on Saturday afternoon. The Iraqi police had reported weapons caches and possible Muj in the artillery positions that had formed part of Baghdad's southern defensive line the year before. But American forces had been so shorthanded that no one had thoroughly searched those gun emplacements and bunkers, which could have provided both concealment for the insurgents and the raw material for IEDs.

We rolled out of the FOB in a six-vehicle convoy half an hour before sunset, what they called the "golden hour" in the movie business because the light was so pure. But snaking between the thickets of reeds and brush along the canals, trying hard to keep proper intervals between the vehicles, I got the dry-mouth feeling that only came with combat, not play-acting with extras dressed up like a SWAT team.

A spicy-sweet stick of Dentyne Fire gum tasted fantastic. I wondered if it would be my last. The Iraqi police were our guides, although they seemed confused about where we were headed, and they just might be leading us into an IED trap.

And it didn't help any that the company CO, Captain Brad Weston, Gunny Naylor, and First Sergeant Graham were along for the ride. If I was going to fuck up, I wanted to do it out of sight of the company leadership. But I had trained my guys well, and they were squared away. And if we hit serious resistance, I always had "Buster," the Marine F/A-18 fighter-bomber pilot assigned as the Warlords' combat Forward Air Controller. Using Marine aviators as FACs was a tradition that went back to World War II, and I'd seen the tons of shit they could call down on the enemy during the first Gulf War.

When we reached the objective, the edge of a harvested grain field next to another thicket of tall reeds beside a canal, I dismounted two squads with one M-240 machine gun and kept the rest of the platoon in overwatch, securing the trucks. I guessed this would be my Infantry Officers School final exam.

We got the squads on line and moved north toward the heaped berms of the old gun positions. Saddam's engineers had bulldozed them up at crazy angles before the 2003 invasion, both to deflect American tank rounds and to disperse the blast shock of bombs away from ammo stacks.

I was jumpy about mines, but a couple of shabby goatherds with yapping dogs moved ahead of us.

"Human EOD," Sergeant "Stick" Word, my First Squad leader, joked.

A hair morbid maybe. But accurate. I looked down the line of twenty-four young Marines. They moved steadily, scanning the low white farm building ahead and the wall of reeds off to our right. Their fathers might have walked paddy patrols in Vietnam.

Before we reached the house, the Marines poked cautiously through old artillery revetments. The 155 mm guns were rusty, some of their breechblocks missing—as if the artillerymen had bugged out in a hurry. But there were still neat stacks of dusty shells, missing their threaded nose fuses. Hundreds of them. Each one held enough high explosive to rip apart one of our vehicles. There were bigger ammo caches than this in Iraq, I knew, including at least one monster bomb-and-rocket dump south of our AO. If they were the Wal-Marts for IED raw materials, *minor* artillery positions like this were Stop & Shop convenience stores for the Muj.

I marked this ammo cache on my map.

EOD would have to sort this out. We had no way of telling how stable the high explosive inside these shells was. But our explosive disposal teams were already tied down day and night, handling IEDs. So the stacks of artillery rounds sat here, unguarded. To me it was just more proof—if any was needed—that we didn't have enough troops in-country to meet our responsibilities.

Two Iraqis were sitting outside the farmhouse, smoking and joking, as we say. They were tough-looking, unshaven guys in their late forties. Both wore dirty *dishdashas*. One had thick, scarred fingers and dead eyes.

A *real thug*, I thought. He definitely knew which end of a battery cable to hook up to somebody's balls. No *"As-salaam alaikum,"* for him.

Through our IP terp, the tough guy immediately started busting my chops.

"Why do you come here to my home for the third time in one week?" he demanded, rudely pointing his left hand—his ass-wiping hand—directly at my chest.

"I've never been here before," I said.

He glared at me with contempt and spit onto the dirt, a gesture of great disrespect. "Yes, you were. I remember your face perfectly. I never forget the face of my enemy."

So much for hearts and minds from this asshole. He'd probably been a career corporal in the Republican Guard's interrogation corps. I smiled at our terp and told him to translate *every* fucking word I said.

"Do you remember me marching your ass halfway across Kuwait with your hands on your head thirteen years ago?" I asked the tough guy.

The arrogance drained from his face.

Hot days folded into cool nights. The number of IEDs picked up—the double-thump explosions becoming almost commonplace—but none of our Marines was killed. Yet. We also took our first mortars around the wire. But none inside. Yet.

All the platoons were working hard, but because my guys were the vehicle cadre, we had to accompany the patrol insertions and extractions and the mobile vehicle checkpoints. Every time we went outside the wire, we had to do a brief and get fully suited up, Kevlar helmets and vests—with the shitty chafing neck protector—ammo, radios, first aid pouches. And, of course, all our weapons. So, instead of sorting out our gear, we hung it all, ready to go, on splintery wooden T-frames slapped together from shipping pallets.

We rarely got more than a couple of hours of exhausted sleep before being called out. Sleep, chow, and briefings took precedence over hygiene. A swipe of your armpits and ass with a baby wipe—hopefully remembering to follow that sequence—replaced showers on most days.

The company and battalion commanders spent a lot of time at the city council in Mahmudiyah, and Easy 3 was often tasked with the security mission. I carried a laminated photo of Jill and Domenico, which I showed to the councilmen who sat around the courtyard. With one hand down at my knee to indicate his height, I'd point the other hand at my chest. "Abu Domenico," Domenico's father. Then I'd curve my fingers across my ammo pouches, the universal symbol of pregnancy. "Madame."

Smiles and mumbled words. What were they saying . . . feeling?

I *was* getting friendly with their security man, Mustafa. He was a young guy with a neat brush cut who carried a cut-down Kalashnikov like he knew how to use it and always seemed happy to see me. I figured from the pistol in the back of his pants that he might have been a former soldier, but we didn't talk about that.

Mustafa liked to learn new English words, which I traded him for Arabic. And he loved *"foo-oot-baal,"* international-class soccer . . . Manchester United, Real Madrid. So did I. He said there were some pretty good players on his security detail, and I replied that Easy Company also had some talent, that two of our lieutenants had played in college, and some of our younger guys were naturals.

"Let's arrange a game," I said after doing the quick math to determine it would take the entire 150-man company to secure an area large enough for eleven Marines to run around without body armor. It would be a great gesture and I knew Captain Weston would buy off on it.

"Yes," Mustafa answered vaguely. "Soon . . . *Inshallah.*"

In the middle of a moonless night at the end of March, I was observing Sergeant Word lead his squad as he set up an ambush position along Jackson north of the FOB, backing up the Marines at a checkpoint on the highway. The plan was to conduct surprise stops and searches on truck convoys moving under cover of darkness. We stayed hidden like cops in a speed trap, letting a few stray cars zip by as we waited for bigger prey.

For an hour, the night was quiet. Then a wild firefight erupted off to our east, small arms, light and medium automatic weapons, streams of red tracers cutting through the dark. The fight looked and sounded close. Tracers arced out in all directions so we stayed down. Word got 2nd Squad on the radio, and they too had heard the fight, but were safely on the other side of our AO. I was glad they were okay and that Staff Sergeant Glew was with them as an "observer."

Glew and I had decided that one of us would always be present on

3rd Platoon's patrols while the Marines acclimated to combat. I really enjoyed the opportunity to go out in small groups and focus my attention on one individual at a time. While the squad leader managed the patrol and perfected his craft, I was helping the young riflemen and fire team leaders perfect theirs.

"Hey, Sims, I see you looking around, but your weapon isn't moving with your head. Fix it."

"Posada, where would *you* hit us from if you were a Muj? Then keep your eye on it."

"Perry, did you do your five- and twenty-meter checks? Oh yeah?"

They would learn my ways, my expectations, and they would hold to my standards. Or they would hear about it.

Third Squad "heard about it" from me all the time, but not because it was manned by bad Marines. The opposite; they had some of my young studs, but I needed those studs to balance their weak link of a squad leader, Sergeant Daniel Coburn.

My relationship with Coburn got off to a shitty start the first time I took the platoon to the field at Camp Lejeune. I had noticed bright orange against the wall of green-camouflaged Marines.

"What the fuck is that?" I pointed incredulously at Coburn's web gear.

"Umm, Gatorade, sir," he answered sheepishly.

"Why do you have an orange Gatorade bottle in your *green* canteen pouch?" I tried shifting rage into a tone of fatherly concern.

"Don't know, sir."

Okay, a ten-year sergeant was making a recruit-level mistake. That was a *problem*.

I had been warned about Coburn's shortcomings, by the company executive officer, Lieutenant Keating, as well as by the CO, but I assured them that *I* could square him away.

"I can get him there, sir," I told Captain Weston. "I just need some time."

That was January in North Carolina. This was March in Iraq. I saw Coburn's flaws every day and night. So did his men. When we were staging at Camp Udari in Kuwait, I'd tried to counsel Coburn, running with him around the perimeter, offering to tutor him and explaining the challenges ahead. His head nodded a lot, but the effort never came, not because he didn't want to, but because he didn't possess the leadership resources. We were in combat now, and I would not allow his fuck-ups to kill my Marines. He was on notice.

Twenty minutes after the firing stopped, I heard that a Golf Company platoon had hit an Iraqi Civil Defense Corps ambush that was supposed to have been set up much farther south. Back at the FOB we found out the Golf Marines had fired over five hundred rounds and only wounded two ICDC.

"Somebody's got to teach those ICDC to read a map, and those Golf boys how to shoot," I told Glew.

"Roger that, sir . . . *and* the FPS and the IP. Eventually, the Hajjis are supposed to be taking over this AO."

"Riii-iiight." I was grateful that Glew and I always made each other laugh.

They're supposed to be taking over security for the whole fucking country, I thought.

The rest of the patrol was quiet. But I did get a rush climbing up to inspect the back of a couple dump trucks. What would I find, a load of onions or manure? Or a squad of Muj, lying prone with their AKs pointed at my face?

I found only burlap sacks of onions. No manure. No insurgents.

A blur of baking days and chilly nights flashed by. Patrol, eat, sleep a few hours. Enemy pressure increased. Now there were multiple IEDs along Jackson and Tampa every day and every night. Explosions around the FOB like summer thunder. But none of the local folks ever saw who planted them. We started taking the odd, badly aimed sniper round driving in and out of Mahmudiyah. The *Inshallah* school of marksmanship.

But the Marines weren't the only targets. Lieutenant "Demo" Dmochowski, my friend from TBS and IOC, brought his platoon back to the base one afternoon, hot and angry at what they'd encountered in town. Demo's Marines had spent four hours in the sun cordoning the front of a school while the EOD team disarmed an IED that had been planted there.

"Some sick bastards, Ilario," Demo said. "Why target kids?"

I thought about Marlon Brando's Colonel Kurtz speech in *Apocalypse Now.* ("We left the camp after we had inoculated the children for polio, and this old man came running after us and he was crying. He couldn't see. We went back there and they had come and hacked off every inoculated arm. There they were in a pile. A pile of little arms.") But I kept my opinion to myself for a change. The IED at the school had been the third found in densely populated areas in twenty-four hours. Local people had to have seen the Muj planting them. Again, nobody had come forward to report the danger, even when children were involved. This was the insurgents' demonstration of power. They—not the U.S. Marines—called the shots on the street.

Sooner than later, I knew, we were going to have to meet violence with violence.

Camp Lejeune
27 April 2005

Reh was asking a final round of redirect questions after Bolling had finished his cross-examination of Schrantz:

> REH: You talked about an instance where you had to cut off the flex-cuffs of certain detainees. Do you remember that?
>
> SCHRANTZ: I do.
>
> REH: Do you remember that day if any of those individuals ended up getting shot?
>
> SCHRANTZ: No, they didn't.
>
> REH: Permission to approach the witness.
>
> WINN: Permission granted.
>
> REH: Handing the witness a copy of the ROE, Investigative Exhibit seven, I believe it is, sir. [to Schrantz:] Read the one that's checked there.
>
> SCHRANTZ: It says, "Comply with law of war. If you see a violation, report it."
>
> REH: Just one last question. You talked a little bit about self-defense; is that correct?
>
> SCHRANTZ: I just read what he provided.
>
> REH: Isn't it also true that, in order to use that guise of self-defense, that, first, a hostile act or hostile intent has to be used against you?

SCHRANTZ: —that threatened your life or the life of coalition forces.

REH: So the answer is yes?

SCHRANTZ: Yes.

REH: No further questions, sir.

WINN: Redirect?

Reh took his seat as Bolling walked around the podium.

BOLLING: A determination of hostile act or hostile intent,
that's a perceived threat by that particular Marine, correct?

SCHRANTZ: It's going to depend on the whole situation. I
suppose someone could perceive a threat but it
would be completely irrational and incorrect.
Rather than say, I think, it would be unper-
ceived, I think it would just depend on the circumstances of the whole situation.

BOLLING: But that's the facts based upon that Marine's
perception?

SCHRANTZ: Based off [on] the situation that he's encountered, then yes. You try to dissect was it appropriately engaged or not. It would depend on
the situation, the totality of the circumstances
and what that Marine was encountering at the
time.

BOLLING: Marines always retain a right and essentially an
obligation of self-defense, correct?

SCHRANTZ: Yes. You're always authorized to defend yourself
and your life.

BOLLING: That need is a matter of judgment?

SCHRANTZ: Based on the entire situation there, you know,
whether or not your behavior is appropriate or
not is going to depend on the situation.

BOLLING: But it's your judgment call on the spot?

SCHRANTZ: You are going to decide how to act. And then if
you behaved inappropriately, then that's going
to be for others to decide.

BOLLING: No more questions.

FOB Mahmudiyah, Iraq
29 March 2004

In late March, our S-2 Intelligence shop spread the message through the battalion: the Shia *Arbaeen* pilgrimage to the holy cities of Karbala and Najaf would reach its peak in the second week of April.

Arbaeen was one of the most sacred holidays in Shia Islam. It ended the traditional forty days of mourning for the Imam Hussein, grandson of the Prophet Muhammad. Imam Hussein was martyred after having been captured by rivals at the Battle of Karbala in 680 A.D.—the treachery called the Day of Ashura. Together, the two holidays defined the Shia, setting them apart from the world's majority of Sunni Muslims. But in Iraq and Iran, Shia were the majority. For decades, Saddam Hussein and the Baathists had stopped them from making their pilgrimages to Iraq's holy cities. But in 2004, the pilgrimage would take place for the first time in thirty years. This year, Arbaeen fell on April 11, also Easter Sunday.

"We can expect at least a million Shia pilgrims coming down Jackson," Captain Weston briefed us. "After the holiday, they'll be heading back north again."

A *million*, I thought. Buses, minivans, taxis, and trucks. Tons and tons of bedrolls and food parcels, which would be impossible to search for weapons and explosives. And all those pilgrims would be passing through our AO, which was Sunni Arab turf. Just to make this a real challenge, many vehicles would transport Shia militiamen, including those of the Badr Brigade, which was anti-American and had ties to Iran. The even less-disciplined, black-clad Mahdi Army militia were equally anti-American and fanatically loyal to their leader, the young cleric named Moqtada al-Sadr.

"We could really step in some shit, Ilario," Demo said as we finished lunch. "You've got the potential for three-way crossfires."

I thought about the goat-fuck between the platoon from Golf and the ICDC. "Maybe *four*-way . . . five-way. Why stop there?"

This was becoming one of those places where you'd go nuts if you lost your sense of humor.

But nobody was laughing on the afternoon of Thursday, April 1. The previous day in the Euphrates River city of Fallujah, about fifty kilometers northwest of the FOB, four American contractors from Black-water Security had been ambushed. The men were cut down by AK fire while still in their SUVs. Then the Muj dragged the bodies into the street and burned them with gasoline. To celebrate, the savages strung up two of the blackened corpses from the steel girders of a bridge.

Now we sat in the FOB chow hall, watching the video play and re-play on CNN. The sickening images made great visuals, and no doubt jacked up the network's ratings.

"That's not just a massacre," I told my guys. "It's 'Fuck America' time up there."

Marines of our parent unit, the 1st Regimental Combat Team, had just assumed operational responsibility for the city from the Army. The Fallujah insurgents were testing the Marines' "No Better Friend" policy.

I drank some cold coffee, wondering if the enemy would now learn the meaning of "No Worse Enemy."

On Thursday, April 8, my platoon was patrolling the northern Zulu sec-tor, an irregular network of dirt roads and highways that formed the perimeter of our AO. From the bridges across Jackson and Alternate Supply Route Sue, we had good overwatch positions on the tens of thousands of Shia pilgrims streaming south to Karbala and Najaf, rid-ing everything from bicycles to flatbed trucks. A couple of times an hour, we'd roll onto Jackson and set up snap checkpoints, just to show we were there and awake.

Another responsibility was mounting foot patrols through built-up areas along the road where Muj might be staging to ambush the pil-grims. Obviously, the Sunni Arabs would love to kill a bunch of Shia pilgrims en route to the holy cities—out of raw hatred, and to demon-strate that they could operate as they pleased in our AO.

To prevent attacks, we patrolled all the farms and built-up areas near the roads where the Muj might hide out. That was why I insisted that the platoon patrol very cautiously, treating every structure as a threat.

One location I found to be a potential danger was an old factory we called "the Brick Yard." These ruins were just west of the Mother of All Battles (MOAB) military-industrial complex, which had been heavily bombed during the 2003 invasion. There was no way to tell if the Brick Yard itself had been bombed or was just decrepit.

Late that hot morning I joined Sergeant Coburn's 3rd Squad, walking along as a rifleman, closely observing his performance. I was puzzled when he called a "security halt," and then proceeded to allow his fourteen Marines to file into an open courtyard between the walls of three buildings. The men flopped down in the shade, and several began mixing red Kool-Aid in plastic Hajji water bottles.

"Coburn," I screamed. *"Get the fuck over here!"* That was a rough way to talk to a sergeant in front of his Marines. And my words would have consequences.

"Everybody else, get your motherfucking gear on and search those goddamned buildings."

Two fire team leaders took charge and began working their men through the rooms that surrounded us.

Coburn pulled his personal equipment together and rushed over.

"Did you clear these fucking buildings before your fucking pigs started chowing down?" I demanded.

He looked sick. "We cleared all the buildings around here last night, sir. And another squad that pulled out of here this morning said the area was clear. I'm in the process of setting up a hasty defense."

Last night. Another squad. Right. This place was a fucking kill box. Days before, his squad had lost a piece of one of our encrypted radios, forcing them to risk a second patrol just to try and find it. They hadn't.

I was furious at myself for letting events come to this. I had failed. If we hadn't been lucky, we'd have been dead.

"You almost put every one of us in a fucking black bag." Coburn stood looking at me, not sure how to react.

"You're fucking *done,*" I seethed.

Now he looked stricken. "Sir . . . I . . ."

"I'm taking over the squad as of right now."

I wasn't even sure if a second lieutenant had the authority to relieve a senior sergeant squad leader, but I knew the CO did. And I knew that Captain Weston realized that Coburn had no business leading Marines in combat.

Coburn walked back to the squad. He was a career NCO. But that career had probably just ended. In peacetime, I would have felt some sympathy for a fellow Marine. But this was war.

Camp Lejeune
27 April 2005

Major Derek Brostek was the second JAG officer witness the prosecution called. He had taught classes of new second lieutenants on the Law of War and Rules of Engagement at The Basic School. Today, Brostek was still in Quantico and was testifying by speakerphone. Assistant Government Counsel Captain Lee Kindlon conducted the direct examination of the witness.

KINDLON: Thank you, sir. Sir, I am holding some documents in my hand. They are labeled "Law of War," "Code of Conduct," and "Rules of Engagement." They are course outlines from The Basic School. In the bottom right-hand corner is a date that says "July 2004." Sir, do you know these documents, sir?

BROSTEK: I do.

KINDLON: Okay, sir. How do you know these documents?

BROSTEK: They are the student handouts that are provided to every TBS student that comes through The Basic School. That particular one is a July 2004 revision of our Law of War/Rules of Engagement curriculum.

KINDLON: And, sir, did you send me today a test inventory report of Lieutenant Pantano?

BROSTEK: I did. A test inventory report comes from our automated system, the Marine Corps Automated Instructional Manual System, MCAIMS.

KINDLON: What did Lieutenant Pantano get on this military law exam?

BROSTEK: A 98, which indicates he missed one question. Further research this afternoon, after calling MCAIMS, allowed us to dig deeper into an archival database to indicate what question he actually missed. He missed question number four, which is a line of duty misconduct investigation question. There are fifty questions on the test, so if you get a 98, they are two points apiece.

He missed one question.

In a classroom in Quantico, ten, twenty . . . *fifty* million years earlier, I had missed one question about the "Law" of war. I pictured the little Iraqi kids with their scuffed leather book bags and dusty sandals, lining up at the school in Mahmudiyah that the Americans had paid to rebuild. I pictured Demo's hot face and sweat-salted T-shirt after he'd come back from that EOD cordon at the school. The IED had been two 155 mm rounds bound together with thick steel cable to increase the kill range.

The fucking *law* of war.

Area of Operations: Warlord
8–9 April 2004

Four more hours into the same patrol in which 3rd Squad had set up a checkpoint along Route Sue, Cobra attack helicopters buzzed us at twenty feet. It was the first time I had seen Marine Air Wing assets in theater. We'd been told they were all tied up with Fallujah, but when knife-like silhouettes appeared with their distinctive *whomp-whomp-whomp,* we all cheered. It was hard to say why. Maybe because the last few days had seen such a dramatic uptick in violence all over the country it was great to see we owned something. If not the ground, then at least the sky. All fourteen of us felt comfort that we weren't alone out in this hellscape.

The joy didn't last long. A convoy of Humvees slowly limped into view along Route Sue. We waved greetings, but none of the Marines waved back. We watched in mournful silence as vehicle after vehicle with bullet-starred windshields thumped by on tires flattened by heavy fire. One Humvee towed another. I saw bandaged Marines inside. There was dark liquid dripping from one vehicle. Transmission fluid? Blood? This looked like a scene from *Black Hawk Down.*

Oh, my God.

The helo gunships hadn't been out hunting as a show of force. They had swooped in to rescue this ambushed convoy of Marines.

I didn't get to feel sick or sorry for long. After dark, heavy fighting literally exploded eight hundred meters north and east of us. Muj were moving near the MOAB ruins. The insurgents were hammering at the six gun-trucks of Combined Anti-Armor Team White on the other side of Jackson—with mortars, RPGs, and machine guns. A huge display of tracers, sailing and looping. Loud smack-flashes of RPGs and mortar rounds landing, like an accident at Fourth of July fireworks. When the Muj forward observers found good targets, they'd pop little white or red flares from signal pistols. Definitely not "All Quiet on the Western Front" tonight. This sounded more like conventional combat than some disgruntled dead-enders.

Nearby Iraqi police and FPS fled south along the highway.

Taking Coburn's former squad, I set up a blocking position on a bridge and rallied the retreating Iraqis, grabbing some by the collar and throwing them into position. The men of the squad held the intersection as RPGs smacked in just in front of us and friendly .50 cal rounds reached out in all directions. I did not try to move forward because I couldn't establish comm with the company on any frequency, and I didn't want to go north and stumble into friendly fire from CAAT White. As bad as it sounded, I prayed that they were holding their own with their heavy machine guns and grenade launchers while we held their flank. We waited through the chilly night. There was firing in all directions, which eventually tapered off, and then stopped. Muj flares, inevitably followed by mortars.

But there was some good news the next morning. Staff Sergeant Glew reported that Zulu 1, Sergeant Word's squad, had "whacked some cunts" near Jackson just after dawn. Word had been at a snap checkpoint when they heard mortar rounds fired and saw a car attempting to speed through their position.

"They lit it up pretty good, sir," Glew said.

"Aw-right!" I felt like a coach whose team had just scored a touchdown.

Later, IPs confirmed that rifle and machine-gun fire from Word's squad had killed two known Muj in the fleeing car.

Third Platoon had the first kills in Easy Company.

That was the good news. The bad news had been coming in for days and was about to get worse.

The convoy we saw belonged to our assistant division commander, General John Kelly. They'd been forced to shoot their way out of a well-organized ambush while taking back roads to the town of Iskandariyah to the south. They had lost one man killed and suffered nine wounded.

Late on Good Friday night, April 9, we were returning to the FOB when we saw two twin-rotor CH-46 medevac helos inside the berm. I had the tired 3rd Squad set up a perimeter to protect the vulnerable aircraft as they sat on the other side of the blast wall, rotors thumping up clouds of dust and gravel.

Then I heard some moaning, and I proceeded to rip new assholes.

"What if we'd just walked right past those helos?" I demanded. "Fuck 'em, right? And if those birds got hit? Then what? Any Johnny Jihad for miles would throw himself into the rotors to kill one of our birds."

I continued, searching for the emotional button to push to make this fight personal, to make it clear to these young men that we were all in this together—"And those helos are probably evacuating *our* casualties for Chrissake."

And they were.

Among the wounded on stretchers, there were two black body bags, one holding a Marine from General Kelly's convoy. The other a corporal named Speer from Fox Company who had been shot in the face down in Latafiyah.

The Warlords' first Killed in Action.

SIX

Article 32 Hearing
DAY TWO

Camp Lejeune
27 April 2005

Major Keane began the prosecution's direct examination of my platoon's corpsman, Hospitalman First Class (HN1) George "Doc" Gobles. Doc was a brave and self-effacing young guy. During the Warlords' first tour in Iraq, he'd saved the lives of probably twenty wounded Marines and Iraqis. And Doc Gobles was tough. He'd almost made it through SEAL training, but had been dropped for a medical problem after developing a severe cellulitis skin infection, a condition he could have used to avoid combat. Instead, he chose to go where he was most needed.

As with Sam Cunningham, I saw Doc's open, unassuming face tightened with discomfort at the need to testify as a prosecution witness about the events of April 15. But obtaining Gobles's complete and honest testimony was vital for both the prosecution and defense cases because he was one of only two Marines who were with me when I shot the two insurgents.

The other was Sergeant Daniel Coburn.

Major Keane first established for the record that I had led a battalion Quick Reaction Force on April 15, 2004, and that Gobles was a member of the unit.

> KEANE: Was the QRF assigned any specific missions
> that day?

As Doc answered, it quickly became obvious that he was nervous, unused to speaking in such a public forum, painfully conscious of the three-member media pool at the rear of the courtroom and the red eye of the closed-circuit television camera.

> GOBLES: That day in particular, yes, we were. What I was
> aware of what we were told is that we were going
> to an insurgent point or a point where a house
> where there was a suspected mortar fire position
> where they were firing mortars at our FOB. We
> were going there. We were told that the insurgents
> were there and that they were taking the family
> that was there, holding them hostage. That's
> where they were firing the mortars.
> KEANE: Was it a completely open area or was there fo-
> liage?
> GOBLES: No, it wasn't an open area. There were houses. I
> would say there were houses in the middle.
> There's foliage all around. There's fences on the
> outside. And on the right side, there's a road. And
> then there's a wash, and trees, and whatnot. So it
> wasn't open by no means.
> KEANE: What did you see as you were moving up?
> GOBLES: As we were approaching, I witnessed the two Iraqi
> males coming out of the house that we were
> tasked to raid—coming out of the house and got
> into the white car or white sedan or white com-
> pact car.
> KEANE: Okay. Go on.
> GOBLES: So as they did that, First Squad—we told them—
> the Marines told them to stop about two times,
> told them verbally, Stop. And then after that, they

didn't stop. They didn't pay attention to that. And
it was a loud—you know, it was loud. And then
after that, they shot warning shots towards the vehicle.

KEANE: Did they stop when the warning shots were fired?

GOBLES: After the warning shots were fired. Yes, they did
stop.

KEANE: Okay. What did they do when they stopped?

GOBLES: Kind of raised their hands and surrendered there.

KEANE: You say they surrendered?

GOBLES: Well, they had their hands up.

KEANE: Okay. What did you do when you saw the car stop
and they had their hands up?

GOBLES: Well, after, I went with Lieutenant Pantano and
Sergeant Coburn, went up there. We approached
the vehicle because we were the only ones left to
do—to do anything, to do this. And First Squad
continued, went into the house.

KEANE: What did these Iraqis look like?

GOBLES: Well, just like any Iraqi. They had their dresses on.
And then they had—I can't recall if they had their
headbands on or not, but just black hair and—

KEANE: How old were they?

GOBLES: One of them was older, like maybe late into mid-
thirties. And the other one was in his young twenties or teens.

KEANE: What did they do when you pulled them out of the
car?

GOBLES: When I pulled them out of the car? Well, they—I
pulled them out. They didn't really give too much
resistance, a little bit but nothing really.

KEANE: At this point, it's yourself, Coburn, and the lieutenant?

GOBLES: Yes.

KEANE: Did the lieutenant tell you to do anything?

GOBLES: Well, we went about—ordered me to search the
vehicle after this. Use the—I believe it was the
older male to help me search the vehicle. It is
what we were taught to do, just had him open up

the doors, opened up the hood, open up the glove box while he was in there, and make sure all the doors are open, and open up the trunk.

KEANE: You were taught to do it that way?

GOBLES: Right. You usually want them to do that because it's—I guess it's safer so you ain't—you aren't the one that's opening things and you don't know what's there.

KEANE: After you pulled everything—you ripped everything out of the car, the seats and the console and everything, did you put that stuff back in the car?

GOBLES: Yes, sir, I did.

KEANE: Who told you to do that?

GOBLES: Lieutenant Pantano, because he felt that it was, you know, I guess, a little disrespectful, so I had it replaced, as well as I could, back in the vehicle.

FOB Mahmudiyah, Iraq
11 April 2004

Easter and Arbaeen fell on the same Sunday this year. Not that the co-incidence of religious holidays mattered. The flood of Shia pilgrims had already passed south through our area of operations along Jackson and those million people were down in Karbala and Najaf, performing their sacred duty. The hot morning began with some haze and the gritty taste of dust in the air. But by noon, the sky cleared to a deep blue transparence that reminded me of 9/11.

The Warlords' chaplain—a gutsy Navy lieutenant named Verhulst—held interfaith services at the FOB. But my platoon, Easy 3, had just taken over the battalion Quick Reaction Force, and I had to keep the men on alert, ready to roll out to protect the explosives disposal teams when IEDs were discovered or to respond to ambushes. We had to give up a squad for guard duty, so the QRF was centered on 1st and 2nd Squads in two seven-ton trucks and two Humvees.

After a quick lunch, I checked with the platoon sergeant for about the third time that day: ammo loads, vehicle and weapons status, fuel, water, medical supplies, extra radio batteries . . . all the shit that was so easy to forget, and which forgetting about could kill you. And we had lots of extra maps. We had never done a QRF mission before, and I was terrified at the prospect of getting lost or hung up on some back road while Marines were in trouble.

I needed to stay busy to stay cool inside: the tempo of enemy operations was definitely peaking. The base had been mortared—no serious casualties—and the Muj were obviously probing us, testing our responses. On Good Friday, while I was bringing my squads back from the Brick Factory, Easy Company's 2nd Platoon ran into some Muj recovering IED parts at the edge of our AO. The insurgents tried to speed away from the checkpoint, but the car stopped after the Marines fired about fifty rounds—some even hitting the vehicle. And what a package of goodies the 2nd Platoon guys found in the car: everybody's favorite, 155 mm shells, detonator cord ("detcord"), picks and shovels, even some weight lifter's belts so the little bastards wouldn't strain their 110-pound asses lugging the heavy shells. It turned out the Muj were recovering the unfired components of a big IED they'd planted, which had malfunctioned.

One of them was hit with an M-16 round, but wasn't hurt bad. Another had some cuts from broken windshield glass. A tough business.

And today I was also glad to have clear tasks at hand because I was still sickened by the image of the wounded from General Kelly's convoy and those two dark body bags being loaded on the helos the night before. But I couldn't let my men see how this had affected me. So, in the steamy heat of the head, I took advantage of the privacy to jot some notes in my journal about the impact that the first death had on the Warlords—and on me.

Loneliness was the strongest emotion.

> *I miss my family. My wife. My babies. God, those last few days before deploying were so terrible. Locking myself in the bathroom in the middle of packing my shit, with my 1.5 yr old son playing with my green socks, not knowing if I was ever gonna come back. I felt like my heart was going to rip itself out of my chest and slither down the toilet like an alien. It hurt so bad. I chose this. I chose to do this to all of them. I didn't have to. I chose to. They must be wrecked with latest news. The Internet café on base is shut off until the family is notified.*
>
> *Damn roosters crow here at every fucking hour of the day and night. Wonder if it's a person giving a signal.*

May Speer rest in Peace.
Peace. Ha.
"Only the dead have seen the end of war."—Plato.

My little Icom radio squawked. "Easy-Three, report to the Big House."

That was the battalion combat operations center, COC. The headquarters building had been a brick-and-concrete poultry processing plant before the war. Naturally, we called it the Chicken Factory. It and the nearby tents were guarded by HESCO barriers—rectangular chin-high boxes of steel mesh and thick plastic sheeting, which front-end loaders had filled with rocky sand. A HESCO could absorb the shrapnel from the direct hit of an incoming mortar or artillery round.

When I reached the COC, a little short of breath from the dash across the base in the afternoon heat, I found a tense and apparently chaotic scene. NCOs and enlisted men were speaking into the handsets of the encrypted tactical radios lined up in a rack along one wall. Radio speakers broadcast streams of frantic, overlapping reports. Some voices were reasonably calm, some near hysterical. The COC this afternoon reminded me of the New York Mercantile Exchange trading pit. But this wasn't a commodities exchange. The radio traffic sounded like people were dying out there. *Something bad going down.*

The Easy Company CO, Captain Weston, and battalion commander, Lieutenant Colonel Kyser, were already in the room. The officers and senior NCOs were studying the big maps mounted on easel boards.

The Airborne had left us some flat-screen, liquid-crystal displays for posting and retrieving SITREPs and POZREPs (situation and position reports), but Marines also still used paper maps (protected with clear plastic), marked off in the traditional military grid system. For us, when it came to managing the battlespace, it was colored pins and grease pencils, not electron beams. If mortars knocked out the generators, maps kept working.

Enlisted men called out information from the tactical radio nets, and watch officers jabbed colored pins in the big area of operations map—the latest POZREPs of friendly and enemy units. Marine assets were also marked with flat-head white pins on which the name of the platoon or company was printed in fine felt-tip pen. Enemy contact (IEDs, firefights, etc.) was marked with red pins and the densest cluster was in and around the town of Latafiyah, twenty klicks south on Jackson. That was Fox Company's AO. And it was where my buddy, Lieutenant Stibb, had lost Corporal Speer, our first KIA, two days before. *Shit.* This did not feel good.

"Okay, Pantano," Major Neil, our operations officer, said pointing at the map. "Here's the situation. Fox Six reports a big Army convoy ran into a heavy ambush, beginning here . . ." His voice was calm, precise, as he tapped the straight north-south line of Jackson on the south end of Latafiyah. "We've got reports of vehicles burning, friendly casualties, and combined arms fire targeting Fox Six's position."

Even as Neil spoke, I heard frightened voices from the Army vehicles over the radio frequency shared by joint forces in this AO: ". . . three WIA, three, two *bad* . . . the fuel tank's gonna . . ." The soldiers were like actors stepping on each other's lines. But I felt a long way from Manhattan TV studios.

"Get the QRF down there fast, Pantano," Major Neil said, his voice even less emotional. "Tie in with Fox and report back. Make sure you've got the wrecker to pull off any disabled vehicles blocking the road. And take EOD because there'll probably be IEDs."

"Aye, aye, sir." I turned to leave, my mouth set in what I hoped looked like determination, not anxiety.

I had literally been preparing myself for this mission for years, but now that I finally got it, I was nearly overcome with emotion. Guilt that I had been given what I had secretly wished for, but at what cost? And dread that I would fail the biggest test of my life.

The QRF that roared out the gate of the base and turned south on Jackson consisted of ten vehicles. My platoon had two Humvees and two seven-ton trucks. CAAT White had four Humvees, two armed with .50 caliber heavy machine guns, two with MK-19 40 mm automatic grenade launchers—which looked like short-barreled machine guns that had been chewing crystal meth for six months. The big green wrecker truck had a swinging crane arm, and also a cab-mounted "Ma Deuce" .50 cal. As always, EOD rode "slick" (unarmed) and fast in a hard-shell Humvee. I mixed the heavily armed and unarmed vehicles along the axis of our convoy, silently thanking God that we made it that far. Just days before, a QRF out west, Ramadi maybe, had been ambushed leaving their base. The casualties from the point-blank RPG attack and a donkey-cart bomb had been heavy.

If the Muj were going to hit us, I wanted to be able to strike back immediately, overpowering their AK and machine-gun fire—even their RPGs—before they had a chance to break us up and pick off the cripples. Our seven-tons, the wrecker truck, and two of the CAAT White Humvees fired .50 caliber armor-piercing incendiary (API) ammo that could rip apart any insurgent vehicle that tried to close on us, and could blow through the thinner walls of the buildings along the road.

The MK-19 40 mike-mike grenades had dual-purpose high explosive, antipersonnel warheads. This belt-fed weapon could lay down bursts of five grenades per second—enough to break up enemy RPG ambushes, which they tended to stage from alleys and side streets, a bunch of lethal cockroaches begging to be stomped out.

We blew through Mahmudiyah, our machine-gunners swiveling their weapons right and left, just to be sure none of the ambushers hadn't already proceeded north from Latafiyah to hit us up here.

As we rolled past the Iraqi police post in the center of town, I called Captain Bairstow, Fox Company commander.

"Fox Six, Easy Three Actual, ten klicks north of your POZ." I recited the map coordinates and gave him our ETA, 1610 hours.

We were past the southern edge of Mahmudiyah, and the typical brush and stands of reeds around canal networks appeared on both sides of the road. This was prime territory for IEDs or an RPG ambush . . . or both those and a close-in ambush with PKM Russian-made 7.62 mm machine guns. I was keeping myself externally calm, braced in the troop bay of the swaying truck with the Marines of 1st Squad.

Two Army trucks and a clump of Humvees approached, moving north as fast as they could with the battle damage they'd taken. Flat, thumping wheels, bullet-starred windshields, that lame-assed Tinker Toy kit armor torn open as if by a big can opener. I tried calling on my radio, but got no answer.

That's gotta be from RPGs.

Lance Corporal Faleris stood behind his .50 cal in the gun cupola of our truck's cab. While some of the other young Marines now looked a little pale under their desert tans, he was grinning like a varsity ballplayer about to be called off the bench. I knew I could count on him. Hell, *all* these Marines would be okay once we actually got into the shit.

"Check that out, sir," Corporal Arnulfo Magdaleno said, pointing his M-16/M-203 grenade launcher combo to the south. Black clouds rose into the blue sky. I counted two . . . no, three, closer to us, and then a greasy, rippling pillar of smoke and flame farther south. This felt so much like looking down toward the burning Twin Towers that I had to shake my head to stay focused.

Rolling at fifty miles an hour, we soon identified the source of the first smoke. North of Latafiyah, there was a line of disabled tractor-trailers, big flatbeds that the military calls lowboys. They could haul anything from an Abrams tank to a bunch of Humvees. All of them were flaming, sooty smoke from the tires mixing with black-and-gray puffs from the engines. I saw no dead or wounded soldiers in the shot-up Army vehicles we'd passed. They'd scrambled to get free while they could. The convoy hadn't had an adequate armed escort, and none of those drivers wanted to end up on Al-Jazeera TV getting his head hacked off.

On both sides of the highway there were the giveaway signs of the IEDs that had stopped the Army convoy: deep, sandy craters rimmed with black.

The blazing trucks weren't the worst sight. It was the cargo. Three lowboys were carrying tracked M-113 field ambulances, their desert-tan hulls clearly marked with big red crosses. Those ambulances burned on the flat trailer beds. One had the neat round impact hole of an RPG just below the red cross. That internationally recognized symbol of medical aid had made a great target. For a second, I pictured the effect of an RPG's armor-piercing warhead. The shaped charge drove a jet of molten metal into the crew compartment, incinerating anyone it touched.

Ahead through the smoke, I saw the minaret of another mosque. Red Cross and mosque. Was this the fucking Crusades? Had we traded swords for M-16s?

The pillar of smoke south of beautiful downtown Latafiyah—probably a finalist for Shithole of the Year along this stretch of Jackson—was obviously from a big oil fire. I might just as well have been back in Kuwait in February 1991. The Muj must have started this fire, too, either intentionally or by accident. Maybe with RPGs, more likely with mortars.

Shit, *mortars*. I was going to have to locate good cover for my men down in Latafiyah. It was a grubby industrial town with one- and two-floor workshops on both sides of the highway—plenty of places to hide PKM machine guns and RPGs. But we would also need good fighting positions once we made contact with the Muj. I didn't intend just to dash into some buildings and hunker down. These bastards were about to find out the true meaning of "No Worse Enemy."

We passed another burning truck and were nearing the northern outskirts of Latafiyah when the enemy opened fire. Pop-pop-pop-*POP-POP-POP* . . . smack-pop-pop . . . pop-smack-*smack-smack* . . . 7.62 mm rounds hitting our titanium-sheet side armor, either AK or PKM rounds. Probably both. The noise was like Carolina hail pounding on a metal shed roof.

On both sides of the road, Muj were dashing around, firing and ducking, firing and diving for cover. They'd be lucky not to hit each other. Maybe they didn't give a shit, as long as they hit us. This was what the old gunnies called a "Polish ambush." I'd better not tell that to Demo, I thought. He'd punch me senseless. We were in the kill zone and still two or three klicks from Fox Company.

"Engage . . . engage, *engage!*" My voice was hoarse. We were in the shit for sure. No time for dramatics. No brave speeches. Just kill the fuckers before they killed us.

Faleris swung the dark barrel of his .50 cal to the right. "*Oh,* no you . . ." He let fly a long burst, and then another, reverse-leading his aim, fighting the g-forces of the swaying truck and the weight of the weapon with its attached 100-round ammo can. His fire sounded like a jackhammer pounding my head. ". . . You . . . *didn't* . . ." The Muj never had the chance to continue firing. Either Faleris killed them or broke up their little jackoff session next to that water tower.

War is a battle of will. And Faleris had just learned that you dominate the enemy by imposing your will.

Along both sides of the truck bed, my guys popped up and cut loose with their M-16s. Three-round bursts, sounding flat and brittle under the .50 cal's heavy thud. I'd taught the platoon to lay down a solid *wall* of suppressing fire, "The Mad Minute." Burn through one magazine, drop it, and load and dump another. All in a few seconds. Again and again. The idea was to blast out solid streams of the little 62-grain green-tip bullets to hit or pin down anyone down range. The rounds wouldn't do shit to the buildings or the reinforced firing positions, but the Muj would know death was knocking at the door.

When I called Fox Six, Captain Bairstow, again, he said the enemy "main force" seemed to be regrouping south of his position in Latafiyah. They were a couple of klicks below the town center around the "T" intersection of Jackson with a paved highway leading west, a road we called Route Temple.

"The heaviest fire is coming from the west and south," he told me.

"Roger that, sir. That's where I'm headed."

The only way I could secure the convoy—my principal mission—was to engage and dominate the enemy. So we blew right by Bairstow's Marines as they rallied convoy survivors along the main drag—with fire from surrounding roofs and storefronts still striking our vehicles. It seemed like every motherfucker in Latafiyah big enough to hoist a weapon was in on the action today.

I was still on the hook with Captain Bairstow when Corporal Magdaleno crawled over the back of my flak jacket, balanced his weapon on my helmet, and let fly a 40 mm round from the M-203 grenade launcher slung beneath the barrel of his rifle. *Cuu-chuunk.* The grenade was in the air about a second when I heard it blast into a rooftop ahead of us.

Magdaleno laughed and shouted something in Caribbean Spanish. The only word I understood was *chinga* . . . "fuck." The mania of combat.

Camp Lejeune
27 April 2005

Major Keane continued his slow, deliberate examination of Gobles. Keane probed Doc for his detailed recollection of the actual shooting. Once more, I hated the necessity of Jill and my mother's presence in this courtroom, hearing these words.

Finally, Keane's questions shifted to the aftermath of the shooting.

KEANE: All right. Did you check to see if—provide medical attention to these two persons?

GOBLES: Yes. Yes, sir. When the firing was over, I assessed the scene, when I came to it. And I went and put on my gloves and went there and checked their pulse, carotid pulse and checked his radial pulse. I just looked for signs of—you know, checked his airway, checked for any breathing or any circulation. I pronounced the first one dead. I told Lieu-

tenant Pantano he was dead. And I went and
checked the second one in the same manner and
reported that he was dead also, so they were both
dead.

KEANE: What did you do next?

GOBLES: Well, next, I just went to Lieutenant Pantano and
he told me—he told me [that] he yelled stop and
they were trying to get away, and then—well, then
I went to the rear of the vehicle. And I saw
Sergeant Coburn. And he came up to me looking
startled, looking shocked, just as I was too. He
asked me what the hell just happened. And I said,
"Don't worry about it." And I said, "The blood is
not on your hands, it's on Lieutenant Pantano's." I
just told him that because it was. So I was trying to
ease his mind, I guess.

Latafiyah, Iraq
11 April 2004

As we blasted through the sprawl of shabby buildings on the south side
of Latafiyah, it became obvious where the concentration of insurgents
that Fox Six had reported was positioned. The huge, crackling oil-tank
blaze was off to our left front—the southeast—and we were taking
small arms and automatic weapons fire from two industrial-type buildings, one on each side of Route Temple, where it intersected Jackson.
Up and down our convoy, the .50 cals and MK-19 grenade launchers
were chopping into windows and roofs of those buildings.

We were not some undermanned Army truck convoy that the Muj
could pick off at their convenience. I intended to slam right into that
intersection and lay down such a wall of fire that the cunts would have
two choices: run or die.

"Main objective on southwest corner," I shouted into my Icom
over the roar of the weapons.

Our seven-ton slammed to a stop only twenty meters from the raw
concrete two-floor repair garage—the insurgents' main position. They
fired straight at us. We fired straight at them. I would have put the truck
right through the wall if it wouldn't have killed us all in the process.

The insanity of the day took on a splintered quality, ripped free from the normal flow of time.

Faleris stood behind his long-barreled gun, his face snarling as he emptied an entire can of .50 cal into the second-floor window.

Streams of 40 mm MK-19 grenades whipped over our helmets to explode inside the building.

My men rose and fired their M-16s, ducked to reload, and rose again to fire.

Just up the road, Staff Sergeant Glew had 2nd Squad in the other seven-ton, and put out such a shitstorm that the Muj in the ambush position on the other side of Route Temple had no chance to return fire—or if they did try to pull the old *Allahu Akbar,* they became instant martyrs.

Faleris burned through another can of .50 cal ammo and reloaded. One of the CAAT White MK-19 gunners was reloading at the same time. I saw the empty rectangular ammunition containers fly end over end through the hot sunlight, hitting the pavement with such force that the impact actually torqued the green steel.

Several seconds had passed since we'd rolled up to the garage. Our fire was smacking around inside the open vehicle repair bays, piercing the oil and grease barrels the Muj had used for cover, ricocheting off the raw concrete walls and the ceiling, twenty feet above. Daylight appeared from an open door at the back of the garage. Movement, men fleeing the building, limping, stumbling.

We had established fire superiority; now it was time to dismount and seize this position. My body moved. I issued commands as clearly and precisely as I could. But as Lance Corporals Davis, Smith, Johnson, Perry, and Braun leapt off the tailgate and took cover beside the truck, waiting for their squad leader, I experienced an unexpected internal pause. They looked up, their young faces a mix of anxiety and determination.

Suddenly I was back at Camp Lejeune again, a month earlier, the platoon formed up, waiting to board buses for the aircraft at Cherry Point—just as I had stood in formation before Desert Storm. My platoon's families were there to see them off, their sons going to war.

I had given those wives, mothers, and fathers more assurance than I had any right to offer: "I promise I will bring your Marines home to you. Maybe a little bumped and bruised, but I will bring them home."

Who had I been to make that kind of promise? On that cool March morning, who could have imagined a five-kilometer ambush, with belt-fed machine guns, IEDs, and RPGs using shaped-charge warheads? This was not security, not stability. It was fucking war.

Camp Lejeune
27 April 2005

Major Keane was still patiently, skillfully working through his direct examination of Doc Gobles.

> KEANE: [indicating photo blow-ups on easel] What are those pictures of?
>
> GOBLES: That's pictures of the vehicle and where the dead Iraqis were. And those are the detainees that we had out of the brown car.
>
> KEANE: So this is after the shooting?
>
> GOBLES: Yes, this is.
>
> KEANE: Who are those guys on the ground right there?
>
> GOBLES: I believe those are the ones out of the vehicle that was approaching us after the shooting, those are the Iraqis that were in it.
>
> KEANE: Okay. And obviously, there's Marines standing around the car. Just one final question. Do you believe this was—the shooting of these Iraqis was justified?
>
> STACKHOUSE [TO INVESTIGATING OFFICER]: Sir, I'm going to object to that. That's your decision, not his, whether it's a justified shooting or not.
>
> WINN: I'm going to let the witness answer, but I want that noted for the record.
>
> STACKHOUSE: Yes, sir. I mean, you're asking him to look into Lieutenant Pantano's mind by asking what—

This was another critical moment, an invisible fulcrum. If Keane scored his point here, he would have established that one of my most trusted men, the combat-tested Doc Gobles—who had literally been

up to his elbows in blood to save the lives of wounded Marines—
thought that the shooting of those insurgent prisoners had not been
justified. I sat very still, rigid.

WINN: No. He's asking in his own mind.

STACKHOUSE: Well, sir, he wasn't even—I mean, the evidence is he wasn't even looking at him when
he started pulling the trigger. I mean, how
could he even make that opinion? That in-
vades the provenance you have here to decide whether it's a justified shooting.

WINN: I'm going to go ahead and sustain that objection. He can't testify to what he thinks Lieutenant Pantano was thinking. And that would
make him conclude what Lieutenant Pantano was thinking. So I'm going to go ahead
and sustain that objection.

Something tight inside me unclenched. But not much.

KEANE: While you were present on the scene, did you
see anything to indicate the need to exercise
self-defense?

STACKHOUSE: Sir, I'm going to object to that. I mean, he's already talked about that. He wasn't even look-
ing in that direction when—

WINN: No. I'm going to go ahead and allow the witness to answer this question. But I want that
objection noted for the record.

KEANE: Did you see any reason to employ deadly
force in self-defense?

GOBLES: Myself, I didn't see any, but—

KEANE: Thanks. No further questions.

Latafiyah, Iraq
11 April 2004

Off the truck, I did a head count, and then pointed at Faleris, who was
hunkered behind his gun, grinning. I waved west down Temple to indi-

cate his lane of fire, and he gave me a thumbs-up. Staff Sergeant Glew had dismounted the other squad to cover our entry and prepared to attack across the street when we could provide cover fire.

I took a breath and rushed inside the garage, Sergeant Word's Marines beside me. There was a lot of brass and concrete chips underfoot. There was some thick red blood, but no dead Muj.

"Doc," I yelled at Gobles, pointing to the shelter of some oil barrels. "Here's your office."

I knew he would need a casualty collection station with good cover before we finished in Latafiyah.

Waving to Corporal Matchett, I indicated where I wanted him to give Doc Gobles the best security. Matchett had an M-203 grenade launcher on his rifle and could make matters difficult for any Muj coming toward us on Temple. He'd do his damnedest to protect Doc, but I also saw that the four CAAT White Humvees were positioned at good intervals among the buildings both north and south of Temple, their .50 cals and MK-19s peeking around the corners to cover both roads.

While we consolidated, the Muj stepped up their fire from the factory. They had retreated to about two hundred meters to the west along the south side of Temple and from their other positions north of us. But heavy machine-gun fire from our trucks and CAAT vehicles suppressed the enemy right across Temple. Staff Sergeant Glew did not hesitate. As I bounded up the stairs of the garage, Glew and 2nd Squad leader "Cujo" Aguirre dashed across the street with their men and did a classic, well-disciplined building entry, shooting high and low to eliminate any stay-behinds.

On the second floor of the garage, Sergeant Word brought me to one of the corner rooms overlooking the main highway. Hot 7.62 mm PKM machine-gun brass littered the floor. Shards of concrete from our incoming fire crunched under my boots. Word handed me a Thuraya satellite phone he'd found in the room. I used to provide these to my journalist teams going to Afghanistan, I thought. A repetitive sequence of digits flickered on the small rectangular display. Middle Eastern Service . . . 979 . . . 4548 . . . 979 . . . 4548 . . .

That had been the trigger code for the last IED. Or was it for the *next* one?

I flipped open the back of the handset and shucked out the battery. The display went dark.

**Camp Lejeune
27 April 2005**

Major Stackhouse began his cross-examination of Doc Gobles, speaking calmly and with quiet precision. My confidence was slowly returning.

STACKHOUSE: Okay. I want to start right where you ended, which is did you see anything that would give rise to self-defense. And you said no, right?

GOBLES: Did I see anything? No, I didn't.

STACKHOUSE: You were not looking toward Lieutenant Pantano when he started shooting, correct?

GOBLES: Correct.

STACKHOUSE: Did you hear anything?

GOBLES: I heard—I heard—yeah. I heard—well, I heard Lieutenant Pantano and—and yell stop, and I didn't really hear anything except that.

STACKHOUSE: You heard him yelling stop in Arabic?

GOBLES: Yes. I heard him. Yes. I heard him yell that.

STACKHOUSE: And—

GOBLES: And in English as well.

STACKHOUSE: Right. I mean, so he at least yelled stop twice?

GOBLES: Yes, he did.

STACKHOUSE: So that might give you some indicator that something was going on, right?

GOBLES: Yes.

STACKHOUSE: And then the fact that he shot—

GOBLES: Correct.

Stackhouse now took Doc Gobles away from the events of April 15, 2004.

STACKHOUSE: All right. I want to start at the beginning with how you met Lieutenant Pantano and how long you knew him before April 15?

GOBLES: All right.

STACKHOUSE: Tell the investigating officer how you guys trained as a platoon working up to the deployment to Iraq.

GOBLES: How we trained? Well, we trained together. We did a lot of training. Lieutenant Pantano gave us the best training in the company. We did VCP's, we did a lot of PT, we did a lot of different other—he had us take—he wanted us to learn Arabic. He had us learn Arabic. He always gave us studying material to learn Arabic and about the culture, about the Iraqi culture, and different things to familiarize ourselves with Iraqis.

STACKHOUSE: And what was his general demeanor when he was teaching the platoon how to interact with the Iraqis? What was his general guidance to you?

GOBLES: Well, I felt that Lieutenant Pantano was very for the Iraqis. He thought it was a good thing that we were going there to free the country and give them the democracy and whatnot. And he was always for the Iraqis, and we should always present ourselves as humanitarians, as we are, and greet them with smiles on our faces, and be kind to them.

STACKHOUSE: Did you do patrols out in the small towns around Mahmudiyah?

GOBLES: Yes. We did patrols all the time, every day.

STACKHOUSE: And did you see Lieutenant Pantano interacting with the Iraqis on those kind of foot patrols?

GOBLES: Yes.

STACKHOUSE: And how did that go?

GOBLES: It went good. He would introduce himself as Lieutenant Pantano. And everyone got to know his name. And when we went to village meetings and councils and things like that in Mahmudiyah. They all knew his name. And

Lieutenant Pantano would always go around and talk to security guards, talk to the cops there, you know, and even little kids that were selling us soda and stuff and bread. It went well, his contact with them. When they asked about somebody, they asked about Lieutenant Pantano. They asked to talk to Lieutenant Pantano because they felt that he was a friend, that he was someone that they could talk to.

Latafiyah, Iraq
11 April 2004

The Muj dropping their satellite phone proved that we had taken them by surprise. Always attack into an ambush. I looked around the room again. A stained blanket. Some dirty cooking pots. What was that along the walls? Christ, there were piles of dried-up turds in here. They had been waiting for days to hit that long Army convoy. And they probably figured knocking out those lowboys had been payday. But we'd already made them pay double, at least five or ten KIAs among the ambushers against one KIA driver and a bunch of wounded soldiers.

There was no time to celebrate. I wanted our M-240 machine guns and SAWs on the flat roofs of both buildings that we held. Those weapons together with some M-203s would give us a dominant position.

I passed the word to Staff Sergeant Glew on the Icom, grabbed the longer-range PRC-119 encrypted radio in its backpack, and headed up to the roof myself. The sun was a weight on my head and shoulders. A mix of stinking exertion and adrenaline sweat rose from beneath the collar of my flak jacket. The oil fire up the road roared like a crazy blast furnace. Small-arms fire crackled, and machine guns pounded.

Through this noise, Fox Six called to announce he was moving vehicles down to my POZ.

"Easy Three Actual," Captain Bairstow said, "I'll set up my gun trucks on the east side of Jackson and roust out any enemy that try to counterattack from that direction. You hold Temple."

"Aye, aye, sir."

No sooner had I put down the handset than the low wall surrounding our rooftop position was hit by machine-gun fire from the factory to the west. We dropped behind the concrete at the incoming fire. Heavy 82 mm mortar rounds burst around us and the vehicles on the roads below. If we took a direct hit up here . . .

Don't think about it. Don't think of your family. You wanted to be here . . . you *had* to be here.

We weren't the only ones who understood suppressive fire. "Here they come," Corporal Magdaleno yelled.

Fuck taking cover. The Muj in the factory to the west were trying to pin us down, to protect a vehicle attack. A rusty orange dump truck sped toward us on Temple. From this height I saw that the back of the truck was jammed with RPG-gunners.

Just as I was giving the command to hit it, the salty old HIET [Human Intelligence Exploitation Team] chief warrant officer who'd decided to ride shotgun on the wrecker cut loose down on Temple with his .50 cal. The armor-piercing ammo tore up the dump truck's cab and sides, ripping the Muj apart, throwing some bodies—and smashed RPGs—onto the pavement. The vehicle spun out of control and slammed into a building down the road.

I couldn't stand up long enough to count the dead Muj because mortar rounds were still exploding nearby.

Now a minivan crammed with Muj swerved toward us, weaving from one side of the road to the other to dodge our fire. The van got close enough for me to see the men inside clutching AKs and RPGs, crowded in like some kind of sick Keystone Kops circus act.

Lance Corporal Davis, a SAW-gunner, fired small pop-pop-pop bursts, hitting the van but not stopping it.

I smacked the Marine on the shoulder. "Put forty rounds into that van, warrior."

"Roger that, sir."

The butt of his 5.56 mm SAW pounded the shoulder of his flak jacket. Two long bursts, three, four. Like the dump truck, the minivan spun out of control and crashed. But there was still motion inside. The SAW fired the same light round as our M-16s. It didn't have the stopping power of a heavier weapon like a 240G.

"Hit 'em again," I shouted.

Two SAWs were firing now, punching clusters of bullet holes in the minivan's sides and roof. After five or six more bursts, there was finally no more movement inside.

The mortars fell. Fire came from the factory. And I repositioned my men on the rooftops, so they could cover both Temple and Jackson. I had fewer than thirty Marine infantrymen, half that number in dominating fire positions.

Christ only knows how many Muj are out there, I thought, but it feels like hundreds.

And they knew the terrain, every piss alley and shed around here. They had already shown suicidal courage and tenacity. We had started the mission after 1600 hours. It would be full night in ninety minutes. I knew they would try to outflank us, to pin us down with mortars and RPGs while they slipped back into the buildings.

The incoming mortars and small-arms fire were almost constant. Across Jackson, the burning oil tanks whooshed and rumbled. Oil, I knew, rarely exploded. But what if one of those big, untouched steel tanks held gasoline?

"Hey, you bastards," I yelled to my Marines on the roof, "bad guys, good guys, all kinds of stuff blowing up. It's like a fucking Jackie Chan movie . . . And you lucky motherfuckers are getting *paid*. Damn."

"Fuckin' A, sir."

"Oohhraah, sir."

There was movement down Temple, Muj darting among the buildings, getting closer before they fired. "Light 'em up when you can," I told my guys. I grabbed the PRC-119 and bounded down the stairs, the antenna bouncing spastically against my left hip.

In the wide door of the garage, I sucked a couple of deep breaths, and then dashed across Jackson to Captain Bairstow's Humvee. I showed him the position of my Marines and reported on the enemy personnel and vehicles we had eliminated.

"Solid," he said. "You've taken pressure off the ambushed convoy. They've limped back to the FOB. Now we've got to hold these positions. Battalion is on the way down." He studied a map a second. "Oh, yeah. We've got air up . . . F-14s. But we probably won't be able to use them. All they've got are two-thousand-pounders so they're supposed to head back to rearm."

I drank some warm water from my camelback. A two-thousand-pound bomb exploding down here in this cluster of workshops and narrow lanes could kill a lot of Marines. For the moment, we were better off fighting on our own.

We'd prevented more Army casualties, kicked the Muj hard enough in the nuts to really piss them off, and now *we* were set up in a good hasty defense. Once the battalion got us what reinforcements they could muster, we would have enough Marines to sweep through Latafiyah, south to north, and drag the surviving Muj out of their ratholes.

All we had to do now was hang in there until reinforced. All the Muj had to do was overrun us and hack off our heads for an Al-Jazeera commercial.

Camp Lejeune
27 April 2005

Major Stackhouse now moved ahead to the QRF and the long Easter Sunday firefight in Latafiyah.

STACKHOUSE: What happened during that firefight?

GOBLES: Well, we responded because they ambushed—I believe it was an army unit. And then when some of our units went down there, they were also getting fired upon. But we were the first platoon to respond down there. And as soon as we got down there, we made contact with them there by a gas station. And vehicles were all burned out that were RPGed and whatnot. And as soon as we got there, we made contact with the insurgents and dismounted the vehicles and there was—just everywhere, they were at the buildings across the street right by us, shooting at us and—what do you want to know?

STACKHOUSE: Okay. And did you see Lieutenant Pantano during that firefight?

GOBLES: Yeah. I was attached to him basically the whole time.

STACKHOUSE: Tell us what you saw him do during that firefight.

GOBLES: I saw him take control. He had the radio on
him at one point. He had the radio on him.
He was issuing orders over the radio to the
other squads, and running around, giving orders, and just making sure everyone was all
right, getting everyone on line, making sure
everyone had their fighting positions on line
and that they were engaging proper targets.
And he was taking command. We set up a
field aid station, guess you would want to
call it, or casualty collection point. And he
posted—he got security for me, posted security. And then he went about—went upstairs
is where the main engagement was going on
from the building that we were on upstairs. It
was—Marines were up there. And they were
engaging another building across the way is
where all the insurgents were. And he went
up there and was just directing fire and issuing out orders.

STACKHOUSE: Did you see him expose himself to fire while
he was involved in that firefight?

GOBLES: We all did. Yes, he did. Yes.

STACKHOUSE: And what was his demeanor during that firefight?

GOBLES: His demeanor, it was focused. It was intense.
It was just, you know—excuse my expres-
sion, but it was "balls out," you know. We
were in a firefight, so it was pretty crazy. He
held his head better than anybody because,
hell, he had to be. He was issuing out orders
to everyone, telling them what the hell to do.
And his demeanor and his attitude was the
best out there. That's my opinion.

STACKHOUSE: And during the month of April, just from your
perspective, did you notice an increase in the
activity of the enemy?

GOBLES: Very much so. By the time we got there
          from—yeah, there was a lot of activity.
STACKHOUSE: Was it a scary time?
GOBLES: Yeah. It was the craziest time of my life. It
          was—it was scary. Yeah. It was every emotion
          you can think a human can feel. It was every-
          thing.
STACKHOUSE: Did you ever see Lieutenant Pantano lose
          control during that period?
GOBLES: No, not at all.

Latafiyah, Iraq
11 April 2004

Down on Temple, one of the EOD guys lay prone on the roof of his
Humvee aiming the team's long M-14 rifle at enemy sniper positions.
EOD guys carried this scoped 7.62 mm infantry weapon in order to
disrupt the circuits of IEDs exposed along roadsides. Now this brave
Marine was disrupting the central nervous systems of the assholes up
in those buildings sniping at us with their AKs.

"Sir," the guy shouted, "I see a . . ."

"Kill it," I yelled back down at him.

"Sir, I see a . . ."

"Waste it."

I pointed along Route Temple to a source of sporadic fire. "Hey,
Faleris, take out that entire floor."

His .50 cal pounded. I just hoped he wouldn't burn out the barrel.

Camp Lejeune
27 April 2005

In our second break today, my family and I, trailed by the defense
team, had to run the usual media gauntlet between the main courthouse building and the legal services section. The reporters and cam-
eramen stayed on their side of a barrier, but jostled for position to get
the best shots. Some of them had digital cameras, and I knew these

latest images would be on the wire within minutes. We had decided our best course was to look calmly straight ahead, as if we did not hear their shouted questions.

In the defense conference room—our war room—a whiteboard presented the witness list and summaries of the testimony we could expect from them. We also had the roster of attorneys on both sides and where they fit into the scheduled testimony.

The war room had a rectangular mahogany table that could have easily seated a twelve-person jury, and which was certainly big enough to give my mother, Jill, Mike Gregorio, and me space to stretch out. On lunch hours we could spread around our Subway sandwiches and joke about who got the turkey breast with mustard when they really wanted mayonnaise.

Today we had laid out several national and local newspapers that discussed the first day of the hearing.

There were also a couple of well-marked copies of *New York* magazine with me on the cover in my dress blues. The headline featuring the article by reporter Steve Fishman was emblazoned in red and white block letters, MURDER AND THE PREPPY MARINE. The actual article was entitled "Hell's Kitchen." Fishman had done an excellent job presenting my background, and he certainly caught the "dynamic" between Jill and me over my obsession to join the Marines after 9/11. He quoted Jill as having said, "If you'd told me I would end up married to a Marine, I would've said, 'You're on crack.'" No one ever said Jill didn't have an opinion.

Fishman's article also devoted a lot of space to Sergeant Daniel Coburn, whom the reporter interviewed at the latter's home near Camp Lejeune. My and Coburn's views on what had happened on April 15, 2004, in particular and our tour in Iraq in general were about 180 degrees opposed.

Jill went to the window and turned her back on the room to use her cell phone. She was calling home, checking in with the squad of babysitters, some off-duty law enforcement officers, some Marines. I noted the cut of her suit jacket and skirt, clothes she hadn't worn since being pregnant with Domenico three years before. Her professional success and sophistication had always turned me on. But now seeing her in a suit only reminded me of the gravity of the situation we all faced. I felt sick and I wasn't alone. As I moved beside her, Jill whispered, "Pino's been crying, and they still can't get him to eat much."

That morning before we left for the hearing, our little Pino had thrown up his hot cereal, a reaction to the silent, invisible stress crushing our home. So far, Domenico had enjoyed the excitement of attentive new grown-ups in the house. But if this went on much longer, I knew he'd discover something bad was happening.

I took Jill's phone. "Hi, Domenico," I said when he came on the line. "Mommy and Daddy are at work. Are you taking care of your brother? Are you being a good boy?"

Domenico explained he was building wooden Tonka models. My friend, Billy, a fellow Marine officer and vet of two combat tours in Iraq, had flown in to lend emotional support. I'd tried to wave Billy off, telling him we'd be busy and didn't really have space. But he didn't give a shit. I'd sent him care packages in Iraq and he had done the same for me. Now he was a human care package—in true Marine fashion, he ran toward the sound of the guns. And I was grateful.

After the break, Major Phil Stackhouse glanced at a note before continuing his cross-examination of Doc Gobles.

STACKHOUSE: And did you have an opportunity even after—during that timeframe, a couple months after April 15th, to observe him in combat?

GOBLES: Yes, I did.

STACKHOUSE: Tell us about that, if you would?

GOBLES: Well, I would say the most significant was when we were—after this week, after that week of QRF, we were basically told that we were going into Fallujah. We went into Fallujah, and we got a FOB outside of Fallujah right along the Euphrates around the outskirts no more than a mile out of the town or the city of Fallujah. And we were told we were going to basically go to war there, we were going to make contact. We were set out there just basically to do recon I guess and—but we did a lot of combat patrols there. All of them were on foot again. And he—as good of a leader as he was the first time—he's—you know, in particular, that week that we were there is when we were told we had tanks, we had Cobras, we had everything . . .

As Doc spoke, I could almost hear the thud of the explosions and the biting turbine exhaust of the tanks.

GOBLES [CONTINUING]: We were laying five hundred-pound bombs, one thousand-pound bombs there. But in particular, we woke up one morning, and it was our—basically our whole company that was told we were going to go in and raid all these houses. There was machine-gun bunkers that were there, because we—our platoon beforehand found this out because we did patrols out there and get shot up by friggin' RPGs and get shot up by machine guns, heavy machine-gun fire, and—but, you know, we did an assault.

STACKHOUSE: How many times did you expect that you saw him leading in a firefight?

GOBLES: Every time, every time, every time he led—

STACKHOUSE: Generally, how many times do you think you guys were involved in a firefight?

GOBLES: Well, that week in particular, I'd say about every time we took contact, pretty much.

STACKHOUSE: More than a dozen?

GOBLES: It seemed that way. I'd say about a dozen. Yeah. Maybe more.

STACKHOUSE: In that week?

GOBLES: Well, yeah. That week in particular was—every time we went out there, we took contact. And every time we were at the base, we took contact. Every time, he was leading the way.

STACKHOUSE: Even though you were in a combat zone when these firefights were going on, did you feel safe when you were around Lieutenant Pantano?

GOBLES: Yes, I did.

STACKHOUSE: Why?

GOBLES: I just felt he was a—he's a damned good leader, you know, and I just felt a sense of security because I knew that—whatever situation arose, I knew that he wouldn't freeze up. I knew he'd be able to take care of it. And I knew that he would be able to lead his squad leaders and the Marines and tell them how to react and—because of his training, you know, given his training and how he trained Marines. I knew that they were all competent, and I didn't feel—I felt the safest with this platoon more than any other platoon in our company because of—more than anything, because of Lieutenant Pantano's—his leadership.

Latafiyah, Iraq
11 April 2004

The sun was lower than I would have liked. And the Muj were still dashing among the buildings, singly and in small groups, maneuvering to outflank us.

In the middle of this, six up-armored Humvees with .50 cals and MK-19 40 mike-mikes rolled onto the street below. The vehicles were an MP QRF convoy from the Army's 1/32nd Infantry, and they were quickly met by machine-gun fire. The officer who jumped down was a full bird colonel. I dashed from the garage to meet him. This was too much: that guy outranked our battalion commander and was coming to my rescue, to follow my orders.

"What's the situation, lieutenant?" he asked calmly.

Quickly explaining, I pointed to a cluster of buildings about three hundred meters off the road where the enemy had rallied and from where they were firing mortars and beginning to volley RPGs. We just didn't have the firepower to beat them up.

The MPs did. In a few minutes they had maneuvered their Humvees and were blasting the shit out of those buildings, sending streams of .50 cal API and MK-19 grenades through the doors and windows. This was not just a keep-your-head-down demonstration. It was an exercise in no-shit kill-your-ass. For about a nanosecond, I almost felt sorry for those Muj. Almost. Maybe Allah was trotting out more virgins about now.

One thing was sure, none of those Muj were going to outflank us now. And, as Captain Weston showed up with part of 2nd Platoon and confirmed that the battalion headquarters was en route, bringing every spare swinging dick, I began to realize that it was us, not the Muj, who would be doing the outflanking this afternoon.

Time passed. The fire in the streets rose and fell. No more enemy approached our position. Overhead, jet fighter-bombers were growling through the sky. The F-14s were back on station.

The battalion headquarters element arrived, having run the Polish shooting gallery that persisted to the north along Jackson. Lieutenant Colonel Kyser and Major Neil began planning the assault with Captains Bairstow and Weston. Sergeant Major Swann looked on, shotgun in hand.

Captain Weston gave me my orders: my reinforced platoon would push west into town and wheel right, putting us on line facing the north as we tied in with Fox Company, which would clear the buildings to the east along Jackson.

After the inevitable fuck-ups and delays, we were finally in assault position. But we'd lost the precious momentum required to slam the door on the enemy.

We eventually started moving forward and the resistance began to scatter. Humvees full of heavily armed Marines, looking like pissed-off porcupines, swept up the road screening our western flank while the two companies moved north on foot. Our main body swung north, like a windshield wiper slapping from six to three o'clock, knocking off bugs.

I did not like this deal. We were way too undermanned to sweep a town with long streets and three- and four-story buildings, so I had to give Doc McNulty—the sweet-faced farmboy corpsman from Montana whom we called "Big Country"—the duty of guarding the sweaty, nasty-eyed prisoners who'd obviously just been trying to kill us moments ago. "If they try to jump you," I ordered McNulty, "shoot the motherfuckers." He was so stunned from all the firing I had to grab him by the back of the neck and tell him again.

Advancing up the trashy streets, checking in with squad leaders and Staff Sergeant Glew as they cleared the houses, I found the most beautiful rosebush. And in the middle of a narrow shit-strewn alley—with dogs barking, small arms crackling, and Marines dashing back and forth—I picked a light pink rose. The thorns were small but dense on the stem, which made the act of plucking the flower even more memorable, a mix of pain and beauty. I opened my pocket notebook, carefully laid out the flower, then pressed it flat and put the book away inside my flak jacket.

"Hey, Big Country," I yelled back to McNulty as he watched over the prisoners, "if I get whacked, please send that rose to my wife."

"Roger that, sir."

(Weeks later, when I tried to send the flower home, the military post office returned it because the dry flower was considered an "agricultural product.")

Staff Sergeant Glew called in from the far left, western, flank of our axis of advance, the direction toward which so many Muj had fled. "Hey, Lieutenant," he said tiredly. "We've got dozens of enemy KIAs layin' in alleys and blood trails on side streets over here."

"Roger," I said. "Just leave them."

Jesus, if they left that many dead behind, how many had we actually killed?

We continued moving north into the heart of Latafiyah, everyone jumpy, strung out with after-action nerves. Except the action wasn't over.

We had to stay alert. A couple of small mistakes, hell, *one* little mistake, could kill Marines.

I had McNulty shoot out the tires of another goddamn dump truck parked to block a side street, and I ordered all the tires to be slashed. We'd already destroyed a number of civilian vehicles that had engaged us, and I wasn't going to let any new ones follow us out of town, launching suicide attacks or planting IEDs after dark.

During the building clearing, family after family lied about the weapons we found and their complicity with the Muj.

"*Maku Ali Baba*," they always said, hands on their hearts. "No Ali Baba here, Boss."

Every house had at least one or more AK-47s. By the end of that long day, we had confiscated hundreds, some still stinking of hot powder and scorched weapons' lubricant. We struggled to bundle so many assault rifles and load them on our trucks. And there were lots of men still mysteriously "at work," leaving their women and children to meet us. I hated the need to deal with these women, kids, and old folks. We'd made a lot of widows and orphans that afternoon. I sure wasn't happy about that, but my duty lay to my Marines and to my country.

Camp Lejeune
27 April 2005

Major Stackhouse took Doc Gobles to the heart of the case. It had been quiet in the courtroom before. Now there was absolute silence, other than the words Stackhouse and the witness spoke.

STACKHOUSE: HN Gobles, I want to talk to you now about the events that transpired on the 15th of April; okay? Do you remember how the platoon was informed that there was a QRF mission?

GOBLES: I don't recall specifically, but we just got word passed down from—I guess, we were already out on another mission, if I remember correctly.

STACKHOUSE: And so from what you know, what was the situation?

GOBLES: Well, from what I knew was that, first of all, it was not an insurgent hideout, but it was actually a family there that was being held hostage by insurgents that were using this house as a position to fire mortars at Camp St. Michaels [FOB Mahmudiyah], which was our base there, of operations. And that is what we were told. So our mission there was to go and raid the house and to find this out, to see if there was [a] cache of weapons or mortars or anything, or insurgents there.

STACKHOUSE: Do you remember where that information came from?

GOBLES: I believe it was—when we got there, I remember there being a HIET team there on the side of the road also. I recall they were interrogating. It was either a man or it was two men there that they were interrogating. It was before we even attempted to go to the house. And what I was told was that these men told the HIET team that their family was being held hostage and there was insurgents in there that were firing mortars at us.

STACKHOUSE: And so these two individuals that were being interviewed by HIET, they were—they actually lived in that house?

GOBLES: Yes, it was their family.

STACKHOUSE: That was being held hostage?

GOBLES: Correct.

STACKHOUSE: And so once that information—once you got there and got that information, what is the very next thing that happened?

Major Keane and the prosecution team watched and listened intently, occasionally taking notes for redirect. I had the feeling that they were worried about the impact of Stackhouse's detailed cross-examination of Gobles on Major Winn.

GOBLES: Well, once we got that information, we were told what we were going to do, got it passed down from the squad leaders. And we were told what we were going to do. That is when I attached myself to Lieutenant Pantano and Sergeant Coburn. And First Squad went about their objective, and Second Squad went about their objective, as well as Third Squad.

STACKHOUSE: And who was Sergeant Coburn?

GOBLES: He was our RTO, radioman.

STACKHOUSE: So you had a sergeant for a radio operator?

GOBLES: Correct.

STACKHOUSE: Was he the platoon radio operator?

GOBLES: He was. He was the platoon operator. Yes.

STACKHOUSE: What rank were the squad leaders?

GOBLES: Squad leaders, we had—we only had one sergeant, First Squad, and then the rest were corporals.

STACKHOUSE: So you had a sergeant squad leader and two corporal squad leaders, and Sergeant Coburn humping the radio?

GOBLES: Correct.

For a few minutes, Major Stackhouse asked Gobles to give a summary of the description of the insurgents' small white sedan leaving the objective house, which he had presented earlier in direct examination.

STACKHOUSE: So while this car, where it stopped, was not in the middle of a bunch of Marines, the area was certainly visible by anybody that was in the area of the house, anybody that was in the area of that intersection to the north; right?

GOBLES: Right, with the exception I don't think the view was too well as far as on the east side because there was shrubs, like you said, there.

STACKHOUSE: —what is going through your mind?

GOBLES: Well, just, you know, I am focusing on—I am aware, and just real cautious as far as coming up to them. You know, I don't know. A little tense.

STACKHOUSE: Is that because they're leaving a house that is a target house of the insurgency?

GOBLES: That and I was just tensed up to any vehicle there because there was so many VBIEDs around there. Just every vehicle I came up to was a tense situation, to me it was.

STACKHOUSE: And you said something about a "VBIED." What is that?

GOBLES: Well, "VBIED," is a vehicle-borne IED, im-
            provised explosive device. I had just—we en-
            countered those a lot, and we heard of a lot of
            reports about them. So every time you come
            up to a vehicle where Iraqis are in, and you're
            aware, that is in your mind. You know, you
            put your mind-set there that this could be a
            vehicle-borne IED.

STACKHOUSE: So what happened when you approached the
            car?

GOBLES: Well, we approached the car, looked around
            it, observed it. I looked at the Iraqis. I just—
            what would go through my head, just did a
            brief check to see if, you know, anything,
            weapons or anything like that. Obviously, you
            can't tell that at first. But I went there and
            just got them out of the vehicle. That is it, ba-
            sically, just get them out of there as quick as
            you can.

STACKHOUSE: What did you find in the vehicle?

GOBLES: Well, I didn't find anything, the only thing,
            like I said, that brought a little bit of attention
            to me was just these nuts and bolts and wires
            in the coffee cans. But besides that, I didn't
            see anything out of the ordinary.

STACKHOUSE: And based upon your training and experi-
            ence, why did that even draw your atten-
            tion?

GOBLES: Well, just because I know an IED is exactly
            what it is. It is improvised. So they can use
            any kind of parts you can think of, you know,
            out of cars, wires, any type of electrical
            equipment, anything you can think of. They
            can use any odd, miscellaneous little tool, or
            screw, bolts, nuts, or anything like that,
            switches.

STACKHOUSE: And the nuts and bolts and things like that
            had you, either in your training or in your per-
            sonal experience over there, become aware

that those kinds of things were also used as shrapnel in IEDs?

GOBLES: Yes.

STACKHOUSE: Were they—did they try to resist you in any way?

GOBLES: No. Just—they were cooperative. The only resistance I had was just me trying to take their hands, you know, and—when I was flexi-cuffing them. But other than that, they were cooperative. Just the only thing is we had to tell them numerous times just to be quiet because they would try to talk to each other.

STACKHOUSE: How many times do you think you had to tell them to be quiet?

GOBLES: Oh, I told them three or four times to be quiet, maybe more, because they weren't— they were talking to each other and going about. I told them to be quiet. That is why we separated them, you know, separated them apart from each other, so they wouldn't talk to each other.

STACKHOUSE: What is the reason that you don't want them talking to each other?

GOBLES: Just it's—it's annoying. I mean, and the fact that there is no reason. You know, just like a regular cop here in the States, you don't want the passengers talking. They could be corroborating something. They could be, you know, thinking up something to do or trying to cover their stories. And because they speak Arabic, obviously, who knows. I just didn't like them to talk.

STACKHOUSE: And you don't speak Arabic; right?

GOBLES: No, I don't. So I would rather not, you know, feel like they were talking behind my back. I don't know what they're saying, so I would rather them just not talk at all unless I am speaking to them.

STACKHOUSE: Right. So you don't know if they're plotting against you?

GOBLES: I have no idea. I have no idea what they are talking about.

STACKHOUSE: If they are plotting an escape? Nothing?

GOBLES: Who knows?

As Gobles described the scene along that rutted canal road, I could almost hear the whine of the mosquitoes as the sunset approached.

Now Major Stackhouse asked Gobles to continue describing the events of April 15, 2004, and to discuss the statements about the shooting he had made to the Naval Criminal Investigative Service.

STACKHOUSE: Were they still trying to talk at this time as well?

GOBLES: Yes, they were.

STACKHOUSE: At some point, you had to yell at them to shut up, didn't you, because they kept talking?

GOBLES: Yeah—yes, sir, there was. Because, like I said, I had to tell them to be quiet numerous times.

STACKHOUSE: Now, after the flexi-cuffs got put on them, what happened?

GOBLES: That is when Lieutenant Pantano told me to search the vehicle again, do a more thorough search. I did a thorough search on it. That is when I went about and took the seats out and just pretty much upheaved everything and checked for everything that I could, because everything came out.

STACKHOUSE: And is this the point when he took them up to speak to the HIET team?

GOBLES: I don't remember that, but that is what NCIS told me. And that is what I found out. But I don't remember that point. I was searching the vehicle. I don't recall that.

STACKHOUSE: Who from NCIS told you that?

GOBLES: This man right here [Gobles indicated Gunnery Sergeant Special Agent Dan Carlin] I forget your name. I apologize.

STACKHOUSE: The individual sitting opposite of me over on the other side?

GOBLES: Yes, sir.

STACKHOUSE: When did he tell you that?

GOBLES: When I was interviewed by him, when he investigated.

STACKHOUSE: Was this out in Iraq?

GOBLES: No, no. This was back here in the States, Camp Lejeune.

STACKHOUSE: So this was the statement that you made in February, the end of February of this year?

GOBLES: Correct.

STACKHOUSE: What other things did he tell you that you weren't aware of at the time?

GOBLES: Well, just, you know, [he] said basically that, I guess, like the movement I saw was just a flinching, it wasn't what I thought, or I guess it wasn't them trying to flee. He said it was just a flinch or reaction to the other guy being shot. Basically, was—I didn't know, I guess, at that point I didn't know that HIET interviewed them. I didn't know that.

STACKHOUSE: So he told you that?

Gobles shrugged but did not answer.

STACKHOUSE: Is that right?

GOBLES: Yes.

STACKHOUSE: Did he tell you what anybody else said?

GOBLES: No.

STACKHOUSE: So the only things that he told you was—is that while you were doing that search, Lieutenant Pantano had taken them up to talk to the HIET team; correct?

GOBLES: Correct.

STACKHOUSE: And that what you had saw [seen] was not them trying to flee, but them flinching?

GOBLES: Yes.

STACKHOUSE: Yes?

GOBLES: Yes, it was. That is what NCIS told me.

STACKHOUSE: Tell us how the second search went, please.

GOBLES: Well, like I said, I just took the seats out and—

STACKHOUSE: The seats came out of the car?

GOBLES: Correct. They were unbolted. They weren't even—they were unbolted. They weren't even bolted to the frame.

STACKHOUSE: And in your training and experience, does that trouble you?

GOBLES: Yes, it does.

STACKHOUSE: Why does that trouble you?

GOBLES: Just because it would be easy to place something in there, because it's so accessible to be able to take the seats out and—as well as the center console and the dashboard, it would just be easy to conceal something in there, conceal a weapon or anything in there, conceal an IED in there, whatever.

STACKHOUSE: Did it concern you when the instrument panel came out of the car?

GOBLES: Yes, it did.

STACKHOUSE: Why would that concern you?

GOBLES: For the same reason as the seats coming up because, again, you could place something in there, anything.

STACKHOUSE: And is it fair to say the same concern—you would have the same concern with respect to the center console coming out?

GOBLES: Yes.

Once more, Major Stackhouse checked his notes. Major Keane and Captain Reh were watching intently from the prosecution table.

STACKHOUSE: If we're going to assume that Lieutenant Pantano took the two vehicle occupants up to speak to a HIET team away from the car, if we're going to assume that, then you would not have been privy to any radio calls he received; correct?

GOBLES: If that was the case, no I would not have heard any radio—anything come over the radio.

STACKHOUSE: So at this point, did Lieutenant Pantano tell you about anything he had learned when he was up the street?

GOBLES: Just what they had found. And that was basically it. I don't recall him telling me anything else.

STACKHOUSE: Did he break down all—break it down to you, all of the different things they found in this house?

GOBLES: I don't remember that.

STACKHOUSE: Do you remember him telling you that they found AK-47s in the house?

KEANE: Objection, asked and answered.

WINN: Go ahead and answer the question.

GOBLES: I don't recall that, sir.

STACKHOUSE: Okay. Do you recall that—if he told you whether or not they found insurgency propaganda, like Osama bin Laden info and things like that, in the house?

GOBLES: I don't remember. I don't recall that either.

STACKHOUSE: Do you remember if he told you whether or not they found IED-making equipment in the house?

GOBLES: I don't recall that either.

STACKHOUSE: Flare guns, money, bulletproof vests, you don't remember anything like that either?

GOBLES: No. Like I said, that is the only thing I knew about it until now, and during the investigation. I didn't really hear too much more about what this incident afterwards [was] about what was found and who those people actually were.

STACKHOUSE: So if he had additional information he didn't share it with you prior to giving you additional orders. Is that fair to say?

GOBLES: It is fair to say I don't recall. If he did, I don't recall it.

STACKHOUSE: So when he came back down from the house, what happened?

GOBLES: Then he told me—we got the Iraqis up on their feet from the position they were in and walked them towards the vehicle. Lieutenant Pantano told me to cut their flexi-cuffs off. I cut them off. And he told me he wanted me to have them search the vehicle and to find something to, you know, to do a search on it themselves.

STACKHOUSE: After you walked them to the car, what did he have you do?

GOBLES: After I walked them to the car, he had me just place them in their position so they can get ready to search it where they were going to search. One was going to search in the driver's side and the other was going to search in the passenger's side. So I placed them there, and then he told me to take security. And then I saw Sergeant Coburn, he was there. He took security as well.

STACKHOUSE: And what were you securing?

GOBLES: I was securing the road that was—the road going down towards the east—excuse me, the west, and up north, and kind of just, I guess you could say, a 180-degree view.

STACKHOUSE: Was your primary concern the road, though?

GOBLES: Correct. The road and the house right there.

STACKHOUSE: And there was nobody covering that road further on down to the west; correct?

GOBLES: Not that I remember. No. I don't—besides,

the First Squad—or excuse me, Second
Squad being somewhere over there. I don't
recall seeing any Marines over there though.
But I didn't see anyone having security on
that road.

STACKHOUSE: And that squad you just mentioned is the one
that was really conducting or providing flank
security to First Squad, going into that house
to the west; is that right?

GOBLES: Correct. That is what they were tasked to do.

STACKHOUSE: So really this road that you were providing security down, nobody is guarding at this point,
until you get there?

GOBLES: Correct.

STACKHOUSE: And the house that is just to the west of the
car, it has not been searched yet; right?

GOBLES: Not that I know of. I didn't see any Marines
go in.

STACKHOUSE: And Sergeant Coburn, do you know really
what he is even looking at [at] this point?

GOBLES: I just figured he was doing rear security. I
don't know what he was looking at though,
because I didn't see him.

STACKHOUSE: Did Lieutenant Pantano tell you in any way,
Hey, Doc Gobles, don't look in my direction,
or anything like that?

GOBLES: No.

STACKHOUSE: How long after you took up that position
until you heard Lieutenant Pantano, in Arabic, yelling the word "stop"?

GOBLES: It wasn't long. It wasn't long. I mean, before I
heard him, before I heard Lieutenant Pan-
tano yell "stop," maybe a minute or two. It
wasn't too long.

STACKHOUSE: Prior to you posting security, did you ever see
the two Iraqi males or the two occupants of
that vehicle on their knees? Or were they on
their feet?

GOBLES: They were on their feet.

STACKHOUSE: And they were just bent over inside the car?

GOBLES: Right, getting ready to—what I perceived as them getting ready to search it. They weren't on their knees. At no time did I see them on their knees.

STACKHOUSE: So at some time between two and ten minutes later, you heard Lieutenant Pantano yell "stop," the first time. And he yelled it in Arabic?

GOBLES: Correct.

STACKHOUSE: And how did you know what he was yelling was "stop"?

GOBLES: Just because of what we were taught, different verbal commands that we were taught. I knew it as "stop," sir.

STACKHOUSE: He was closer to the occupants of the vehicle than, say, he was to you; correct? Lieutenant Pantano that is.

GOBLES: Yes.

STACKHOUSE: And you heard it fine; correct?

GOBLES: Yes, I did.

STACKHOUSE: And how long after he yelled stop in Arabic was it that he yelled stop in English?

GOBLES: It was basically in unison. I heard stop in Arabic and then stop in English.

STACKHOUSE: And what is the next thing that you heard?

GOBLES: I heard shots fired.

STACKHOUSE: Was it right at that point that you turned and looked in his direction?

GOBLES: As soon as—yes. As soon as shots were fired, I turned.

STACKHOUSE: And from your perspective from your security position, did it appear to you that they were attempting to flee away from the vehicle?

GOBLES: It appeared to me that the passenger—or not the passenger, but the driver, who I mostly had the view of was, what I thought was, yes, him trying to flee, like I showed the position

that he was in. From the position I saw, I perceived it as him trying to flee away.

STACKHOUSE: You told Special Agent McMorris that you
saw—or you observed the two detainees attempting to flee back in June. Did you see
them both doing something?

GOBLES: I just—I mainly remember seeing the front
guy flinch—or the movement that I showed.

STACKHOUSE: Flinch is what Special Agent Gunnery
Sergeant Carlin told you?

GOBLES: Right.

STACKHOUSE: Okay. In one of the statements that you gave
in June to Special Agent McMorris, you said,
Lieutenant Pantano yelled stop, and then I
heard shots being fired; right?

GOBLES: Correct. That is what I said. Yes.

Major Stackhouse read from the statement.

STACKHOUSE: "And then I quickly turned in the direction of
the vehicle and observed the two Iraqis
on their feet attempting to flee." Is that a
fair statement of what you observed as
well?

GOBLES: That is what I put there. I—it's basically the
same thing. I mean, seen them—I seen that
guy trying to—what it looked like, trying to
flee. And they were—they were bent down in
the vehicle, still on their feet, yes, but they
were bent down, kneeled down in the vehicle, just like I showed.

STACKHOUSE: How fast was Second Lieutenant Pantano
shooting?

GOBLES: How fast was it? It was quick. It was quick as,
you know, a rifle, an automatic rifle spits out
bullets.

STACKHOUSE: Okay. So you checked for vital signs and both
of the vehicle occupants were dead; right?

GOBLES: That's right.

STACKHOUSE: And you reported that to Lieutenant Pantano?

GOBLES: Yes, I did.

STACKHOUSE: And he told you that they were trying to get away add [and] run towards him and he warned them to stop before he shot?

GOBLES: Yes.

STACKHOUSE: After he told you that, what happened?

GOBLES: I believe that is when I said what I said to Sergeant Coburn. I think that was—excuse me, that was afterwards. And I told Sergeant Coburn that, you know, that the blood is not on his hands, and not to worry about it. And then I just went back towards the vehicle. And that is when we saw the brown vehicle come down the road—the brown car, and just the same thing, the same events that I already said.

STACKHOUSE: So you told him something like, Don't worry about it, and that the blood is on the hands of Lieutenant Pantano; something like that?

GOBLES: Yeah.

STACKHOUSE: Why did you tell him that?

GOBLES: Well, it was basically the truth. I mean, I just told him, Hey, don't worry about it, because he was just—I mean, he was shocked by it, you know. And I didn't know if, you know, he was questioning it. He didn't know what just happened. I said, Well—that was just the first thing that came out of my mind. I don't know. I was just trying to offer him some kind of, you know, comfort, I guess, or to calm him down, because he was—he seemed like he was freaking out by it. So that is what I said.

STACKHOUSE: Was it a pretty dramatic scene at the car?

GOBLES: I guess you could say that, yes. Dramatic, I guess it was dramatic.

Latafiyah, Iraq
11 April 2004

My men were doing the hard work of searching and questioning, as I moved from team to team, regulating their steady IV-drip of rage, fear, adrenaline, and exhaustion.

Of the hundreds of homes that we searched well into the night, there was one house where I gazed into a kind of psychic mirror. The thirty-year-old man was tall and well groomed, proud even as he lay facedown on the ground. The man's mustache was trimmed as neatly as my own. His traditional black man-dress stood in contrast to the shining yellow Honda Accord in his paved driveway.

He denied possessing any weapons, *"Maku . . ."*

Right. Bullshit. We found a new folding-stock AK and a magazine pouch full of tracers. You needed tracers to fight wars, not to protect your home.

Sadly, the discovery was not that unusual at this point in the war. So, without any further evidence of insurgent activity, we couldn't detain him. He knew it. And I knew it. What he displayed was an intangible hardness. Not day-laborer-dig-a-canal hard. The kind of hard edge that told me that this professional with a clean home and a nice car had done the cold, rational calculus, months or maybe years before, that he had no choice but to oppose me. And I had no choice but to oppose him.

My men jostled tiredly around me, oblivious, as I dragged the Iraqi to his feet by his collar. Our eyes locked as we reflected on the decisions that put me standing in his home six thousand miles from my own. We smiled at each other like friends sharing a secret in a public place. We knew that we would kill each other one day. And that would be that.

Camp Lejeune
27 April 2005

At this stage in his cross-examination of Gobles, Major Stackhouse shifted back to the subject of Sergeant Coburn.

> STACKHOUSE: How much observation did you have of Sergeant Coburn in Iraq?

GOBLES: Quite a bit, up until the point that he left our platoon or left our company.

STACKHOUSE: You gave us some general impressions earlier in your testimony of Lieutenant Pantano. Do you have any impressions of Sergeant Coburn and his actions in Iraq?

GOBLES: Basically what I have already written down. I didn't feel that he was a competent sergeant. At one point, I guess he was—I can't remember him being a squad leader. He wasn't competent to do that. He got demoted from that. And then he went to [be] an RTO. I never felt that his leadership, even from the time I first met him, I didn't think his leadership as a Marine, or his capabilities as far as leading an infantry platoon, were up there or up to par as, you know, they should be. And—as a sergeant, as a squad leader, or even a platoon sergeant. I don't think he had the capabilities of that.

STACKHOUSE: And did you observe him under fire as well?

GOBLES: Yes, I did. I don't remember him—honestly I don't remember him ever firing a round. I remember him particularly in Fallujah, and I don't remember him ever firing a round, even when we were taking bullets.

STACKHOUSE: I mean, were there times when Lieutenant Pantano was firing his weapon and Sergeant Coburn was right there not firing his?

GOBLES: Yes.

STACKHOUSE: Did Sergeant Coburn ever talk to you about his views of the war in Iraq and how things should be done?

GOBLES: Well, not necessarily his views of how things should be done, but there were certain instances that came up when we did searches or went into the houses that, you know, he didn't feel that, you know, things should have been done the way they were, or that we shouldn't treat Iraqis—you know—or you know, he didn't really—I don't know, seem to feel like being there, you know. He didn't think it was a good cause, us being there, or how we were going about it, I guess, how Marines in general were going about it.

STACKHOUSE [TO MAJOR WINN]: May I have just a moment, sir?

Stackhouse leaned over the defense table and spoke quietly to Charlie Gittins and me. "I think we're almost there." Gittins and I both nodded. Stackhouse returned to the witness.

STACKHOUSE: HN Gobles, is it fair to say that this incident that happened on the 15th of April was the first close-in killings that had been witnessed by the Marines on the scene?

GOBLES: This—well, no. Because beforehand we saw Latafiyah. There was a lot of dead people there.

STACKHOUSE: Right. I mean—

GOBLES: This up close and personal?

STACKHOUSE: Yeah, exactly.

GOBLES: Yes.

STACKHOUSE: And you said earlier that Lieutenant Pantano was five feet or maybe ten feet away from the car?

GOBLES: I don't know, whatever they—three to five feet, three to four feet, where they placed him.

STACKHOUSE: Thank you.

Major Keane began his redirect of Doc Gobles, working mainly without notes.

KEANE: You said you found—during your initial search and the subsequent search, you found—some bolts and switches in the trunk?

GOBLES: Correct. That's what was in the cans.

KEANE: You said they could be used in explosive devices?

GOBLES: Yes.

KEANE: You'd also need explosives, wouldn't you?

GOBLES: Well, correct. That is just why I said they could be used in explosive devices.

KEANE: You didn't find any explosives?

GOBLES: No.

KEANE: Did you find any blasting caps?

GOBLES: No. I didn't see any blasting caps.

KEANE: No blasting fuses?

GOBLES: No. Just wires and switches. I didn't find anything else like that.

KEANE: On cross-examination, you talked a lot about Lieutenant Pantano. And it became pretty clear that you have a lot of respect for Lieutenant Pantano?

GOBLES: Yes, sir.

KEANE: And it's hard for you to talk about a lot of these facts?

GOBLES: Sure it is. Yes.

KEANE: You actually said in previous statements that you don't want to stab him in the back?

GOBLES: Right. I wouldn't, no.

KEANE: You don't want to be responsible for being the guy that gets him in trouble?

GOBLES: No, I wouldn't.

KEANE: Because you look up to him?

GOBLES: Correct.

KEANE: You follow his example?

GOBLES: I thought he was—I still think he is a good leader.

KEANE: You mentioned that the accused was nice to the Iraqis that he came across?

GOBLES: Yes, sir.

KEANE: Was he nice to the Iraqis in that car when he slashed their tires?

STACKHOUSE: Sir, I'm going to object. It's an argumentative question.

GOBLES: They—

WINN: Can you—go ahead and rephrase your question, Major Keane.

KEANE: Did you perceive it as being nice when he slashed the tires on these guys you ended up letting go?

GOBLES: No, sir.

Keane was speaking quickly, probably attempting to muddle Doc Gobles's answers.

KEANE: You had seen him slash tires before and after that?

GOBLES: Well, when it was called to disable a vehicle, it was done.

KEANE: You turned around as soon as the shots started firing; right?

GOBLES: Yes, sir.

KEANE: And you never saw any rounds hit anywhere else but the back?

GOBLES: Besides hitting various parts of the vehicle.

WINN: Doc, can you speak up a little bit? I couldn't hear.

GOBLES: Besides hitting various areas of the vehicle. That is what I witnessed, vehicles towards the back—or excuse me, shots towards the back.

The long volleys of direct, cross, redirect, and recross examination of Doc Gobles were finally winding down.

WINN: Major Stackhouse?

STACKHOUSE: Do you have any idea where the rounds were

impacting the occupants of the vehicle when Lieutenant Pantano started shooting?

GOBLES: When he first started shooting, no, because as soon as I turned, that is what I seen. I saw them going towards the back.

STACKHOUSE: Had you seen people being hit by rounds before?

GOBLES: From a far distance. Yes.

STACKHOUSE: Does a body move a lot when they're being hit by rounds, or were you close enough to even tell?

GOBLES: No. I wasn't that close.

STACKHOUSE: One of the other lines of questioning you just went through was whether you had a lot of respect for Lieutenant Pantano or not. Do you remember that just a minute ago?

GOBLES: Yes.

STACKHOUSE: Why do you have a lot of respect for Lieutenant Pantano?

GOBLES: Well, just the way he deals with people, you know, he deals with human beings. His interaction with people. That, and, you know, his leadership as a Marine, a Marine Corps officer, an infantry officer, just the way he leads his people, led his Marines. That is where my respect grew out of, you know. It's hard not to show respect for Lieutenant Pantano.

STACKHOUSE: Have you lied about anything on the stand today?

GOBLES: No, I haven't.

STACKHOUSE: So as long as you've told the truth while on the stand, do you feel like you stabbed him in the back?

GOBLES: No, I don't.

FOB Mahmudiyah, Iraq
11 April 2004

The shower water wasn't very warm this time of night. But I'd felt a desperate need to clean the stinking grime off my body. Dressed in a clean set of desert cammies, I stared into the mirror. The real, foggy stainless-steel mirror. Not the eyes of that Iraqi in the man dress.

My hands moved to my face. In a moment, the shaving cream was on my upper lip. And the dark hair of my mustache was washing down the drain. Into the sewer. Into the Euphrates.

SEVEN

Article 32 Hearing
DAY TWO

Fallujah, Iraq
25 April 2004

When I'd briefed my recon patrol plan to Captain Weston that morning, we carefully studied the map of Fallujah. This was an essential but dangerous mission.

Easy Company's Combat Operations Center was in a derelict admin building beside a concrete dam across the Euphrates. To me, this ten-room structure on the east bank seemed like a cross between a Foreign Legion post and a squatters' camp. Marines who'd been on night duty slept on the floor wherever there was room. Outside, others scraped up dirt to fill sandbags. Here in the "lounge" where the CO worked, crates and metal containers of ammunition were stacked high.

This little Forward Operating Base was only about two klicks south of the city itself, closer to the outlying buildings. As we finished setting up here the day before, the Muj had hit us with mortars and RPGs. An RPG-7 had an effective range of only about nine hundred meters, and some of those rounds had passed overhead. That was how close the enemy was.

Our 150-man company had taken over this outpost from a single platoon that had been trying to guard the entire southern side of Fallujah—a town of over four hundred thousand. A single fucking platoon of forty Marines. And people in Baghdad wondered why the insurgents were constantly infiltrating reinforcements into the city.

This close to the water, there was a lot of vegetation. The air was humid, the night nasty with mosquitoes.

Captain Weston leaned above the map. Nearby, radios squawked over the tactical net, detached voices of tired men. Small arms tapped and mortars chug-thumped far to the north.

"I want a thorough recon," Weston said. "We've got to determine where their automatic weapons, mortars, and strong points are to get some air on them before the assault."

"Aye, aye, sir."

He looked at me closely. "Okay. But you will *not* become decisively engaged today. This is not Latafiyah, and I don't want to send out the entire company as a QRF to extract your patrol from some kind of shit-storm."

"Roger that, sir."

We reviewed my planned patrol route. A bermed-up road ran north along the riverbank from our compound. But the elevated packed-dirt surface was exposed both to fire from the buildings on the city's southern fringes and to plunging fire from the nine-story hospital and mosque minarets farther north. In fact, my friend Demo had taken fire and a few casualties on the first probing patrol along that road the day before.

"Sir," I told Captain Weston, "we'll move below the riverbank, using the road berm as a defilade."

"Looks good," he said.

We examined the map more closely. "Here's the 'townhouses,'" I said.

They were a row of solidly built, multistory brick residences—almost like waterside vacation homes—that ran from the road down to the river, most of their rear courtyards sharing common walls. Metal barricades with rusty wrought-iron spikes extended into the river, providing the homeowners some protection from thieves. The town-houses had been reserved for well-connected residents of Fallujah—

Baath Party members who'd gotten rich on the smuggling trade west to Jordan and Syria.

Westies on the River—the Euphrates, not the Hudson.

"We'll clear the townhouses first, sir. Then we'll continue north into the city itself."

"I concur," Captain Weston said. "Let's review your strength."

I was taking Sergeant "Stick" Word's 1st Squad, reinforced by an M-240G machine-gun team; a three-Marine section armed with a Shoulder-Launched Multipurpose Assault Weapon (SMAW) from Weapons Platoon; "Buster," our Forward Air Controller (a Marine F/A-18 pilot named Captain John Bailey, who'd flown combat strikes in OIF I); and a four-man fire team from 3rd Squad. Counting my command section, which included Doc Gobles, and Sergeant Coburn as my new RTO, the patrol would total twenty-five Marines. We were about as heavily armed as possible for a dismounted patrol: one 7.62 mm machine gun, 5.56 mm SAWs, M-203 grenade launchers, an AT-4 anti-tank rocket launcher, and the SMAW with plenty of extra rounds.

Today's patrol was big enough to kick serious ass if need be, but small enough to move quietly and fast.

"Good hunting," Captain Weston said, handing me back the patrol roster.

He hadn't needed to emphasize the importance of my mission. Moving north into Fallujah, we would recon Easy Company's avenues of advance for the multibattalion assault that we all expected would go down within days.

Since the ambush and murder of those four Blackwater security guys in Fallujah on March 31, the city had become *the* symbol of the insurgents' fuck-you defiance. The 82nd Airborne had returned to the States. The 1st Marine Regimental Combat Team had replaced them, and—augmented by Iraqi forces—had tried to advance into the city center. But the Marines had been pulled back when Muj resistance got bad and our Iraqi Civil Defense Corps allies had bugged out. For twenty days, the Marines had been ordered to hold off while the generals and high-ranking civilians in the Coalition Provisional Authority negotiated with the local sheiks for a peaceful solution. That solution included the Iraqis' Fallujah leaders turning in the butchers of the Blackwater guys.

This hadn't gone down well with the grunts.

Negotiate. *Right.* Every PFC fresh out of boot camp had heard of the Tet Offensive '68. Every serious Marine officer had studied the failure of the negotiated Tet New Year's truce. Under cover of that truce, the NVA and Viet Cong had infiltrated thousands of regular troops and guerrillas into the cities of Vietnam.

And it had been Marine grunts who had fought and died recapturing Hue City.

Here in Fallujah, the Marines I'd heard bitching about the April 2004 negotiations were pissed off and scornful.

"Hey, Sheik Butt Fuck, will you please, please, pretty please turn over those naughty little boys who slaughtered our people, burnt their bodies, and strung them up from that bridge?"

"Why of course, Excellency. Certainly. Immediately. This very day. Tonight . . . tomorrow . . . next week . . . without fail, *Inshallah.*"

While the negotiators talked, the Marines continued to take casualties from skyrocketing cease-fire violations.

And the Muj inside the city had just dug in deeper, slabbing up their machine-gun bunkers and mortar pits with fresh concrete. They had plenty of food—most of it relief aid—and all the water in the river to drink. And about two Iraqi army divisions' combat load of ammunition left over from the good old days of Saddam.

Hue City on the Euphrates.

For three weeks, the 1st Marine Regimental Combat Team had cordoned off Fallujah. It was clear that the negotiations had failed. Now—augmented by the Warlords, Army units, tanks, and artillery—the 1 RCT was ready to attack: 2/1 from the north, 3/4 from the east, 1/5 from the southeast, and 2/2 from the south. When General Mattis gave the order, about 5,000 Marines and soldiers would advance, blasting the estimated 2,000 hardcore Muj out of their fortified positions in houses, schools, office buildings—even in mosques and hospitals.

The mission of the 1 RCT now was to kill or capture every one of the enemy in Fallujah. And not lose half our men in the op.

After the final head count and ammo-load check, my patrol moved out past the company's sandbag barriers. We used the cover of the building to slip-slide down the riverbank and move slowly north, our boots sucking in the stinking black mud.

Mesopotamia. The Land Between the Rivers. Cradle of civilization—if you could call the motherfuckers who hoisted charred human carcasses onto bridge girders and danced around chanting *"Allahu Akbar"* civilized. For a couple of million years, half the silt of western

Asia had been picked up and dumped along the banks of the Euphrates. And *all* the cow shit, donkey shit, camel shit, human shit from upriver had made its way into this silty mud. Now we were up to our ankles, our knees in it. "It's a treat to beat your feet . . ." *Right.*

Our boots popped like wine corks. We teetered under our loads of ordnance. The damp heat rose to our faces. Flies bit our sweaty necks.

I had briefed the men that this patrol would be as abso-fucking-lutely "tactical" as possible. No grab-assing. No whispering. No talking. All radios off or on earpiece. All loose equipment and ammo secured to the max degree possible. Movement commands would be hand and arm signals.

And that was how we worked our way north, watching where we stepped, scanning the tall reeds on the riverbank road berm above us to the right.

We were getting closer. Ahead, the human slaughterhouse bridge stood out clearly, dull aquamarine steel above the swirling brown river. None of the TV images of those strung-up bodies had captured the weird color of those girders.

At the southern wall of the first of the five townhouses, I finger-signaled *one-two-three*.

And Sergeant Word had three men, sprawled on top, crushing the sharp blades of broken glass studded into the concrete—Third World deadbolts—with their Kevlar vests. Follow-on Marines were right behind. We cleared that townhouse and the next. They were both empty.

But beneath the wall of the third, we could smell cigarette smoke and hear Arabic voices, some soft, others boisterous. The wall was about six feet. Not tall by the standards of the OCS obstacle course.

One, two, three . . .

In a tumbling rush, half the patrol was over the top, with Word at the river end, me in the middle. The rest of the Marines straddled the wall, weapons pointing down.

The six Iraqis in the courtyard were shocked. But none of the trim young men showed much fear, no panic for sure. They hadn't been expecting us to come over that wall, but were too disciplined to run.

Military discipline, even though they wore Hajji knockoff button-down shirts opened loosely at the neck. Untucked and casual, like a Gap ad. Flies buzzed. The sun was painful. I studied their faces. Some stubble. If it hadn't been for their bad teeth, they could have been Italian professional soccer players. Or my cousins in Calabria. The one with the mustache seemed to be their leader.

"*As-salaam alaikum,*" I said, peeling back my muddy Nomex combat glove to shake his hand.

The man returned the formal greeting. And then his eye flitted back to our weapons, silently counting, maybe figuring his odds. Bad fucking odds, Mohammed.

While I exchanged the hello-how-are-ya bullshit with the others, Corporal Spencer Stringham from 3rd Squad went into the house, keeping his M-16 ready at belly level.

"Sir," he called, "better check this out."

From the open doorway, I saw the heap of discarded ICDC chocolate chip cammies in a corner.

I pointed at their chests, and then inside at the pile of dirty uniforms.

"Are they yours?"

Two of the young men carefully withdrew their Iraqi Civil Defense Corps identification cards.

We're the good guys here, Mistah.

I pictured the nasty firefights along Route Jackson during Arbaeen when Muj wearing this same ICDC cammie arrived in fucking *ambulances*—each marked with the Red Crescent—to ambush the Marines of CAAT White and Black from mosques and minarets along the highway. Assholes wearing the uniform of their country, attacking from the sanctuary of holy sites—almost daring us to respond, but knowing that we would not.

These were not men. Not civilized men.

While Sergeant Word's men spread out, searching the townhouse rooms, I conducted a cursory interrogation.

"*Maku Ali Baba?*" I asked. "No insurgents?"

"*Lah . . .* no." Mustached Man pulled the hand-on-heart routine. "*Maku Ali Baba.*"

I displayed my dog-eared Show-and-Tell interrogation card that had pictographs of AK-47s, RPGs, and machine guns, each identified with an Arabic caption.

"No weapons?"

"*Lah . . . lah . . . maku.*"

Right. Without a fucking doubt.

"No food in the house, sir," Sergeant Word reported, no bedding. What were these Iraqis doing here, just a couple of klicks from our base?

I glanced around the courtyard, toward the second floor. There was a cistern outside, probably another in the kitchen . . . a typical concrete water tank on the roof. In any souk in Iraq, you could buy big plastic containers with watertight lids. Great for storing flour and dates . . . fantastic for hiding stripped-down AKs and RPK light machine guns.

But we didn't have time for a full search.

During the first firefights in Fallujah after the Marines arrived, the ICDC had deserted left, right, and center and gone over to the Muj—taking their weapons and radios with them.

These guys were part of that bunch. But there was no way to prove it. I smiled and patted the black plastic stock of my M-16 where I'd taped a laminated photo of Jill and Domenico.

Mustache Man smiled. And then his eyes darted from the beautiful dark-eyed woman and our son to the black steel magazine of my weapon.

My men were looking around nervously, not forgetting for a second the butchery on that bizarre blue bridge just up the river. We were all scared, but I made a point of projecting strength to these Iraqis.

We are here to help, but make no mistake. We *will* kill you. *I* will kill you—if you force our hand. Look, here is my wife, my son. Look, I am a man just like you.

They spoke to each other in Arabic and snickered. Maybe they were appreciative, but more than likely they were whispering obscene comments. I had exposed a vulnerable human part of myself to them. I wanted, no, I needed, them to understand. This will end badly. Please do not force us to kill you.

And then we were off, pushing farther into the most dangerous city on earth.

Camp Lejeune
27 April 2005

On this second day of the hearing, Assistant Government Counsel Captain Lee Kindlon began the direct examination of Sergeant "M," a

Marine counterintelligence specialist who had served with my batal-
lion at FOB Mahmudiyah in April 2004. On either side of me, Gittins
and Stackhouse watched intently.

KINDLON: Sergeant, what unit are you currently with?

M: Second Intel Battalion.

KINDLON: And what is your MOS?

M: 0211, counterintelligence specialist.

KINDLON: What kind of training have you had?

M: Marine Air Ground Task Force, basic counterintelligence course, interrogation training, SERE
school, strategic debriefing course, counter-
surveillance/surveillance detection course, and
various driving and shooting packages for personnel.

KINDLON: Have you ever had any detainee training
courses?

M: Definitely, sir.

KINDLON: I want to take you back to the last year, April of
2004. Where were you?

M: Mahmudiyah, Iraq.

KINDLON: How do you know the accused?

M: The lieutenant was [a] platoon commander for
Easy Company. And I worked with him.

Captain Kindlon took the witness through the circumstances of
the QRF mission on the afternoon of April 15 and asked him to describe what had led to the stopping of the insurgents' white sedan.

KINDLON: Sergeant, to your knowledge, were these men
searched?

M: Yes, sir.

KINDLON: Did they have any weapons?

M: No, sir.

KINDLON: When you were questioning them, what kind of
things did you ask?

M: Name, where they were headed. It was unnatural for [to] me for them to be moving through a
cordon area when they knew the Marines were

there, it was unnatural. I asked them if they had
any affiliation with insurgents in the area, if they
knew of any attacks, were there any weapons in
the house, stuff of that nature, sir, interrogatives.

Right, I thought. *Maku Ali Baba.*

KINDLON: When you were talking to them, did they ever
threaten you?
M: No, sir.
KINDLON: Did they ever threaten any of the Marines?
M: No, sir.
KINDLON: Did they threaten the lieutenant individually?

Gittins was on his feet.

GITTINS: Objection, leading.
WINN: Sergeant, in your presence, did they ever
threaten the lieutenant?
M: No, sir, not in my presence.
KINDLON: Other than trying to leave the cordon, did they
do anything suspicious?
M: They were flexi-cuffed behind their backs, sir,
they couldn't really do anything.
KINDLON: Did you receive a call over the radio?
M: Yes, sir.
KINDLON: What did this call say?
M: The call was basically just—not specifically to
myself, just broadcasted over a comm channel,
that they'd found various items in the house,
mortar stake, flare gun, insurgent-style vest with
extra magazines, extra AK-47s. They are only allowed one AK-47, sir. There was three found
with fully loaded magazines, various propaganda
CDs and DVDs of Chechnyan rebels, Saddam,
beheadings, and Osama bin Laden, sir.
KINDLON: Where—did you go anywhere after you got this
call?
M: Shortly after I got the call, I relayed to the lieu-

tenant, I recommend we take these guys back.
Just initially after they were trying to do the cordon, I had planned on taking them back. And I
was going to immediately head into the house
with Corporal "O" and start exploiting everything
inside.

KINDLON: What did you find inside the house?

M: I found everything that I just mentioned, sir, and
I found various passports and IDs of nobody in
the house: none of the names matched.

Fallujah, Iraq
25 April 2004

We cleared the last townhouses—each a dry hole—and moved farther
north, still keeping the riverbank as a defilade. Captain Bailey—
"Buster"—went up on a house roof and used his laser target designator
to get the exact coordinates of the bridge, its road approaches, and the
tall block of the hospital nearby. He also pointed the invisible laser
beam at some mosque minarets and likely-looking apartment blocks.
When the assault began, we all knew the Muj would use those structures as observation posts or actual fire positions.

With that task completed, I still had to determine the location of
the enemy's outermost ring of defensive positions. In Infantry 101,
there's a maneuver called "movement to contact." In other words, keep
probing until you draw enemy fire.

We were in the narrowing streets of the city now, and I had orders
not to get pinned down. I figured we'd been under enemy observation
for a long time, but they didn't want to show their hand. We turned
back south to link up with the Marines I'd left in fire-support positions
down behind the road berm and in houses along the riverbank.

But just to make sure the Muj knew we were out here, I had the
four Marines with me on the road fire into the dirt ahead and into the
dried-mud fields and vacant lots to the east, our left flank.

The ruse worked.

An Iraqi in a man dress came out of a house down the road, walked
casually along the street, and went into another house. Ten seconds
later, he popped out of the door in the blank concrete wall and cut

loose at us with an AK on full auto. Then everything went to hell. A machine gun behind us to the north hammered away. And there were more weapons firing from the townhouse where we'd bullshitted with Mustache Man and his buddies.

Camp Lejeune
27 April 2005

KINDLON: What happened after you heard the gunshots?

M: I took a knee, sir, and I just realized that it was M-16 fire. I stood fast and I saw a little bit of smoke.

KINDLON: What did you—after you took a knee, what did you do?

M: I just gave it a little bit of time, like thirty seconds, sir, then I went ahead and went out of the driveway. I took an immediate left, which I saw a lieutenant and another Marine running directly north, and I immediately took a left, going west to a little side road. Then I heard "halt," so at that time I started running down that way.

KINDLON: As you were running down, I guess north—so up, as you were running up towards this road, did you see anything?

M: Yes, sir.

KINDLON: What did you see?

M: As soon as I took about—about ten meters north, I noticed two Iraqis I had just spoke to up in the vehicle, just hanging out. I realized what happened, that they [had] been shot. I continued, I walked right past, or basically jogged right past them, continued north, and then headed to assist the lieutenant with the other guys.

KINDLON: Sergeant, how many bullet wounds do you think you've seen over your career?

M: Ten to fifteen, sir.

KINDLON: Do you know the difference between an entry wound and an exit wound?

M: Yes, sir.

KINDLON: How?

M: Entry wound is typically smaller, pinpoint size, and the exit wound is simply bigger.

KINDLON: Based on your experience, where were these men shot?

M: From what I saw, sir, they were all in the back, entries.

Fallujah, Iraq
25 April 2004

"Stick," I ordered Sergeant Word, shouting over the swelling noise of ambush. "Hit that fucking place with the AT-4."

Word told a young Marine named Smith—I had two of them in my platoon—to put an anti-tank rocket up the ass of that Muj House. Smith ripped off the safety, pre-firing the round, rose to his knee—enemy bullets kicking up dust and gravel around him—sighted, and pressed the trigger. Click. Nothing. Misfire. He tried again. Misfire. And again.

Sergeant Word grabbed the AT-4, made sure the weapon was armed, and pressed the trigger. Another fucking misfire.

I signaled Word to get rid of it. The armed AT-4 was now more dangerous to us than to the enemy. He gave it to a Marine who slid down the bank and threw it into the river.

I'd kept two four-man fire teams static to cover the movement of the third in a technique called bounding overwatch. I'd used it as a TOW-gunner, and now I was doing it as a platoon commander. Once a fire team had dashed across a dangerous open space they would set up behind the cover of the road berm and watch carefully with their weapons aimed toward the most likely enemy threats while another element moved.

This had better work because we were so outnumbered.

The volume of small-arms fire rose.

The thunder boom of RPGs.

Crack-crack-cra-*acck*. Machine guns firing straight at us.

"Contact left!" AK and RPK fire.

"Contact rear!"

Shit, interlocking fields of fire. Bullets were dancing up and down the road like in the old war movies when a Messerschmidt would do a low strafing run and you could trace the path of the rounds in long sweeping columns of kicked-up dust and rocks. A miracle we didn't lose anybody right then and there. I had the squad on both sides of this bermed-up road, one side facing the city, the other facing the river. As the fire erupted, the Marines scrambled to consolidate on the river-side. The only good news was that we weren't taking fire from across the Euphrates. That would have required an immediate air strike, because our only real cover was the road embankment.

Basically, our asses were in the breeze. That was okay. We'd given them a little something to remember us by. One of the Muj firing positions was a farmhouse across the road with a corrugated metal roof. I got up my SMAW gunners with their big bazooka-like weapon.

"Hit it," I yelled. With a crackling whoosh-roar, Lance Corporal Brown nailed the left side of the house, putting an 83 mm rocket right through the wall. The explosion was so powerful that the metal roof blasted up from the overpressure. The roof panels seemed to levitate a foot in the air, jiggling in the afternoon sun, shimmering and shaking. Spooky.

The roof resettled crookedly in a shroud of dust and smoke. *Tatatatatat.*

"Fuck. They want some more. Hit it again! Other side this time!"

"Yes, sir."

The rusty metal jumped up and fell again. No more fire from that house.

And there it was, the crux of the lesson: if it doesn't work the first time, don't give up, hit the motherfucker again.

There was a platoon commander in the battalion famous for the time he'd screamed for 60 mm mortar support in conditions less serious than this—as if those little rounds would have done shit. Every second he'd waited with his face to the ground, the enemy had gotten stronger, bolder, and had consolidated their positions. Fucking lucky he hadn't been overrun.

The teams along the road were pouring M-16, SAW, M-240G fire, and 203 grenades through the windows of that townhouse. But behind us, more Muj had joined the strung-out ambush. My Marines along the road laid down suppressing fire, covering us as we scuttled down the side of the berm. A poorly aimed grenade from one of the Marines'

M-203s exploded about fifteen feet ahead of Doc Gobles, but he was covered by the defilade of the road. Finally the firing stopped.

I checked with the squad and fire team leaders over the Icom. No casualties.

"We're good to go, sir," Word reported.

But go where? I wanted to attack the line of buildings to our north and east. But we couldn't take the risk. There was just too much open ground, and my orders were not to start the invasion today.

Today wasn't Easter Sunday in Latafiyah, Captain Weston had reminded me. But I had a sick feeling in my gut that the situation could get almost as bad.

Camp Lejeune
27 April 2005

Charlie Gittins conducted his careful cross-examination of Sergeant "M."

> GITTINS: Okay. Corporal "O" is not a trained CI [counterintelligence] member or wasn't on the 15th of April; correct?
>
> M: He is not, sir.
>
> GITTINS: He was simply acting as your translator; correct?
>
> M: Yes, sir.
>
> GITTINS: It was you who made the judgments about intelligence value; correct?
>
> M: Yes, sir.
>
> GITTINS: It was you who evaluated the potential for whether or not these individuals should be detained; correct?
>
> M: Yes, sir.
>
> GITTINS: He wasn't trained to do that; correct?
>
> M: No, sir. His job is basically a mouthpiece, sir.
>
> GITTINS: Okay. When you questioned the two detainees that had been detained by Lieutenant Pantano, you did not know at that time what materials had been found in the house; correct?
>
> M: Initially, sir?

GITTINS: Correct.

M: No, sir.

GITTINS: And that was the only time you talked to those detainees; correct?

M: Yes, sir.

GITTINS: So when you questioned the detainees, you did not have knowledge, for example, that mortar-aiming stakes had been found in the house; correct?

M: No, sir.

GITTINS: That information had not been passed on the radio or you would have heard it; correct?

M: Yes, sir.

GITTINS: And the demeanor of these individuals concerned you; didn't it?

M: Yes, sir.

GITTINS: You believed that they were not telling the truth; correct?

M: Definitely, sir.

GITTINS: That was your evaluation; correct?

M: Yes, sir.

GITTINS: As a trained CI guy?

M: Yes, sir.

GITTINS: How many people do you suspect you interrogated or had interrogated in Iraq by 15 April?

M: Close to a hundred, sir.

GITTINS: And based on your experience in Iraq, you concluded that these guys were bad guys; didn't you?

M: Yes, sir.

GITTINS: Probable insurgents; correct?

M: Yes, sir.

GITTINS: Not innocent Iraqis who just happened to be driving out of this house; correct?

M: Yes, sir.

GITTINS: It was your intent to recommend to Lieutenant Pantano, and you did, that he should take these people back to the FOB; correct?

M: Definitely, sir.

GITTINS: They were not going to be released, to your understanding; correct?

M: I couldn't make that call then, sir. I just knew I wanted to take them back for further questioning.

GITTINS: You made that recommendation to Lieutenant Pantano though; correct?

M: Yes, sir.

GITTINS: When Lieutenant Pantano and your QRF group arrived at the checkpoint, you observed him give his five-paragraph [SMEAC] order; correct?

M: Yes, sir.

GITTINS: And you observed it to be done in a thoroughly professional manner; didn't you?

M: Yes, sir.

GITTINS: His demeanor never changed throughout this entire operation; did it?

M: Not that I saw, sir.

GITTINS: You never saw him upset in any way?

M: No, sir.

GITTINS: The briefing you observed was by the Marine book, wasn't it?

M: Yes, sir.

GITTINS: SMEAC; right?

M: Yes, sir.

GITTINS: Situation, mission—what are the others? I don't even know the others. It's been a long time.

M: —execution, admin/logistics, command/control.

GITTINS: What you did tell Lieutenant Pantano after you interrogated these Iraqis was that you recommended they be transported and that he cut the flex-cuffs and cuffed them in front for transportation; correct?

M: Yes, sir.

GITTINS: So it was your expectation that they would have their flex-cuffs removed; correct? Or at least briefly?

M: Yes, sir. I recommended. It's easier to transport them, basically.

GITTINS: With their hands in front?

M: Yes, sir.

GITTINS: And that was your recommendation to Lieutenant
Pantano; correct?

M: Yes, sir.

GITTINS: And after you interrogated these two Iraqis and
concluded that they should be transported, and
made that recommendation to Lieutenant Pantano, Lieutenant Pantano told you he would take
care of it; correct?

M: Good to go.

GITTINS: Good to go?

Sergeant "M" nodded but did not speak.

Fallujah, Iraq
25 April 2004

We continued our bounding overwatch another eight hundred meters
south down the road berm. About three hundred meters to the east,
the city side of the road, there was a squat windowless concrete building, some kind of industrial or agricultural deal we'd called the "Refrigerator" in our patrol brief. It had a flat roof and would command a
360-degree field of observation as a support-by-fire position during the
battalion assault. I had to check it out.

Then machine-gun fire and slow, badly aimed sniper rounds
ripped into the hard dirt of the road. At least for the moment, that
sniper hadn't gotten the range. We dove for cover.

"Sir," Word asked, "you still want to go over there?" He nodded toward the flat, weedy ground between the road and the Refrigerator.

"Set up a base of fire," I yelled to Corporal Fulton and his M-240G
machine-gun team. "Suppress the shit out of that stuff."

Fulton was a tall, blue-eyed farmboy who could have played Super-
man in the movies. He had the gun pounding, traversing the enemy fire
positions in well-disciplined bursts that poured out a stream of metal
but did not burn through too much ammo—or melt the gun barrel.

"Stay with the gun team," I ordered Coburn. If the Fridge was
booby trapped or if we got hit during the recon, he could call for a
QRF. I trusted him to do that much. I always kept him hidden behind
berms; that long antenna made him a valuable target.

While Fulton kept up his suppressing fire, I pushed a fire team toward the building, hoping it was empty and we wouldn't have to de-louse it at close quarters. Nobody liked that shit.

Approaching the structure, Corporal Stringham fired on a Muj with a few rounds from his M-16, and the man went down in the waist-high grass. As I neared the building I stumbled on the guy String-ham had shot. He'd been hit at least once in the left leg and had taken his checked scarf and wrapped it. He had an OD military web belt and ammo pouch. My thoughts slowed; my perceptions and actions went to Auto.

The man wore a black robe and his face was swarthy beneath the crusted dirt. His beard was long and dirty, with bits of grass from where he'd fallen and maybe bits of food from the previous weeks of fighting. Yemeni? Definitely some type of jihadi. He didn't look like many of the Iraqis that I'd ever seen. His hands were filthy, and he was older and weathered, maybe in his forties. Maybe a grandfather even. He was as shocked to see me as I was to encounter him.

I had just been firing at a house where we thought one of the enemy was shooting at us, trying to suppress while the fire team checked out the Fridge, so my weapon was already up. Oily smoke lifted off the bolt where lubricant and carbon from the rounds made a slimy film that sprayed across your face after too much firing.

The man was fumbling with his AK-47. Maybe changing a maga-zine. Maybe it had jammed. Maybe he was just slow on the draw. I wasn't. Weirdly, he was smiling, probably thinking he was about to kill an infidel. Our eyes met and held for an instant and his smile immedi-ately changed to a grimace as I fired into his chest from less than fif-teen feet away. Two bursts. Three. The rest of the mag.

I couldn't take the chance of approaching him. The word was that some of these jihadis tucked armed grenades under their web belts at the small of the back, so the enemy would get blown away when they stripped the body of ammo.

Whatever the truth, I thought, this motherfucker would *not* be get-ting up again. Even with massive trauma it takes seconds for the body to die. I would have blown his head off with a shotgun if I'd had one.

Inserting a fresh magazine, I continued firing on the houses to our north. Firing into Fallujah. Trotting up to the Fridge, I got the word that it was clear. I told the men to hold a perimeter and try to identify the source of the fire and suppress it while I headed up to the roof. Right, just swing on up there, Tarzan. The only stairs were bare concrete treads on the north wall, no railing, completely exposed to enemy fire from the city.

"How are your boys for ammo?" I checked with Corporal Trent of Third Squad.

"Okay for now, sir."

I always lugged a dozen magazines, so I could hand them out like treats to my guys when they "done good." As I bounded up the stairs, bullets smacked into the concrete behind me with each step. I stuck my weapon up and fired over my head before cresting the stairs. No one on the roof. I slithered on my belly and caught my breath. It took a while for my ragged breathing to settle down. What a fucking day. And the big invasion would be tomorrow or the next day? And then on to Ramadi.

Wonderful. I studied the photo taped to my rifle stock. Would I ever see Jill and my babies again?

The flat roof of the Refrigerator lacked the traditional protective wall. I felt bareass naked up on top. Like I was on a stage. Rounds impacting the side of the building but from where? The fire was slower. More deliberate. More dangerous.

The sniper saw me through the scope of his 7.62 x 54 mm Dragunov rifle. I knew a little bit about snipers and their prey.

Camp Lejeune
27 April 2005

Gittins continued his cross-examination of Sergeant "M."

GITTINS: After you interrogated these two suspected insurgents, that you concluded should be transported, you learned that they had assault vests in that house; correct?

M: Yes.

GITTINS: That they had a flare gun, which is a signaling device, which in your experience had been used to initiate ambushes; correct?

M: Yes, sir.

GITTINS: Three AK-47s with magazines; correct?

Easy Company 2/2, "the Warlords," at FOB Mahmudiyah, September 2004.
Artillery positions, helicopter loading zone, and Hesco barriers in background.

Nineteen-year-old Lcpl Pantano digging a hole with gasmask nearby during Desert Storm, 1991.

Standard-issue tough-guy war photo. On the Kuwaiti border (Lcpl Jackson, Lcpl Dejessie, Lcpl Foley, Lcpl Pantano, Cpl Vargas, Sgt Ocasio), 1991.

Head Hunter 1 and 2 (Cpl Pantano, Cpl Howard, Lcpl Dethridge, Cpl Rivers, Lcpl Decker, and Lcpl Johanneson) at the Royal Army training facility on Gibraltar. The Rock is in the background, 1992.

Cpl Pantano, Scout Sniper Platoon 1/6, role-playing an "insurgent" against conventional infantry units during training at Camp Lejeune, North Carolina, 1992, with AK-47 and RPG-7.

Mother and son at home in New York, 1988.

Father and son in Central Park,
New York, 1975.

Making dad proud as a "Master of the Universe" in training at the "21" Club,
New York City, 1995.

Celebrating good times with mom and aunt Lynda, New York City, 1995.

Jill and me with my "new" haircut, at our wedding rehearsal dinner,
New York City, October 2001.

Training actors in Amsterdam for the feature film *The Shaft*, 2000.

Production Assistant on the set of *Lateline*, New York, 1998.

A final meal with family before leaving for Iraq, February 2004.

Four prior enlisted officers at IOC who all went to Iraq. Erasmo (left) had his legs shattered by an IED, Rex (second from right) took shrapnel in the face and eyes, Bill (second from left), a Harvard grad who has gone to Iraq twice, and me in the black cap on the right, December 2003.

Meeting Colin Powell during a charity fundraiser at the Plaza Hotel, New York City, 1998.

Mustafa, head of security, and I at the town council of Mahmudiyah, March 2004.

Doc Gobles and Doc McNulty manning radios and filling sandbags at our platoon patrol base, April 2004.

SSgt Glew and I preparing to insert night ambush patrols at FOB Mahmudiyah, April 2004.

Fighting out of an ambush in Fallujah, April 2004.

A CNN Chevy Suburban ambushed outside of FOB Mahmudiyah. Translator/Producer Duraid Isa Mohammed and driver Yasser Khatab were shot to pieces, 2004.

Writing in my journal and smoking a cigar after a firefight in Fallujah, April 2004.

The machine gunners of Easy Company. Lcpl Benny Cockerham, center, was awarded the Purple Heart on this day in June, 2004. On October 25, 2005, he was killed by an IED on his second combat tour.

Lcpl Keuchner, a three-time Purple Heart recipient engaging the enemy. Behind him is Lcpl Jernigan, who would later be robbed of his eyes and part of his skull and face by an IED, April 2004.

Easy Company finishing up a pre-dawn raid in Fallujah with tank rounds firing overhead, April 2004.

2nd Lt Nate Dmochowski hamming for the camera with the *Time* magazine article about our operations in Fallujah. The picture under his left fingers show him briefing his squad leaders, May 2004.

Lcpl Posada holding the walkie-talkie detonator of an IED that barely missed us, May 2004.

1st Sgt Graham watching Capt Weston negotiate funds for a school project in the suburbs of Fallujah, June 2004.

Lt Col Kyser awarding Lcpl Faleris the Purple Heart at FOB Mahmudiyah. 1st Sgt Graham and Capt Weston look on at left, August 2004.

1st Squad getting ready to head off on a patrol a week before the ambush that would cost Lcpl Johnson his arm and put shrapnel into Lcpl Smith's brain, June 2004. Top row: Lcpl Dunham, Lcpl Johnson, Lcpl Brown, Sgt Word (no helmet), Doc Gobles, and Lcpl Chicas. Bottom row: Lcpl Perry, Cpl Braun, Lcpl Davis, Lcpl Sacchi, Lcpl Smith, and Cpl McPherson.

Image from the threat-site that originated out of Pakistan, February 2005.

HE DESERVED IT

246-18

Puma, Gucci, and Glock. Jill and I practice at a four day defensive handgun course at Front Sight in Nevada, 2005.

Mike Gregorio, Marine Vietnam veteran and commander of American Legion Post 10, wears a DefendTheDefenders.org T-shirt during a fund-raising fish-fry at the Legion hall in Wilmington, North Carolina, April 2005.

Checking roof-top security during a recruiting
event for the Iraqi Police (Rasheed), August 2004.

In my dress blues.

Homecoming at Camp Lejeune, North Carolina, October 2004.

Fallen Warlords immortalized on the wall of the "Chicken Factory" in FOB Mahmudiyah, September 2004.

M: Yes, sir.

GITTINS: Which violated the rules; correct?

Sergeant "M" nodded again.

GITTINS: They had ID media for people who didn't live in
that house; correct?

M: Yes.

GITTINS: That would be an indication of insurgent activity,
wouldn't it?

M: Yes, sir.

GITTINS: And would probably be; correct?

M: Yes.

GITTINS: Those were kind of the things you learned about
as you—as you lived through this insurgency; correct?

M: Definitely.

GITTINS: In addition, you found pro-Saddam propaganda;
correct?

M: Yes.

GITTINS: And you also found pro-Chechnyan rebel propaganda; correct?

M: Yes.

GITTINS: That is consistent with Iraqi insurgents; correct?

M: Yes.

GITTINS: And also Osama bin Laden propaganda; correct?

M: Yes.

GITTINS: And Osama bin Laden, we're talking about the
same guy that ran airplanes into the World Trade
Center; right?

After more than three years, I could still see the billowing smoke
and the debris tinsel floating in the bright September morning sun-
shine.

M: Yes, sir.

GITTINS: Not some other Osama bin Laden; right?

M: No, sir.

GITTINS: And after you learned that all of these proposed—potential insurgent materials were found in the house, you were outside and you heard the gunshots; correct?

M: Yes, sir.

GITTINS: And as soon as you saw Lieutenant Pantano after that shooting stopped, he was running toward another vehicle—correct?

M: Yes, sir.

GITTINS: And when Lieutenant Pantano got down to that vehicle, you arrived and you made a determination that those guys were probably not threats; correct?

M: Yes, sir.

GITTINS: The five painters or whatever—however many there were.

M: Yes, sir. You could tell their demeanor.

GITTINS: They seemed like innocent Iraqis; correct?

M: Yes, sir.

GITTINS: And just to be clear, when you recommended to Lieutenant Pantano that these innocent Iraqis be released, you had them walk away; correct?

M: Yes, sir.

GITTINS: They didn't drive away in that vehicle, did they?

M: No, sir.

GITTINS: You personally observed them walk away from the area; correct?

M: Yes, sir. I escorted them probably fifty meters north.

GITTINS: You escorted them?

M: Yes, sir.

Fallujah, Iraq
25 April 2004

Although the roof of the Fridge was naked, it did give me a good view of the city. Murphy's law of combat: if you can see them, they can see you. The sniper's precision fire intensified, striking the rooftop around me, but I wasn't alone in this predicament. I had left orders that I was to go up by myself to check out the vantage point, but two of my men had followed. Against my orders, but to protect me. Corporal Stringham was firing his M-16/M-203, trying to suppress the enemy sniper.

Meanwhile a round glanced off the Kevlar helmet of PFC Smith. He looked a little shaken, but kept firing north.

"How many 203 smoke rounds you got left?" I asked Stringham.

He patted the multipouch grenade vest. "Only one, sir."

"Put it into the field between the sniper and us." The smoke popped, a thin yellow wisp.

I radioed for the other teams to pick up the volume of fire, and Smith was dashing down the stairs. Stringham kept firing north. I lobbed a red smoke grenade, which we usually saved for emergency "cease-fire" signals. By now, my men knew to keep on firing until the enemy was dead. So the red cloud became a surreal presence as we scrambled off the rooftop. Sniper and AK rounds followed us down the stairs, impacting above and beside us. Close.

Dashing and crawling, we made it back to the squad at the road berm and continued the patrol south. A cigar was going to taste good tonight.

But before I thought too far ahead, I conferred with Buster and we made sure to mark all the confirmed enemy fire positions on our maps. I was especially eager to get that sniper who'd nearly clipped my men and me. As soon as 1 RCT gave the go-ahead, I wanted to be back up here, watching some two-thousand-pound bombs hitting.

Burn, bitches.

No worse enemy.

Camp Lejeune
27 April 2005

Gittins's cross-examination of the intelligence sergeant ground relentlessly ahead.

GITTINS: When Lieutenant Pantano was dealing with the second vehicle, did he seem to be—have the same demeanor he had before he dealt with the first two Iraqis?

M: Yes, sir.

GITTINS: There had been no change in his demeanor?

M: No, sir.

GITTINS: When Lieutenant Pantano—I'm sorry. After the rounds had been fired from the—in a very rapid way, you heard the lieutenant on the radio saying it was friendly fire; correct?

M: Yes, sir.

GITTINS: Acknowledging and announcing that he was doing the firing; correct?

M: Yes, sir.

GITTINS: Now, prior to April 15th you were aware, and it was general knowledge, that this area from which this cordon and raid was going on was a place where Marines had killed Iraqi insurgents who were firing mortars at FOB Mahmudiyah; correct?

M: It was a known point of origin, sir. We had taken mortar fire from that position several times. Our snipers had actually caught two individuals setting up a mortar position and went ahead and killed those guys.

GITTINS: So this was an area where there had been insurgent activity, and Marines had obtained kills by using snipers; correct?

M: Yes, sir.

GITTINS: Prior to April 15th you also—you were present on the Easter Sunday firefight; correct?

M: Yes, sir.

GITTINS: Approximately four-to-six-hour firefight?

M: Yes, sir.

GITTINS: And Lieutenant Pantano was the QRF platoon commander for that fight?

M: Yes, he was.

GITTINS: You accompanied him, you were among the first guys on the scene; correct?

M: Yes, sir.

GITTINS: You observed Lieutenant Pantano in combat under the hazards of combat; correct?

M: Yes, sir.

GITTINS: And you observed him to be a highly professional
officer; correct?

M: Yes, sir.

Major Keane and his colleagues at the prosecution table were exchanging notes.

GITTINS: Conducted himself—accorded himself appropriately into combat?

M: Yes, sir.

GITTINS: A very dangerous situation?

M: Yes, sir, very dangerous.

Fallujah, Iraq
27 April 2004

Lying prone in the observation post we'd set up on the concrete dam, I was sighting through the day-night scope of an M-16 on a person I could only describe as a "Ninja." Black robes, head to ground, maybe a female. But walking funny. That robe was too full. Like a man balancing heavy IED components under an *abaya*. And she . . . he was shuffling along to a white Toyota pickup truck on the east bank. I couldn't let him get away.

My right thumb clicked the rifle's selector switch off SAFE to single-round. My trigger finger took out the slack and I expelled a lungful of breath. Now . . .

I lifted my finger. A little boy, maybe a few months older than Domenico, appeared from beneath his mother's robe. Shorts and a T-shirt, ripped plastic sandals. I clicked the safety back on and pushed the weapon away from my body. I almost threw it with revulsion at the sin I had nearly committed.

What a fucking war.

Casualties were mounting. We'd taken seven WIAs in two days. The Muj in Fallujah were not stupid. They knew we were still indecisive and would not retaliate against their sniping and IEDs.

Someone had smelled blood in the water in Fallujah. Last night at 0100 a sixtyish British *Time* reporter named Paul Quinn-Judge showed up with his Korean photographer, Sungsu Cho. They were here because of our firefights and had planned to push up to us this afternoon, but that was expedited after news of our recent casualties. Yesterday was guard, and today we rotated to QRF standby.

Neither assignment was what I'd been hoping for. I wanted the big attack, an end to this "not decisively engaged" shit that was emboldening the Muj further. We had to take ground and hold it and blow the fuckers out. Period. This half-ass shit was getting boys hurt.

I didn't want this fucking reporter coming with me. I didn't need a camera on my back when I was trying to fight and kill the enemy any way I could. As often as I could. As quickly as I could. I didn't need anyone to see that or write about it, or us, for that matter. No real soldier wants their actions recorded for posterity. I didn't want my family to know. I didn't want my children to learn about bloodlust and fear and shit and killing. There was nothing good in it. There was nothing good that came out of war.

You didn't come back more. You came back less.

Camp Lejeune
27 April 2005

Gittins was finishing his cross-examination of Sergeant "M."

GITTINS: You indicated that you saw the two bodies, you were running by the bodies; correct?

M: Yes, sir.

GITTINS: You looked at the bodies here in the photographs [gesturing to easels]; you didn't spend much time looking at them when you were running by [them] though; correct?

M: No, sir.

GITTINS: The wound on the guy in the white, who was in the front seat—can we show it to you again?

M: Sure, sir.

GITTINS: If I may, that wound is not consistent with what you believe to be an entry wound; correct?

M: No, sir. It's an exit wound, sir. This blood-smear was on the back of the man dress.

GITTINS: You believe that to be an exit wound in the back of that individual; correct?

M: Yes, sir.

GITTINS: That is not a small point of entry, is it?

M: No, sir.

GITTINS: It's a blown-out back, isn't it?

M: Yes, sir.

GITTINS: No further questions, sir.

Now Major Winn examined the witness.

WINN: You also testified that there was propaganda found in the house?

M: Yes, sir.

WINN: How did you know—you said there were CDs?

M: Yes, sir.

WINN: How did you know what was on the CDs?

M: Our corporal, Corporal "O," read the CDs.

WINN: So there was writing on the CD itself, or the cases that said—

M: Correct.

WINN: —beheadings or—

M: Correct.

WINN: —Osama bin Laden?

M: Well, they actually had printouts of the Chech-nyan rebels on the front of the disk, Osama, Sad-dam, there was actually printouts, like little slide-ins.

Fallujah, Iraq
29 April 2004

At 0400 we finally crossed the line of departure to attack north to de-stroy enemy in the vicinity of Target 2. We were the main effort of the big assault that came after three weeks of negotiations. Supported by tanks, CAAT units, snipers, and a day of air prep.

The previous afternoon, I'd had the raw, hateful pleasure of watch-ing Marine F/A-18s and Harriers as well as Air Force F-16s drop precision-guided five-hundred-pound bombs on the targets that Buster and I had identified on the recon patrol. Fantastic. Fourth of July on the Euphrates. Our FAC had coordinated the bomb drops with Captain Weston.

Buster told *Time* reporter Quinn-Judge, "We've got to rebuild this fucking country sooner or later. We don't want to blow up too much of it."

Now we were moving through the humid darkness up to the objective, about three klicks north. First Platoon, which had set up a combination blocking and support-by-fire position with CAAT Red, came on the tac net. "We got two AKs and an RPG setting up . . . Engaging."

I was the only one in my platoon that heard this over the company net, and then as soon as I passed the word to the platoon, CAAT Red began firing. Just as we were passing through their position.

Awesome volume of fire, .50 cal, MK-19s, even a TOW shot. They took out the Muj observation post on a rooftop bunker that we had marked. It looked like all of our reconnaissance work had paid off. But now the enemy knew that we were there.

"Double time," I called, and heard the boots thudding behind me toward the objective.

We'd definitely taken the initiative by killing those bastards on the roof, but if we didn't move quickly, the enemy would seize the initiative back from us. Some of my guys had been so surprised by the fireworks from 1st Platoon and CAAT that they almost pissed themselves.

"C'mon, bitches," Staff Sergeant Glew yelled. "That's friendlies." Tracers screamed past above. Like a net of light cast over our heads. Awesome!

The signature "Pop! Whoosh! Boom!" of a TOW missile fired from the top of a Humvee . . . something I hadn't heard in combat for thirteen years. The Pop was the initial charge sending the missile out of the tube without burning the gunner's face off. The Whoosh was the flight motor kicking in a safe distance out to send it careering downrange to deliver its shaped-charge payload. The Boom. Ahh, the Boom was the music of incineration. The sonata was bad guys and their weapons doing the chicken dance at 2,000 degrees Fahrenheit in a billowing fireball.

Whether it's a tank or a mortar position that is dropping rounds on you as in my first war, or a terrorist fighting position that has shot your men up for the last few days, the feeling is the same: like a badly needed air strike, like Christmas.

We passed through 1st Platoon's position: they had set up almost an hour prior to ensure that they could infiltrate slowly and quietly and have the targets identified in time for our party. We moved through their lines and absorbed their energy. The volume of fire propelling us gave us momentum through the chute. We turned down a dirt road heading east, paralleling the south edge of the city, into a series of massive stone structures collectively and benignly known as Objective A. They formed the southern defense of the city, sitting there like sultans' palaces with balcony after balcony overlooking a no-man's-land of open swamp—machine-gun alley for the fodder dumb enough to cross that shit to lead an attack. That would be us.

But we came prepared. Not only did the previous day's air strike prep the target, a sniper team had been out hunting all night. And today we had a little surprise in the form of two sixty-ton M-1A1 Abrams main battle tanks. Early in my Marine Corps career as a young anti-tank guy I had learned reverence for these beasts. In fact, when I'd joined, the Corps didn't yet have them. Only the "high-tech" Army did. We'd only had had the venerable M-60A3. ("Hell, if it was good enough for Marines in 'Nam, it's good for me.")

The M-1's self-stabilizing gun could not only track a moving target while the tank was moving, but onboard sensors could detect an impending collision with a tree, deftly turning the barrel away and then back to the target, not just where the target was, but where it should be, based on a million variables like the target's speed, direction, and distance all relative to the tank. Technology that would have helped us crush the Russians. Here, in the chaos that was urban guerrilla combat, a tank was worth a hundred martyrs.

The Muj had tried to take out the tanks with heavy mortars as soon as they lumbered up to our positions, days before the assault. The presence of the tanks signaled the seriousness of what was to come. When the mortars didn't work, they tried to sneak up and lob RPGs. Sadly for those goat fuckers, our men were a lot more afraid of their sergeants and corporals than they were in need of sleep. So our boys on guard were always ready, and every time the bastards tried to get close, the Marines would cut them down.

One of the interesting stories from the siege of Fallujah came from the Psyops unit attached to us before our invasion of the city. They had big speakers on the roofs of their Humvees that were particularly good at playing tanks' noise. The high-pitched mechanical "whine-and-clank" of metal on metal was like a martyr mating call. They came dashing out with RPGs and Molotov cocktails at the ready and down they went in streams of accurate machine-gun fire. When you know the enemy wants a tank, you give it to them, not on a plate, but up their ass. We'd play the tanks' noise with the Humvees, keeping the tanks off at a safe distance watching and waiting for targets with their thermal imaging. Sometimes you'd win the lotto and it would be a bad day for Johnny Jihad. And sometimes they got one of us, like when they killed my friend Lieutenant Stern, a tank platoon commander, with an IED.

Now we were moving up onto 2nd Platoon's position, leapfrogging, each platoon a rung on a human ladder that intertwined the lives of 150 men in a desperate climb to the top. What was the top today? We would find out soon enough. As we trotted through the predawn darkness, panting beneath the weight of our weapons, ammo, and equipment, we left the light show of tracers and explosions behind us. That wild display had been the wake-up call for every Muj in the area—shit, for half of Al Anbar Province. They would think that the invasion was coming and it was their duty to die opposing it.

The deep roar of our crew-served heavy machine guns brought us comfort. The old Ma Deuce M-2 fired .50 cal rounds almost half the length of a man's forearm. It probably wasn't even supposed to be used against human targets without violating a law of war. But war violates the laws of nature . . . so fire 'em. We did . . . and as often as we could. And finally the Bam-bam-bam-Pause-Boom-boom-boom of the MK-19 lobbing grenades almost a mile at such a high arc that you could put them over a wall directly into the sun roof of a getaway car. The time of flight was so long that there would be complete silence, and apprehension, as you waited to see the explosive zipper of grenades explode downrange, opening up whatever was in its path.

We pushed past 2nd Platoon and were by ourselves now with nothing between us and the objective but dark air and the opportunity for the enemy to kill us. In a moment the darkness was gone. Tanks were firing into some nearby houses where hostiles had begun the counterattack. We dashed the last hundred meters of what was now totally open ground around the houses, and that's when 1st Squad began taking fire from the top window of a house.

Sergeant Word lobbed a frag into the window and the assault team kicked the door. *Boom.* First Squad and then 2nd Squad took the house. Flashlight beams swept the rooms as gunners looked for more targets in the darkness. The flashes of the initial gunfire had killed their night vision. Now we were going to white light. Not your first choice when you have surprise, but you had to accept it. Most of the men had purchased flashlights themselves (or had their families mail them) and, if they were like me, the lights were attached to their hi-tech rifles with duct tape.

We proceeded with a technique called the Bump. Once Aguirre's 2nd Squad had the roof, Word's 1st Squad went on to the next structure, Building 2. When Trent's 3rd Squad came in out of the swamp, they "bumped" 2nd Squad out to take another house of its own: Building 3. I was giving my CO updates in real time as we progressed. The technique is good for four men, forty, or four hundred. You didn't advance until the follow-on forces moved. It was the best way to ensure no gaps in a seamless offense or defense.

But the maneuver could be a little confusing, especially in darkness with lots of fire. That's why squad leaders, all leaders, had to be so damned disciplined about accountability. You didn't want your machine-gunner leaving his security position to go clear a building with another squad that he doesn't belong to. That would fuck up everyone's numbers, and during the millisecond it took to unfuck that mini-catastrophe, the machine-gunner's original sector would be left uncovered. People die unnecessarily and for what? Because someone got confused?

This kind of combat was as much mental as brutally physical. Focus, goddammit, and move!

I marked the rooftop with a chem-light so tanks would know where we were. The radio sputtered with reports of movement. Left, right . . . it was like the scene in *Aliens* when all the sensors are screaming that the bugs are everywhere, but the victims can't see a thing.

"There . . ." I'd hardly shouted when the narrow alley crackled with more AK fire. I wanted to dominate the situation with an AT-4 instantly. Nothing spells fire superiority like a rocket. We'd been ordered to allow the exodus of "innocent civilians" for days, so I wasn't worried about Iraqi friendlies. I wanted an AT-4 down their throats *now.* More firing and the insurgents spilled out the back to get help. You bring a knife. I bring a gun. Sooner or later they won't want to play anymore.

But not today. Up on the flat roof of a house, Lance Corporal Gillian had the AT-4 on his shoulder, calmly aiming. A dull click. Shouts. Chaos. "What the fuck? *Fuck.* Misfire!" It wasn't exactly fun to fire a rocket from a rooftop. Everyone had to be careful not to get blown off by the back-blast. Now we had a dud that could fire and explode at any moment.

"Goddammit," I yelled. "Shit. Fire it again!"

The gunners knew what to do. Half the time the yelling was just to reinforce the lessons to the younger troops who were struggling to understand what the fuck was happening around them. They would be tomorrow's leaders if today turned out to be a bad one for the older guys. The Marine Corps was prepared for that. In the battle of Montezuma we'd lost 90 percent of our sergeants and officers . . . a loss immortalized in song and the cut of our dress uniform with the red blood stripe on the pants of NCOs and commissioned officers. Everything has a reason.

My brain was swarming with information that I struggled to process in the priorities that had been beaten into me in TBS and IOC.

So much data, sights, smells, sounds, positions, locations, directions, angles, fires, rooftops, basements, windows, doorways, donkey carts, car bombs, human bombs, down, left, right, around corners, over walls, where are the friendlies? Where is 2nd Squad? Where are they pointing their weapons? Did the enemy get in between us? Was that us or them? Who's shooting? Why? Where? How much ammo? Who's hurt? How much time? Where is the sun? Was that a call for prayer or attack from the minaret? What's the difference? Was that a grenade landing at my feet? How many rounds left? Where is the corpsman? Why isn't that fucking building clear yet? Who's taking so fucking long on the radio?

"Clear the goddamn net!" I listened. "What?"

What was that last bit about binoculars? Will these steps hold, is the staircase rigged? Is that a trigger? A booby trap? Where are the bodies? Look at all of these shoes! What's the head count? What did the tanks just see?

"Yes sir, we are finishing on the objective." What was the fucking brevity code for that?

Shit! Moving, grabbing. Tracer or laser? NVGs are foggy. . . . Are they broke? Where is the handset? Fix the fucking handset. Give the report. You know what the fuck is going on! Tell 'em. Pushing. Screaming. Firing. Shadows. Dawn light. Cooking fires. Oil fires. Bodies on fire. Dogs barking. Dogs chewing on bodies. Dogs getting shot. Corporals barking. I'm barking. My CO is barking. His CO is barking. *His* CO is barking . . . Somewhere, probably, the president is barking.

We recovered machine-gun ammo, three pairs of binoculars, and thumb-size 7.62 x 54 mm rounds for the sniper rifle. Clearly some guys had been killed in the air strike, but even turned to rubble, these buildings still offered cover. The sun was rising, hot and ugly. And it was time to get the fuck off the objective. I led the way in, and the platoon sergeant was in the rear with the extremely important job of keeping accountability. Now he would lead them out and I would take the rear. In many ways we were complements to each other, interchangeable, if need be.

The Marine Corps hadn't become the ultimate fighting force by accident. Our combat tactics were born on the battlefield and honed over two hundred–some years of vicious and unforgiving classrooms. In the organization of a fighting unit, the simple leadership objective was to put yourself wherever the most friction or complexity arose. You didn't need to be leading the easy shit, you needed to seek out where your men were being challenged, either by a tough enemy or a complex problem. That was where your role as mentor, father, and example was combined to move the platoon along. To obtain results.

Getting to the objective undetected had been the first challenge of the day. The last would be getting off unscathed. We were always at our most vulnerable when withdrawing. Exiting meant you were facing away from the enemy. And any enemy, particularly a guerrilla force, will take advantage of your back (note how many guys get shot in the ass). You had to make sure your opponent was really knocked out before you turned your back. If you were still trading blows with the opponent in anything resembling a one-to-one ratio, you could not turn your back or you would get killed.

Too many dirty fights with too many junior gangsters taught me all I needed to know about the sucker punch. When it was time for us to move off the objective, it was also time to suppress the enemy to cover our movement. Nothing in the world is better for that than tanks.

"White 4, White 4, this is 3 Actual!" I screamed over the mayhem. "We are out of the eastern buildings. Only friendlies are in the building with the chem-light that I am flashing to you now . . . Do you see me?"

"Roger 3 actual, we've got you. The place is crawling with 'em."

White 4's tone was distant and mechanical inside the whine of the tanks.

"Roger, fire up everything to my east with the Coax." The 7.62 mm coaxial machine gun mounted next to the main gun benefited from the computer targeting and stabilization that the bigger weapon enjoyed. This made it the most accurate machine gun in the world. And today, I had two of them, and the gunners were eager to go to work.

Tracer fire erupted as the tanks began to slash apart the enemy that was massing as we pulled off the objective. Bullets poured in and bricks blasted apart. First Squad was out and heading down the road, back into the open, the scariest place in the world. Second was close behind. Both squads moved a few hundred meters and then dove into shit-mud canals on the sides of the roads. I came out last with 3rd Squad ahead of me. I had taken the glowing ruby chem-light from the building and stuck it in my helmet so tanks would be sure where the last friendly was.

"Okay, 3 Actual is last element with red chem-light on helmet. We are moving west. Engage anything behind me." That was the kind of order tankers wait their whole careers to hear, and in this war, tanks had been getting that order a lot. They began to hose any motherfucker that stuck his head out.

As we moved back, both the tanks' and the enemies' fires followed us to the west. We passed through the position of 2nd Platoon, which now became the tail element. At this point, we were out of range of the original Muj shooters in the buildings, but the rest of Fallujah was waking up, so RPGs and machine-gun rounds started coming from the north and east.

Hoarse from screaming orders and thirst, almost deaf from the hours of gunfire, I led the platoon into the Easy Company FOB. All my guys were drained, their cammies stiff with sweat-salt, with dried shit from the ditches. Flies swarmed. But nobody cared. We'd made it back without a single casualty that day. White toothy grins shone under muddy faces. Every weapon in the company—mortars, rockets, machine guns, and sniper rifles—had been firing. And we'd had two tanks attached to us, under my command, as well as a platoon of CAAT Red with Ma Deuce .50 cals and TOWs under 1st Platoon's command. Captain Weston had the FAC with him and air was on standby.

(Later, when *Time* wrote up our attack and cited all the damage we'd inflicted on the enemy, the Muj would come seek out our unit specifically for retribution.)

Third Platoon had been the main effort, and as a result we were able to rest after we cleaned our weapons. I slept deeply . . . none of the sleepless preplanning jitters and coordination nightmares of the night before: Did we get this? Is that ready? Have we rehearsed enough? But you could never be too prepared for combat.

Camp Lejeune
27 April 2005

The prosecution called former Lance Corporal Greg Thompson, who served with the Warlords before completing his enlistment. Thompson, whom I had heard rumors about, had been kicked out of 3rd Platoon before I assumed command in 2004. He testified from Lexington, North Carolina, by speakerphone. Major Keane began the direct examination.

> KEANE: All right. You can have a seat if you've got a chair handy. Could you state your name and spell your last name.
>
> THOMPSON: My name is Greg Thompson. My last name is spelled T-H-O-M-P-S-O-N.
>
> KEANE: Were you once in the Marine Corps?
>
> THOMPSON: Yes.
>
> KEANE: Have you ever deployed to Iraq?
>
> THOMPSON: Yes.
>
> KEANE: How many times?
>
> THOMPSON: Twice.
>
> KEANE: Do you know a Sergeant Coburn?
>
> THOMPSON: Yes.
>
> KEANE: At any point while you were in Iraq, did he discuss with you an incident where two Iraqis were shot?
>
> THOMPSON: Yes, he did.
>
> KEANE: Okay. What did he tell you about what took place?
>
> THOMPSON: Sergeant Coburn, Lieutenant Pantano, and

the corpsman, held security on a vehicle. They searched the vehicle. They searched the two civilians inside the vehicle. Everything was good to go. Then Lieutenant Pantano shot the two civilians with a magazine and a half to two magazines.

KEANE: Upon learning that information from Sergeant Coburn, what did you do?

THOMPSON: The next morning I went to tell Sergeant Major Swann.

KEANE: Did anyone else become involved when you reported it to the sergeant major?

THOMPSON: The sergeant major then told the battalion executive officer, Major Dixon.

KEANE: Why did you feel you needed to report the incident?

THOMPSON: For one reason, it is going against our whole operation of SASO, Security and Stability Operations. And it is a war crime.

KEANE: Did you have any interaction personally with Lieutenant Pantano?

THOMPSON: Yes. I worked with him in CAAT Platoon.

KEANE: Did you work with him enough to form an opinion about it?

THOMPSON: Yes, I did.

KEANE: What is that opinion?

THOMPSON: That he was mentally unstable and he was little too gung-ho.

KEANE: Your witness.

Fallujah, Iraq
30 April 2004

We got the word that 1 RCT's big assault into Fallujah had been put on hold—indefinitely. It seemed that our heavy probing of the city's southern fortifications—especially our eagerness to blast the Muj out of their holes with bombs, tanks, and dismounted Marines—had convinced the enemy that it was time to negotiate, *again*.

"Motherfuckers," I said.

The 1st Marine Expeditionary Force headquarters and local Other Government Agencies (CIA), along with Iraqi intelligence weenies in Baghdad, had come up with a compromise. A goddamn Sunni former Republican Guard general named Jassim Mohammed Saleh was taking command of what would be called the "Fallujah Brigade." They'd have responsibility for keeping the peace in the city. Right. Of course, certainly. Three bags full.

Saleh lasted a couple of days—until the Shia and Kurds in the governing council in Baghdad had a shit fit. And then he was relieved and replaced with another former Saddam officer. But the Fallujah Brigade was not stood down. I had no doubt whatsoever the unit was about 110 percent hardcore Muj—the extra 10 percent being foreign jihadis and terrorists like that blackbeard I'd killed.

Easy Company followed orders. We reinforced our little FOB and took comfort in small pleasures. Care packages from home began to catch up. Jeff sent garlicky salami to slice into my MRE spaghetti. Heaven. My dad sent my Ninth Avenue Special cigars that an old Cuban guy wrapped by hand.

Jill's parents and family were terrific, sending articles and cutouts from my favorite papers. I was always starving for news, about the markets, about fashion, about film, about anything except the fucking war. Mom sent me the entire Sunday *New York Times,* which I gobbled up like porn. And sometimes it would make me laugh with the zany triviality of life in New York. Debutante balls and twenty-dollar martinis. The newest steakhouse or a sale at Bloomingdale's. Meanwhile people were dying over here, Iraqis and Americans. What an amazing disconnect. We were truly legionnaires on the frontier of an empire. Back in "Rome," they were sipping Pinot Grigio at a tapas bar or downing Buds at Hooters, all without fear of a bomb going off in the restaurant. It was a beautiful thing.

I studied the brightly colored coupons for computers at spring sale prices at Circuit City. Boy, a plasma screen sure would be great, I thought, as I took my boots off for the first time in five days—just to let my toes air out so I could repowder them and pack them back into to crusty socks and wet boots that would always be on when I slept . . . always ready to fight.

With the sweaty heat down inside the building, it was more pleasant—and more dangerous—to sleep up on the roof. Lieutenant

Brian Hampton, another urban badass from Philly, was also sleeping
on the roof, and so was the *Time* magazine reporter, Paul Quinn-Judge.
We talked a lot, about family and wine and past wars. Paul had been
covering Vietnam before I was born and had seen more than I could
ever imagine. (He would become my friend and write an important
story on my case the following year.) But that was a million years away,
and right now we were just trying to stay alive and I was one of the guys
making that happen for him. His photographer, Cho, was one of the
bravest/craziest sons of bitches I had ever seen. His camera never
stopped, which was a great thing, because I didn't even bring my camera to Fallujah. I expected to be so busy—and I was. But Cho was
catching the rounds blowing up all around us. His pictures captured
the heat and the fatigue of the men in war and we were all so grateful
that he was able to immortalize that intense time of our lives for us.

Word came down from regiment to battalion: we were pulling out.
There would be no assault. The Marines were leaving the city in the
kind hands of those Iraqis loyal to whoever was the most intimidating
and barbaric.

     Now we had to rip apart the solid little FOB we'd sweated so hard
to fortify. The nitty-gritty work of breaking down all the green nylon
sandbags was under way. We couldn't just cut a sandbag. We might
need them later. So each one of the thousands had to be methodically
untied and emptied.

     As we were pulling out, it was painfully obvious that a family that
lived nearby, who had trusted us, who had pointed out bad guys fleeing
the city, would be executed. The old man with the lumpy nose, the
barefoot little kids . . . all of them. They were collaborators and the
Fallujah Brigade was clearly a bunch of thugs.

     *God, this is so stupid. We could win this thing now . . . and every one
of us on the ground knows it.*

     As we were breaking down the outpost and coordinating the entry
to Fallujah of new allied Iraqi forces, I vented my bitterness to Paul
Quinn-Judge. "Does this remind you of another part of the world in the
early seventies?"

Camp Lejeune
27 April 2005

Gittins began his cross-examination of Greg Thompson.

> GITTINS: Sir, my name is Charles Gittins. How are you
> doing today?
>
> THOMPSON: I am doing fine.
>
> GITTINS: Can you please tell me what rank you were
> when you had the conversation with Sergeant
> Coburn?
>
> THOMPSON: I was a lance corporal.
>
> GITTINS: So Sergeant Coburn came to you looking for
> advice?
>
> THOMPSON: No, he didn't.
>
> GITTINS: Okay. He wasn't looking for advice, but he was
> talking to you about this event?
>
> THOMPSON: Yes.
>
> GITTINS: So what happened—the way it went down was
> you talked to Sergeant Coburn, then you re-
> ported it to the Sergeant Major and Major
> Dixon, and then NCIS came around to you at
> some point to get a statement from you; cor-
> rect?
>
> THOMPSON: Yes, I did.
>
> GITTINS: Do you remember telling the NCIS agent that
> "Easy Company, Third Platoon, was falling
> apart" is what Coburn told you?
>
> THOMPSON: Yes.
>
> GITTINS: So Sergeant Coburn told you that E Com-
> pany, Third Platoon, was falling apart; cor-
> rect?
>
> THOMPSON: Yes.
>
> GITTINS: And he told you that Lieutenant Pantano killed
> two cleared innocent Iraqis; correct?
>
> THOMPSON: Yes, he did.
>
> GITTINS: So he told you the Iraqis had been cleared and
> they were innocent; correct?
>
> THOMPSON: Yes.

GITTINS: And Sergeant Coburn told you that Lieutenant Pantano was being nuts; correct?

THOMPSON: Yes, he did.

GITTINS: Now, you said Lieutenant Pantano appeared to you to be mentally unstable; correct, sir?

THOMPSON: Yes, he did.

GITTINS: Sir, do you have any medical training?

THOMPSON: No, I don't.

GITTINS: Do you have any psychological training as a psychologist?

THOMPSON: No, I don't.

GITTINS: Have you graduated from college in any field, sir?

THOMPSON: No, I haven't.

GITTINS: Did you graduate from high school?

THOMPSON: Yes, I did.

GITTINS: Any additional education beyond the high school level, sir?

THOMPSON: No, I don't.

Gittins kept his tone even, but was ratcheting up and down the pace of his questions.

GITTINS: Do you know a Corporal Walls, sir?

THOMPSON: Yes, I do.

GITTINS: Did you brag to Corporal Walls that you brought down the Third Platoon commander in Easy Company?

THOMPSON: No, I didn't.

GITTINS: Did you say to him that you brought down the Third Platoon commander in E Company?

THOMPSON: No, I didn't.

GITTINS: Is Corporal Walls a truthful person?

THOMPSON: No, he is not.

GITTINS: He is not? Sir, did you ask to get out of going to OIF I and II by saying you were sick, and a mental mess?

THOMPSON: That I said I was sick?

GITTINS: Yes.

THOMPSON: No, I didn't.

GITTINS: Did you tell Sergeant Word that you killed a guy in a judo competition?

THOMPSON: Am I being prosecuted here?

GITTINS: Did you understand my question, sir?

THOMPSON: Yes, I did.

GITTINS: Did you tell Sergeant Word you killed a guy [in] a judo competition?

THOMPSON: Yes, I did.

GITTINS: Was that true?

THOMPSON: What is that?

GITTINS: Was that true?

THOMPSON: No, it wasn't.

GITTINS: So that was a lie; correct?

THOMPSON: Yes, it was.

GITTINS: Were you a lance corporal when you lied to Sergeant Word?

THOMPSON: Yes, I was.

GITTINS: Did you also tell Sergeant Word that you were a member of a gang, either the Bloods or the Crips?

THOMPSON: I can't remember.

GITTINS: So you don't remember if you told Sergeant Word that?

THOMPSON: No, I don't.

GITTINS: Were you a member of the Bloods or the Crips, sir?

THOMPSON: No, I wasn't.

GITTINS: Is Sergeant Word a truthful guy?

THOMPSON: I don't know him personally.

GITTINS: Okay. But you knew him well enough to say you killed a guy in a judo competition; right?

THOMPSON: Again, I don't know him personally.

GITTINS: But you knew him well enough to tell a lie to him, that you'd killed a guy in a judo competition; correct?

THOMPSON: I have said my share of lies.

To the surprise of all of us at the defense table, the prosecutors looked at each other and started chuckling. Thompson's words would have been funny to me too if they were on Court TV. But my life was at stake in this case.

GITTINS: What other lies can you tell us about that you've told?

THOMPSON: None come to my mind right now.

GITTINS: How about any lies in respect to your duty performance, any lies you can think of that relate to your duty performance, sir?

THOMPSON: No.

GITTINS: Are you in the military right now?

THOMPSON: No, I am not.

GITTINS: Who are you employed by?

THOMPSON: A place called Daddy Rabbit's.

GITTINS: Daddy Rabbit's. In what city?

THOMPSON: Lexington.

GITTINS: While you were in Iraq, did you threaten to kill yourself?

THOMPSON: No.

GITTINS: So you never did that?

THOMPSON: No.

GITTINS: You never threatened to kill yourself?

THOMPSON: Not in Iraq.

GITTINS: Where did you threaten to kill yourself?

THOMPSON: When I was like ten.

GITTINS: So certainly not while you were in the Marines?

THOMPSON: Not while I was in Iraq.

GITTINS: Not while you were in Iraq. When, not in Iraq, did you threaten to kill yourself while you were in the Marines?

THOMPSON: Before my first deployment.

GITTINS: Before your first deployment, you threatened to kill yourself because you didn't want to go to OIF, isn't that true, sir?

THOMPSON: That is correct.

GITTINS: That was a lie to get out of a deployment, wasn't it, sir?

THOMPSON: That was a cry for help.

GITTINS: That was a lie to get out of going on a deployment, wasn't it, sir?

THOMPSON: No, it wasn't.

GITTINS: So you did intend to kill yourself?

THOMPSON: No, it was a cry for help.

GITTINS: So you didn't intend to kill yourself, but you said you were going to?

THOMPSON: Yes.

EIGHT

Article 32 Hearing
DAY TWO

Camp Lejeune
27 April 2005

I watched Sergeant Daniel Coburn walk stiffly to the witness stand. Passing between the defense and prosecution tables, he kept his eyes straight ahead.

Coburn wasn't fat or even noticeably out of shape. But there was a softness about him, like he was out of focus.

But there was a hard fact about Coburn: as the prosecution's key witness, his testimony here today would go a long way in deciding my fate.

Coburn turned, raised his right hand, and took the oath that Major Keane administered.

"Do you swear or affirm that the evidence you will present at the hearing now in session will be the truth, the whole truth, and nothing but the truth, so help you God?"

COBURN: Yes, sir.
KEANE: How long have you been a Marine?

COBURN: Ten years, sir.

KEANE: What assignments have you had in those ten years?

COBURN: I have been a SAW gunner, team leader, squad leader, platoon guide, platoon sergeant, platoon commander, police sergeant, training chief, armory custodian, sir.

KEANE: How many combat tours have you had?

COBURN: Two, sir.

KEANE: To Iraq?

COBURN: Yes, sir.

Now Major Keane took Coburn through the 3rd Platoon's QRF raid on April 15, 2004, and the subsequent search of the two insurgents' white sedan. Coburn noted that I'd ordered the car's interior stripped.

KEANE: Did Doc Gobles comply with that order?

COBURN: I did not notice the seats being ripped out, because I was watching to the north. But when I looked back every once in a while, I did see things flying from the vehicle. So he was ripping things out of the vehicle, yes, sir.

KEANE: Did Doc Gobles find anything of interest in the vehicle?

COBURN: I think he found some wire, sir, but that was about it.

KEANE: What happened after this search was completed?

COBURN: The search was complete. A call came on the radio, the Icom that was on his shoulder, from the house, stating that they found a mortar-aiming stake.

KEANE: What happened after that came over the radio?

COBURN: Lieutenant Pantano got mad and said, "These are the motherfuckers that were mortaring us," took out his K-bar [fighting knife], slashed the rear driver-side tire, and then to the front driver-side tire, then around the vehicle, slashing all four tires. He put the K-bar away, then he butt-stroked the rear driver-side door, the window, the front-left headlight, the rear passenger window, and then the rear driver-side taillight.

KEANE: Did HIET have anything to do with these two guys?

COBURN: Yes, sir. HIET came over, interviewed Doc Gobles's person first, gave them back to Doc Gobles, came over to me and grabbed my guy, and then interrogated him also.

KEANE: How long did their interrogations of these two individuals last?

COBURN: A few minutes.

KEANE: Did you hear any of the comments made by the interrogators or any of the HIET team to Lieutenant Pantano?

COBURN: No, sir. They were away from me. I didn't hear the actual interrogations of the two individuals.

KEANE: Okay. What happened after they were interrogated?

COBURN: One of the interrogators went over to talk to Lieutenant Pantano. I heard them say that basically these two individuals are going to be let go because they had nothing on them. There is no proof that they had anything to do with the house.

KEANE: Okay. What did Lieutenant Pantano do upon hearing that?

COBURN: He looked a little upset that these guys were going to get off.

Gittins sprang up.

GITTINS: Objection. This witness can't possibly know what my client was thinking.

WINN: He said, "looked upset." From his perspective that is how the facial expression looked.

KEANE: Continue on.

COBURN: The interrogator walked back to the HIET vehicle. Lieutenant Pantano was walking around. He looked like he was mumbling to himself, talking. I heard him say that he was thinking about having the two individuals go back and search their vehicle. He said it again. Then he clarified it and said, "Yes, I want these two individuals back and to search their vehicle."

KEANE: What happened once you got back to the vehicle?

COBURN: Got back, stopped back at the rear bumper. I held the individuals; Doc Gobles cut off their flex-cuffs.

KEANE: Why did he cut off the flex-cuffs?

COBURN: Because Lieutenant Pantano told us to cut the flex-cuffs off so the two individuals could search their vehicle.

KEANE: What did you think about the fact that you were having these you [two] guys search the vehicle again?

COBURN: I was not pleased with the fact that we had detainees in our possession and they were searching a vehicle that was already searched.

KEANE: Do you think it was strange?

COBURN: Yes, sir.

KEANE: All right. What happened after you cut the flex-cuffs off?

COBURN: Lieutenant Pantano grabbed the one that—as soon as the flex-cuffs were cut off, took the one, put him in position to the front driver side, put him on his knees, and grabbed the other one, put him on the rear driver-side on his knees while they opened doors.

KEANE: What did you do after these guys were put on their knees in the car?

What's he talking about? Were we even at the same car? Gittins and I leaned forward in our chairs.

COBURN: I just watched Lieutenant Pantano. He told the two individuals what to do, explained to them what he wanted them to do.

KEANE: Did he explain to you what he wanted you to do?

COBURN: Yes, sir. He told me and Doc Gobles to face and flank, cover the house.

KEANE: Did you do that?

COBURN: Yes, sir.

KEANE: What happened after you faced away from the vehicle?

COBURN: A few seconds after I turned away, I heard gunfire. I immediately turned around and saw Lieutenant Pantano shooting into the vehicle.

KEANE: What did you do when you saw him shooting?

COBURN: Kind of confused. I stared at him. Looked at the two individuals, saw no movement from the individuals, looked back at him. He was still firing. I was trying to figure out when he was going to stop. I looked back at the house in case there was movement, and I just kept on looking back and forth.

KEANE: Could you tell which guy he shot first?

COBURN: It appeared to me that the person in the rear was shot first.

Gittins was on his feet again.

GITTINS: Objection. The witness has no basis to—wasn't watching, no factual basis, no foundation laid for how he could tell who was shot first.

WINN: Did you see who he shot first?

COBURN: I did not, sir. The shots were fired, and then I turned around.

WINN: Okay.

KEANE: All right. After you saw these guys getting shot, what did you do?

COBURN: I asked Doc what the hell just happened.

KEANE: What did Doc tell you?

COBURN: Doc told me that it was out of my hands and not to worry about it.

KEANE: Then what did you do?

COBURN: Lieutenant Pantano told me to go back to my

north position, covering [the road] and the field, and I complied and went back to the north.

KEANE: What happened when you took up that position?

COBURN: Doc Gobles, I believe, checked the vitals to see if there was any life in the two. I covered the north, verified there was no movement coming at us.

KEANE: Did you observe anything that would lead to the use of deadly force in the situation?

COBURN: No, sir. The car was clear, the individuals were clear, there was no weapons in the area. So no, sir, I did not.

KEANE: Did you observe any hostile acts?

COBURN: No, sir. The two individuals were placed on their knees. And when I turned around, they were moving into the vehicle.

KEANE: Did you see any hostile intent on their part?

COBURN: No, sir.

Patrol Base Impact
Zaidon Province, Iraq
6 May 2004

Easy Company had established a small patrol base in the guest house of Qusay Hussein's bombed-out pleasure palace southeast of Fallujah. The actual palace was a mound of rubble from several direct bomb hits: probably GBU thousand-pounders, judging by the small chunks of concrete. The floor was knee-deep with bronze-mirrored tiles knocked from what was left of the ceilings. There were a couple of dry swimming pools with decorative moldings and some dried-up fountains. All this shit was shattered, and what the local people couldn't steal, they smashed—pulverized was a more accurate term. We had shoveled most of the loose debris into the pools, nearly filling them.

The company had called the base Impact, both for the bomb damage and for the mortars that the Muj kept dropping on us.

The guest house was laced up and down with bullet holes of various sizes. Somebody had done a little killing here—or tried to—probably American Special Operations forces striking ahead of the main invasion force in 2003. I'd seen those guys out at our Fallujah FOB next to the dam. Dudes in faded Levi's and Kevlars, dusty beards, lugging folding-stock M-4 carbines they'd spray-painted tan. They'd bullshitted with our terps in Arabic, conferred with our intel section, and then driven off in their up-armored Humvees, each armed with a long-barreled Ma Deuce.

While the rest of 2/2 pulled back to Camp Fallujah, 3rd Platoon was selected to QRF for the entire regiment encircling the city during the first week after the withdrawal. I was equal parts excited, honored, and terrified to be attached to a company of tanks as their dismounted security unit while we waited like a 911 operator for something bad to happen in a place where bad things happened all the time.

We got a mission, but after the initial pants-crapping, realized that we were just augmenting the under-strength cordon at the northern edge of town. We attached to 2/1 near the rail yard overlooking the Jolan district, where we watched through our binos and scopes as the new Fallujah Brigade and the Muj mingled openly. They'd probably been assessing the damage we'd done with the air strikes and tank probes and were planning how to reinforce the place.

It wouldn't be Hue City anymore. We'd be looking at a fucking mini-Stalingrad on the Euphrates. A lot of Americans and Iraqis would die, I knew, when we finally got orders to retake that place. But I kept my opinion to myself.

When I'd showed up with my platoon at Patrol Base Impact, Captain Weston had been kind of cold toward me. Might have been his reaction to the battalion losing Gunny Baum, KIA, but I suspected it involved the *Time* magazine article. Evidently, it had blown a lot of gaskets in Higher. Paul Quinn-Judge had described one of Easy Company's Marines humming the circus clown tune as we waited to pull out after the assault was canceled.

And, of course, the reporter had quoted my *brilliant* comment comparing our withdrawal with abandoning South Vietnam. Second lieutenants weren't supposed to voice such views in international news magazines. That gave heartburn to colonels, generals, and to those unnamed "senior Pentagon officials" you were always reading about. When Higher got heartburn, ass-chewings ensued, ripping down the echelons, level by level. I could hear it: "Who the *fuck* does that second lieutenant think he is?"

But Captain Weston and I respected each other, and the coldness between us passed.

We settled into life at this primitive Forward Operating Base. Food was MREs. Drink was Gatorade or Hajji bottled water. But the Weapons Platoon machine-gunners had worked hard to make this shithole their home. True Marine ingenuity and creativity at its finest. They'd fashioned a wide tile mosaic of the Marine Corps emblem, the Anchor, Globe, and Eagle, using bits of Qusay's palace. Talk about pride and brotherhood.

One hot afternoon when the sun was setting, a few junior officers and senior NCOs were sitting in the shade, opening the care packages that had just arrived from our families. We all wore Kevlar vests and helmets because an 82 mm mortar round had struck about ten meters outside the wire an hour earlier.

It was an indication of our exhausted mental state and frayed emotions that the conversation focused on the merits of wet wipes versus toilet paper.

Staff Sergeant Glew held up a crushed box of wet wipes. "I think I'm going to get my wife to stock up on these."

"Yeah," Lieutenant Demo said, "but they need to be tough so your fingers don't push through."

From there, the conversation dropped a couple of rungs into scatological humor. Grown men, combat leaders, joking like preadolescents at summer camp. But sometimes keeping our heads empty was a very good thing.

Captain Weston thought that if he assigned each platoon its own shitter—plywood outhouses built by the Seabees—that they would take good care of them, pride of ownership. Didn't happen that way. First Platoon did just shit in the burn barrel; 2nd drew humorous graffiti; and of course my guys in 3rd punched out the screen, and the door broke. They were pissed off at having to wait three or four in line to crap in our shitter when the other two were empty. And nobody liked the flies and stench. Even dragging out the burn barrels twice a day and stoking them with diesel left a shitty haze of smoke over the FOB.

One thing that did amuse me was the only graffiti in our crapper: "In this land of sun and fun, we never flush for Number One."

The day after our wet wipes debate, some cunt dropped another mortar round on the base, and our snipers shot him. A max-range, fucking-A great shot. Hit the guy, knocked him down, but did not kill him. The Muj managed to drag himself to a car and speed off. A couple of klicks down the road, a Marine patrol stopped the car. But they let him go. He claimed that he'd been shot by accident in Latafiyah. To half the scumbags in Iraq, Latafiyah had acquired such a bad rep for Muj casualties that it was easy to say they'd been shot there—and people would believe them.

The grunts in Easy Company had taken to calling it *"Shoot*afiyah."

Probably that wounded Muj had shown up at a Baghdad hospital moaning that trigger-happy Americans had gunned him down, just an innocent peasant. He'd appear on the *CBS Evening News,* solid proof that American troops were out of control. Right, an Iraqi farmboy who just happened to know how to aim and fire an 82 mm mortar.

It was time for the news media to pile on. While Easy Company had been attacking the fortified Muj positions in Fallujah, *60 Minutes* and the *New Yorker* had broken the story that U.S. Army Reserve military police guards at Abu Ghraib Prison had tortured and abused detainees. But the pictures in the media showed intimidation and humiliation, not actual Baathist Party–league torture. Saddam's thugs had ripped out people's tongues, flayed prisoners alive, and jammed them into wood chippers feet first. The detainees in the *60 Minutes* digital photos had been sexually humiliated in an effort to trade violence for embarrassment. It seemed like we were running out of tools, and yet our boys kept dying.

Crushing a little of their Arab machismo by having some female MP corporal ridicule the size of their dicks might seem like a war crime back in New York and Washington. But the fact was such techniques had probably helped obtain information that had saved both American and Iraqi lives. The news media at home failed to realize that the "prisoners" in Iraq were not the same as Martha Stewart serving a few months in a federal playpen. There were no pickpockets, or tax evaders. If you made it to Abu Ghraib, and I knew this by how many of the vermin I detained never did, then you must have done some grisly shit.

Maybe butchering scores of Shia civilians wasn't considered a crime against God to some people. Maybe the term "mortar" or "IED" had been sufficiently overused that someone's calculated decisions to obtain, construct, and emplace the weapon, based on weight, cost, time, opportunity, and the ideal method of transforming Americans into stinking clouds of bloody vapor, were no longer considered evil. Oh, I couldn't forget those pesky Iraqi women and children or the hundreds of police recruits, or peaceful worshippers at the wrong mosque.

People back home just had no idea what evil really looked like, but it sure wasn't Johnny Walnuts serving 5–10 for boosting cars.

But I also realized that damning pictures were spreading across the blogosphere, and that Al-Jazeera was succeeding in firing up the usual America haters.

So, when I'd read the Internet accounts of the exploding Abu Ghraib scandal, I'd been soundly pissed off. A handful of rear-echelon prison guards had thought it would be amusing to take a bunch of pictures of their interrogation techniques to show how tough they were. Fucking *Reserve* MPs. I retained some of my prior enlisted hatred of them. Then I remembered the 1/32 MPs who'd rolled into Latafiyah in their Humvees and kept my platoon from being outflanked and overrun.

After dark in base Impact, the brevity code word "NASCAR" usually sounded over the tac net, signaling a patrol was departing friendly lines—Captain Weston was a big car-racing fan. While a patrol mounted up, other Marines got ready to watch a movie. It was important for all of us to remember that there was more to our lives than this armpit of a country.

We'd set up a portable TV set and hooded it with cut-and-taped MRE cartons to cloak the light from the screen and not draw mortar fire. But, just in case, everyone in the audience lugged his flak, helmet, and weapon, which they'd piled in the dirt between their feet. War and entertainment. J-Lo and a clean rifle bore.

The key to keeping balanced here was being able to unwind just the right amount of tension on the tight internal spring. After Latafiyah and Fallujah, we all realized Iraq had become an unforgiving meat grinder, a kill box the size of California. And we were facing seven months of that. Without wanting to do it, I'd find myself looking at a Marine opening a tray rat or MRE packet and wondering, *Will that kid go home in a bag?*

Paranoia? Maybe. But as an officer, my challenge was to keep the platoon vicious—as they'd been in Fallujah—yet compassionate toward innocent Iraqi civilians, paranoid yet steady. The adage "Just because you think someone is trying to kill you doesn't mean that they aren't" certainly applied. Every day and night. In the case of Easy Company, the enemy was definitely trying to kill us but wasn't succeeding.

A few days earlier, when Captain Weston had come out to this AO, his reconnaissance took him to the site of a Marine convoy that had been hit with a suicide car bomb, which had left a crater four feet deep. The bomb had flipped a LAV-25 and killed two Marines. The hood of the car was blown three hundred meters away, and charred pieces of the jihadi had been blasted up and down the road.

April 2004 had been the bloodiest month of the war to date, which included the multidivision combat of the invasion. In February 2004, twelve Americans had been killed, thirty-three in March. But Coalition KIAs had soared to 127 in April, with 1,200 more wounded in action. The number of mortar attacks, IEDs, and suicide car bombs was mounting steadily.

But with a couple of exceptions, no one at Higher seemed to have a clue about how to stop this. Certainly turning Fallujah over to *friendly* Iraqi forces had been moronic. In the most critical moment of the war, we'd been punked out by the fear of a disintegrating coalition. A useless one at that. The first order of business after a year of missteps should have been establishing security through strength. We'd been handed the opportunity to crush the enemy in Fallujah, and instead we had blinked.

All that the Fallujah handover had accomplished was to buy a few weeks' grace while the politicians in Baghdad pulled their thumb out of their collective ass and prepared to take on "full sovereignty" in June. But it actually also accomplished something else: abandoning Fallujah had revealed the United States as an ineffective occupier. It had telegraphed to the world we didn't have the stomach to inflict the kind of pain required to beat the resistance out of an enemy, a people.

I'd heard all the complex arguments, but I had learned my lesson about pain compliance in the ring. Getting ready for OCS, I sparred with an ex-Marine named Jason who fought semipro in Atlantic City. He outweighed me by almost fifty pounds, but as long as he went soft I could fight him all day. I'd never really hurt him, but I'd tire him out. Then one day, like an idiot, I goaded him into laying one on me. He found his opening and cracked two of my ribs. I fell to the floor like I was going to die. There was no more dancing around. I learned in the ring that things are only lengthy and complicated if you choose to make them that way.

Later, more sophisticated and respected voices than *this lieutenant* would trumpet a particular "oil spot" theory, or that insightful poll, all the while failing to reflect on the most successful counterinsurgency in history, the American Civil War. Chaplain Verhulst, our chaplain, used to remind me that had Sherman not made the pain of rebellion so excruciating, we might still be at war with the South today. Nothing brings a Marine's spirits down like a Navy chaplain telling you the war-fighting plan is being run by pussies. By politicians.

"Right, yes, certainly, Sheik This, Sayyid That, and Ayatollah The Other One. You shall soon be free to practice democracy."

Free? Who was going to guard the new Iraqi freedom from the ani-mals who targeted pilgrims and schoolchildren with their IEDs?

Would Fallujah be free and democratic after June 30, the date when sovereignty would revert to Iraq? Fallujah was an insurgent can-cer. And we'd stuck a little piece of gauze over the putrid lesion and an-nounced that the malignancy had been healed.

Meanwhile, Easy Company patrolled Main Supply Routes Tampa and Mobil, as well as the local side roads, trying to guard the ground between Camp Fallujah, Abu Ghraib, Baghdad International, and Mahmudiyah. A force of 150 Marines was given a mission that would have required a regiment.

And the enemy was quick to recognize that we couldn't protect our logistics routes. They blew bridges and attacked convoys with IEDs and suicide bombers, effectively squeezing off the flow of munitions and food along the road networks. While we tried to choke them, they tried to choke us. After the fighting in April, Easy Company did not have enough 5.56 mm or heavier caliber ammo, mortar rounds, or smoke grenades for extended offensive ops. MREs were down to about a week's supply. It would take time to rebuild the reserves of ma-teriel we'd used up at Fallujah.

The insurgents who had accomplished this tactical success were not disorganized rabble but rather a well-led, well-supplied irregular force that usually matched or surpassed our strength. Most of them were Sunni Arab former soldiers who knew how to read a map, use weapons, move tactically, and exploit our weaknesses.

The worst thing was that we couldn't tell the good guys from the bad. *Maku Ali Baba.* We'd shuffled too many units, too quickly, too many times. We needed more *ownership* of the AOs in order to estab-lish relationships with the locals. Jumping around so much, we couldn't develop the intel needed to conduct raids, so we could not ex-ecute basic security.

Too many promises that we couldn't possibly keep. One thing was sure: we left behind the civilians who'd come over to our side, who'd believed in us. I would always remember that family living next to our company FOB at the Fallujah dam. And I would hope that they had died quickly at the hands of our *allies* in the city.

Who would ever trust us? Until we'd won this war, anyone who'd sided with us would be marked as a traitor.

Every Muj in Iraq knew we were in an entirely *defensive* posture.

Our force protection measures advertised that we were intimidated. And they were not effective. Hey, Abdullah, want to plant an IED or drop a few mortar rounds? Have at it, buddy. The Americans can't stop you, *won't* stop you. The Iraqis now recognized that we would always move on once we'd set up a base. Fill those sandbags and HESCO barriers; rip 'em down and dump them. Mount up. Move out.

Out here in the desert west of Baghdad, our terps brought us the same message from the local people: "We are glad Saddam is gone, but we want you to be gone too. You bring Ali Baba. They come to fight you. But we die."

I watched Jennifer Lopez shaking her ass to a hip-hop beat and thought about the Iraqis' message. That was a tough premise for a liberator to swallow.

Camp Lejeune
27 April 2005

Major Keane now asked Coburn to describe what happened when we stopped the second vehicle, the brown car on the canal road near the arms cache house. Coburn said he and Doc Gobles had removed the Iraqis from the vehicle.

KEANE: All right. What happened when you pulled them out of the car?

COBURN: We were told to take them back up in front of the white sedan, lay them down, search them, and check them out. Me and Doc Gobles took them back up, laid them on their faces, and searched them.

KEANE: Could they see the dead guys?

COBURN: Yes, sir. On the way up, they noticed the vehicle and the dead individuals.

KEANE: What was their demeanor on seeing this?

COBURN: There was about three of the five that were crying. They were a little scared. They had no idea what was going on, sir.

KEANE: What happened after you put them on the ground over there?

COBURN: HIET came up, they talked to them, one or two of them. They said that they didn't know what was going on, that they were painting a house down the road.

KEANE: Did he [Pantano] do anything to the vehicle?

COBURN: The five individuals got in the car. And before they started pulling off, he popped the rear-right tire.

KEANE: How did he do that?

COBURN: With his K-bar [fighting knife] again, sir.

KEANE: Did they drive off on a flat tire?

COBURN: Yes, sir.

KEANE: What happened after that?

COBURN: After that, the items in the house started coming out. I walked back up to where the seven-ton was and helped load up the items.

Patrol Base Impact, Iraq
9 May 2004

I got back to the small base late at night, smoked from a long day, humping in the sun, village to village, cordon and knock . . . *Maku Ali Baba.*

Just outside the company COC, I dumped my gear, watching sweat drip from my face onto the dusty floor. There was stinking steam wafting from my flak jacket. My grenades clanked on the concrete, a sound that once might have been disturbing. Here, it was just part of life. *What the fuck.* That had become our mantra.

Some sleep. When I woke, I was curled up in my flak jacket. No matter how much it stank, I always wrapped it around my head in case an incoming round landed close while I slept. Water and a greasy

MRE beef patty and tepid Mexican macaroni and cheese. I was getting low on hot sauce again.

We were alerted for a night ambush patrol. Intel had read the smoke signals and concluded that some crazy Syrians were escaping Fallujah and planned to hit our camp on the way out. That was the kind of shit I could believe. The Muj with the wild beard whom I'd killed near the Refrigerator wasn't an Iraqi. And back on the Zulu perimeter north of FOB Mahmudiyah—a couple of weeks and a billion years before—a checkpoint had stopped a Syrian in a shiny black Land Cruiser, carrying $500,000 in U.S. hundreds.

So I briefed the squads and we double-checked our weapons, ammo, and gear. I had ten free minutes, so I took off my boots and socks and dropped my sweat-stiff pants. Time to dig out the plastic Gold Bond container and powder my feet and crotch. The treatment was so strong that my nuts burned. Better than open sweat sores.

The "NASCAR" call came over the tac net.

We set up a decent L-shaped ambush—two SAWs, and four M-203s—along the approaches to a bridge. But I didn't like the exposure out here in the moonless dark. So I had one squad lay out claymores to cover our naked asses and I pushed another out on continuous security patrols. We waited all night. No Syrians. In the morning, we found that one of the claymores had its THIS SIDE TOWARD ENEMY business end facing a little school near the highway. That was what happened when you established an ambush at night. As we gathered up the claymores, I knew that the Muj were capable of attacking us from a village school, and that they'd probably have welcomed us tripping a claymore that sent out hundreds of steel balls to slice apart children.

But the image just made me feel sick.

Camp Lejeune
27 April 2005

KEANE: At some point did you—did you write a letter to your wife concerning these events?

COBURN: Yes, sir, approximately three days later.

KEANE: Three days after?

COBURN: Yes, sir.

KEANE: Is that [the] letter you sent to your wife [showing Coburn a copy of the exhibit]?

COBURN: Yes, sir.

KEANE: Why did you send this letter to your wife?

COBURN: I wanted to tell my wife what just happened. I couldn't tell her on the computer or on the phone. So I wrote a letter to her explaining the situation, how important the situation was that I witnessed, and more of a security measure for myself, just in case something happened to me.

KEANE: What do you mean by that?

COBURN: We're in an environment where we are shooting all the time. At some point somebody could realize that I know some information and take it upon themselves to silence me, sir.

KEANE: What was your relationship with Lieutenant Pantano like?

COBURN: We had our ups and downs, sir. We disagreed sometimes, but otherwise we were pretty good to go, sir.

KEANE: Did you sleep near him at night?

COBURN: Yes, sir.

KEANE: Did you have any good times with him?

COBURN: Yes, sir. We had a pretty good relationship.

I glanced at Gittins and Stackhouse. Their expressions were neutral.

KEANE: Did you have a conversation about the facts of that day or the incident that took place with a Lance Corporal Thompson?

COBURN: Yes, sir.

KEANE: How soon after the incident did you have that conversation?

COBURN: With Lance Corporal Thompson, it was about two to three months later, sir.

KEANE: And what did you tell Lance Corporal Thompson?

COBURN: Basically, [I] told him the situation on what happened. I wanted to see what his views were also.

KEANE: What did he do with that information?

COBURN: He worked directly for the battalion commander and the sergeant major, and he passed the information up.

KEANE: Did you request that he do that?

COBURN: I did not, but he said that he might. I told him that whatever he wants to do with the information is up to him.

KEANE: Are you trying to get Lieutenant Pantano—or—why—why—bring this up?

COBURN: Again, sir, I didn't bring it up. I questioned it. I talked to a couple individuals, questioning the situation. I wanted to get their input on what happened. One of those individuals then passed the information up.

Stackhouse wrote on his pad: "use on cross?" Gittins nodded, keeping his eyes on Coburn.

Patrol Base Impact, Iraq
17 May 2004

We raided a water plant on another failed IED hunt. But at least the locals saw us out there. Back at the company FOB, the night was almost cool, the sky full of stars. I was in the mood to chat, to decompress from the raid. Glew was in his bag on the deck by the rubble-filled pool, prepared to roll in if the incoming started. Hamps was underneath the cammie netting, so we couldn't see him and just barely hear him. I had my cigar, lying on my back looking up at the Big Dipper, thinking about how I was going to look at the stars one day with my son. Domenico. My boy.

We shot the shit about the war—about "the exit." We all wanted this to turn out right, but we were worn out, fucking exhausted, and we had only been there for three months.

We joked about starting a rumor. "Hey, if after the June 30th for-sovereignty date, if the Hajjis don't want us here, out we go."

Roger that.

What a difference from the days of World War II. When GIs got on those trains, they weren't coming back until the war was won. The only exit was victory for us, unconditional surrender for the enemy.

The Muj weren't going anywhere. So we patrolled. We pounded on doors and asked our questions. We dug up gardens and turned over hay bales.

A new captain came out with us on patrol and was appalled at our tactics.

"Do you really have to do that?" he'd asked, pointing at a donkey manure pile we'd scattered, searching for mortar rounds and IED parts.

"Yes, sir. Gotta do it. The dumb Muj are dead. We're not gonna find anything under a mattress."

The captain looked skeptical.

"Sorry, sir," I said. "But you haven't been shot at or mortared yet, you just got here."

We continued the patrol. At each house, it was the same deal, *"Maku Ali Baba."*

The people hadn't heard mortar rounds firing, they sure as hell hadn't heard explosions.

But when my terp, Jack, a former Baathist bodyguard, pressed them, more came out. He wasn't one to fuck around. Jack had begged me to kill him before I let the Muj capture him.

Yes, they'd heard the explosions at our base. But they had no idea where the rounds came from. Fucking A, Sherlock. *Lah* . . . the hand on the heart. They never, ever seemed to hear or see the guys firing, but they knew that we were getting hit.

Maybe I wasn't asking the right way. I went back to the first house and began to spread a new message. I began heavy and oppressive as hell, but after five or six houses refined my approach to a message of patriotism and motivation that drew on the famous Iraqi male ego. My spiel went something like this:

"I have a problem." I pointed west. "My base has been mortared from this area four times. Two of them happened yesterday. I know the mortar rounds came from here. My spotters have seen them and the only reason we have not bombed you is that we do not want to hurt your families."

Some of the men stared into my eyes, some watched the chickens scratching in the dirt.

"Here is my problem," I continued. *"I know that you know about* these attacks and you are not helping me. This is a small community, a village. You are all related. Someone knows something . . . So this is what I am going to do . . ."

I paused, letting the tension expand.

"If we are attacked again from this area . . . if rounds are shot from your fields . . . I will arrest every man. Every single one of you will be cuffed and blindfolded and marched away in front of your family to Abu Ghraib. All of you. Every man in this area."

The words "Abu Ghraib" definitely got their attention.

"My problem will become your problem," I said in a reasonable tone. "*You* can solve this by taking charge of your lives, your destinies. You each have an AK-47 to protect your families. You all know each other. You know who belongs and who doesn't. You know who is firing mortars. If he is your friend, *stop him.* If he is a stranger who drives here, *kill him."*

This wasn't what most of them wanted to hear. But they were going to listen.

"It is time for you to take responsibility for your homes," I continued. "This is your freedom. We have fought for it in your place. Now you must stand up and fight for it yourself. If you are not willing to fight for it, to protect your homes and communities, then we will take that freedom away."

This argument always grabbed their attention.

"I will put you in jail in front of your families. The choice is yours. Be a strong Iraqi man. Solve this problem . . . I don't care how. But if you do not, then *you* will suffer with *me."*

After Jack finished translating my civics lesson, it was remarkable how many people started to talk. To speculate. There had been strange "trucks," "one afternoon," late "one night," "over here," "over there." It turned out that the Muj roaches were everywhere and now these people were willing to help.

Back at the base, I wrote in my journal:

EVERYONE RESPECTS FORCE. EVERYONE. YOU DON'T HAVE TO LIKE IT. BUT YOU CAN'T DENY IT.

Camp Lejeune
27 April 2005

KEANE: When he was firing his weapon, do you recall what mode the selector switch was on?

COBURN: The weapon was on burst, sir.

KEANE: Do you recall how many rounds he fired?

COBURN: Two magazines worth, sir, approximately sixty rounds.

Major Keane addressed Major Winn. "At this time, I would like him to demonstrate what he observed shooting, using the ISMT trainer."

This was a full-size M-16 training simulator that operated on compressed gas, which made sounds similar to, but not as loud as, an actual weapon firing. Following Keane's order, Coburn lifted the ISMT trainer.

KEANE: Sergeant Coburn, stand where you observed Lieutenant Pantano—assuming this is still the car, stand where Lieutenant Pantano was standing.

Coburn stepped forward and stood three or four feet from the table representing the hypothetical vehicle.

KEANE: All right. Load the magazine in the weapon.

As Coburn inserted a simulated thirty-round magazine, Gittins rose and addressed Major Winn.

GITTINS: Sir, I object to this.

WINN: Note the objection for [the] record.

GITTINS: This witness has a motivation not to fire as fast as my client. And we don't know that he is as qualified as my client.

Now *that* was the truth.

WINN: I am going to allow the demonstration to continue.

KEANE: Okay. When I give you the word, start firing as you observed it. Go.

Coburn began firing, slow, deliberate bursts, with definite pauses in between—almost like he was on the range.

COBURN: He switched magazines.

Coburn continued firing, soft puffs of compressed gas. Popp-oppop . . . another. Another. I could hear the clickety-click of the court reporter's keyboard. As Coburn neared the end of the second mag, he actually seemed to slow further.

KEANE: Thanks, you can return the weapon and have a
            seat. No further questions.

Patrol Base Impact, Iraq
18 May 2004

We went out on counter-mortar patrol that afternoon. The sun was like a heat lamp, and the ground that had been moist enough for the farmers to plow a few days earlier was now hard as concrete.

The first place we headed was the house we'd tossed ten days before. Then, we had found two AKs, an assortment of ammo, some Saddam Hussein fan-club pictures, and a photo of a young dude in Republican Guard cammies proudly holding a Dragunov sniper rifle. Supposedly, that portrait dated to the first Gulf War. Just ancient history.

Right, without a doubt. And, of course, the guy in question was "working." Only the wife and five children had been at home when we'd arrived that day. But I expected Abdul the Sniper to appear before dark.

"Honey, I'm home, killed two Americans today and maimed seven more. What's for dinner?"

Well, when daddy-o did show up he didn't know anything about the photo of him with the sniper rifle or the pictures of Saddam.

But common sense told us that this guy was a problem, or at the very least he needed to be watched closely. Other than having an extra AK, however, he hadn't broken any law, so he was innocent until proven guilty—just like this was Iowa or Tennessee. I confiscated his

ID card and showed it to my guys. "Study this shitbird's face." We'd probably want to chat with him again if we started taking well-aimed fire.

He was thirtyish, impassive, tough, and unflinching. For over a week, I carried that guy's ID card because I knew he was a threat.

He was a sniper and could be damned dangerous. And if any of my guys started dropping from 7.62 mm fever, I was coming right back to the village and burning the whole fucking house down. I looked at the picture often, feeling his power and his rage. He had a vaguely Russian look. Thick, coarse, and widely spaced features that had a hint of Mongol or Asian influence. Maybe his father had been a Soviet advisor or something intriguing. Probably not.

Now, ten days later, neither the Sniper nor his wife was there, but the kids and their granny were. The kids. I felt a wave of pity and nausea. The youngest baby's face was badly bitten by flies, and they were swarming all over its snot-running nose and eyes. A malnourished three-year-old carried the baby. She looked like a stunted doll holding an even smaller doll. The baby, wrapped in a stinking blanket, was trying to suckle on the three-year-old.

The old grandmother with her tattooed chin and forehead gave me a song and dance as we asked about weapons and Ali Baba and things of that nature.

She told me that Saddam had killed "four of my five children."

I could not tell if she meant those sons had been executed or had died in the long string of Saddam's wars, starting in the 1980s during the bloody struggle with Iran. Sniper Joe the Dragunov Man was her last surviving child. But, she said, I'd been intimidating him in order to find weapons. How could I possibly be like one of Saddam's thugs, trying to shake him down?

I looked at Jack. *Can I believe her?* He remained silent. How could she explain the pictures of Saddam? Had the local imam put him up for sainthood?

She shrugged. "From before . . ." Unspoken was the explanation that the portraits of Saddam were protective totems against the Muj.

And here I was, leading heavily armed men into this crappy little farmhouse.

Exactly how am I different than the Baathists? They would have taken the suspect out and shot him on the spot. I wanted to win him over . . . or at least get him to shift into neutral, so that he didn't kill any of my guys and I didn't have to write letters to the parents to explain that I'd done my best—but failed—to save their son's life.

But am I the problem now? Had I become the beast? Or was I doing what I had to do to save lives?

Like the other villagers to whom I'd taught my little civics class, that young man had a choice. He could help us fight for a new Iraq. Or he could be part of the problem, part of the old way, and he would surely die.

How dare he employ his mother, trying to make me feel guilty for doing my job and keeping my boys alive? But I did feel guilty that this old woman had to explain herself, plead, to bob and weave for me and spin tales, bat her eyelashes and show her painted face in front of these young men, my Marines. A wrinkled courtesan with a court of stinking foreign troops.

The stooped widow had to use her stunted grandchildren as props in her dance. Her black *abaya* was her stage, her tattoos her makeup. Her voice actually became lilting, and she laughed as she wove her story, as she tried to befriend me to make sure that I would not take her son away. Just as so many beasts had done with her other sons before me.

No. Don't you understand, we are here, willing to give our lives for you. For your freedom. We are not the monsters that the war makes us. We just want to help.

But can I believe her?

She had given this dance before, a mother defending her son. No one was going to take her baby. Maybe *she* felt guilty that she had not fought harder or resisted before, maybe this time he really was all she had left and it wasn't fair that Allah could let the mother outlive her children.

I felt my anger and resolve soften and pulled back the Velcro tab to open my flak jacket. The hard layers of ceramic and sweat-soaked Kevlar parted to reveal my spongy wet interior. I reached into the chest pocket on my blouse that was three shades of sweat darker, soaked entirely through. With all the dried salt at the collar and arm holes, I felt like a margarita glass, as I withdrew the ID card with the damp and dog-eared picture of her son.

The old woman was ecstatic. Obviously, I knew what it was to love a son.

I found myself compelled to mumble an apology for any *misunderstanding* about her boy.

But as we formed up the squad to move out into the hair-dryer heat of the afternoon, I still couldn't decide if I'd made a friend or had instead been conned by a pro. Either way, I still had a mission, a duty to my troops.

I asked Jack to translate carefully. "If there is another attack, I will take your son to Abu Ghraib," I said, emphasizing the name of the prison.

She stared at me, her tattooed face slack. Could the widow be moved by the earnest threats of a clean-shaven foreign soldier when her family had already suffered so much under Saddam?

She and her son had lied to me about weapons, and I had judged them to be hostile. But given their history, how could they ever trust a government or a soldier? Any government? Any soldier? How could she be expected to tell the truth? Did she even know what the truth was?

Camp Lejeune
27 April 2005

Charlie Gittins began his cross-examination of Coburn, speaking softly and slowly, but with a certain cold precision.

GITTINS: I believe you were asked if you had—you said, you served two combat tours in Iraq, in response to trial counsel's question?

COBURN: Yes, sir.

GITTINS: On your first tour to Iraq in OIF, did you actually leave the ship?

COBURN: No, sir. We did anti-mine ship laying [missions], sir.

GITTINS: Did your battalion leave the ship?

COBURN: Yes, sir. I was the senior armory custodian at the time and stayed back with the weapons.

GITTINS: So when you responded to the trial counsel that you had done a prior combat tour in Iraq, that is not true; is it?

COBURN: It was a combat tour. Yes, sir.
GITTINS: In Iraq, sir?

Gittins's voice was rising, his words coming more rapidly.

COBURN: OIF I is considered a combat tour, sir.
GITTINS: Did you serve a combat tour in Iraq, sir?
COBURN: I was on the outside of Iraq, considered Iraq, sir.
GITTINS: So you didn't actually land, did you?
COBURN: I did not land. No, sir.
GITTINS: You remained behind as the ship's representative for your ship's spaces; correct?
COBURN: Yes, sir. I was the senior man.
GITTINS: So my question was, you were not involved in combat operations during OIF I; correct?
COBURN: No, sir.
GITTINS: You liked working at the armory because you were on your own and nobody is going, "I want this done now," correct?
COBURN: I liked working at the armory because it was me. There was really nobody in charge of me, everything was up to me.
GITTINS: Right. You don't like people telling you what to do; correct?

Coburn began to roll his tongue against the inside of his cheeks, a nervous tic that made him look like a chipmunk.

COBURN: I don't like people telling me what to do when I am already doing it, sir.
GITTINS: So the armory was the right place to be because you could do what you wanted to do when you wanted to [do] it; correct?
COBURN: Yes, sir.
GITTINS: You want to get out of the infantry because it does not complement your personality; is that true?
COBURN: That is what my wife says. Yes, sir.
GITTINS: Have you said that?
COBURN: I agree with her.

GITTINS: Have you said that? My question was, Have you said that?

COBURN: Not in those words. But I do agree with that sentence, sir.

GITTINS: You feel like it doesn't complement you because you don't need to show yourself like a lot of people do to scream and yell to be effective; isn't that true?

COBURN: That is true, sir.

GITTINS: You have wanted to be assigned to some other duty that would complement your personality better; correct?

COBURN: Yes, sir.

GITTINS: Would it be your testimony that you believe that your platoon sergeant, platoon commander, and company commander thought you were weak because you didn't yell?

COBURN: I was not given that interpretation, sir.

GITTINS: There was another reason, besides the fact that you didn't yell, that they thought you were [a] weak performer?

COBURN: I didn't know they thought [of] me as a weak performer until I had my fitrep, sir.

GITTINS: You didn't know that until you had your fitness report, sir?

COBURN: Yes, sir.

Gittins studied his notes.

GITTINS: Is it true, sir, that on the 8th of November, 2003, you were counseled by your company commander for your lack of leadership due to improper accountability of Marines in the platoon, false numbers, and accountability of morning reports to the company and platoon commander, ultimately rosters and info to platoon commander, not informing platoon commander of what is going on in the platoon on a daily basis, and overall lack of confi-

dence and leadership in regards to your handling
of junior Marines?

COBURN: Yes, sir. I did have a Page Eleven [performance
counseling report].

GITTINS: So you were counseled? So before you received
your fitness report, your company commander did
counsel you on 031108, that would be November
8th, 2003; correct?

Coburn was rolling his tongue inside his cheeks again.

COBURN: Yes, sir.

GITTINS: You were also counseled on the 3rd of November,
five days before, for the following deficiencies:
poor leadership, poor communication skills toward the chain of command, and not performing
to the standards of your pay grade. Specifically,
"subject named Marine failed in his duties as
platoon sergeant to properly brief his Marines so
that they could plan for future training evolutions?"

COBURN: Yes, sir.

GITTINS: That was Captain Weston as well; correct?

COBURN: Yes, sir.

GITTINS: He was your company commander at [the] time?

COBURN: Yes, sir.

GITTINS: So is it your testimony—my question to you before was, were you aware of other reasons why
your platoon sergeant, platoon commander, and
company commander thought you were weak?
And you said, Not before you received your fitness report. That was inaccurate; wasn't it?

COBURN: I didn't consider myself weak; so . . .

GITTINS: Is it your testimony that, prior to Lieutenant Pantano arriving in your platoon, you were doing a
good job as a squad leader?

COBURN: Before he showed up, I was not a squad leader at
the time.

GITTINS: Have you told anyone that Lieutenant Pantano has a split personality?

COBURN: Not that I recall, sir.

GITTINS: Not that you recall? Did you tell Mr. Fishman on the 15th of March, "He had a split personality. He would come up to you and talk all nice and say, 'Hey, how you doing?' Not to say anything bad, but when he talks to you one-on-one or quiet-like he sounds kind of gay. The tone in his voice, he would always ask me—I don't understand it. He would always ask me, 'Hey, how are you doing? You okay?' 'Yeah, I am doing fine.' Where the hell did that come out of? Am I looking like I am not? But he would always ask me in a quiet voice, 'You okay? Any problems going on?' Leave me alone. Even back in the rear, he got pulled out of the unit, and I saw him and he was like, 'How you doing?' " Do you remember saying that to Mr. Fishman?

COBURN: Yes, sir.

Patrol Base Impact, Iraq
25 May 2004

"It's so hot, I'm three degrees away from hell," Staff Sergeant Jason, the Amtrack section leader, yelled over the clanking roar of the "armored" personnel carrier. Even in the dark, the metal of the vehicle radiated back the long day's soak in the sun.

I'd been scrambled at 2100 hours to take a squad and a section of Tracs and link up with one of my squads on patrol. Battalion wanted us to have a platoon-size force out. Show some muscle along the MSRs. Fuck the careful rest rotation plan I'd drawn up for my tired men.

We'd pushed out in the Amtracks, feeling pretty strong until we remembered that they were just bigger targets. Amtracks couldn't survive IEDs or RPGs, so as Captain Skaggs, one of our Abrams tank officers, put it, we were just "neatly packaged for destruction." Cheery thought.

We set up an overwatch of the highway and began to take some small-arms fire. I was confident from the sounds that it was friendly, probably just M-16s and SAWs. But I remembered those LAV 25 mm chain-gun rounds zinging by my head so long before in Kuwait.

Are there any LAVs out here? Nobody knew shit. I was feeling old.

Then I saw four Humvees sneaking up a trail with their lights off. The squads were dug in around these big steel-and-aluminum coffins and I was up on the roof watching these Humvees through my NVGs. At first I was concerned they might have been stolen. A lot of American gear had been disappearing after attacks, and my biggest fear was having some *American* patrol roll up on us and having them blow a "friendly" bomb. Real friendly. After a Mexican standoff, I sent a team out to approach the vehicles and make contact.

My guys started flashing their IR signals and got no response. They flashed red-lens. No response. They continued to approach until they were right on these jackasses, and finally they were noticed. Thank God they weren't shot. Turns out, in an effort to beef up security, that our battalion had been given a new "partner," although no one knew it, not even the battalion.

We'd been on the radio the entire time asking who the fuck these Humvees were, and they were as curious as we were. In fact the unit, led by a Lieutenant Gunn, was with the 45 ADA (Air Defense Artillery), and they had just received the mission to patrol Tampa.

Well, shit. I said, "This is our turf. We're 2/2, baby, the Warlords."

Jesus H. . . . They didn't even have maps or really understand what they were doing. So we set them straight and sent them on their way, another bump in the night, just grateful that the firing earlier hadn't hurt anybody.

The next day we searched some houses and found some unexploded rockets in a farmer's field that required us baking in the sun for six damn hours while we waited for EOD to come from another site where they had been blowing up bombs to come blow up these munitions. EOD, the hardest-working guys in Iraq. Work all day, all night. Make one tiny mistake and you are hamburger.

We searched some houses. Sun, dust, baking heat. *Maku . . . Maku . . . .*

And then later that afternoon, we set up a checkpoint across from a ghetto-like village near Abu Ghraib. We started receiving sporadic small-arms harassing fire from some housing projects on the far side of the six-lane highway. It wasn't a sniper because no one went down, but the dust puffs were close, and it really pissed me off.

Here I was with clumsy, supposedly powerful armor, yet there was nothing I could do. I couldn't cross the road, because that was not my AO over there, and those buildings were too close to the prison for me to shoot up with our M-240s and M-203s. And I didn't want to take my two squads as dismounts and get sucked into an ambush in a ghetto with one of those APCs burning for the news cameras.

If I'd felt that we would have been supported, been able to call on forces to cordon off the area and attack, I would have moved out smartly. But that wasn't our mission and we did not have the man-power. Period. And Mission has priority, even over killing the enemy. I didn't want to stay out here at the checkpoint just to show them I had bigger balls. That wasn't true. I *totally* wanted to remain here, but I knew if one of my kids got hit and we had nothing tactically to show for it, I would be wrecked.

So, short of firing heavy machine guns and 40 mm grenades into a housing complex, I had no choice but to move farther down the road. Here I was, representing the greatest military power in the world, and I was being displaced by a lone gunman—even though I had superior forces and weapons. In combat, there are no good choices. You are constantly choosing between two or more bad things. We pulled back five hundred meters, and soon we were relieved by 2nd Platoon, who came to play with the Tracs.

We took over 2nd's Humvees for the return trip. As we were cruising back in a tactical column, I was in the tail vehicle with Corporal Trent. We passed the Four Corners Intersection with its usual spread of vegetable stall carts and bullshitting vendors. About another two klicks down the road and I was picking up the handset to my radio when, Ka-BOOM.

"What the fuck was *that*?" I shouted to Trent. I was on the radio: in fact, it could have been my radio call that set it off.

Fuck!

IED.

Ambush?

Why aren't I dead?

Why wouldn't those other fucking vehicles stop so we could get in the fight? Didn't they hear it? Goddammit, *stop*.

I was the tail-end Charlie, and no one in our truck seemed to be wounded. We set up security as the other trucks wheeled in to cordon. The bitch about IEDs was the secondary or tertiary attacks that often accompanied them. Sometimes these were more bombs, sometimes they were ambushers with RPGs.

In this instance, our cordon found nothing but country roads and lots of berms and canals. It was easy to see the crater in the road and there was still red det cord sticking out of the ground.

Det cord was explosive fashioned into a line, so that a piece could be wrapped around a tree to cut it in half, or a Muj could run a hundred-foot length of it from a detonator up to a motorcycle battery to a firing device inserted into the nose cones of three South African 133 mm artillery shells.

Our IED today hadn't been the usual three-shell blast. So there were probably at least two shells still in the ground. That explained the partial det—when only some of a firing system or an IED went off, leaving the bulk of the explosive live and ready.

That was why I was still alive. Because they fucked up, not because they didn't try. They just weren't as lucky as I was that day.

After the Boer War, Churchill commented, "There is nothing more exhilarating than to be shot at without result." In other words, the only thing that kept you alive was the enemy's misfortune.

Sergeant Word located the det cord and the demo charge, and we called in the IED report to Easy Company. EOD was dispatched and it would no doubt take hours to get there and then hours more to do their magic. They would run a robot out to the site and drop some fresh explosive with a time fuse in order to blow the still-buried shells.

I had to face the ugly truth that I'd done a lot of stupid shit that day. Maybe I was tired from being shot at twice and waiting for EOD all afternoon. Maybe it was hot, and maybe I just didn't give a shit anymore. But I had walked up to that IED and I'd looked at the crater that was blown and found the wires that led away from where the det cord explosion had started back to the motorcycle battery hooked up to a Motorola 5620 Talkabout handheld radio you could buy at Wal-Mart or RadioShack—or any souk in Damascus. Who would ever imagine they'd be blown up by a toy whose "batteries were not included." Wow. Some cunt had sat in the weeds, or an oncoming car, or at the little soda stand two klicks up the road, and when my truck got to just the right spot, they'd pushed the button. In that moment they should have killed me and the other four Marines in my lightly armored Humvee.

Instead, the IED sent a shower of shrapnel and rocks but not enough to break skin, and the real killer payload remained dormant and buried in the roadside. That day someone had deliberately tried to blow me up. Once again, I was feeling the personal nature of war. It wasn't big blue arrows on a digital screen. It was personal.

And yes, when I got back to the base that night and dumped my reeking flak jacket, we were mortared. In *twenty-four* hours: shot at twice, IED'd, and mortared. That kind of shit happened in one fight all the time, but this was theoretically by different people in different places. *That's a lot of hate.*

I'd been feeling pretty lucky, but I was never more glad to see the chaplain. He gave a small sermon in the shade of a guard tower, his altar a stack of MRE boxes. There were only three of us there; the rest were on patrol, on guard, or preparing to do one or the other.

"Juice or wine?" Lieutenant Verhulst asked.

I couldn't have blurted out "Wine!" any faster.

Camp Lejeune
27 April 2005

GITTINS: So you did tell Mr. Fishman that you felt Lieutenant Pantano had a split personality; correct?

COBURN: Yes, sir.

GITTINS: The first personality was that he was quiet and he would ask you how you are doing; right?

COBURN: Yes, sir.

GITTINS: You didn't like that, did you?

COBURN: I didn't like somebody coming up to me asking me if—it seemed like I had a problem and I didn't know about it.

GITTINS: You didn't like Lieutenant Pantano, your platoon commander, coming up to you and ask, "Hey, how are you doing?"

COBURN: Not every—not all the time. No.

GITTINS: You understood that your platoon commander's job was to take care of the welfare of his Marines; correct?

COBURN: Yes, sir.

GITTINS: And you didn't like him to do it; did you?

COBURN: Not—not all the time. No, sir.

GITTINS: You thought it made him sound gay because he talked to you and asked you how you were doing; isn't that true?

COBURN: I didn't use that as a reference to Lieutenant Pantano.

GITTINS: Sir, did you say, "Not to say anything bad, when he talks to you one on one or quiet-like, he sounds kind of gay." Did you say that to Mr. Fishman on the 15th of March 2005, sir?

COBURN: I did, yes, sir.

GITTINS: You have also told—the other part of the personality was, quote, "the frigging hard-core personality, his General Patton personality. He had his mix. Every once in a while, he would break back into his enlisted and say, this is bullshit. General Mattis had this freaking gas mask Wednesday thing. We had to wear gas masks on Wednesday, like Wednesday is the only day of the week we are going to get gassed." Lieutenant Pantano made you PT in a gas mask, isn't that true?

COBURN: Yes, sir.

GITTINS: You didn't like it because you thought gas mask Wednesdays, that General Mattis determined were appropriate, were not appropriate; correct?

COBURN: I did not think that gas mask Wednesday had any relevance to our mission in Iraq. No, sir.

GITTINS: Did you tell Mr. Fishman on the 15th of March that you see Lieutenant Pantano as the type that would hang out in the Village, one of those thespian-type people, one of those artsy, I am going to hang out at a drama club. I see him hanging out in the Village with those kind of people, hanging out, a lot of freaks down in the Village. Did you say that to Mr. Fishman?

COBURN: Yes, sir.

GITTINS: Sir, do you understand that it is [a] violation of the Uniform Code of Military Justice to be dis-

respectful toward an officer in the United States
Marines?

COBURN: I was not being disrespectful, sir.

GITTINS: You don't think it is disrespectful to call your—a
lieutenant in the Marines, "He is quiet like he
sounds kind of gay." You don't think that is disrespectful, sir?

COBURN: No, sir.

GITTINS: You don't?

COBURN: No, sir. He was talking to me quietly.

GITTINS: What is a "thespian-type" person?

COBURN: More of a renaissance type of person, someone
who likes art, all that kind of stuff, theater.

Patrol Base Impact, Iraq
June 2004

Higher seemed determined to demonstrate that we had successfully
tamped down enemy resistance in this part of Zaidon Province. So we
conducted groundbreakings at schools and paid to repair mosques
damaged in the April fighting. The public works stuff had been rewarding. Or so it seemed.

One day I met with Sheik "Tommy Gun" Turfa, my grunts' epithet
for the slippery tribal leader. That night Sergeant Word was on a
counter-IED patrol, which meant walking along the shoulder of the
road with flashlights, looking for fresh digging or wires. Word's squad
found an IED and then promptly set up a VCP to see who they could
catch. Within minutes, they'd stopped a car with an AK between the
driver and passenger and a shovel with freshly caked dirt. Our two
Iraqis were lucky twice: first, the dirt didn't match the mud around the
IED, and second, Sheik Turfa rolled up.

I cut off their hand-on-heart denials and began the whole empow-
erment/responsibility shtick: "What kind of sheik are you that you
can't even stop an IED being buried three hundred meters from your
house? What kind of man lets that happen?"

Back and forth. He claimed someone was trying to "poison" our relationship. More specifically, grab the $30,000 of U.S. taxpayers'
money we'd just given him to rebuild a school.

I was angry. The school project was going to be announced the next morning, and this IED was clearly meant for us. We started banging on all the neighboring houses and the sheik was clearly disturbed and trying to help us get to the bottom of this shit. We let the two drivers go, after the sheik's assurances they were just farmers. I reempowered him by letting the two men know that the sheik was the only reason they were not going to Abu Ghraib for driving around with an AK-47. That was illegal. But I wouldn't have driven around unarmed, day or night. This was a dangerous neighborhood.

The sheik took us to a house directly across from the IED. Even in the dark we could see the red det cord leading into several shells. We didn't have a choice. We had to scour the area—very carefully—and make sure we knew no one was waiting to blow the bomb before we got EOD in here.

We knocked on the house, weapons ready. The scene was just as tragic as I could imagine. There was a twelve-year-old boy inside, shaking in fear at the sight of our weapons. Why was he guarding the Muj detonator? Because he'd been coerced: insurgents had just machine-gunned the boy's father in front of the family. True? Coincidence with the IED? Probably not. Poor kid, if what he was claiming was true at least. We disarmed the detonator and moved on.

BBC-TV had been rolling with us for a week. They got to show their audience footage of us getting mortared. The word was that some of their segments had been seen on BBC International back at Camp Fallujah. Paul Wood, the correspondent, and I had a mutual friend. Chris Cobb-Smith was managing security for the "Beeb," the job he used to do for me.

I told Paul to pass a message for me: "Isn't it great that I'm now protecting Chris's journalists in Iraq after he protected mine in Afghanistan and Pakistan?"

But I found it weird how Europeans always sought a way to criticize us. I had Paul and his cameraman out on a patrol with us, and he was constantly fishing for comments from me. Finally, he made a claim bound to piss us off: "You Marines are good, but a British patrol would have done things much differently."

"Really?" I said. "Paul, how long have the Brits been fighting in Northern Ireland?"

"Thirty years," he said.

I pounced. "Seems like a long time. How do *you* define success?"

That was my most direct rhetorical trap. Another more subtle demonstration of the European reporter's bias came in the form of a simple question. "Paul, what do you think will happen here in three months? And in three years?"

I sure wasn't prepared for the intensity of his diatribe. He launched into a pent-up rant about how *all* of the U.S. Iraqi appointees would soon be assassinated and that in three years Iraq would be a "failed state." So much for objectivity.

After about ten minutes of walking in silence, he asked the same question, and I replied simply, "I don't know."

And the realization of his bias washed over him. After that my men started calling me "Paul Revere."

On the night of June 18, Fox News announced the details of Saudi terrorists shooting and beheading an American defense contractor in Riyadh. The anchor was breathless. This was good for the news business.

An hour later, Captain Weston got an urgent call over the tac radio net. I was to return ASAP to Battalion Rear at Camp Fallujah. Naval Criminal Investigative Service personnel were conducting an "investigation" of the April 15 shooting.

"How long will I be there, sir?"

"Until this gets sorted out."

I felt like *I* had just been beheaded.

Early that morning, I packed using the red-lens flashlight. Your basic fucking thief in the night. I hated it. This was not how I was supposed to leave Easy Company. Not packing silently in the predawn hours, so I didn't wake the others, not like this.

Getting ready to catch a ride to Camp Fallujah, the sprawling headquarters of all Marine forces in Iraq, I encountered clusters of my men . . . Williams, Andrado, Anderson, Perry, Aguirre . . . Glew. They hovered around me, and it was hard not to cry.

I took off my grenades and my pop-up flares and gave them to Staff Sergeant Glew.

"Hope you won't need them. I hope you guys are gonna stay loose out here."

As a gag, one of my men had written Coburn's name on a grenade. My gut contracted. Coburn had already been pulled out of the platoon, but just seeing his name scrawled on the apple-shaped grenade made me sick. With all the heat coming down on me, that was the last thing I needed. I scribbled furiously over the name with black marker. Trying to make the entire situation disappear.

Captain Weston had told me something awesome, one of many things that he would say or do over the coming months that saved my soul from the pain and humiliation of being torn from my men. Weston had spoken to the battalion commander, who'd asked him if he needed a new platoon commander lieutenant.

"No, sir," Weston said he'd replied.

That was because I had done such a good job with the platoon and with Staff Sergeant Glew that they would be fine until I returned. Another saving grace was that Major Neil, the operations officer, was eager to put me to work in the battalion COC. Feeling wanted in an environment of extreme loss was more important for my emotional survival than I would ever know. And I would never be able to sufficiently thank these two fine officers for the trust they had placed in me.

That week I was also able to talk to my son on his second birthday. Domenico was buzzing about his party and his Thomas the Train cake. The whole family had converged in New York. And as great as it was to hear everyone's voice, it was hard to tell them, "Everything is fine."

Fine, right. One day, I was in combat leading forty Marines, and the next, I had been taken from my men to be investigated.

Later that day, I heard that 3rd Platoon had suffered its first casualties. And I hadn't been with my guys.

I was in the chow hall at Camp Fallujah eating lunch with Mulvaney, one of my fellow platoon commanders from TBS and IOC. He got buzzed on his radio to fire up the Quick Reaction Force. Off he went. I wallowed in my uselessness, dumped my tray of uneaten chow, and headed to the COC to see what was going on. Then I heard a captain yelling in the hallway, "Easy has taken casualties." I raced down to the COC, which was getting crowded as news spread of Marines in contact. The unit log looked like this:

> 1215 EASY MORTARED FROM SOUTH
> 1220 EASY MORTARED FROM NORTH

Twice. Hadn't seen that before

> 1223 EASY 3 QRFS
> 1227 EASY 3 AMBUSHED

My heart was thudding, slow, then fast. I wanted to scream.

My boys had been ambushed QRFing the mortars. CAAT Blue swooped down from the north in their gun trucks, and initial reports of enemy KIAs had the room cheering. Then elation subsided, as all that was found were blood trails. The enemy, once again, had faded away, dragging their dead and wounded with them. By all accounts it was a platoon-plus–sized element, at least thirty.

(Later investigation revealed that the insurgents had dug fighting holes for their crew-served weapons. One was a 12.7 mm heavy machine gun that was able to punch through the titanium armor on the big truck. That was what wounded our Marines.)

A platoon of insurgents . . . *Why?* My only thought was that they hoped the BBC was still with us. If they could kill some Marines in front of a news crew, a European news crew no less, they knew they would score big points. The Marines had been notoriously tight-lipped about the where, when, and how of our casualties. Usually, the only information we released was that Marines had been killed or wounded "conducting security operations in the Al Anbar Province."

That was our way of hiding the blood trails.

Much later, I got a note from Sergeant Word describing the ambush. His message carried the ragged immediacy of an ambush and counter-ambush.

FOB took mortars that were very well adjusted. So the CO told Glew to get someone out and find them. So Glew told 2nd squad to load up, but after a couple of min. they were taking too slow so 1st squad loaded the trucks Victor 1: Word, McPherson, Chicas, Brown, Gocadack. Victor 2: Magdaleno, Sacchi, Perry. Victor 3 (7-ton): Doc, a driver, Smith, Johnson. Victor 4: Braun, Davis, Dunham. We went to the south found nothing & went to the north at FOB exit north on "Bristol." We held there to get a grid from the CO when all hell broke loose. They started the ambush with an RPG aimed at Victor 1 which bounced off the front of it, then it was pure hell. Chicas' bolt blew up. He switched to his 40 mm and had a direct hit on two guys, it was a great shot. Then the 7-ton hauled ass out of the fight and we moved to block the rounds while it went back to the FOB. I knew something was wrong but did not know what. But what happened was Johnson was trying to jump over the center set to get where he could fire got hit several times in the right arm and he went down. Smith then stopped firing and started to treat Johnson while his truck was under heavy .50 cal [12.7 mm] AK-47, RPG, and 7.62 machine gun rounds. A .50 cal armor piercing round went through the side of the truck and fragged and several pieces of frag hit him in the face and he fell. Johnson tried to help him out. Doc saw what happened and pulled the machine gunner down and grabbed his medic bag and crawled through gunners hole and started to apply life saving aid. He had a tourniquet on Johnson and field dressing on Smith by the 3 min drive back to the FOB, that was when I heard on the net that they were calling in a medevac, we were still in the fight when dust off came, no one knew what happened but me until we got back to the FOB.

Reading the message, I could almost hear the sounds and feel the wild frenzy of the ambush.

Johnson and Smith were both urgent casualties and air-casevaced to the surgical hospital in Baghdad. Johnson was in risk of losing his arm and Smith's helmet and eye protection had disintegrated into his face.

That night, among the squawking radios in the battalion COC, I thought about the ambush and my platoon. Had I been there, maybe just maybe I could have made a difference in the outcome. On the other hand, maybe we would have been casualties whether I'd been there or not. Or maybe I would have been killed trying to press an attack.

Maybe Domenico's birthday present was that his daddy was still alive. Maybe the wretched truth in sitting here on a folding chair in a Camp Fallujah tent, while my men fought for their lives, was that this April 15 shooting investigation had saved my life. Maybe killing those two insurgents at the white car beside the darkening canal had saved my life twice. That day, and this day, Father's Day.

Camp Lejeune
27 April 2005

Gittins continued his cross-examination of Coburn, who was now obviously shaken.

GITTINS: You have been given an order not to talk to the press; true?

COBURN: About the case. Yes, sir.

GITTINS: Who gave you that order?

COBURN: Major Keane did, sir.

GITTINS: Just Major Keane?

COBURN: And Public Affairs.

GITTINS: So two commissioned officers, in February 2005, gave you an order not to speak to the press about this case?

COBURN: Yes, sir.

GITTINS: Did you believe you had [a] duty to follow those orders?

COBURN: Yes, sir.

GITTINS: At that time you were interviewed by Mr. Fishman from *New York* magazine, you were under an order that directed you not to talk to the press about this case; correct?

COBURN: About that case, but not about me, sir. Yes.

GITTINS: Is it your testimony, given here today under oath, that you did not talk about this case with Mr. Fishman on the 15th of March 2005, sir?

COBURN: I mentioned no details of this case.

GITTINS: Is it your testimony given here today under oath, that on the 15th of March 2005, when you spoke to Mr. Fishman, you did not talk about the case?

COBURN: I did not talk about that case. No, sir.

GITTINS: That is your testimony given under oath, here today, subject to the penalty for perjury; correct, sir?

COBURN: Yes, sir.

GITTINS: You understand that the penalty of perjury is maximum punishment of five years confinement and a dishonorable discharge; correct, sir?

COBURN: Yes, sir.

Coburn shifted on the witness chair.

GITTINS: So we can rely on your testimony that you did not talk about this case with Mr. Fishman to the same degree that we can rely on the testimony that you have already given here about the shooting, sir?

COBURN: Yes, sir.

GITTINS: It is just as truthful?

COBURN: Yes, sir.

GITTINS: On the 15th of March 2005, your wife actually reminded you about the order that required you not to speak about this case; correct?

COBURN: Yes, sir.

GITTINS: So when you spoke to Mr. Fishman, you were clearly aware that you had an order not to talk about the case; correct?

COBURN: Yes, sir.

GITTINS: You could have followed that—it is your testimony that you did follow that order; correct?

COBURN: Yes, sir.

GITTINS: Do you remember talking to Steve Fishman about this case, after you were given a lawful order not to talk about it, sir?

COBURN: Yes, sir.

GITTINS: So you knew, when you were talking to Mr. Fishman about the case, that you were violating a lawful order given to you by a commissioned officer; correct?

COBURN: At the time it didn't seem relevant to me, sir. I was talking about myself.

GITTINS: You had been given an order by two officers in the United States Marine Corps not to speak about this case; isn't that true, sir?

COBURN: Yes, sir.

GITTINS: You also talked to Betty Chin from CBS News; didn't you, sir?

COBURN: She had called. Yes, sir.

GITTINS: And you talked to her about the case; didn't you?

COBURN: I talked about myself again, sir.

GITTINS: Did you tell Betty Chin from CBS News that Lieutenant Pantano shot the Iraqis while they were on their knees?

COBURN: It is common knowledge. It is out there, sir.

GITTINS: Sir, my question was to you, did you tell Betty Chin from CBS News that Lieutenant Pantano shot the Iraqis while they were on their knees?

COBURN: I don't recall our conversation, sir.

GITTINS: You don't recall it, sir?

COBURN: No, sir.

GITTINS: Did you talk about the case with Betty Chin, sir?

COBURN: Not that I recall.

GITTINS: You told Ms. Chin that you could not do an on-camera interview because you had been given an order not to talk to the press; isn't that true, sir?

COBURN: Yes, sir.

GITTINS: But you did agree to talk to her off camera; isn't that true, sir?

COBURN: No, sir.

GITTINS: You talked to her on the telephone; correct?

COBURN: Yes, sir.

GITTINS: And even though you didn't appear on camera, you did speak to Betty Chin about the case; correct?

COBURN: About myself, yes, sir.

GITTINS: You actually talked to her about the case; didn't you sir?

COBURN: I don't recall.

GITTINS: Is your recollection about whether or not you spoke to Betty Chin about the case as good as your recollection of April 15th, 2004, a year before?

COBURN: No, sir. I remember the case better.

GITTINS: You were also interviewed for and talked to the *New York Daily News* published on or about March 5th or 6th, 2005; isn't that true, sir? *New York Daily News,* sir, do you remember that?

COBURN: I might have. I don't remember.

GITTINS: Was it after the February order that you were given not to talk about the case, sir?

COBURN: Yes, sir.

GITTINS: And you were quoted in the *New York Daily News* on that day; correct?

COBURN: I don't remember, sir.

Camp Fallujah, Iraq
June 2004

We got word that a four-man observation team from 2/4 Marines near the city had missed a fifteen-minute comm check. By the time the QRF got there they were all shot dead. Their gear was taken, including two sniper rifles. These Muj assholes were getting braver.

When I thought of this, it was hard to keep my mouth shut. So I wrote in my journal:

> *Four Marines are executed, probably in their sleep and I'm being investigated for Murder? What a bunch of bullshit!*

The cover of the June 19th *Stars and Stripes* newspaper had a gritty green NVG-type image of a bound hostage in an orange jumpsuit. "American Beheaded" was the headline. On the page, right above the "Messages of Support" section, the article noted, "One of the three photographs posted on the web site showed a man's head, face towards the camera, being held by a hand. The other two showed a beheaded body lying prone on a mattress with the severed head placed on the small of the back. The clothes underneath bloodied."

Once more, I picked up my journal:

> *Now tell me again why I'm not leading my platoon?*

That night, my boys came back to Camp Fallujah. The NCIS investigator questioned two squads. They lined the hall, standing next to the crossed flags of the battalion. They stood like real Warlords, proud of themselves. They were killers. They had been tested. They had survived. They stank of fear sweat. Pungent. Finally, indoors, they took off their helmets, and their hair was just a dirty patch of spite.

They all wanted to reach out to me, as I did to them. But I was on some other plane. I was clean. I smelled good. I had been absent. Their leader had not been there when they'd needed him, but they had found their own way.

Lance Corporal Marty McPherson, who'd always been the grinning joker, approached me. He needed to vent. He needed my approval. He looked as though he might still be in shock. His eyes were jumpy. I thought they might break with tears. Hell, mine too. I was so glad to see my Marines, my brave sons.

"Sir, it was pretty bad. It was Fallujah . . ."

That was the only word necessary. Fallujah.

"I know. I was in the COC. Listening." I didn't add *praying*.

He told me about the FOB getting mortared from different directions. First Squad had been mounted in three Humvees and a seven-ton. They were saved by coming at the ambush from the "wrong" direction. The enemy had planned to take them from the flank, but chance had it that they approached head-on. They saw a guy standing near a building. It felt fishy. Thirty seconds later a barrage of RPGs and machine-gun fire cut loose. They held their ground and 2nd Squad with Staff Sergeant Glew QRF'd. But by then, 1st Squad had fire superiority, which saved the day.

I had drummed into these knuckleheads that the only way to survive a well-laid ambush was to attack into it, hard. The lesson of Latafiyah, of Fallujah. They had learned that lesson.

Then McPherson asked for a high five, and he got it. His big Cheshire cat grin shone through the sweat filth on his cheeks.

Corporal Magdaleno, whom I used to call my "bodyguard" after he fired his grenade launcher by balancing it on my helmet as I was talking on the radio down in Latafiyah, came up to me. He, too, had stories about the ambush day that he wanted to share. And he had a PX card for Smith and one for Johnson that he asked me to sign. I was so touched. What do you write to two kids who have given up their eyes or their arms? I think I wrote something about being strong, about the biggest challenges still lying ahead of them.

Easy Company XO, 1st Lieutenant Keating, came up and pulled me aside. He asked how I was. I explained my pain and anger at being absent from my platoon and their first casualties. *Jesus!*

That's when he said it. "Your boys did what they did out there because of you. Because of what you taught them. Because of your words which echo in their ears."

They had assaulted a three-to-one superior enemy and the only reason they survived and took so few casualties was because they were as aggressive as hell.

"They were Devil Dogs out there," Keating said, referring to the Germans' description of the Marines during the fierce fighting in Belleau Wood in 1918.

Now *that* made me feel better.

But Gunny Naylor, with his raspy drill instructor's voice, said it best. "Hey, sir." I turned to look into his tired eyes. "That ambush was fucking beautiful." He paused for effect. "If it had been any other platoon it would have been a disaster . . ."

Thank you, Gunny. You don't know how much I needed that right then. Or maybe you do.

Camp Lejeune
27 April 2005

Gittins continued relentlessly. Coburn shifted in his chair, rolling his tongue. Chucky the Chipmunk in a wire cage trap.

GITTINS: You have actually downloaded news reports about this case; have you not?

COBURN: Yes, sir.

GITTINS: You knew on or about March 5th when your quote was published in the *New York Daily News* that you had violated the lawful order that was given to you by both Major Keane and the PAO [public affairs officer]; correct?

COBURN: What was the question again, sir?

GITTINS: You'd rather do what you wanted; is that true?

COBURN: No, sir. Because—

GITTINS: People were smearing you, and you were going to talk about this case; isn't that true, sir? Isn't that what you testified to earlier, you were smeared?

COBURN: Yes, sir.

GITTINS: And you wanted to talk to the press; didn't you?

COBURN: I wanted to, but did not.

GITTINS: Well, you didn't talk to the press?

COBURN: I did not seek out the press. They called my house.

GITTINS: And after you were given the order not to speak to

them, when they called your house, you did speak to them about the case; correct?

COBURN: I spoke to them about myself.

GITTINS: Sir, is it your testimony that you only spoke to them about yourself?

COBURN: Anything relevant with me.

GITTINS: Relevant like did you—let me ask you. Would a description of the wounds that you saw be speaking about yourself, or do you think it would be speaking about this case?

COBURN: About the case.

GITTINS: Did you describe the wounds to Ms. Chin?

COBURN: I don't recall, sir.

GITTINS: Did you describe the wounds to Mr. Fishman?

COBURN: Again, I don't recall.

GITTINS: So now, after we have just gone through the—these questions, you don't remember the conversation at all?

COBURN: There were three different reporters that contacted me. And I don't remember who I talked to about what.

Gittins glanced at his notes. I knew what was coming and fought to remain impassive. I felt like I was holding a virtual claymore detonator. Just waiting to squeeze.

GITTINS: On February 14th and February 17th, 2005, did you post on an Internet blog site?

COBURN: I don't recall the dates, but yes I did, sir.

GITTINS: Did you post using the name, Marine That Knows?

COBURN: Yes, sir.

GITTINS: That was using your COBURNDL@AOL.COM address? You are aware that your personal e-mail address and unique computer address are recorded when you post; correct?

COBURN: Yes, sir.

GITTINS: You didn't use your name when you—when you—

you didn't use your name when you posted on the Internet; did you?

COBURN: No, sir.

GITTINS: Did you say on the Internet, "Here is a little advice. Before you make stupid comments, get the whole story. All you people have read is his side of the story. I must say that the lawyer was very smart in putting in a false statement. Now, all the stupid people that think they know something about what happened will have his story in their heads and think he is telling the truth. What person that is up on charges is going to tell the truth that will put them away. They all lie. How about you all wait until the Marine Corps makes their statement. Until that happens, I cannot tell what I know. If you know anything about the military, you would know that a service member is not authorized to make a statement unless authorized by the legal department"; correct?

COBURN: Yes, sir.

GITTINS: At the time you posted that, you were under order not to contact the press; isn't that true, sir.

COBURN: Yes, sir.

GITTINS: That is why you said, if you know anything about the military, you would know that a service member is not authorized to make a statement unless authorized by the legal department; correct?

COBURN: Yes, sir.

GITTINS: You knew when you posted that on the Internet that you were violating a lawful order that you had been given; correct?

COBURN: I wasn't discussing anything, sir.

GITTINS: You don't think you were discussing about the case when you made that post, sir?

COBURN: No, sir. I was defending myself.

GITTINS: You don't believe that that was a post about the case?

COBURN: No, sir.

Gittins read aloud from Coburn's web posting.

GITTINS: "Now, all the people—all the stupid people that think they know something about what happened will have his story in their heads and think he is telling the truth," you don't think that is about this case, sir?

COBURN: Not directly. No, sir.

GITTINS: Did you also say on the same Web site on February 14th, "nothing that has been in the news about this case is true. The facts are all wrong. The prisoners were never a threat. And they had nothing on them. They were shot after the car was searched, long after. So before you start talking trash about the case, learn the facts," or words to that effect.

Coburn did not answer. He seemed stunned. The operators of the blog site Euphoricreality.net were two patriotic female vets who had been following my case closely. Kit and Heidi thought it was suspicious that someone who claimed to have information on the case was posting anonymously and they forwarded his information to my defense team. So much for his accusations not being *personal*.

GITTINS: Did you post that, sir?

COBURN: Yes, sir.

GITTINS: You knew at the time that you were under an order not to comment about the case; correct?

COBURN: Yes, sir.

GITTINS: So we have identified at least five different violations of that lawful order that you were given by two different Marine officers; correct?

COBURN: Yes, sir.

GITTINS: So a total of ten violations of a lawful order. Five from—you violated Major Keane's order on five separate occasions. And you violated the order of the PAO five separate occasions; correct?

COBURN: Yes, sir.

GITTINS: You are a sergeant in the Marines; correct, sir?

COBURN: Yes, sir.

GITTINS: You are expected to follow orders; isn't that true?

COBURN: Yes, sir.

GITTINS: "What person that is up on charges [is] going to tell the truth that will put them away? They all lie." Is that what you believe, sir?

COBURN: Yes, sir.

GITTINS: That is what you believe, that every person who has been accused of something will lie?

COBURN: If there is a shred of evidence or a shred of thought that they could get off of the case, then yes, sir.

GITTINS: Sir, I have just accused you, basically established the evidence beyond a reasonable doubt that you violated a lawful order. Are you lying, sir?

Keane jumped up.

KEANE: Objection. Speculation.

WINN: Note that objection for the record.

GITTINS: Are you lying, sir? I have established beyond a reasonable doubt that you have violated an order on ten separate occasions. Are you lying, sir?

COBURN: What, that I stated people lie?

GITTINS: They all lie.

COBURN: Okay. No, sir. I don't.

GITTINS: As long as you are under oath, sir, would you tell me what other Internet blog sites you have posted on?

COBURN: I don't remember anything, sir.

GITTINS: Are there others, sir?

COBURN: Not that I can remember.

GITTINS: Not that you can remember? Other than on February 14th, at 8:15 P.M. and February 17th, at 6:38 P.M. did you post on the Internet about this case?

COBURN: I don't remember, sir.

GITTINS: Sir, this is probably a good time to take a break.

Gittins went to discuss an important legal matter with Major Keane and Major Winn.

Ten minutes later, Major Winn addressed the hearing.

WINN: This hearing will now come to order. Sergeant Coburn, before we continue any further, because of the testimony you gave earlier, I'm going to need to read you your rights under Article 31.

Sergeant Coburn, no person subject to the UCMJ may force you to incriminate yourself or answer any questions if the answer may tend to incriminate you. You have the right to remain silent. If you choose to make a statement in any form, or answer any questions your statement or answer may be used against you in a trial by court-martial.

There was a long pause while Coburn appeared to struggle to understand what was happening to him.

WINN: Do you understand these rights I just read to you?
COBURN: Yes, sir.
WINN: Do you wish to speak to a lawyer?
COBURN: Yes, sir.

Coburn rose from the witness chair and walked from the hearing room, his head down.

There are many things I've seen and done in my life that you could never understand, I thought, watching him leave. *And I don't need you to. You are a sheep that I protected from the wolves. Not by any fault of your own, but by your nature.*

But one thing that you and I will share for the rest of our lives is the revulsion and horror of being read your rights.

Now you know how it feels, you son of a bitch.

NINE

Article 32 Hearing
DAYS THREE AND FOUR

Camp Lejeune
28 April 2005

The prosecution was concluding its case. In Charlie Gittins's opinion, they had opened as many false trails and raised as many red herrings as they could get away with, trying to convince Major Winn to recommend a general court-martial. Maybe they had succeeded. Maybe not.

This morning, one of the government's witnesses was a former member of my platoon, Corporal Spencer Stringham. The platoon sergeant and I had had to put our boots in his ass on more than one occasion for pulling dumb JV shit. But he'd also shown the makings of a good combat Marine and he knew his way around a gunfight.

Captain John Reh handled Stringham's direct examination for the prosecution. He established that Stringham was at the site of the April 15, 2004, QRF mission, but had no knowledge of the details of the vehicle search. Reh then widened his line of inquiry.

REH: Are there any other instances that stand out in your mind with respect to Lieutenant Pantano during your time there in Iraq?

Assistant Defense Counsel Captain Brandon Bolling rose and addressed Major Winn.

BOLLING: Sir, I am going to object. He is asking about uncharged misconduct.

WINN: I am going to overrule. I don't see him asking for misconduct. He is just asking for opinions of the performance of the accused. Go ahead, Captain Reh.

REH: Go ahead.

STRINGHAM: Just one where there was a vehicle checkpoint and Lieutenant Pantano—we found a fully loaded AK-47 magazine in the car. And Lieutenant Pantano kind of gave that driver a hard time, the guy, more or less, threatening him, you know, trying to find out some information about insurgents in the area. After—we were pretty sure that he didn't know anything. He was crying, and he didn't seem to give up any information. So Lieutenant Pantano took his bayonet and had the magazine and said, "For this, I do this," and slashed his tire and had him drive away.

REH: Do you remember him saying anything to him prior to that?

STRINGHAM: He said a lot of things, sir. They weren't specific.

REH: Well, if I provided you with a copy of your statement, would that refresh your recollection?

STRINGHAM: Sure, sir.

REH: I am handing to the witness—do you recognize that document?

STRINGHAM: This is my statement to the NCIS.

REH: Well, does that refresh your recollection as to what happened that day?

STRINGHAM: Yes, sir.

REH: Can you describe, for the investigating officer, what happened?

STRINGHAM: We found a magazine inside of the vehicle. Lieutenant Pantano gave the driver a hard time, trying to get some information out of him as far as insurgents in the area. Lieutenant Pantano was joking with the—well, not joking with the driver, but we knew he was joking. He was keying the mike on his—or pretending to key the mike on his radio saying, "Captain, Captain, this is lieutenant, request permission to execute an individual." And we could tell the guy, even though he said he didn't speak English, [w]e could tell he knew what he was saying.

REH: How could you tell that?

STRINGHAM: Because he immediately started saying "No, mister; no mister," and proceeded to cry.

Brandon Bolling began the defense cross-examination.

BOLLING: Corporal Stringham, isn't it true that, when you are talking about this keying of the radio, there was actually two Iraqis in that car?

STRINGHAM: I believe there were four, sir.

BOLLING: You were questioned by an NCIS agent?

STRINGHAM: Correct.

BOLLING: Was he asking you to try to think of reasons or think of things that Lieutenant Pantano had done incorrectly, in your opinion?

STRINGHAM: I believe so, sir.

BOLLING: Now, I am reading through your statement in here. And it doesn't say anything good about Lieutenant Pantano. Did he ever ask you any of those questions?

STRINGHAM: Not that I can recall.

BOLLING: So it was a negative interview, essentially, they were looking for dirt on Lieutenant Pantano?

STRINGHAM: I guess, sir.

BOLLING: All right. Now, we are talking about this keying of the radio at this vehicle checkpoint. Until Lieutenant Pantano had done that, this Iraqi had been pretending like he didn't speak English; correct?

STRINGHAM: Correct.

BOLLING: All right. So this actually worked?

STRINGHAM: Worked as far as—

BOLLING: The guy immediately began speaking English?

STRINGHAM: Broken, yes, sir.

Bolling now asked about relationships among the members of the 3rd Platoon and its squad leaders.

BOLLING: You thought Lieutenant Pantano was too motivated?

STRINGHAM: I wouldn't say "too motivated," sir. Our—I am not going to say "our profession" but we have our word. He was "motarvated," which is so motivated that—we joked that it is so motivated to a state of retardation, sir.

BOLLING: All right. So that isn't too motivated to you?

STRINGHAM: In some areas, yes, sir.

BOLLING: You remember telling me that not only was he too motivated in garrison, he was actually too motivated in the area of operations as well; correct?

STRINGHAM: To be vague, yes, sir.

BOLLING: Because he always volunteered for missions; correct?

STRINGHAM: Yes, sir.

BOLLING: Because he didn't know when you thought the squad or the platoon needed a rest; correct?

STRINGHAM: Yes, sir.

BOLLING: Because he was a micromanager; correct?
STRINGHAM: Yes, sir.
BOLLING: Because you thought Lieutenant Pantano always tried to be a cop and investigate anything that came up while on a patrol; right?
STRINGHAM: Yes, sir.

FOB Mahmudiyah, Iraq
26 June 2004

I had now been officially assigned to H&S company (Headquarters and Support, the "Hide and Slide" to the grunts). As I went to bed this morning in the swelling heat after standing the night shift as watch officer in the COC, I listened on my Walkman to a tape Jill had sent me. She'd had the recorder on in the car as she talked to Domenico. His little voice, not much more than a piping squeak from his car seat, made me smile in my sleeping bag.

Jill was saying, "Daddy is going to take you to the firehouse when he gets back."

In our home, firemen were the biggest heroes. I purposely deemphasized military life. If he chose that path on his own, fine, but I would not push him.

"I can drive, Mommy," the two-year-old chirped.

Dust was landing in my face as the FOB shook from incoming. It was heavy. Two and then five more. Probably 82 mm, maybe bigger. Well, that got my attention. I took off my headphones and sat up. I was in my OD shorts and T-shirt wearing my boots, carrying my weapon as I headed to the toilet.

I saw men dashing around at the battalion aid station, which was unusual for 6:00 A.M. A corpsman was straining to hear his radio.

"Did we take casualties?" I asked as casually as I could.

"Yes, sir."

Shit. I headed back to my bunk and pulled on all my gear for another attempt at pissing, now fifty pounds heavier.

I felt more vulnerable here at the FOB than I ever had on patrol or attacking into an ambush. Being trapped here inside the berm, inside the wire, made me feel helpless. I didn't command a means to affect the enemy *directly*, and—despite the weight of this "battle rattle" on my head and torso—was naked, vulnerable to these random explosives from the sky.

An hour before sunset, we got mortared again. "Sunrise . . . sunset." Fiddler on the fucking roof. An 82 mm fiddler. That was our life in this particular ghetto.

After Easy Company finally rolled into the FOB, I told the leadership about the suicide car bomb that almost killed CAAT Red. An old Hajji sedan was going south on the east side of Jackson while Red's gun trucks were rolling north. The Iraqi driver pulled a sharp U-turn, looking for a target of opportunity. He found it with CAAT Red. Almost across the junk-strewn median, the car got hung up on a guardrail—just as it was about to merge into Red's column of Humvees.

The premature detonation killed four Iraqi bystanders and destroyed a nearby civilian vehicle.

"The old neighborhood is going to hell, guys," I said.

Earlier in the week an Iraqi dressed in a crisp blue-and-white uniform had walked into a police station and detonated a suitcase full of explosives, nuts and bolts, killing four Iraqi police officers and wounding dozens.

Meanwhile, Lieutenant James "Milky" Lindler was being investigated for shooting a motherfucker who'd run his checkpoint after an IED wounded five of Lindler's Marines. This was insane. Five Marines were bleeding out. A Humvee's *armor* was crushed, and a "civilian" vehicle made a U-turn and came racing back toward them. Of course they fired.

We need to start investigating people for not *shooting,* I wrote that night in my journal.

FOB Mahmudiyah, Iraq
29 June 2004

Sovereignty! The Coalition did a surprise handover. Brilliant! Two days early to catch the terrorists unprepared. We finally did something smart. And for once, we got the word right after the event.

Outside the wire, sovereign Iraq looked, sounded, and smelled a hell of a lot like it had presovereignty. Trash on the highways. The sewer stench of the canals. The smack-thud of mortars.

Every day, mortars, IEDs, and ambushes. Marine casualties were mounting again.

On July 2, CAAT White got hit with a homemade RPG fashioned out of PVC pipe and nine-volt batteries. The best part was the washing-machine timer that let the terrorists set it and dash off, so if the Marines *had* fired back, they would have at best hit nothing, and at worst, wounded or killed innocents.

On the night of Wednesday, July 7, I learned that the NCIS team investigating the April "shooting incident" had arrived at the FOB. I was on duty in the COC when I encountered a confused, scruffy, un-shaven dude in khakis, a sweaty T-shirt, and body armor with the straps all undone, like tentacles hanging off of him. He had a Kev-lar askew on his head, an M-4, and an OD towel around his neck—Charlie Sheen in *Platoon*. Seeing a stranger saunter into the COC while I was in command instantly triggered a challenge.

"Hey," I shouted, my hand gripping his arm. "Who are you?"

"Good on ya for challenging me, lieutenant," he said with a grin. "I'm NCIS."

"Well, let me know if I can do anything for you, sir." It took all of a half a second to flip from wanting to stomp his guts out to licking his goofy Nike jogging shoes.

Grreeaaat. I wondered if he had already known that I'd be up here and was just looking to take my pulse. If he didn't like my reception, Hajji gave him an even warmer one. The FOB took six rounds of 82 mm mortars a few minutes later.

In the morning, I was sick in spirit, almost nauseous. I just couldn't believe that after wasting those two fucks on the canal road this could possibly be happening. Was I supposed to let them kill me? I'm sure they were great guys. I bet the older one could play the hell out of a mandolin and make a zesty flat bread, and the younger one . . . Oh, the clever jokes he could tell. I bet he could make his little broth-ers and sisters laugh. His parents must have been so proud of him, standing up to the infidel. But in a splintered moment, they made a choice to fight for something they believed in. And it hadn't worked out so well for them. It didn't always work out for us, either.

Yesterday, a 28,000-pound LAV-25 was flipped like a bottle cap—killing all four crewmen—when it ran over a stack of land mines piled like poker chips. Four sets of mothers and fathers, sisters and brothers.

Maybe even a few kids and a wife or two. All that had been left behind, because men made a choice to fight for what they believed in.

Now there were NCIS agents here to question my character? It hurt. It really hurt—worse than any physical pain I'd ever suffered. I had to turn in my M-16. They were taking it with them. And I wasn't sure why. Something about tests. I felt stripped, weak, and naked without that weapon. It had saved my life in Latafiyah, all along the Zulu perimeter, and in Fallujah.

Now they'd seized it from me. What if there was a big QRF? What if my former platoon stepped deep into the ambush shit and we had to send every spare Marine who could shoot a rifle to save them? What would I shoot?

The priceless irony of course was that the dirty, beat-up 9 mm Beretta pistol I was issued to replace my M-16 had come hot off the thigh of Lance Corporal Simental. The soft-faced boy, always quick to help, had kept Easy Company's communications running until he had been blown up by an IED. He had lost his leg, so he wouldn't be needing a pistol anymore. Well, here's to you, Simental. We were bonded forever. The word on the street was that you were trying to speed your recovery so you could come back to us. You are a lion of a man. All of these boys were lions. America's greatest resource was the courage and tenacity of her young troops.

On the night of July 9, I was able to speak to Jill for twenty minutes. It was a little mental vacation from the war, spiritual R&R. She was making my dad a veal Francese dish with lemon zest, Parmesan cheese, and breadcrumbs. My son was getting older, she said. Domenico was starting to manipulate the way we all do: sugary sweet when he wanted something and gruff and tough when he didn't. I couldn't wait to see him.

My God. What if this whole thing goes sideways and I get scapegoated and never see my kids again.

Camp Lejeune
28 April 2005

At 10:37 that Thursday morning, the defense began to present its case by calling a series of witnesses who testified by phone from the Marine base at Twentynine Palms, California, where they were training for the Warlords' next deployment to Iraq.

I should be out there with them.

The first defense witness was Lance Corporal James Faleris, the shaven-headed, utterly fearless machine-gunner. He and the other witnesses in California were testifying from a tent in a beating downpour that we could hear over the speakerphone.

Major Phil Stackhouse had Faleris outline our platoon training and then asked him to describe the Easter Sunday fight in Latafiyah.

FALERIS: —we were getting in the firefight and was moving down the road, and [t]hen we stopped. Lieutenant Pantano pushed my victor up so I could suppress the target that we were engaged from, and he went and took his platoon or the react force that was there and went in and assaulted the target that we were getting ambushed by. Lieutenant Pantano was always—he was always all over it—he was always all over everything. He was getting everything done out there. He was always a hands-on officer.

STACKHOUSE: So, did you observe his actions during that firefight?

FALERIS: Sometimes, sir. He wasn't always around me. He was mostly with his Marines during that time, but he'd run up every now and again to make sure I was all right.

STACKHOUSE: Do you remember anything else about that firefight?

FALERIS: I don't know, sir. What do you mean, sir?

STACKHOUSE: Do you remember any other interactions with Lieutenant Pantano during that firefight? Did he have any conversations with you? Did he tell you anything? Did you observe his platoon do anything when he was commanding his platoon?

FALERIS: I remember a lot after the firefight, he talked

to me a little bit, because that was the first
time I had been in a firefight before.

STACKHOUSE: What did you talk about?

FALERIS: He was just—he just kind of like—when we
were back at the berthing area, sir, he just
was making sure we were all right, you know.
He asked to see if we needed to talk about
anything, we could talk to him. He made sure
we were okay, like we didn't get—I don't
know, like jarred by the whole incident or
anything, make sure we were still good to go
and on track. I think that's about it, sir. I don't
really remember a whole lot about it like his
particular—what was going on with him, sir,
where he was at and stuff.

STACKHOUSE: And did you see him interacting with Iraqi
civilians while you were over there?

FALERIS: Yes, sir. One time in particular, I remember
him buying soccer balls with his own money
for some of the kids in the area. There was a
little shop setup that had soccer balls hanging from the windows, and he went and
bought some soccer balls and gave them to
the kids in the area. We used to go around
and get boxes of toys and stuff. I don't remember where we got them from, but we had
a box of toys, and we went out passing out
toys to the kids. He used to tell us to bring
the Charms and stuff from our MREs or bags
of Skittles or any kind of candy we got in
packages to give to them and stuff like that.

I could picture those little kids snatching up the candy from our
ration pouches and kicking their new soccer balls down the rutted,
trashy streets. And when I saw them, I'd always thought of my father in
the ruins of the bombed Calabrian villages.

STACKHOUSE: Did you ever see him interacting with any
adult Iraqis?

FALERIS: Yes, sir.

STACKHOUSE: Why don't you tell us about that?

FALERIS: He was always respectful. Once again, I kind of think about this one time we were on patrol, and we ended up snapping a VCP on a car that we had seen a few times pass by with a—It turned out the guy—I was one of the Marines that stopped the vehicle, and I was asking him if he spoke English, and the guy told me, "Yes, PFC," and that kind of threw me back, and as soon as he did that, Lieutenant Pantano came up and started to talk to him. It turned out that he was a former Iraqi general. I think he was like a brigadier general for the Iraqi army, and Lieutenant Pantano talked with him. Since he was kind of a higher-ranking guy and he still was well respected, could we talk to him. He told him that they needed to have lunch and stuff and talk about the area and talk about bad people in the area and certain activity and stuff like that. He told him they needed to have a lunch or something like that.

STACKHOUSE: A couple more areas I'd like you to talk about. One is just your general overall impressions of Lieutenant Pantano's leadership?

FALERIS: Sir, he was—he was an outstanding leader, sir. He demanded a lot from us. He demanded for us to know our jobs. He demanded us to do our best out there. He wouldn't take anything other than that. He wouldn't give you anything but his best at the same time, and there was like nothing that he would tell you to do that he wouldn't do himself. He's an outstanding leader, sir.

STACKHOUSE: And if you were going to characterize his actions in combat that you observed in one word, what would it be?

FALERIS: I'd say inspirational, sir, make you want to be
like him.

I had been fighting my emotions from the moment Faleris started speaking. Just hearing the youth in his voice made me think of my sons. My body convulsed, I was crying so hard. Those words, his words, were the most excruciating thing for me to hear in this entire process. They had called me a murderer in front of my wife and mother, but it was the devotion of this tough, war-hardened, but articulate young man that racked my body with sobs.

Hearing Faleris's praise, I knew that I had finally found my way in life. But his words delivered in a courtroom also meant that my career was over. Regardless of the outcome, my reputation had been destroyed. I was finished, and it made me think of a scene from *An Officer and a Gentleman*. Richard Gere's agonizing plea not to be drummed out of flight school, "Don't you do it . . . I got nowhere else to go!"

It wasn't true, but it was how I felt. I could go anywhere, and in my short life I had already scaled slopes that most people only dreamt about. But this was where I had to be, serving my country in time of war. And all that had been stripped from me, just as the scruffy NCIS agents had confiscated my rifle. The pain was like a sudden and violent accident robbing me of a loved one. I was isolated, trying to recover in the loving arms of a family that could never fully understand the journey that I had been on.

I stared at the Marine Corps flag and I wept at my sorrow and my loss. Tears ran hot and salty down my face and pooled on my legal pad as I bowed my head. Captain Trombly put her hand on my shoulder, but I couldn't stop crying.

FOB Mahmudiyah, Iraq
17 July 2004

That morning a massive car bomb hit the Iraqi National Guard compound I had visited the day before. One ING soldier was killed as he tried to stop the car's advance by firing his AK-47 from the hip. His counterattack was effective—for everyone but him. He was killed when the bomb blew early, but the compound and the hundreds of ING soldiers inside were spared.

That was heroism, honest-to-God, Medal of Honor valor. But how was his family rewarded? That summer, we'd learn that it would be months before—if ever—they would receive his insurance payment.

But more importantly, I thought, there should have been a statue dedicated to him. *Rename the base for him.* He was a hero and Iraq desperately needed heroes right now. Was that going to happen?

Not likely. But there were plenty of brave Iraqis. Every time a bomb exploded at a police recruiting line, the survivors dusted themselves off. They just wiped away the gore, fingertips, and eyelids of the guy who'd been standing in front of them and soldiered on.

That kind of courage helped a few Iraqi police and troops perform their duty. But we had to convince more than just the few. We had to reach the majority. There had to be a cultural mind shift in the role and pride of the new Iraq and the new Iraqi security forces. Right now all the kids saw the insurgents as glorified gangsta-rapper drug barons—or maybe hot-shit Westies. They had the money, the violent power, and the fame.

And even if people didn't like the insurgents, they still feared them more than they feared us. That was squarely a failure of two American policies: our reluctance to use decisive and overwhelming force, *and* our inability to capitalize on and publicize our victories. Iraqis, I thought, needed an image, an icon like the flag raising on Iwo Jima, even if it had to be restaged. Especially if it had to be restaged. We had to give them the tools to believe in themselves and that went much deeper than a paycheck. We had to purge the image of a man in uniform, the negative stereotypes of Saddam's regime.

If we don't get this right, I thought, heading for my rack one baking July morning, *my son will be fighting in Fallujah in twenty years.*

Camp Lejeune
28 April 2005

The next defense witness was one of my fellow Easy Company platoon commanders, Second Lieutenant Nathan Dmochowski.

STACKHOUSE: Would you give the investigating officer your general impressions of him [Pantano] during OCS, TBS, and IOC, each independently?

DMOCHOWSKI: OCS, he definitely stood out because he was always good at PT, also very outspoken, sometimes a little bit too much for the sergeant instructors there but very witty, a leader. He always did a real good job, a stellar performer there.

At The Basic School, as I said, we were in different platoons, so my observation time there was not as close, but it—at the Infantry Officer Course, it was very close. You worked closely together and conducting operations and such. There again, he was class commandant chosen by his peers for that position. His peers held him in high regard. I, myself, voted for him. Again, he excelled there and did very well [at] the operations. Both when I worked with him and—also, he worked for me and I worked for him.

It's a strange dynamic. You're either working for him or he's working for you depending on what billet they put you in, so he's a very over—very much an overachiever in all the respects that I observed him in those three courses.

STACKHOUSE: You went to SASO training together prior to your deployment; is that right?

DMOCHOWSKI: Yes, we did.

STACKHOUSE: If you would, tell us about SASO training.

DMOCHOWSKI: I'm actually at the same training right now. It's a place called Matilda Village. It's abandoned Air Force housing at March Air Force Base [California]. It's about a kilometer square that they have—that they use. They have aggressors here, about one hundred of them, and it's set up as an Iraqi village. The aggressors dress in Iraqi garb, speak a little bit of Arabic, and they run you through ten days worth of training and a three-day field evolution where they basically—you're in an Iraqi village in a company base, and you run operations out of it and interact with the locals and do all that sort of stuff that you do in Iraq.

STACKHOUSE: When you went to SASO training the first time, I'm going to direct your attention to a debrief that you received for NCOs and up.

DMOCHOWSKI: Okay.

STACKHOUSE: Would you tell the investigating officer about that, that debrief and that subject in the debrief?

DMOCHOWSKI: Okay. We had been talking—the buildup to it's always the complex environment that SASO presents, and one of the things I remember from the brief that stuck in my head was the first go-around in OIF-I when they were doing the push up to Baghdad, they had had a lot of trouble in this particular village. They kept getting attacked. They had set up a small presence around the village but kept getting attacked, kept taking fire. Finally, one day, I guess they had gotten into an engagement, and there were some enemy KIA, and they put a sign by them with General Mattis's motto, "No better friend, no worse enemy" by the bodies as sort of a deterrent to the rest of the people.

STACKHOUSE: Now, at this time, you and Lieutenant Pantano had been with your first infantry unit, as officers anyway, for how long?

DMOCHOWSKI: At this time, maybe a month and a half.

STACKHOUSE: Did you and Lieutenant Pantano talk about that class and that subject?

DMOCHOWSKI: Very briefly. I just remember sort of saying, "Hey, that probably would be a good deterrent. That's something that sounds like it would work."

Stackhouse directed Demo to recall security operations at the
Mahmudiyah Town Council and interactions with the locals.

STACKHOUSE: How was he interacting with them?

DMOCHOWSKI: He took the—we had been sent over there
with the guidance, you know, wave tactics,
get to know the people, follow their customs
and courtesies, win them over hearts and
minds, and he took that very, very seriously,
almost to the point where he would endan-
ger himself. I remember particularly, we
dismounted—we were with an Army convoy
at that point. They were still showing us
around. He just sort of went up to a couple of
houses and was shaking hands with people
and trying to be friendly and all that stuff,
and the Army guys were pulling him back because he went by himself. I just remember
him being very, very adamant about that.

STACKHOUSE: What was your general impression in those
instances that you interacted with him
when you were on missions?

DMOCHOWSKI: Again, very proficient. It's the way he
needed to be there, and he did a very good
job with that. He moved from SASO and
meet and greet and stuff like that to full
combat in Fallujah, and he proved to be very
good at that as well. He's proficient in both
respects in my opinion.

STACKHOUSE: Do you recall speaking to Lieutenant Pantano after he came back from a Quick Reaction Force mission in April?

DMOCHOWSKI: Yes. When he came back from that engagement, at that time, none of us had really
seen any action. Of course, I was jealous
that he got sent out to that mission and all
that stuff, because to that point, we had
been doing security for meetings, vehicle

checkpoints, basic security patrols. There hadn't been any real missions with intelligence involved so to speak. I was jealous. When he came back from it, if I remember correctly, it was at night, and I just sort of asked, "What happened? How did it go?" He said, "Yeah, we got [a] weapons cache and a couple enemy KIA," and I remember sort of being jealous. "Hey, good job. I wish I had been sent on that mission." That's what I remember from it.

STACKHOUSE: Do you remember him talking to you about this sign and how that worked out for him?

DMOCHOWSKI: I remember him mentioning something about putting it out there or wanting to, but it was cancked [canceled] by higher.

STACKHOUSE: Has anybody talked to you since about the appropriateness of putting up signs like that?

DMOCHOWSKI: Yes. When I was questioned by NCIS, that subject was addressed.

STACKHOUSE: At the time back in April of 2004, did it strike you as inappropriate that he would put a sign up like that?

DMOCHOWSKI: No, not at all. Again, that environment we were in was especially hostile in that area, and the Mahmudiyah area itself, it wasn't exactly—it wasn't secure. When we patrolled through it, you didn't feel safe. There were still IEDs being detonated. There were small-arms engagements, things like that. Yes, at that time, I thought that would have been a decent deterrent.

STACKHOUSE: What's your general overall impression of Lieutenant Pantano's military character?

DMOCHOWSKI: His military character is impeccable in my opinion. He's somebody that I would definitely serve with in combat again, and that's not something I would say lightly. I would want him on my flank per se, and I think his military character is impeccable.

STACKHOUSE: And you say that as you're getting ready to deploy back to Iraq?

DMOCHOWSKI: Yes, sir.

For the prosecution, Captain Reh refocused on the sign during his cross-examination.

REH: You would agree with me, would you not, Lieutenant Dmochowski, it's wrong to desecrate dead bodies?

DMOCHOWSKI: Absolutely, sir.

REH: Do you believe in your opinion that placing a sign over a body is desecrating a body?

DMOCHOWSKI: I don't believe that's desecrating the body itself, sir.

REH: You don't?

DMOCHOWSKI: No, sir.

REH: So, you wouldn't consider that a law of war violation?

DMOCHOWSKI: I wouldn't, sir. I consider the enemy not wearing uniforms and conducting attacks after we help them violations of the law of war, sir, and cutting our heads off and hanging bodies from bridges as well.

REH: Very well. Did you ever create any signs and place them over dead bodies?

DMOCHOWSKI: I did not, sir.

REH: Why not?

DMOCHOWSKI: I never had an engagement where that would have been something that I would have done, sir.

REH: So, you're saying that you do see a reason then to leave a sign?

DMOCHOWSKI: Well, if nothing else works, sir, when you've been in that environment and you've handed out money for civil affairs projects, you've built things for them and you've also

been in an engagement and killed the
enemy and detained the enemy and questioned them, if nothing else—if nothing
seems to be working, you have to figure out
ways to enforce your will upon the enemy.

"... *enforce your will upon the enemy* ..." Demo had just offered
the quintessence of war in six words.

FOB Mahmudiyah, Iraq
21 July 2004

I was on watch in the COC after midnight when four new NCIS
agents arrived by helo. They were older than the last bunch, in their
late thirties and forties. This was the senior crew, the head gumshoes.

Amid the static and cacophony of the tac radios, one of them
leaned close.

"Did you get the report that our helo took fire?" he asked urgently.
"And that we returned it?"

Receive fire and return fire, the criteria for the Combat Action
Ribbon. That was what this pogue was fishing for.

"No," I said, glancing at the Significant Events radio log. "Can't say
we did."

I hoped that he never had to see real combat. For his sake.

The next day, Captain Weston gave me some great gouge (verified
intel) about the ambush that hit our boys near Patrol Base Impact on
June 19. The Muj had specifically targeted Easy Company.

"They knew our unit," Weston said. "They wanted a piece of us from
when we smoked them in Fallujah, or maybe from the *Time* article."

It turned out a local official who felt bad about the whole affair
wanted to do something good for the CO.

"Do you need food, Captain?"

No. Got plenty.

"Information?"

"You bet. Can always use that."

And we got it.

Maybe the ambush *had* been revenge for Fallujah, I thought. But I still figured the Muj commanders wouldn't have minded killing some of our boys on camera for the BBC.

That week, Weston boosted my spirits. I'd wanted to turn in my NVGs so a Marine in the company could use them, and he wouldn't let me.

"Hang on to them, Ilario," he said. "You'll need them when you come back."

"When," not "if."

That little demonstration of faith and optimism kept me going.

Major Neil, with his confident trust in letting me run my COC, also kept my head straight. If I wanted to launch QRFs, maneuver platoons, or call in artillery or air he always supported my play after walking me through the variables. He groomed me like an apprentice as he orchestrated the battalion's fight. His fitness report said that I was the "best second lieutenant in the battalion," the best he had seen in seventeen years in the Marine Corps. The unwavering support of my command didn't stop the rumor mill from churning as Marines from other companies speculated wildly about my case. One Marine in Golf company was fond of suggesting I had taken bound and blindfolded prisoners into a house and had shot them in the head with a pistol. It was a reckless way to pass the time, but gossip was one of the few pleasures to break the tedium between combat patrols.

The new NCIS agents were shaking down my men, looking at their journals and computers. With everything that was going on— IEDs, ambushes with wounded Marines, increased mortar attacks— that just felt a tad disrespectful. These boys had nothing, some worn-out utilities, boots with holes in the soles from humping long patrols, and sore asses from trying to eat, digest, and shit out there in the dust and flies. But they were giving everything they had and didn't need to feel intimidated by these motherfuckers, shaken down or second-guessed.

They don't need to begin doubting themselves out here. But the men of my platoon were resilient and demonstrated their solidarity and character in ways that made me proud. Back at the FOB, they started drawing up T-shirts that read "Free Easy 3 Actual." Then on the night of July 27th, while searching with flashlights discovered a five-hundred-pound bomb, buried and waiting for them on the side of a road in Latafiyah. Once more, the EOD guys saved a lot of lives.

A *five-hundred-pounder*, I thought. A big, fat aerial bomb left over from the good old days when Saddam had fighter-bombers. Jesus, if they'd had nukes, they'd have been using them.

In the three weeks we'd been back in Mahmudiyah, the battalion had suffered one KIA and several dozen wounded. The enemy had taken one KIA and a handful of wounded.

Those weren't good numbers when the locals were sitting on the fence looking to join the winning team.

Camp Lejeune
28 April 2005

Phil Stackhouse began the direct examination of the next defense witness, Staff Sergeant Jason Glew. He was one of the bravest, most dedicated Marines I'd ever known. The speakerphone crackled as the circuit was opened.

> STACKHOUSE: Staff Sergeant Glew, this is Major Stackhouse.
> GLEW: Sir, how are you?
> STACKHOUSE: I am doing well, thank you. Are you okay?
> GLEW: I am doing good. Cold, wet, but I am doing fine.

God, I missed my wiseass platoon sergeant. I got so lucky with him. So did the men. When I left, he took over smoothly even as the boys struggled with my absence and the shame of the investigation. He'd done a truly phenomenal job.

> STACKHOUSE: Now at some point one of your squad leaders got relieved?
> GLEW: Yes.
> STACKHOUSE: That was Sergeant Coburn?
> GLEW: Yes, it was.
> STACKHOUSE: We will talk about what precipitated the relief in a minute. But what are your general impressions of Sergeant Coburn? And what do you know of him?
> GLEW: As far as his competency as a squad leader, filling the role of a squad leader as an infantryman, he was incompetent. He was un-

decisive and the decisions that he would make it seemed like they didn't include judgment whatsoever. And it always boiled down to little things like accountability and just knowing your Marines. And he didn't do any of it. And as far as knowing him, I didn't know him on [a] personal level. Professionally, I know him.

STACKHOUSE: What about when you got into Iraq, what kind of things were you noticing?

GLEW: Well, initially before we even got into Iraq, when we were at Kuwait, we had one to two weeks to acclimate, to rehearse, to go over some rehearsals in squads and platoons, that is initially when Lieutenant Pantano and I were discussing relieving. Even during rehearsal he [Coburn] had no control of his squad. His—just the whole squad. In particular his team leaders. Their confidence and trust in him was gone. The morale was low. It was all from his indecisiveness. And the young subordinates ate that up. Because they knew he couldn't make a decision.

STACKHOUSE: Well, did you and Lieutenant Pantano just leave him to hang out to dry or were you trying to work with him at this time?

GLEW: We could have easily hung him out to dry but we didn't do that. We were trying to work with them [him].

STACKHOUSE: Was he responding? That is: Was he taking your advice? Was he taking your counsel? Was he taking your training?

GLEW: I'd have to say no. Because he never really changed when it come to leading a squad. You know—you know, when I'd give him— you know, as a staff NCO when I would give him advice and I tell him how it should happen—you know, he would respond by shaking his head yes and he would say, Yeah,

I understand. But then fifteen minutes later when he would go to do, what I just told him to do, he would screw it up. So then no, I guess he wasn't responding.

STACKHOUSE: And you were talking about his ability to handle relatively simple tasks inefficiently: is that why he was made the radio operator?

GLEW: Yes, because he couldn't run a squad.

STACKHOUSE: I want to now direct your attention to the company and the platoon.

GLEW: Okay, sir.

STACKHOUSE: Your platoon was routinely the main effort in company operations?

GLEW: Yes, sir. Most of the time it was.

STACKHOUSE: And your company was routinely the main effort in battalion operations?

GLEW: Yes, sir.

STACKHOUSE: So is it fair to say that on a majority of the occasions these things led your platoon to be at the tip of the spear for the battalion?

GLEW: That is correct, sir.

STACKHOUSE: Staff Sergeant Glew, if you had the choice of whether to go with Lieutenant Pantano to war again would you want to?

GLEW: Yes, sir. I would in a heartbeat.

FOB Mahmudiyah, Iraq
6 August 2004

Just when I thought things were getting maximum cover-your-ass stupid, my friend Lieutenant Dempsey handed me a report.

"Check this out, Ilario," he said. "They ought to investigate these guys for being morons."

Ten Marines had been involved in trying to stop a vehicle that ran a checkpoint. A Marine had literally run beside the vehicle, screaming "*Kuff*" at the driver.

Fucking idiots, I thought. How castrated had we become that we were more afraid of being punished than of being killed? Some bleeding heart would love the story about the heroic Marines that had risked their lives to ensure innocents weren't hurt. I would have fired the squad leader and put every one of those Marines on guard duty, never to leave the wire again. Inappropriate sentimentality could kill an entire squad. *And who would have been court-martialed then?*

Naturally, the media and any number of opportunistic elected officials would have surely jumped on such an incident, claiming that we should have done more to protect those Marines. But the truth was, we had all the protection we needed. We just needed our balls back. We didn't need more armor, this wasn't Camelot. Our shit weighed too much as it was. We lacked the resolve to do the hard things. Instead of investigating Marines and asking if there'd been spike strips across the road and stop signs in two languages—only two? Why not Kurdish, too?—we had to fight the goddamn enemy. What the fuck was this, *CHiPs?*

We needed to punish those who were not aggressive enough. Instead, we were defanging ourselves. And this would have consequences.

Camp Lejeune
28 April 2005

Our next witness was Easy 6, the company commander, Captain Brad Weston. Just hearing his voice on the speaker reminded me of all those missions with him on the other end of the "hook." His crisp diction reflected years on the debate team at Vanderbilt. And his mental precision displayed months as a combat leader. A sharp guy who didn't fuck around.

Major Stackhouse had him recount my performance from when I first checked into the company to our subsequent arrival in country. Captain Weston had actually thought me to be a "little soft" in my early interactions with the Iraqis. He went on to exhaustively detail the battalion's intensifying combat operations in Mahmudiyah and later in Fallujah.

The prosecution team listened passively to Weston's account. Here was an officer speaking from memory, after a long, wet night on an exhausting training exercise. I thought that they recognized Weston was not a guy to screw with on cross.

STACKHOUSE: Do you have any observations that you can provide the investigating officer of Lieutenant Pantano after you pulled out of Fallujah and were in the Zadan [Zaidon] area?

WESTON: While we were in the Zadan area again, his performance was exemplary is the best I can say. He—I could rely on him to get the mission done.

The time that Third Platoon was up there, Lieutenant Pantano established rapport with the local populace. It was a small town. He was able to coordinate with one of the locals who agreed to let us use their house.

The times that he wasn't up there his platoon performed superbly. There is one time that his platoon was—one of his squads was ambushed. Two Marines were injured. They carried on the fight, allowing me to direct other units onto the objective to assault through the ambush and move forward. So his platoon had obviously gone—from the time that we left Camp Lejeune as probably my worst platoon to obviously to one of my most—one of my most proficient platoons and that was due to the efforts of both Lieutenant Pantano and Staff Sergeant Glew. Really, really, developing the platoon and giving them the means to be successful.

STACKHOUSE: So by the time—the end of May early June timeframe, this was the best platoon in your company?

WESTON: I would say that, yes, sir.

STACKHOUSE: So if an outsider, from outside of the company even, said that Third Platoon was falling apart, would they be wrong?

WESTON: Yes, sir, I would say that they were wrong.

STACKHOUSE: Do you know Sergeant Coburn?

WESTON: I do, sir.

STACKHOUSE: How do you know him?

WESTON: Sergeant Coburn had been in my company from the day I took command of Company E, sir.

STACKHOUSE: When Sergeant Coburn was relieved as a squad leader were you in the decision-making circle of that decision?

Captain Weston explained that there had been a long history of back-and-forth discussion during which I'd assured him that I "wanted to give Sergeant Coburn the opportunity to improve himself." That I felt that I "could fix the problem."

STACKHOUSE: At some point after that he came to you about relieving him?

WESTON: That is correct. We had a couple instances when the Arabe'en [Arbaeen] incident started to develop, [that] our troop-to-task became very complex. We had Marines going really twenty-four hours a day. The rotation that I had originally developed was there would be one platoon providing a counter-mortar fight, while one platoon was on rest, one other platoon was providing security in Mahmudiyah for Arabe'en.

Lieutenant Pantano had approached me—originally his platoon was doing the—doing the counter-mortar fight, which is what we called, Zone Zulu, he approached me and said, "Hey, sir, I think I have a better way that we can handle this. That will alleviate some of the troop problems that we seem to be having." His solution was to leave his platoon entirely on the Zone Zulu, the counter-mortar fight, and he would run it, which would allow the other platoons to do their job.

And by far it did work out much better. I bring that out because what happened at that

point, he was going out on twelve-hour patrols with two squads at a time; during one of
those patrols, Sergeant Coburn was in charge
of the patrol, and due to [a] situation that developed at hand he made some bad judgment
calls and Lieutenant Pantano was on scene
to see those. Radioed into me that he was assuming control of the patrol. I—at which
point [I] realized that Sergeant Coburn was
not the right man for the squad leader position.

STACKHOUSE: So you backed the relief of Sergeant Coburn?

WESTON: Yes, sir, I did.

STACKHOUSE: What about your first sergeant?

WESTON: My first sergeant did as well.

STACKHOUSE: Is it fair to say that in your opinion, Sergeant
Coburn is a weak Marine?

WESTON: Yes, I would say that that is fair.

STACKHOUSE: Is it also fair to say that if you combine the official counseling and just the verbal unofficial
counselings that there had been multiple
counselings?

WESTON: Yes, I would say that is the case.

STACKHOUSE: Is it fair to say that in an operation like a QRF
mission, that the commander on the scene
has to make judgment calls based upon the
totality of the circumstances?

WESTON: Absolutely, sir.

FOB Mahmudiyah, Iraq
14 August 2004

On my way to our makeshift gym to work off some steam, I got the
word from Dempsey that one of the intel officers had told him
"they"—the Hajjis—were rioting. I didn't get it. Last night the Iraqis
had won their first international soccer match in fifteen years. Against
Portugal—a real team—and they weren't grateful? So now men were

streaming from every corner of the country for a violent demonstration—against what . . . who? About eight hundred of them were said to be assembling to our north, in the Army's AO. We began getting reports of sniper fire and mortaring.

You've got to be fucking kidding me!

The fresh intel indicated that the soccer riots were a Muj ruse. They knew we were spread thin with all the shit Moqtada al-Sadr's Shiite Mahdi Army was pulling in Najaf. So our old buddies the Sunni Arab Muj wanted to surge and overrun some of our bases.

Police stations were being looted; the weapons, body armor, and radios that America had provided were disappearing. We couldn't guard every damn Iraqi police or National Guard compound.

Maybe we *were* thin, but the Muj were in for a nasty wake-up call. Here at FOB Mahmudiyah, we were so thin, so on the ropes, that we had a 155 mm artillery tube and a 120 mm tank main gun pointed at our front gate from the inside. Had these assholes ever heard of a beehive round? They might blow us up with their remote-control bombs, but had they ever seen what kind of hamburger a .50 cal Ma Deuce could chop out of dumb shits trying to climb a berm? Were we shitting ourselves, waiting for the dreaded "gooks over the wire" call? Not likely, Jack.

They should have feared us. But instead, the Muj apparently thought they could overwhelm our bases. That came from the stupidity of the proportional response. The fact that the insurgents could even consider massed assaults meant that we had not been sufficiently brutal.

As Ambassador Paul Bremer later told both Tim Russert and Charlie Rose, we had become an "ineffective occupier" and not because of the number of troops, he argued, but because of our overly restrictive Rules of Engagement and our discomfort with killing the guys that needed to be killed. If we had shot looters and laid down the law up front, we would have had order because we would have had respect. This was a fancy-suit diplomat talking, and even he saw the problem. Instead of solving it, the horse had left the barn, and Marines were waiting for their bases to be overrun. Awesome.

On August 18, we got word that the Warlords would be going back to Fallujah as part of the inevitable multibattalion kick-ass to clear the city of insurgents. Planes, tanks, artillery, every fucking bit of it. We'd been penciled in as the main effort, again the tip of the spear. If that went down, I *had* to find a way to get back to my men. Screw NCIS. If they wanted Combat Action Ribbons so bad, let them come up with me into those shit alleys, through the booby traps and snipers.

I'd be perfectly content to get off the plane in North Carolina wearing handcuffs if that were required. But if my men were going into combat I had to be there.

I pitched and pleaded with Major Neil, "Sir, I believe I add value to the COC, but if we go back into Fallujah, I'd add more value with a platoon."

He replied coolly and professionally, but in that response there was grave comfort. "I know this." In another life we could have been drinking buddies. We had been lance corporal grunts in the first Gulf War. But now, with both of us in our mid-thirties, I was four ranks beneath him. He directed the company commanders who, in turn, ran the platoon commanders like me. I was way out of my league just seeking his private counsel, yet he always made the time.

"So, how do I pull it off, sir? Is it appropriate to speak directly to the colonel?"

"Yes," he replied, "but wait until this thing firms up, until it's imminent." He was as eager to go back and smash Fallujah as I was.

Camp Lejeune
28 April 2005

The defense now called Marty McPherson, a former corporal and fire team leader in 1st Squad. He was a civilian now, but the minute he entered the courtroom, I remembered his quick, mischievous grin. Charlie Gittins began the direct examination.

> GITTINS: What did Lieutenant Pantano do to prepare your new guys who hadn't seen combat for that experience?
>
> MCPHERSON: Well, he would try to tell us what to expect, not just like the things that you would see, but the things that you were going to end up feeling as a result of it, and gave pointers on how to try to calm that stuff down because,

you know, you don't want to get too nervous
and too scared from the whole thing to shoot
your weapon. So he gave us good pointers
and stuff like that, and told them that—what
they need to do if they can't—he emphasized
more of the small unit leaders, like squad
leaders and team leaders who had more experience, to maintain good composure so that
the junior Marines who would be more easily
rattled [would] see that if the more senior
Marines are calm then we have nothing to be
nervous about ourselves, and they can calm
down themselves that way.

GITTINS: What, if anything, would you normally do
prior to April 15, 2004, when a vehicle had
been searched from which detainees had
been taken?

MCPHERSON: You are either going to take that vehicle with
you or you are going to disable it and make
sure that it is not going to go anywhere.

GITTINS: How would you disable a vehicle?

MCPHERSON: Whether you shoot its tires out or cut some
wires in the engine compartment, just whatever you had on hand, whatever you had time
for, to make sure that car wasn't going to go
anywhere.

Charlie transitioned from procedures to personnel.

GITTINS: And what, if anything, did he [Coburn] say
about being fired from that squad-leader
billet?

MCPHERSON: He was really pissed off about it. And he,
kind of, made it known. And he felt that taking up a radioman's job was kind of a slap in
the face to him because, you know, typically a
lance corporal or PFC or a junior Marine
would have had that job. And he as a sergeant
who had been in for—been in, reenlisted. I

am not exactly sure how long he had been in at that point but it was over eight years I believe. So he was very ashamed, I would say, by it.

GITTINS: And he was vocal about it with other platoon members?

MCPHERSON: Yes.

GITTINS: What, if anything, did Sergeant Coburn say about Lieutenant Pantano and his prior combat experience?

MCPHERSON: He said his prior combat experience was irrelevant to the war we were currently fighting.

GITTINS: From your experience, having been in Lieutenant Pantano's platoon, did you think Lieutenant Pantano's prior experience was relevant?

MCPHERSON: Yes.

GITTINS: Did you ever come across any hidden compartments in any vehicles?

MCPHERSON: Once.

GITTINS: Tell the investigating officer about that?

MCPHERSON: There was a car that I was searching. It was actually after we had shot it. It had tried to run through a VCP that we had set up. My first time through there, I didn't find it. But something didn't sit right with me about that car. So I went back and searched again. There had to be something that I missed. I just felt it. So I looked and looked more, and there ended up being a tray that unfolded underneath one of the seats, under the passenger front seat, I believe it was, that housed an RPG sight. And that was pretty much the only time I found a compartment like that.

GITTINS: But you did find one?

MCPHERSON: Yes.

GITTINS: Sir, I understand that you are out of the Marine Corps now. But if you were called upon to come back into the Marine Corps and go into combat again, would you want to go into combat with Lieutenant Pantano?

MCPHERSON: Yes, sir.

GITTINS: Why?

MCPHERSON: Because he is a great Marine. He had the attention to detail that you need to get out there and do things safely, to bring back your men alive. He had great motivation. He knew exactly what to do and when to do it. And it was just a good experience working with him.

GITTINS: I have one last question. Before today, were you interviewed by Naval Criminal Investigative Service?

MCPHERSON: I believe I might have, one time near Fallujah.

GITTINS: Did they ask you to write a sworn statement to describe some of the things that we just talked about here today?

MCPHERSON: I don't think so.

GITTINS: Did you tell them, kind of, the same things you told us here today?

MCPHERSON: Yes, sir.

FOB Mahmudiyah, Iraq
21 August 2004

The roof of the Chicken Factory was a jumble of microwave comm dishes and antennae and provided an excellent view over the surrounding towns and highways. Sandbags rimmed the ledges and a few plastic chairs made for a relatively comfortable smoking lounge. I'd puff on the cigars my dad sent and Tyler Boudreau would smoke Marlboros while we discussed everything from Noam Chomsky to the amount of exotic beer his wife Suzi had stocked in his fridge. Tyler had enlisted in the Marines at the same time I had and worked his way through the ranks to become a captain.

"Suzi was at a party in Jacksonville and she overheard a conversation." He paused and took a drag. The ember flared for a moment. "A couple of Marines were talking about 2/2 so her ears perked up. One of them gasped, 'Oh, they've got that rogue lieutenant. Have you heard? He's going to get fried . . .'"

Beautiful. *What if that shit gets to Jill?*

The next night, Sunday, August 22, the Iraqi Olympic soccer team beat Australia in Greece. The score was one–zip, a hell of a game. By 2200 hours, we could hear the AK-47 fireworks show beginning. Right through the concrete walls of the COC.

Good, I thought, they were getting a chance to take their pride back. That was important . . . for all the Iraqis to regain a sense of national identity.

Easy 2, Lieutenant Lindler's 2nd Platoon, went out on patrol after first inserting a sniper team down in Latafiyah. James wasn't thrilled to begin with, having to run the "gauntlet," as we now called Jackson. Tonight James would be ordered to do it twice—twice the risk.

The Iraqi police reported that they were taking fire at the Mahmudiyah police station. Easy 2 showed up, and the firing, if there even was any, had stopped and now the IPs were emboldened and wanted to tag along on James's patrol. The real motive, they claimed, was to remove a body that was found down in Latafiyah earlier, which supposedly had a bomb underneath it. The story was convoluted and the discussion had been going on for hours. James begrudgingly agreed to let them follow his vehicles, as his basic mission was to help the IPs any way he could. The IPs followed, chatting on their unsecured Motorola walkie-talkies the entire trip. The same type of radio the insurgents had stolen hundreds of times.

As the strung-out convoy was approaching the oil depot in Latafiyah, a Marine shouted that he spotted a blinking LED light on the side of the road. In Iraq at midnight, that was a *very* bad sign. The patrol stopped, spread out, and began to search. The results were not good: a cordless phone rigged to a battery and det cord . . . IED. This was right in the area that the "suspicious body" reports had been coming. Again, the Iraqi police were claiming that there was a bomb under the body.

I listened from the COC, acutely aware of what was going down. The hot night, the barking dogs, Muj or their sympathizers watching from the shit-block apartment buildings.

Everyone was on edge and it now seemed that we had not one IED, but two. We were in the process of dispatching EOD and then . . . crack-BOo-ooom.

A terrorist had detonated the phone IED while the Marines were setting up their cordon. Whoever said it was better to be lucky than good might have laughed that night. The terrorists, in their haste or in the darkness, had rigged the primer charge to a dud or inert round. So when the detonation was "called in," the detcord blew the dud out of the stack onto the road where it bounced and wobbled harmlessly. The four other live 155 mm artillery rounds lay dormant underneath. A near miss for Easy 2.

We sent out EOD with CAAT Red at about 1:00 A.M. to detonate the remaining explosives.

That's a wake-up call.

Meanwhile Easy 2 was searching for this famous body, and, although they could all smell burnt flesh, there was no body to be found.

Easy 2 then continued their patrol along Jackson. On their way back up, a vehicle went down. The men had been in Iraq a long time and were seasoned. They set security, rigged the disabled Humvee for towing, and were on the move moments later.

They're good to go, I thought, listening to the radio traffic.

A few minutes later, Corporal Chris Belchik, a formidable squad leader who always had his Marines' welfare at heart, was murdered when his vehicle neared the playground in Mahmudiyah.

The explosion was so powerful that Chris, riding in one of Easy Company's few up-armored Humvees, was blown to little pieces. Corporal Krell, his close friend, got showered with shrapnel and the bloody remnants of his buddy. Lance Corporal Jernigan, the fast-talking, *Cigar Aficionado*–reading bullshit artist, lost part of his skull, his eyes, and some fingers, and his knee was mangled. Blown clear of his vehicle and blind with stumps for fingers, he was frantically searching for his weapon—after all, he was a Marine and they were under attack. As Jernigan started to stand, a quick-thinking corpsman, whose ears were still ringing from the explosion, restrained him. Hospitalman Chris Thompson worked hard, coolly, professionally, and he saved Jernigan's life. (Doc Thompson would be murdered by an IED almost a year later during the Warlord's next combat tour.)

CAAT Red pushed out to link up with Easy 2 and start the hard business of bringing back vehicles and bodies. Staff Sergeant Maguire returned with the first wounded Marines. He was shaken in ways that I would never know. Lindler had gone ultracalm on the radio. The first report of casualties had all the names wrong. "First reports" in combat have never been worth a shit. Some things didn't change. I called for Captain Weston to come to the COC. He arrived as I was having them respell the KIA's name "Bravo-Echo-Lima-Charlie-Hotel-India-Kilo." We looked at each other, and the reality washed over us. My eyes teared, but I immediately suppressed the emotion.

They got the dead Marine back to the FOB, but there were more pieces still out there. It took three trips in all. "No glass. No blood. No nothing," Major Neil ordered. "Wash it all away. We aren't giving these fucks any satisfaction."

Easy 6 and I traded pats on the arm. It was as close to a hug as we would get.

Jernigan and another Marine were medevaced out by helo that night. And after my shift, I went up to the roof to have a cigar, half hoping a sniper would try and shoot the glowing ember out of my mouth, or put a bullet in my eye socket. I was twanging with rage. I was thinking about an article I'd just read in the *New York Times* that said revenge was like feeding a hunger, an actual pleasurable sensation for the brain. I wanted to take a platoon down to Latafiyah and raze the entire town. To the ground, the smoking ground.

From Mahmudiyah, I heard the first buzzing crackle of the dawn prayer over the mosque loudspeakers. *Allahu Akbar,* my ass. They were probably sending out orders on where to plant the next IED, just as they had in Fallujah.

I'd seen this attack coming. I should have stopped it. It wasn't my decision to make, but that shouldn't have stopped me from making it anyway. I should never have let the Iraqi police patrol tail Easy 2's vehicles. You didn't command-detonate an IED at 2:00 A.M. without a lot of planning and real-time intelligence. The IPs were compromised and I was afraid it might happen, but our mission was to train and to trust them.

I went to brush my teeth at dawn before heading to my rack, hoping to sleep. A young Marine from Easy 2 was in the shower.

"Tough night, Devil Dog," I said through a mouthful of foam.

"Yes, sir, worst night of my life," he sighed as he hung his M-16 next to his stall.

"I'm sorry" was all I could say. "I'm sorry."

Camp Lejeune
28 April 2005

The next defense witness was former Sergeant Judd "Stick" Word, who was now enjoying life outside the Corps. I almost broke into an inappropriate grin, seeing him march up to the witness stand.

Charlie Gittins asked Word to describe the events of the long Easter Sunday firefight, beginning with the QRF vehicles heading south on Jackson toward Latafiyah. Then Gittins asked Word to provide details of the fighting.

> GITTINS: Were you outnumbered?
>
> WORD: Yes. We were heavily outnumbered.
>
> GITTINS: And for how long did it take before you got more people there to relieve you?
>
> WORD: It was about, I would say, an hour to an hour and a half.
>
> GITTINS: And how was the fighting, up until the point where the battalion arrived?
>
> WORD: It was heavy, intense, just going street to street getting on a roof, and then just holding a strong point until we got reinforcements there.
>
> GITTINS: How did Lieutenant Pantano—what was his demeanor in this combat situation?
>
> WORD: He kept a cool head, was directing where he wanted everyone to go, and then trying to get us more assets down there.
>
> GITTINS: When not in combat like Easter Sunday, when you were on patrols, how was Lieutenant Pantano's interactions with Iraqis?
>
> WORD: It was good. He loved to play with little kids. He always carried candy and stuff like that. Kids would come up to him all of the time. He would give them candy and stuff like that. And he was always asking the elders of the tribe or village or wherever we were at, what they needed or anything we could help them with or anything like that.
>
> GITTINS: Did you participate in stopping—vehicle control points and things like that?

WORD: Yes, I did.

GITTINS: And patrols to seek out insurgents?

WORD: Yes, I did.

GITTINS: We'll get to that.

WORD: Okay.

GITTINS: Okay. Prior to that action, when you seized detainees from vehicles, what would you do with the vehicles?

WORD: If they were known to be insurgents or suspected insurgents, we would disable them.

GITTINS: How would you disable the vehicle?

WORD: Shoot their tires out, slash their tires, take their keys, shoot the engine block, anything we could to disable it.

GITTINS: What was the reason that you disabled the vehicles?

WORD: So the insurgents couldn't use them.

GITTINS: Who taught you to disable the vehicles of suspected insurgents?

WORD: It was passed down from the unit that we relieved.

GITTINS: What was your understanding of the ROE regarding the use of deadly force?

WORD: Deadly force, if you feel threatened or someone is threatening any Coalition forces, you have the right to defend yourself or Coalition forces.

GITTINS: Did Lieutenant Pantano reinforce that ROE to you?

WORD: Yes, he did.

GITTINS: Did you have the opportunity, while you were in Iraq, to engage that ROE and use self-defense?

WORD: Yes.

GITTINS: When you engaged and used deadly force, did you feel threatened at the time?

WORD: Yes, I did.

GITTINS: Were you scared?

WORD: A little bit. Yes, sir.

GITTINS: Did you participate in vehicle searches?

WORD: Yes, I did.

GITTINS: How often would you use Iraqis to search vehicles?

WORD: Any time I felt threatened or unsafe about the vehicle, I would have them search it.

GITTINS: Were there times when you had uncuffed Iraqi prisoners who had already been flexi-cuffed?

WORD: Yes, several times.

GITTINS: Tell the investigating officer about that.

WORD: We had two individuals that we had pulled over and stopped. We flexi-cuffed them. We believe they were insurgents because an IED just went off. So we had flexi-cuffed them. But then, when we went to search the car, there was a button with wires coming from under the seat. So we uncuffed them and made them search the car and press the button.

GITTINS: Did you have both of the Iraqis do it at the same time?

WORD: Yes. We uncuffed both of them.

GITTINS: What was your job on the 15th of April, sir?

WORD: My job was to take down the house. I was the assault squad leader. I was [in] the assault section. My job was to get inside of the house, search it, and find any detainees or bad people in the house.

GITTINS: Take the investigating officer—how did that proceed? Tell the investigating officer how the mission proceeded?

WORD: We breached a hole in the fence. We started slowly walking up to the house. Once we started walking up to the house, these two gentlemen were standing next to the house. They ran for the car. They got into the car [and] sped off. Myself and Corporal McPherson fired warning shots. When the car didn't stop, we tried to disable it by shooting the engine block and the tires. And then I radioed to Lieutenant Pantano. I told him what we had. He told me to continue on mission, and he will go take care of the car and search it.

GITTINS: So you actually saw the two Iraqi individuals that were in the car; correct?

WORD: Yes.

GITTINS: And you saw them leaning against the wall initially?

WORD: Yes.

GITTINS: And then you saw them run to the vehicle?

WORD: Yes.

GITTINS: You personally saw that with your own two eyes?

WORD: Yes.

GITTINS: And then they got in the vehicle and they drove away?

WORD: Yes.

GITTINS: And what was your conclusion about what they were trying to do at that time?

WORD: They were trying to get out of there.

GITTINS: Would you want to go to combat with Lieutenant Pantano again?

WORD: I would go to combat with him any day.

GITTINS: Were you interviewed by NCIS before you gave your testimony at some other point?

WORD: Yes, I was, several times.

GITTINS: For how long did NCIS interview you?

WORD: One time, it was just a quick briefing. They just wanted to know about Lieutenant Pantano's character. And the second time they interviewed me, they wanted to go through the details of what happened that day.

GITTINS: When they interviewed you about Lieutenant Pantano's character, did you tell them the things that you told me today?

WORD: Yes, I did.

GITTINS: Did they ask you to create a sworn statement at that time?

WORD: They asked me to. The NCIS guy said he was going to type it up and bring it back for me to sign, but he never did.

GITTINS: So he never brought you anything to sign?

WORD: No.

GITTINS: Did he ask you—when you were interviewed by the NCIS back—do you remember when that was?

WORD: Honestly, I don't. It was about two months after the incident that happened.

GITTINS: The shooting incident?

WORD: Yes.

GITTINS: Did they ask any questions about Sergeant Coburn's character?

WORD: No, they did not.

GITTINS: So all they wanted to know was about Lieutenant Pantano's character?

WORD: Yes.

GITTINS: And you told them the good things that you told us here today?

WORD: Yes, sir.

GITTINS: And they never brought you a statement to sign?

WORD: No, sir.

GITTINS: That is all I have, sir.

WINN: Government?

Major Keane had been conferring with Captain Kindlon, who was leaning forward at the table, tensely waiting his chance.

KINDLON: How far away were you from the Iraqis when you asked them—when you forced them to push the button?

WORD: We were about 150 meters away behind the vehicle.

KINDLON: Were you afraid it was a bomb?

WORD: Yes, we were.

KINDLON: And you forced the Iraqis to push that button?

WORD: Yes.

Charlie Gittins immediately saw the prosecution's play unfolding and rose to preempt the maneuver.

GITTINS: He is not in the military.

KEANE: Sir, I think you need to read him his rights. It's a law of—

Bullshit. I started to stand. Stackhouse whacked an arm across my chest like a father protecting his toddler during a car wreck. The days of constant assaults on my character had become unbearable. But now the government lawyers were trying to portray my boys as criminals for protecting themselves from those suicidal terrorists? I could *not* accept this kind of shit. These prosecutors in their cammie utilities that had never been stained with blood had no idea what was going on out there or what the bottom of a jaw landing at your feet smells like while the engine block is smoking two hundred meters away in another direction. Too many Marines had died from stupidity like trying to follow rigid, predictable procedures at vehicle checkpoints. And I was determined to make that point, here, *now,* in this courtroom. But Phil restrained me while Charlie held Major Winn's attention.

"Stick," the combat-seasoned door kicker, was visibly shaken at the prospect of ending up on the wrong side of the law. Just like me. We'd had too many weapons in our faces, and I was furious that our own side, the U.S. Marine Corps, had pulled this one on him. Wasn't I enough?

> GITTINS [TO MAJOR WINN]: He is not in the military. He is not
> subject to the Uniform Code of Military Justice.

That fuse had sputtered and gone cold.

> KINDLON: Do you understand that the use of self-defense
> needs to be reasonable; right?
> WORD: Yes.
> KINDLON: So when this car tried to run you over, that self-
> defense was reasonable?
> WORD: Yes.
> KINDLON: When you had these two Iraqis push that button,
> were you acting in self-defense when you did
> that?
> WORD: Yes. I was protecting myself and my men.
> KINDLON: And you also put them in harm's way?
> WORD: Yes.
> KINDLON: Did it ever occur to you that this violated the five
> S's and the T [the detainee handling protocol]?
> WORD: Yes. It did violate the five S's and the T.

KINDLON: I thought you said earlier that Lieutenant Pantano said you could never violate the five S's and the T?

WORD: Well, every situation is going to dictate what you can do. You are not supposed to—you are not supposed to go off of them. But in rare incidents, you have to.

And that was basically all the prosecution could wrest from Judd Word. Now Charlie Gittins rose and addressed Major Winn.

GITTINS: Sir, at this time I would like to have marked as the next investigative exhibit in order, Naval Criminal Investigative Service report of screening interviews dated 22 July '04, which indicates that those two witnesses who just came in here and testified had no information relevant to this investigation.

I looked at Keane and Kindlon. *That's gotta hurt, boys.*

FOB Mahmudiyah, Iraq
25 August 2004

"Do not be angry that he is dead, rather thank God that he lived," the chaplain told us.

The company was formed into its platoons for Corporal Belchik's memorial service. And the Marines, all of us, were shaken, subdued. There was a pyramid of neatly stacked sandbags at the heart of the formation. We were due to leave Iraq in a few weeks. Who got killed outside a playground, of all places? And the guys who survived?

Good thing Doc Thompson wrapped those fingers up with Jernigan's hand. *Hope that works out for him. Microsurgery and all that.*

There were a lot of Marines from the other companies there, too. Even if those Muj bastards dropped mortars and rockets on top of us right now, no one would have moved. The chaplain did his thing, and the battalion commander did his, and then it was Captain Weston's turn to speak.

"We will help the Iraqis when we can, but if an enemy presents himself, we will put him in the ground." *Amen.* "Honor Belchik. Take care of each other. Be brave," he concluded. Corporal Belchik's friends and fellow squad leaders gave their tributes, and then it was time.

First Sergeant Graham had taught drill instructors how to terrorize recruits and simultaneously be models of Marine professionalism, so when it was his time to close the ceremony, it was perfect. With measured cadence and in a powerful tone, he announced, "Corporal Christopher Belchik, 1974–2004." Then a procession began to peel off, one at a time. The Marines of the honor guard planted his weapon—bayonet first—into the sandbags. Then they placed his helmet on the rifle and his boots—the clean, extra pair—at the bottom. Somewhere in the process a pair of dog tags got hung on the rifle's pistol grip.

But the traditional closing of the ceremony was the most wrenching.

We came to attention and the CO called for the first sergeant, who, in turn, faced the company and shouted out the names of the 2nd Platoon squad leaders: "Sergeant Crutcher. Corporal Capucccio.

"Corporal Belchik . . . Corporal Bel-*chik* . . ."

Like he was lost and we were going to find him. *Goddammit!*

Silence. The ringing of a bell. Taps.

And then I began to cry. I was standing behind my platoon. Staff Sergeant Glew was up front, the platoon commander now. I was just a spectator. A friend of the family. Some of my boys were clearly shaken and I put my arms around them and gripped their hands. I told them to stay hard and that it would be okay. They said that they missed me. Some even said they were scared. I couldn't stay. The grief was overwhelming, engulfing me.

Camp Lejeune
28 April 2005

The final event of the afternoon was watching my interview with Stone Phillips on NBC's *Dateline*. It was the one piece of evidence that both the prosecution and the defense wanted to present. We darkened the courtroom and sat back as Stone's voice took me on a little trip.

I'd flown up to New York to shoot the interview at the Women's Republican Club near Rockefeller Center. The bookish parlor effect was maximized by dramatic lighting. This gravitas was a nice touch, since the show's other segment would be Drew Barrymore talking about the rigors of turning thirty.

As I'd finished makeup and sat in the interview chair, I'd felt isolated, alone . . . naked. I dreaded what my family would see when the editors finished clipping and pasting the tape.

Now the courtroom television monitor flickered and the *Dateline* segment played.

Stone Phillips's earnest anchorman's voice was reading the setup.

> *The following is Lieutenant Pantano's version of what happened just four days later. On April 15, his unit got a tip from some Iraqis in a town south of Baghdad. They identified a house where they claimed insurgents were hiding out and storing weapons. Pantano says he smelled a setup.*

PANTANO: The most critical clue was that the people who gave us this information drew a map. We had never had that kind of a windfall of information. So this thing smelled like an ambush immediately.

PHILLIPS: Sounded too good to be true to you.

PANTANO: Absolutely. We went in heavy. We had machine guns with us because we fully expected we would be ambushed by some larger force as we had just seen just days prior.

PHILLIPS: You were not taking this lightly.

PANTANO: Not at all.

The interview continued to recount the details of the raid and led the viewer to the final confrontation.

> *Lieutenant Pantano ordered his radio operator and his corpsman to take up security positions. While they kept their eyes on the surrounding area, Pantano, armed with an M-16, watched the Iraqis as they began to search the car, one the front seat, the other the back. Almost immediately, he says, they began speaking*

to each other in muffled tones in Arabic. What happened next unfolded in a flash.

PANTANO: I give them a command in Arabic to stop. They continue and then there was this moment of quiet. I felt, I could feel like the oxygen getting sucked out of my lungs. I could feel that this thing was happening. There was this beat and they both pivoted to me at the same time, moving towards me at the same time and, in that moment, of them, of them disobeying my command to stop and pivoting to me at the same time, I shot them.

Pantano's concern was that they might have grabbed a hidden weapon or were lunging for his. From just ten feet away, he emptied one magazine from his M-16 rifle, then reloaded and emptied a second, firing a total of fifty to sixty shots.

PANTANO: I didn't wait to see if there was a grenade. I didn't wait to see if there was a knife. And, unfortunately, there are a lot of dead soldiers and Marines who have waited, too long. And my men weren't going to be those dead soldiers or Marines and neither was I.

PHILLIPS: And the idea of maybe firing a warning shot?

PANTANO: There wasn't time for warning shots. There was time for action and I had to act. It becomes very personal. It stops being about war and moving blue arrows and little pieces and big pieces and hold this bridge and take this ground. These guys tried to kill me. That's what I'm feeling and the language that's going through my head at that point was no better friend, and no worse enemy.

. . . But, even if Pantano did act in self-defense, the number of bullets he fired and his reason for doing so raised serious questions.

PHILLIPS: You emptied a magazine. And emptied a second magazine.

PANTANO: The speed it took me to wipe the sweat off my brow is how quickly you fire and reload a magazine. I shot them until they stopped moving.

PHILLIPS: Fifty rounds, sixty rounds to stop them?

PANTANO: Stone, unfortunately, combat is a pretty ugly business. What's the right number of rounds to save your life? I would say it's until there is no more threat.

The monitor went dark. When the lights came up, I could see we had impressed Major Winn with the exhibit.

The clips of burning Humvees and chanting insurgents brandishing RPGs had done precisely what the prosecution was trying to avoid. It had placed the shoot into the context of war. A war that was painfully familiar for Major Winn.

AO Warlord
September 2004

On September 6, something very bad happened. A suicide car bomb hit a convoy from 2/1 (the guys I'd worked with north of Fallujah). The bomb obliterated a seven-ton truck—completely smoked it, killing seven Marines and maiming or wounding six more. The word was it had been another five-hundred-pound bomb and some 155s. The thing that really chapped my ass was that the car had come up from behind. The driver had picked his target, accelerated, and detonated.

The only reason the jihadi had been able to pull that off was that the goddamn division had been hammering us hard on shooting vehicles that get too close to our vehicles. Watch that order get rescinded now.

Four days later, Easy Company was spending forty-eight hours continuously patrolling Latafiyah. And they found five IEDs. *Five!* Five bombs. Many of them quite elaborate. The entire bridge going into the town of Latafiyah was wired as one big booby trap with shells and det cord everywhere.

Fox Company found a house with no roof, just some pullover cammie netting over the top. And the rocket launcher tubes were built into the concrete of the walls! The whole house was a fucking concealed weapon. Who could believe this place?

On September 20, Tyler came to tell me some good news. "Easy shot a car bomb," he said, grinning like a coach who'd just scored a touchdown. "A newish white four-door turned on to Tampa by the Mixing Bowl highway interchange [where they were not allowed]. An ING trooper tried to wave off the car, but it knocked him aside."

Tyler was getting into it now.

"The car barreled toward a checkpoint bunker. But the young SAW-gunner put about a hundred rounds into the car and it finally stopped with the driver slumped dead. The story gets better: the kid then kneels down to wake up the other Marine on post with him and as he does so the bomb detonates, blowing the engine block into the fucking HESCO barrier."

We needed this, sadly. After all of the vehicle checkpoint shootings that had been questioned, we'd stuck to our guns, and after six probings on Tampa alone, the seventh had been a car bomb. That was a persistent enemy. The best part of the story was that Easy 2 deserved a victory. James Lindler's platoon needed it, and they got it. God bless them.

Meanwhile our replacements, 2/24, a Marine Reserve battalion, arrived and were "observing," to see for themselves what we were up against—especially in the face of the insanity from our higher command. They also needed to see how fucking ruthless these Muj were. I hoped the lesson today at the Mixing Bowl saved some of their lives later, too.

The new guys brought a joke from the States:

"What does OIF stand for?"

"Only *IF* I have another division."

Camp Lejeune
4 October 2004

My forehead pressed against the tinted glass. Tires squealed and the bus lurched as it negotiated the traffic circle at the heart of Camp

Lejeune. Yellow ribbons hung from trees. Bedsheets with spray-painted love letters and cardboard signs welcomed the Marines. Some promised sex and cold beer. Some declared the love of mother and child. A few swore to never forget the fallen.

Hard turn as the big tour bus strained to make "E" street without clipping the stop sign. Marines in green cammies and orange vests guided the vehicles to a stop at the red-and-white tents set up in our battalion area. Tyler sat next to me scanning the crowd for his family. As the brakes whined, he flashed me a big smile. We had often talked about this moment as we sat on the roof of the Chicken Factory, counting the tracers. Now the war was over. For him. I tucked a little stuffed puppy toy up my sleeve as I scanned the crowd, too. I wasn't smiling. I was looking for MPs.

The joy of homecoming had been eclipsed by a sour, growing terror of what might happen back here. In Iraq, no one had seemed able to tell me the status of the NCIS investigation, which was now entering its fifth month. With each day that the battalion drew closer to home, my dread had grown at the prospect of what might lie ahead. Abu Ghraib was still a smoldering stain on the war, and the upcoming presidential election was only a month away. Would I become a political casualty, a blood sacrifice? Was I already?

Every morning in Mahmudiyah, I'd woken with nausea and anxiety. Every night I went to bed wondering if the next day I would be ordered to lead my men in combat again in Fallujah, or be led away in cuffs and leg chains. While my brothers were fighting just to stay alive in Iraq, I was fighting my own fear of tomorrow. And all that just for trying to keep my men alive. The war had been surreal even before the investigation, but afterward, it became a Kafkaesque nightmare.

I'd tried to stay optimistic that my name would be cleared with a thorough review and that soon I would be able to resume my career. One night in September, I had asked Lieutenant Colonel Kyser if he would write me a recommendation to his old unit, the 2nd Force Reconnaissance Company, and he warmly assured me that he would "sing your praises to anyone who would listen." After all, my record would speak for itself.

I remembered the wise advice of a senior Navy SEAL commander as we worked together one August night in the Mahmudiyah COC. He was intrigued by my situation and had quickly determined that I should be out of wire leading Marines, not running the maps and radios. I explained that there was an ongoing investigation into one of my shoots and he snorted.

"As the saying goes, Lieutenant, *'These things too shall pass.'*" He clasped my shoulder. "I was investigated once myself. Now I'm the senior SEAL in Iraq."

We laughed about breaking eggs to make an omelet and by the end of his mission, for a brief moment I had my confidence restored that everything would be okay. I stopped him while he was leaving the COC and awkwardly asked if I could have the American flag off his arm. He pulled the muted black-and-tan patch off the Velcro and handed it to me with a smile. I felt giddy, like the little boy from the Mean Joe Green seventies commercial. I don't think the SEAL had any idea how much our exchange had meant to me. Something to remember that night and to bolster my faith.

"God Bless America" flooded in as bus doors hissed open. The cheers from outside were met by our cheers from inside.

Maybe the cars are unmarked. Maybe it'll be plainclothes NCIS. I didn't know what to expect, so my training and DNA as an infantry officer prepared me for the worst. Here I was, at a triumphal moment for everyone around me—my second homecoming as a warrior for my country—and the best I could hope for was not getting cuffed in front of my wife and kid.

"Hey, Pantano," a uniform yelled from the side of the bus.

My fists clenched. I had to get to Jill first.

I pushed my way through the crowd, upsetting some family members as their loved ones were knocked out of their arms. I barreled ahead and an arm caught me from behind.

"Ilario, wait!"

Get the . . .

"*Frank,* holy shit. What are you doing here?" I croaked as I hugged my buddy from TBS. The blood was hot in my cheeks.

"C'mon, Jill and Domenico are over here. Whoa, that belly is huge! Man, I'll tell ya she looks great for nine months. Almost time, right? Wow, two Pantanos. You're gonna have your hands full. You almost got yourself a fire team. Man, Domenico is so talkative. Holy cow, you are one lucky guy. That kid'll be at Harvard in no time."

I felt dizzy.

So much movement. So many emotions. There they were. And everything became quiet. The universe became small. I could see

Domenico pointing me out to his mother. Jill was sobbing, as I hugged her, trying to find my way around this bulging heartbeat that sat in between us. I was glad I hadn't even hinted anything about my lingering nightmare. This deployment had been hard enough for her as a pregnant mother with no husband in the house. She didn't need the weight of worrying about the future.

That was my job. I picked up Domenico and we hugged all together. And then he wanted down, to look more closely at the big green trucks that followed the buses and were delivering our gear. *Oh, my love, there will be plenty of time to talk about seven-tons.*

"Come, give Daddy another hug."

He smelled like the cherry ice that had drizzled down his crisp white shirt. Jill lifted her sunglasses to wipe the tears that would not stop. I was too nervous to cry, as I continued to scan the crowd. Most of the faces were strange. Because I'd been the night watch officer in the COC, I hardly knew any of the Marines in H&S Company and I certainly didn't know their families. Not like my boys in Easy Company who were coming in on a separate flight. I pulled the puppy out of my sleeve, but Domenico was more interested in the four-foot-high truck tires. Now I knew how my dad must have felt thirty years before.

I held a jumbo bag of Lay's potato chips at just the right angle for Domenico to reach in. Soon we were feeding each other chips and making a mess as Jill drove us off base. His car seat elevated him to my eye level and I looked at a little face that was already different from the month-old pictures I carried in my pocket.

Small talk at first. Her mother's recent visit. My dad's planned one. The house. The dog. The baby shower Matt and Tina threw at Sara's house with Jenny, Steve, and Ian. Frank's wedding to Kelly, who looked so beautiful. Big Frank was so proud. Debbie was so radiant. Season five of *The Sopranos* was so good. Had I seen the presidential conventions on TV? What did I want for dinner tonight?

I tried not to look forward. Only down. Every time I saw the road I would start scanning for IEDs. Detcord, dead dogs, a pile of trash . . . Every car was a threat. The month prior we'd had thirty-two car bombs. Nine in one day.

Nine.

In one day.

I looked into the foil bag. The rich, oily smell was grounding me in this new reality even as my mind continued to run its old survival drills.

Jill saw me go quiet and she stopped talking. She was having a hard time containing her relief. Weeks before we came home, a rumor had circulated among the wives that we would be extending to do Fallujah a second time. *We* had all hoped so. Leaving Iraq with Fallujah still festering was like leaving a mess for someone else to clean up, and we all felt ashamed and disgraced by it.

The bigger shame was our reason for coming home: there wasn't enough equipment in the theater to go around. Our radios, trucks, and heavy weapons all had to get turned over to our relief, the 2/24 Marines, so there was just no gear for us except our rifles and our packs. Even the machine guns and radios that we had brought from Camp Lejeune had been handed over. Equipment was breaking, being used up, or wearing out faster than it could be replaced. The cupboards were bare. A sorry state of affairs for the nation's premier fighting force. But selfishly, this meant I would get to witness the birth of my son, Pino.

Jill's second pregnancy had been harder than her first. I'd tried to provide constant support, as had her parents. But I'd also forced her to live through a long-distance war with images of dead and wounded Marines streaming across every newscast. She'd never known if one of the Marines in "Al Anbar Province" had been me.

In the family briefs she attended before my homecoming, career military wives with multiple deployments under their ample belts warned the first-timers to give their husbands some space.

"What you've been through at home is hard. We know it," said a wrinkled fortysomething key wife volunteer. "But you can't compare. There's no tit for tat. Your pain and his pain are different."

The lectures had tried to prepare the wives for the anxiety and anguish that their men would experience on returning from combat duty.

But nothing could have prepared Jill for what happened next.

TEN

Article 32 Hearing
DAY FIVE

Camp Lejeune
30 April 2005

After three days, Sergeant Daniel Coburn was granted the immunity he'd sought in order to continue testifying. He was scheduled to be the last witness, and then the prosecution and defense would make their closing arguments.

The previous day had been taken up with defense witnesses giving testimony on my behalf and with the submission of thirty letters of character reference from officers and staff NCOs who had served with me.

Sergeant Coburn showed little emotion as he took the witness stand for what we all expected to be a long morning. Coburn now had his own military lawyer, a JAG lieutenant named Androski.

WINN: Sergeant Coburn, you may take your seat. I remind you that you are still under oath. Lieu-

tenant Androski, did you go over with your
client the terms of the grant of immunity?

ANDROSKI: Yes, I did, sir.

WINN: Did he understand it?

ANDROSKI: Yes, sir.

WINN: Okay. Mr. Gittins?

GITTINS: Now with respect to the immunity grant, is it
your understanding that the grant of immunity
applies to any testimony you give from now—
from the date it was signed onward?

Coburn remained silent. Was he confused already?

GITTINS: Let me ask it another way. Do you believe that
this grant of immunity protects you for lies you
may have told on Wednesday?

COBURN: It should.

Riiight.

GITTINS: So you believe that any lie you may have told on
Wednesday would be protected by this grant of
immunity; correct?

COBURN: Yes, sir.

GITTINS: Tell me what lies you told me on Wednesday?

COBURN: I don't recall of any lies I told you, sir.

GITTINS: You don't recall of any?

COBURN: No, sir.

GITTINS: So you may have told me some lies, but you just
can't recall what they may have been?

COBURN: I am saying that that covers Wednesday.

GITTINS: Okay. My question was, "You can't recall the lies
you may have told me on Wednesday"; is that
true?

COBURN: If I did, I do not recall.

Wilmington, North Carolina
November 2004

"Ilario, would you turn the TV back on please? *Please?*"

I had barely managed to squeeze onto the couch as I took Jill's hand.

Her pregnancy was at the stage of permanent discomfort that could be relieved only by delivery. Until then, nothing felt good, and we were still weeks away.

I would have waited until the baby was born to tell her about the investigation, but I was trapped. Now stateside, my paranoia was fueled by the lack of news and the silence of my commanders, who earnestly shrugged their shoulders. No one was telling them anything, either, and I'm sure they felt like NCIS was looking at them, too.

Jill needs to know, but how do I do it gently? I didn't want yet another complication from this war ruining my marriage. How did I tell her she wasn't sharing her bed with a monster without scaring her to death?

"Babe, it's important that you understand some things . . . about me and about . . . ." She adjusted her back on the couch, alarmed by my tone.

"I'm still your husband, right? . . . You've had a few days to . . . ."

"Yeah."

"It's still me, right?" We both marveled at how quickly we had resumed life where we left off seven months before. "I mean, you've had a chance to see me with Domenico . . . I'm not sleepwalking or . . . I haven't grown hair or fangs, right?"

"Uh-huh."

"I mean, things seem . . . pretty normal, right?"

"What's so normal about you leaving your family? What the hell is rational about kissing your two-year-old son goodbye for seven months? If you even come home at all? What standard of normal are you talking about? Honestly, there is nothing normal about that, Ilario. There just isn't."

Okay, I'd had that coming, but she realized that she had gone too far.

"I'm sorry. Yes, Ilario, you're not a drooling vegetable that barks at the moon every Wednesday. Congratulations." Wiseass. She still thought that being pregnant was harder than fighting. She was probably right.

"You understand that bad things ha—"

"Good. Does that mean you want to hang up your 'gun-belt' so we can go back to New York?" She pointed her index finger at me and cocked her thumb. I was always too wordy, and she wasn't cutting me any slack tonight.

"Yes-s-s," she continued. "I know that you kill people. Yes-s-s, I know it's terrible and you see people die and stuff like that. Is that what you mean?" I felt like a dad trying to tell his smartass teenage daughter about sex. She knew the words but had no idea what they actually meant. Just like me talking about birth. I took her hands in mine.

"Honey, bad things happened to us. And I had to do bad things. I don't regret them, but I regret having to tell you about them. Things that I wish to God you would never have to know about. But you do.

"Do you remember the movie *A Perfect Storm* with the fishing boat lost at sea? You know, the one with Diane Lane, that chick you look like?"

"I don't look like her, but yes . . ."

"Well, do you remember the scene when that little boat is caught in a monster of a wave, like a hundred-footer or something?" I let go of her hands to demonstrate the small boat angling upward as the wave towered over it.

"Yeah, I remember."

"Well that scene, that horror of being overwhelmed and surrounded by danger . . . That was Iraq in April 2004. That was my world. The wave kept getting bigger and we were sliding backwards. The world became unhinged."

She was quiet, watching me as I spoke.

"Jill, we were running out of ammo. We were running out of food. Our twenty-first-century army was being ground down by these savages. They cut our supply lines, they attacked . . ." I was losing her and I had to stop myself. That was enough for tonight. She needed to learn the truth, but she didn't want to know details. My case was all about the details. If I didn't want her to recoil in shock and fear, I needed to break her in slowly to the reality of war. She just wasn't equipped for it. Who was? Jill was still envisioning the little boat climbing against the swelling wave. I was seeing it, too, only my wave was on fire.

In the end, I was weak or maybe just stupid. I offered up my journal thinking that "if and when" she was ready, she would look at it. Her pace. No pressure. No secrets.

The next day I had Domenico at the playground so his mother could have a chance to rest in quiet. My cell phone rang. It was Jill.

"What the hell is going on?" She was hysterical.

"What do you mean?" I looked at Domenico to make sure I hadn't forgotten his shoes or something.

"Are you crazy?" She began to read through her sobs, struggling with my tiny handwriting and letters scribbled by flashlight.

9/24 Spoke to Jill today—Whenever she says something like "We have something to talk about . . ." or "A lot is going on . . ." I get nervous. I get nervous that she has been told something or she has heard a rumor. I'm particularly concerned for my unborn baby . . .

"Ilario, what's going on? What is this?"

I think I have done the right thing by keeping the details from her. The shock to her system could be catastrophic for our baby. Can you imagine the trauma of:

A) Your Husband is in a war . . .

B) Finding out some fucking rumor or allegation is causing him to be prosecuted . . .

C) His future is in jeopardy? The entire rest of your lives together threatened, the bad name for you and your family . . .

"Hon, honey. *Honey.* Stop. I'll be home in five minutes." I clicked off the phone.

Jill was sleeping peacefully in the dim light of her hospital room as images of filthy troops dragging wounded comrades flickered on the television. I didn't need the volume on to know what was happening. After a painful wait, the inevitable occurred in the week after the presidential election. Jill gave birth to Pino, and U.S. ground forces swept Fallujah.

Coming home from Iraq in time to witness the birth of my second child was a blessing, and yet I felt ashamed that others were fighting my battle. Even worse, I felt a sense of profound self-loathing for a man that couldn't surrender to the joy of a newborn and the warm touch of his wife.

My mind seemed unable to escape the savage brutality on the other side of the world.

Here I am stuck in a maternity ward.

Oh, Christ. How could I even think that?

The live-or-die—kill the other bastard before he kills you—simplicity of combat was so seductive. For days, *and* for longer nights, I had been struggling with a rancid chemical soup in my brain. I was in clinical withdrawal from the powerful neurotransmitter adrenaline, the sustenance that had nourished us in Iraq. But now my mind was corroding in an acid bath of anxiety that had nothing to do with IEDs, RPGs, or incoming 82 mm rounds. This mental assault came from the NCIS.

To top it off, seven pounds of fresh anxiety was sleeping noisily in a crib three feet away.

Am I more afraid of failing as a father than I am of dying?

Hoping to crush these ideas, I inhaled deeply, taking in the dull antiseptic odor of the room and the mustiness of the dozens of men who had waited anxiously in this very same chair. I hoped that they hadn't had to endure the same tormented night. I was discovering one more dimension of war that I could never talk about. Who would understand its dark pull on my soul?

As my son was taking his first breaths, some of my brothers were gasping their last. This tragic irony was particularly poignant for an eager warrior who had been out of the arena for only a month. Waging war had come easily to me. Now it was the "peace" of home that I struggled with. I wrapped myself in the news accounts of Fallujah. Their grim familiarity was weirdly comforting. In the tales of two deaths, I saw echoes of my own life.

Marine Corporal Nick Ziolkowski grew up near downtown Baltimore, and, like me, had no shooting background before he became a sniper. Killing three guerrillas in one day, he took his helmet off to scan for targets from a rooftop position inside Fallujah and was shot through the head. The jagged oval gash from the bullet that had glanced off PFC Smith's helmet was still a fresh, scary image in my mind.

I remembered our discovery of the heaped chocolate-chip cammies when I read about guerrillas in authentic ING uniforms being signaled by an American patrol. When the Marines exposed themselves, the turncoats opened fire and killed Corporal Nathan Anderson, who, like Corporal Ziolkowski, was a member of Bravo Company, 1/8. For the hundredth time, I felt the impotence of not becoming "decisively engaged."

I was startled—a cold jangling mental splinter—by the dark shape of the nurse as she came in to check on Jill and Pino. The light from the corridor revealed her colorful uniform and I'm sure she said something pleasant. I smiled, but I wouldn't have heard her if she'd screamed.

Camp Lejeune
April 30, 2005

> GITTINS: On 15 April 2004 you were no longer the squad leader for Third Platoon; correct?
>
> COBURN: Yes, sir.
>
> GITTINS: Sergeant Trent had been appointed to the squad leader by that time; correct?
>
> COBURN: Yes, sir.

I was about to write Charlie a yellow Post-it note until I realized he had set a trap.

> GITTINS: I am sorry, it was *Corporal* Trent who was made the squad leader; right?
>
> COBURN: Yes, sir.
>
> GITTINS: It wasn't a sergeant, he was actually a corporal; correct?
>
> COBURN: Yes, sir, a corporal.
>
> GITTINS: Among the sergeants in your platoon where did you lie in order of seniority?
>
> COBURN: I was still the senior sergeant.
>
> GITTINS: You were still the senior sergeant?
>
> COBURN: Yes, sir.
>
> GITTINS: Sergeant Coburn, let me show you what has been marked Investigative Exhibit 65. Is that your fitness report covering the period of April 1st, 2004, to June 15th, 2004?
>
> COBURN: Yes, sir.

GITTINS: And that fitness report covers the period in which you have been relieved as a squad leader; correct?

COBURN: Yes, sir.

GITTINS: On Page One of that fitness report, sir, if you look at Item Four, duty assignment, what does it say?

COBURN: Radio operator, sir.

GITTINS: You were relieved of your duties after a patrol that occurred a few days prior to April 15th; isn't that true, sir?

COBURN: A few days, yes, sir.

GITTINS: On that patrol Lieutenant Pantano took over that patrol because he believed that you put the patrol in danger; isn't that true?

COBURN: Yes, sir.

GITTINS: You stopped your patrol in an area of buildings known as "the Brick Yard"; correct?

COBURN: I don't know what the area was called.

GITTINS: But there were buildings all around it; correct?

COBURN: It had a few rows of old dilapidated buildings, but yes, sir.

GITTINS: Lieutenant Pantano walked up and found that your Marines had not cleared the buildings and the rest of your squad was sitting around resting; right?

COBURN: My first fire team was in the process of clearing.

GITTINS: Had they cleared the buildings while your platoon was resting in the middle of a kill zone?

COBURN: We weren't in the middle. We were on the outskirts.

GITTINS: Lieutenant Pantano reported, "this is exemplified by his failure to use the guidance provided to him in his past two fitness reports [and] the formal counselings and [that] MRO [Coburn] reports never to have received. Startlingly bad judgment was repeatedly observed during the conduct of combat patrols. On one occasion during the volatile Arabe'en [Arbaeen] offensive in Latafiyah the platoon commander assumed command of the patrol after the MRO failed to clear potential kill boxes where he had placed his Marines for a rest halt. MRO has since been tasked to be the platoon's RTO where he no longer leads Marines."

That is what was reported; isn't that true?

COBURN: That is what was reported, yes, sir.

GITTINS: And Captain Weston reviewed the circumstances of your relief following that incident; didn't he?

COBURN: Yes, sir.

GITTINS: He was required to investigate it; correct?

COBURN: Yes, sir.

GITTINS: And he concurred with Lieutenant Pantano; didn't he?

COBURN: He did, sir.

GITTINS: What you said in your rebuttal was, "Lieutenant Pantano lists that I made a bad judgment call by failing to clear a potential kill zone. That potential kill zone was a group of deserted buildings that have not been lived in for a long period of time. My squad was there the night before and found nothing to indicate that anyone was staying there."

Sir, did you rely on the fact that there had been nothing there the night before as an indication that there was nothing there the morning that you were out on patrol?

COBURN: The squad that just left that area briefed me that there was no movement, no activity in the area. They just left that position. We were going back to that position. So we were there the night before the squad came in that area, after we left and we came right back in that same area right after they left.

GITTINS: Sir, in your fitness report rebuttal you say that [the] potential kill zone was a group of deserted buildings that had not been lived in for a long period of time.

COBURN: My squad was there the night before and found nothing to indicate that anyone was staying there.

GITTINS: So you don't think your platoon commander was right? You were right; he was wrong, is that your testimony?

COBURN: That was my belief, yes, sir.

GITTINS: You don't believe that demonstrated startlingly bad judgment?

COBURN: No, sir.

GITTINS: You don't believe that justified your relief because you had endangered Marines in combat?

COBURN: No, sir.

GITTINS: Do you know Captain Weston?

COBURN: Yes, sir.

GITTINS: Do you believe him to be a competent officer?

Coburn paused, wary now.

COBURN: Yes, sir.

GITTINS: Do you have a question about that? The way you shook your head kind of maybe, maybe not. Do you have a question about whether he was a competent officer, sir?

COBURN: No, sir.

GITTINS: Your reviewing officer stated, "Sergeant Coburn has continually demonstrated the inability to handle the responsibilities required of a Marine of his rank and grade. This has become especially apparent during times of combat where his judgment and initiative have brought his abilities into question. Not only does he fail to take action in the absence of orders but also continually fails to seek self-improvement. This is exemplified by his failure to use the guidance provided to him in his past two fitness reports, the formal counselings the Marine Reported On reports never to have received."

He also stated, ". . . it has been my observation the reporting senior has given Sergeant Coburn every opportunity to be successful and he has squandered it. In an effort to resolve the inconsistency and disagreements between the RS

[Reporting Senior] and the MRO statements I have taken the follow actions:

"First, I interviewed the Marines that served in Sergeant Coburn's squad while he was squad leader.

"Second, I interviewed Sergeant Coburn's platoon sergeant during this reporting period.

"Last, I reviewed the past patrol reports, specifically those written by Sergeant Coburn. In the course of my inquiry, it was apparent that none of the MRO's claims could be verified. To the contrary, everything reviewed, and all but one Marine interviewed, substantiated the RS's comments in terms of the Marine Reported On's initiative and judgment.

"Additionally, I found that the personal statements made concerning the reporting senior were not appropriate for this forum and are issues more timely handled through an Article 138 complaint. Last and most disturbing is the fact that the MRO failed to realize that his removal as squad leader and reassignment as the platoon radio operator was a signal that he had lost the faith and confidence of his chain of command. As the senior sergeant in the platoon, in accordance with the MOS manual, his duties lie either as a squad leader or platoon guide. As a result, I find Sergeant Coburn's comparative assessment unsatisfactory. And therefore, the Marine Corps should not retain him."

Is that the report you received from Captain Weston?

COBURN: Yes, sir.

GITTINS: And you believe him to be a competent Marine officer?

Coburn was staring at a spot on the far wall, his face puffy.

COBURN: He is competent. Yes, sir.

GITTINS: Okay. You believe those two fitness reports together are career-enders; do you not?

Coburn swallowed, but kept his tongue still inside his cheeks.

COBURN: The last one is.

GITTINS: Okay. So you understand that when you use the term "career-ender," that means you understood that you were not likely to be promoted; correct?

COBURN: Yes, sir. It was an adverse fitrep.

GITTINS: And if you are not promoted, you are not going to be permitted to remain in the Marine Corps, correct?

COBURN: At my max Time in Grade.

GITTINS: Which will be?

COBURN: Thirteen years.

GITTINS: And Colonel Kyser's response to what you put in your rebuttal was that you believed you were—he believed you were being disingenuous; isn't that true?

COBURN: I would have to read it again, sir.

GITTINS: Colonel Kyser reported in a fitness report submitted to Headquarters Marine Corps, in an official record that you were unaware of your deficiencies in Colonel Kyser's opinion, disingenuous; correct?

COBURN: In his opinion. Yes, sir.

GITTINS: And he is the battalion commander responsible for everything, welfare and efficiency of your battalion; correct?

COBURN: Yes, sir.

GITTINS: Disingenuous—you told us the other day what "thespian" is. Do you know what "disingenuous" means?

COBURN: I do not.

GITTINS: When you got the fitness report, when your battalion commander referred to you as disingenuous, did you get out the dictionary to read what it means?

COBURN: No, sir.

GITTINS: You didn't bother?

COBURN: No, sir.

Camp Lejeune
1 February 2005

The day had been a blur of training meetings, phone calls, and urgent e-mails that had accumulated while I was in the field. The late January weather had been relatively mild, which played a big part in the perceived success of the training op. The corporals and sergeants who had been selected from their sections to attend my three-day NCO course actually enjoyed it. I built a curriculum drawn from the hard lessons learned in Iraq, a place we would be returning to in July. We needed to make sure that the NCOs of H&S Company had confidence in their ability to act as infantrymen, even if their actual job was comm-chief, admin-clerk, or cook. That was one lesson we'd learned in Latafiyah. Not so secretly, the training served as an excuse for me to strap on my pack and weapon and be a grunt instead of just an office pogue.

We practiced land navigation, ran patrols, and dug fighting holes, but imparting the warrior spirit took more than a lecture or a foot movement through the woods. After a long day of training and field exercises and a fireside chat on leadership, I didn't have to tell the NCOs twice to get some sleep. They were all snoring in minutes, cozy in their bags as ice crystals formed on their boots. Once my support team had everything in place, we woke one student at a time and I ordered the dazed and confused NCO to stand at attention in just his trousers and blouse.

"Do not say a fucking word . . ." I'd whisper in my most sinister tone. "Put this blindfold on. A guide will take you to your next event." Their bodies would start to tremble from the midnight chill and the anticipation. The guide would then run them one at a time down a three-hundred-meter trail and sit them on a soft patch of cleared ground. Moments later another disoriented student would be placed in the "ring" and once they were back to back they received an order they would never forget.

"*Fight.*"

The challenge for these young men was to summon their interpersonal violence from a deep sleep to overcome an opponent they couldn't see while they were under physical and mental duress of cold, fear, and fatigue. Going from 0 to 60 was easier for some than it was for others, but they learned a lot of lessons that night under the watchful supervision of Gunny Trotter, our black-belt instructor. After all the Marines had fought, we lit a bonfire and read Medal of Honor citations from World Wars I and II where Marines and soldiers had to kill dozens of enemy with nothing more than bayonets or hands. This put their experience into perspective. It was part of their job.

That had been last week. Today my job demanded that I clear off my desk and write some training plans for the next few months. I had finally stopped procrastinating, when a clerk walked up to my desk and told me to go see the battalion XO, Major Dixon.

"Good afternoon, sir. Lieutenant Pantano reporting as ordered, sir." I was a little extra stiff and half joking. We had a good relationship after so much time under the gun in Iraq.

"Siddown, Ilario," Major Dixon replied into his computer monitor, careful not to look up. Then, as an afterthought, "Close the door." I almost tripped over his flak jacket and helmet in the small office as I made my way back to the chair. He opened a file on his desk, scanned it, and then looked up at me. The color was gone from his face but his eyes were completely neutral.

"I'm supposed to read this to you . . . but I can't." He passed me the folder. "Here."

Medals for my guys?

"Murder?" I almost shouted.

No. This can't be right. Let me read it again slowly.

The word hadn't disappeared from the page.

"Murder?" I couldn't close my mouth. It actually hung open stupidly as my head sagged toward the documents.

Noooo. This cannot be right.

The charge sheet read:

Violation of the UCMJ, Article 92. In that second Lieutenant Ilario Pantano, U.S. Marine Corps, 2nd Battalion, 2nd Marine Regiment . . . who knew of his duties at or near Mahmudiyah, Iraq, on or about 15 April 2004, was derelict in the performance of those duties in that he willfully failed to properly safeguard the physical health, welfare, and treatment of [detainee #1] as it was his duty to do by . . . Relieving Sergeant Daniel Coburn, U.S. Marine Corps and Hospitalman George Gobles, U.S. Navy, from their assignment to guard detainees . . . Telling Hospitalman Gobles to remove the flex cuffs . . . Telling Sergeant Coburn and

*Hospitalman Gobles to take up posts facing away . . . Shooting
[detainee #1] in the back with an M16A4 service rifle; and leaving [detainee #1]'s body on display in order to send a message to
the local people.*

The charges went on and on for two pages of articles 109, 118, and
133. Words like ". . . with premeditation, murder . . . by means of
shooting him with an M16A4 service rifle . . ."

I looked up, my eyes running with tears. I had to shake my head to
clear the disbelief and went back to reading.

*. . . on or about 15 April 2004, willfully and wrongfully damage
an automobile by slashing four (4) tires, smashing headlights and
taillights, and smashing the rear window, of an aggregate value of
less than $500.00.*

"Sir, they are charging me—" I had to take another breath. "They
are charging me for disabling a bomber's car? Sir, they . . . five hundred dollars . . . Sir . . . Do they . . . ?" Another breath and an internal
scramble to regain my composure. "Sir, do they know how many
Marines these things kill every day? What's happening here? Has anyone told them there is a war going on out there?"

My voice was now more outrage than disbelief.

"Ilario. I'm sorry."

Then he added, "Get a lawyer."

"There's good news and then there's bad news," the senior defense
counsel at Camp Lejeune told me.

"Well, sir, I'm in the bad news business today. What have you got
for me?"

That might have sounded glib to Major Stackhouse, but I was trying to pull myself together and phony bravado was all I could muster.
Phil had been an enlisted Marine who worked his way through the
ranks to become an officer and ultimately a well-respected attorney. In
the coming months, this father of two, with premature white hair,
would become my priest, my friend, and my champion, but right now
he was just a messenger.

"This Article 118 charge, or I should say these two Article 118
charges are premeditated murder. That's capital," he paused.

"Capital, like . . ."

"Capital like death penalty."

This wasn't the moment for reflection or even processing. I was simply absorbing. Absorbing the framed diplomas. Absorbing the legal volumes. Absorbing the mounted fighting knife that had been a gift from his old platoon.

"Now, if this actually went to court-martial and they got a conviction it's unlikely the government would press to execute. In that case, we're probably looking at life with a possibility of parole . . ."

Every business has a language, and the technical jargon of the law sounded kind of cool in my detached state. I heard things like that on TV shows, and now someone was on the other side of a busy desk and his lips were moving and sounds were coming out. Instead of registering that I was the object of those neat words, my coping mechanisms were triggering fantasies of becoming a lawyer.

". . . but since it's a double, they could be consecutive sentences, which would kind of suck." He finished with a smile like a doctor trying to soften the blow of a cancer diagnosis.

"Yeah. Kind of," I shot back smiling. "Whooooeee. Now how about that good news?" Our grins almost turned to outright laughter at the absurdity of my situation: the absurdity of facing death because I chose to face death.

"Mmmm. The good news . . ." He twisted at the waist, retrieved an inch-thick binder from a pile on the floor, plopped it on his desk, and smiled.

"This is your case."

I blinked. There was nothing innately comforting about that small binder. Stackhouse bent down again and struggled to retrieve another one crammed with about seven hundred pieces of paper. It thudded onto his desktop with the hefty authority of three phone books.

"This is one of my drug cases. The knucklehead tested positive for marijuana." He patted them both and continued, "Yours is capital murder and it's barely a fraction of this one." He lifted my case file. "It might just rank as the worst investigation I've ever seen. And I've seen a few." He shoved the drug case off his desk and flipped open my binder.

"There are no interviews with any of your superiors, not yours and not Coburn's. They didn't even speak to Captain Weston, the one guy who signed both of your fitness reports. Heck, there are no fitness reports! Not a one for either of you." He shook his head with a frustrated grin.

"Maybe that's a good thing, sir. If we request them, maybe it'll force them to dig a little deeper. Then they'd see what this is about and they'd turn it off," I said hopefully.

"Nah. Not now. Once the process starts, there isn't much anyone can do. And it's started. Now what's the deal with this statement you gave to the XO of RCT 1?"

"Well sir, he asked about the shooting and I told him. We'd been through so much combat that no one could even remember what day it was. I probably spoke with more gusto than I should have, but I figured he was a Marine, so I talked to him like a Marine, not a lawyer."

"Yeah, it reads kind of arrogant. Did he say you could ask for a lawyer?"

"I didn't want a lawyer sir. I didn't do anything wrong and I figured they'd see that. If I lawyered up then and there it would have created a big stink and the press would have gotten involved."

"Blown up? Like right now? You should have thought of yourself first and worried about the institution later. You've been around long enough to know that."

"Sir, we'd just been through Fallujah. Hell, I had gotten IED'd two weeks before. Was I supposed to be apologetic for killing these guys? Was a platoon commander supposed to tell his senior officer he had been scared? How would that have gone over?"

"Probably better than this." He held the statement up.

"I didn't even write it. He did."

"You didn't type it?"

"No sir, he typed it from his notes."

"Well, that explains that."

Phil was moving on to another part of my file.

"We've got these grainy black-and-white photos to work with. You can't see anything of forensic value, so I'll get the originals. Of course we'll request the bodies right away, but you know what this report says? It says NCIS has been trying to recover them since last summer, but they're in an insurgent cemetery in LAH-TA-FIIYAH and they can't get near 'em."

I nodded, looking down at my hands as they balled into fists.

Phil continued to connect the carnage. "That's part of the 'Triangle of Death' where they kicked the dead Spanish intelligence agents through the streets, right?"

"Yeah. Just a few months ago, they found execution videos and torture rooms with all those blindfolded bodies. Nice place."

Latafiyah.

I thought of Corporal Michael Speer, Lance Corporal Brian Kelly, and Lance Corporal Nicholas Morrison, who had all been killed there. We probably took one hundred wounded in Latafiyah, and Easy Company had found those five IEDs in one day. Phil looked up and shook his head and smiled at me sadly.

"NCIS said, 'It's too dangerous.' "

I sat lifeless on the couch with both hands on my lap. Without even enough energy to channel surf, I watched the yellow text march across the bottom of *Headline News*. Images flashed. Scores. The Dow. The weather. Pope John Paul II was hospitalized. The two-year anniversary of *Columbia* disintegrating on reentry. Where was my disintegration upon reentry?

Where *was* it? My thoughts began to echo. Bursts of traffic on a tac net that only I could hear. And the messages were bad.

Hit me, you motherfuckers.

Hit me, like you mean it.

They already had, but somehow I needed to see it on TV to believe it. I was like a knife fighter who's cut, but doesn't know how bad he's bleeding until it's too late. But the blood, the proof, was in my hands.

Just look down. Just look.

Manila folder. Plain. One of millions. Two front- and back-typed pages. Military form #DD458, CHARGE SHEET.

This wasn't personal, man. This was a form. Stay cool.

NAME OF THE ACCUSED, PANTANO, ILARIO.

Oh, and now I was CASE 05-034. *Okay.*

The Corps has to protect itself. It has to. America has to protect itself. It has to. You know that. You are part of that defense. If you were offered up on the battlefield, that would have been okay, right? Glorious even by your macabre medieval standards. The Hall of Arms and Armor. Isn't that your favorite line: "We're all gonna die. Will it be on your feet or on your knees?" Ver-rry macho. That's your credo, right? Well, how does it feel?

How does it feel to die? No, silly, not on the battlefield, that's not where we need you, young man. We need to offer you up here. At home.

We need the world to be absolutely certain that America only wages clean war. Nothing dirty, pal. They will like us better if we can make them absolutely certain that we are clean. And nice. Americans are not rough. Americans play fair. Americans are not monsters. You, PANTANO, ILARIO, *with your basic pay per month, $4168.20, listed on line 7, you are not paid to be a monster. You are paid to follow orders, to do what you are told. You are paid to accomplish the mission.*

No, we don't care how, just get out there and do it.

Well, we didn't really mean, "We don't care how." We just meant we didn't want to know *how. Because if we know how, then we have to do something about it.*

You, PANTANO, ILARIO, might really think *that you needed to "survive." And no one is saying that you are guilty or innocent, pal. That's for a court to decide. No one's rushing to judgment here, but . . . but honestly, it doesn't look good.*

Appearances. Very important, like shined boots and a well-shaved head. Marines look good.

No, really. This doesn't look good. It looks sloppy. It looks out of control and chaotic. War's not supposed to be like that anymore. That was the past. The bloody lagoon at Tarawa, the bloody snow at Frozen Chosin, the bloody Citadel at Hue. That was Old War. This is New War. You can understand that, right? No one put a gun to your head. No one made you go. You had to twist arms and bend rules. Now look at what you've done.

You happy now, you sick fuck?

Was this what you had in mind when you dragged your family from their home to relocate three times in one year so you could follow your dreams? Who the fuck dreams of going to war? Don't you have enough sex? What, were you beaten as a child? Anger issues? Depression? Penis size?

Here's the situation, PANTANO, ILARIO:
YOU ASKED FOR IT.
BUT THERE ARE CONSEQUENCES, PAL.
WHAT, DO YOU THINK ONLY THE BAD GUYS GET FUCKED?
OR BURNT OR BROKEN OR DESTROYED?
NO, IDIOT. EVERYONE DOES. YOU. ME.
LANCE CORPORAL BAGADONUTS. JOHNNY JIHAD.
MOTHERS. FATHERS. WIVES. SONS.

ACTIONS HAVE CONSEQUENCES.

FAIL TO ACT. CONSEQUENCES.

ACT. CONSEQUENCES.

SHOOT. CONSEQUENCES.

DON'T SHOOT. CONSEQUENCES.

BREATHE. CONSEQUENCES.

What? Would the big bad Marine rather be dead? Would the tough ole "L-Tee" rather have stayed home and watched your war on TV?

This was your war, right?

They hit your city, right? The Big Fucking Apple. Your home, right? You've done this thing in the desert before right? You know all about this, right?

You're going to save lives, right?

WHOSE LIFE ARE YOU GOING TO SAVE NOW?

You like being the tip of someone else's spear?

Well, what happens when that tip breaks?

What happens when you break?

What happens when you ain't so sharp?

What happens when you get thrown away?

SO YOU CHOSE TO BE THROWN AWAY, RIGHT?

The front door unlocked with a snap and opened slowly. Small fingers curled around the edge. Plastic bags rustled. Domenico ran in and jumped onto my lap. Jill came behind him, holding Pino in the car seat, her other hand shifting from house keys to grocery bags.

"Hey, can you bring in the . . ." She saw my cheeks running with tears and went silent.

The three boys were pacified watching a *Baby Einstein* video while Mommy was making dinner. I sat with Domenico on my lap, and little Pino was beside us in his special infant seat that reclined him at just the proper angle. The pinwheels sparkled and spun, the fish bubbled noisily, and a soft voice cooed words in different languages. This stuff was supposed to make kids smarter, but the truth was that we loved the half-hour of infant zombification it bought us.

I took a swig of my Heineken, careful not to shake Domenico out of his reverie.

Whack-whack-whack and then the rush-sizzle of hot oil on fresh vegetables. Onions sautéing. Another long pull on the beer. What a day. I had been watching *CNN Headline News* for hours when Jill had walked in on me. I had been in a mental and spiritual free fall, but I managed to catch myself when I saw that little hand come around the door. I crawled back from the abyss, the way that parents had to when the audience was their children. There were many times during the war and after when I felt that my family had saved my soul.

Tonight they had saved my life.

Camp Lejeune
30 April 2005

GITTINS: On the prior deployment to OIF, where you stayed back on the ship, you were not awarded the Combat Action Ribbon?

COBURN: No, sir.

GITTINS: And you only fired your weapon in Iraq on one occasion. Isn't that true?

COBURN: Yes, sir.

GITTINS: When was that?

COBURN: During an ambush, we were on QRF down in Latafiyah.

GITTINS: That Sunday was the only time you ever fired your weapon in Iraq?

COBURN: Yes, sir.

GITTINS: Did you shoot your weapon in Fallujah?

COBURN: No, sir.

GITTINS: Not a single time?

COBURN: No, sir. I never saw a target to shoot at.

GITTINS: You ever see any of the members of your platoon firing in Fallujah?

COBURN: I saw them fire. I didn't see what they were shooting at.

GITTINS: Okay. You never got into a firefight; right?

COBURN: Not with my squad, no.

GITTINS: In the Easter Sunday firefight, were you—did you actually aim at people to try to kill them?

COBURN: There was a building I was aiming at. Our squads were in a building. They were shooting at that building. We could not see where we were getting shot from. I saw a window, I pointed to the left of it and I fired some rounds in that area.

GITTINS: Some rounds in that area?

COBURN: Yes, sir.

GITTINS: Was that a pretty serious firefight?

COBURN: Yes, sir. The whole battalion got called up into it.

GITTINS: So that happened in April?

COBURN: Yes, sir.

GITTINS: So that would have been an example of something pretty hot happening in April, huh?

COBURN: Yes, sir.

GITTINS: Okay. So it wasn't—when you told me earlier, like in the very beginning of your testimony today, that April wasn't too bad, that was an example of it was pretty bad, wasn't it?

COBURN: That was one occasion.

GITTINS: One occasion.

COBURN: Other than that it was pretty quiet.

GITTINS: Other than that, it was pretty quiet. How about two days before, on the 9th of April, where the battalion had a KIA. Do you remember that?

COBURN: Yes, sir.

GITTINS: Was it pretty cool then too?

COBURN: That Marine came around the corner, got shot in the head by a sniper. It was the only casualty.

The investigating officer visibly blanched. I pushed back in my chair and almost got up, only to be steadied by Stackhouse. We'd had a dozen Marines wounded within that ninety-six hours. Everyone in the room was aghast that Coburn was blaming the victim.

GITTINS: After April 15th, you were assigned to guard detainees in the FOB; correct?

COBURN: Yes, sir.

GITTINS: And the reason you ended up getting assigned over there, let me see if I have got it right. There had been an escape from the prisoner enclosure a couple of days before; right?

COBURN: Yes, sir.

GITTINS: A guy who had been flex-cuffed escaped from the facility and actually they found his underwear in the wire; right?

COBURN: Yes, sir.

GITTINS: He escaped, not only from the prisoner enclosure, but he also escaped from the FOB; correct?

COBURN: Yes, sir.

GITTINS: And this was somebody who had been caught, detained, captured, returned to the FOB, placed in confinement in the FOB, and he managed, somehow, to escape; correct?

COBURN: Yes, sir.

GITTINS: And when he did it, he was actually flex-cuffed; right?

COBURN: Yes, sir.

GITTINS: So you're entitled to use deadly force to protect your own life or to prevent the escape of a detainee; correct?

COBURN: Yes, sir.

GITTINS: Now, the shoot in this case really bothered you; didn't it?

COBURN: Yes, sir.

GITTINS: And you wrote that letter a couple of days later; right?

COBURN: Yes, sir.

GITTINS: And in your letter you stated to your wife that, quote, "His actions were not justified"; correct?

COBURN: Yes, sir.

GITTINS: You were still in a state of shock right after the shooting; correct?

COBURN: I wouldn't say state of shock, it was more of a, I didn't know what just happened. I was pretty much confused about the situation and how it happened.

GITTINS: So right after it happened, your immediate inclination was, I don't know what just happened; correct?

COBURN: Yes, sir.

GITTINS: So you didn't really understand what had just happened, did you?

COBURN: No, sir.

GITTINS: And you—when you had that thought, what just happened, I don't know what just happened, you had been as close as you were ever going to be to that incident, in time; correct?

COBURN: Yes, sir.

GITTINS: Three days later, though, when you wrote your wife, by then you'd decided it was not justified; correct?

COBURN: That was when I wrote the letter about it, yes, sir.

GITTINS: Okay. What just happened is different than that wasn't a justified shooting, isn't it?

COBURN: If it was justified in my mind I wouldn't have questioned it, sir.

GITTINS: Did you ever use the term "two innocent detainees"?

COBURN: They were deemed innocent before proven guilty, so I might have.

GITTINS: They were deemed innocent until proven guilty?

COBURN: Yes, sir. They're detainees. They were brought back. They were supposed to be brought back for questioning.

GITTINS: At the time that you saw this occurring, you believed that the detainees—is it your testimony that you believed the detainees were going to be taken back for questioning?

COBURN: Yes, sir.

GITTINS: Isn't that something you just read in the newspaper in the last two days, sir?

COBURN: I don't know, sir, they are detainees. They come back with us. That is the way we do things. You detain them. You flex-cuff them, you bring them back.

GITTINS: In fact, you believe that those—you believed at the time, that the detainees were going to be let go. Isn't that true?

COBURN: That is what I heard from the counter-intelligence.

GITTINS: Did you ever speak to counterintelligence? Do you remember saying on direct examination two days ago, on Wednesday, "They were going to be let go because we had nothing on them?" Do you remember saying that, under oath, on Wednesday in this court, in response to Major Keane's questions?

COBURN: Yes, sir.

GITTINS: So it's your testimony that you actually heard Sergeant "M" report to Lieutenant Pantano that these individuals were going to be released?

COBURN: Yes, sir.

With Major Winn's approval, Gittins used the lunch break to obtain a partial transcript of Coburn's Wednesday testimony in order to "clarify" exactly what he had said under oath earlier. Now, referring to those transcript pages, Gittins continued.

GITTINS: Did these individuals indicate, the HIET individuals indicate in your presence that they considered the Iraqis to be innocent?

COBURN: They didn't say anything about being innocent.

GITTINS: They didn't say anything about innocent; correct?

COBURN: Yes, sir.

GITTINS: Can you tell me why then you told Lance Corporal Thompson that they were innocent Iraqis?

COBURN: Because they were caught actually doing nothing wrong.

GITTINS: You believed these were innocent Iraqis, didn't you?

COBURN: I believe there wasn't any evidence on the scene yet to point that these were actually insurgents.

GITTINS: Is your testimony about that as accurate as your testimony that describes the shooting incident you claimed to have observed with Lieutenant Pantano?

COBURN: That I heard the HIET say he was going to be released?

GITTINS: Yes?

COBURN: Yes, sir.

GITTINS: So it's your testimony—it was your testimony the other day that it was Lieutenant Pantano who actually took the individuals over to the vehicle, put them in the positions where he wanted them, including putting them on their knees; correct?

COBURN: Yes, sir.

GITTINS: That is your best recollection of what happened; correct?

COBURN: Yes, sir.

GITTINS: It was not Doc Gobles who did that?

COBURN: No, sir. He was cutting off the flex-cuffs.

GITTINS: So you're certain that Doc Gobles did not put the two individuals, pick which individual went in which door, and placed them in the doorway; correct?

COBURN: It was Lieutenant Pantano who did that.

GITTINS: It was Lieutenant Pantano? And you're sure of that; correct?

COBURN: Yes, sir.

GITTINS: And you're as sure about that as you are about the rest of the shooting incident; correct?

COBURN: Yes, sir.

Camp Lejeune
2 February 2005

By 8:00 A.M., there was still nothing on the news. Nothing on the web. Silence. I just didn't get it. I was in civilian clothes driving in to the base to meet with Phil Stackhouse and talk strategy. He had given me the scoop on how aggressive Public Affairs officers could be. Managing the image and protecting the institution was their job, and in many of Phil's cases the press release had been issued before the charge sheet. But not now.

If it weren't for the overzealous and repugnant nature of the charges, I might have thought the Corps "team" was giving me a pass. That would have been believable if this had been framed more benignly as a *possible* wrongful death investigation where they were just trying to dispel a volatile allegation. But that was not the case here. Someone, somewhere had made a decision to run with this thing and press for the max, so the prosecutors had drawn up and signed a charge sheet labeling me a double murderer. With premeditation. A capital crime.

A death penalty crime.

There was no way in hell that my Marine Corps was going to sit around and hope that no reporter would sniff out something this explosive. No one was giving PAOs journalism awards and Donny Deutsch wasn't snatching them up to hear their out-of-the-box thinking on *The Big Idea*. Still, PAOs had to realize they needed to be proactive on this thing. What were they doing?

I swung out and accelerated past a slow-moving truck, and then the insight smacked me. Phil had said that the gravity of the charges had surprised all the lawyers at Legal Services. It did seem fucking crazy, not just a little crazy, but a lot crazy. I mean, was I the first person in history to be walking around, unconfined, facing double murder charges? Well, if it surprised them, maybe it had surprised the PAOs too. Maybe they were prepared to go one way and the quarterback had made a different call, and now the team had to adjust. Drafts reworded. Releases reapproved. I slid back into the slow lane so I could avoid the speed traps as I raced down the highway. After a ten-month investigation they'd finally decided to charge me but now the machine had gotten stuck on something. But *what*?

Smiling for the first time in almost twenty-four hours, I felt a plan begin to crystallize. My beloved Corps had fumbled the initiative, and I was going to seize it.

No Better Friend, No Worse Enemy.

I had a brief moment to make a choice and neither one was good. I could stay home and pray that all of this would go away, but I had been doing that since June of last year and it hadn't worked. Or, I could take matters into my own hands and make sure that the PC-driven bullshit that was threatening my life wouldn't threaten anyone else's. I wasn't some kind of criminal, and if they could do this to me, who else would they do it to? Who would they offer up next to make the television audience feel better that we had superheroes instead of soldiers? That

war was clean and precise. Laser-guided and heat-seeking. That the
mission was accomplished and we were just cleaning up dead-enders.

This is bullshit.

I wasn't the first and I wouldn't be the last. I remembered the
young Marine who'd shot the wounded Muj in a Fallujah mosque back
in November. The outcry, the collective chagrin. The hand-wringing
because the act had been captured on videotape.

I must have seen the Marine Corps emblem on every cable news
show a dozen times a day as they tried to give us a black eye. Where
was the outcry that those five fighters in the mosque had been using a
holy site, a house of worship, as a firing position? Where was the outcry when a Marine had been killed and five had been wounded as a
booby-trapped Muj body had been turned over. A body that had died
secretly and vengefully clutching a grenade. Where was the outrage
that the supposed call to prayer was being used to issue orders to terrorists, maneuver forces, and adjust their mortar fires? Where was the
outrage over executions of aid workers, women like Margaret Hassan
who had dedicated their lives to helping the innocent?

Fuck the outrage, where were the investigations? How many terrorist names had NCIS uncovered on the sons of bitches that killed
and maimed my brothers? The Warlords had taken 160 casualties with
six KIA, and we didn't have one single fucking name of anyone responsible.

Not one. *Maku.*

But we were able to spend millions of dollars and thousands of
man-hours and send dozens of investigators to draw up charges that I
had killed some fucking terrorists. A killing that I reported? How many
up-armored Humvees could we have bought with the money that went
into investigating my shoot? But even worse than the waste was the alternative. If the Marine Corps hadn't taken all the steps they did to
publicly stage-manage an incendiary claim like Sergeant Coburn's, the
media would have eaten us for breakfast. The Corps would have been
buried under the avalanche of "cover-up" accusations and Seymour
Hersh would have been writing a new book.

I wasn't a murderer and I wasn't a criminal. I was a soldier, a Marine officer. Killing my country's enemies was my job and I was *not*
apologizing about it to anyone. Maybe I was a necessary evil and we
could debate the "evil" part all day long from the comfort of an air-
conditioned TV studio, but the "necessary" part was undeniable. Just

ask twenty million dead Russians, six million dead Jews, or a million dead Rwandans who were hacked to death by machetes.

Cruising down the highway, I continued mulling the arguments, sometimes talking out loud in my empty car. Sometimes screaming. I had to be harshly frank with myself: would mounting a vigorous defense to prove my innocence help or hurt our cause? By that I meant America's global fight against terror. Was I prepared to go away quietly, for a crime I had not committed, to protect the institution? That was mob loyalty, and it had its place. If I had genuinely believed that it would have helped the men on the ground, I would have done my part for the mission. After all, our sons and daughters gave their lives and limbs every day as surely as I was prepared to give my own. I could do some time if it saved lives in the end.

But in the twenty-four hours since I had been officially labeled a murderer for defending myself against suicidal fanatics, I realized the danger wasn't only to me. It was to all the men and women who were on the line, doing the hard things in the dark places. The danger was to my family and to my children, that in the frenzy of blame America first, we were squandering our national power and our national security. We were trading our national resolve in a broken gamble to curry favor with the very people bent on destroying us.

Not on my watch.

Is no one paying attention? Does no one care? Do we really think the world will like us better if we are nicer? No. The world will like us better if we win. *Period.* We had killed hundreds of thousands of Japanese men, women, and children with nuclear blasts unleashed to save the lives of our invading troops, and millions more Japanese soldiers and civilians. And we are considered "just" victors. Only because we won. Only because we had won. If we had lost, we would be barbarians who had perpetrated an Asian holocaust. But our resolve hadn't wavered. Instead, we'd rallied and we had won.

I needed someone who wouldn't waver and could fight as hard as I could. Someone who wasn't afraid, who had skin in the game, whose character was unimpeachable. I needed tough, smart, and compassionate. Someone who understood that this was bigger than me. It was about all our fighting men and women. It was about all of America's sons and daughters. Someone who understood that this wasn't about fighting the military, it was about saving it.

I delicately balanced my cell phone as I worked the keypad and sped along. Agility. Fire superiority. Violence of action. I was doing the mental math to get ready for combat. I was in my happy place as I prepared to unleash hell.

"Hello?" a voice said, still a little sleepy.

"Hey, Mom . . . I need your help . . ."

Camp Lejeune
30 April 2005

GITTINS: You said in your letter to your wife—well, tell me. After Lieutenant Pantano spoke to the HIET team and the Iraqis, what did the HIET team do?

COBURN: They went back over by their vehicle.

GITTINS: Okay. Did you hear Lieutenant Pantano give them any order?

COBURN: No, sir.

GITTINS: Okay. Can you tell me then why you told your wife, "after about twenty minutes he sent the counterintelligence guys, which were right behind the car we just searched, up the road out of sight"? Is it your testimony that Lieutenant Pantano ordered the HIET team up the road and out of sight, sir?

COBURN: No, sir, I was mistaken in that comment on this letter.

GITTINS: You were mistaken in the letter?

COBURN: Yes, sir.

GITTINS: And this is the letter you wrote approximately three days after this incident, when it was still fresh in your mind. Isn't that true, sir?

COBURN: I did not give her every exact detail.

GITTINS: Well, you just gave—you just admitted that you gave her a detail that is not true. Isn't that correct, sir?

COBURN: Yes, sir.

GITTINS: That wasn't true?

COBURN: No, sir, it wasn't.

GITTINS: But you thought it would make it sound like the

lieutenant had this already planned. Isn't that true? If he sent these counterintelligence guys away?

COBURN: No, sir.

GITTINS: That is what you were trying to get across in this letter, is that Lieutenant Pantano planned to kill these people. Isn't that true?

COBURN: No, sir.

GITTINS: Well, then why did you say it at the very bottom, "He had this all planned out"?

COBURN: Because when he was questioning if he wanted to send the guys back to search their vehicle, I considered that at the time, a plan.

GITTINS: To have—you considered that he was going to have the guys search a vehicle, that was a plan to kill them?

COBURN: Yes, sir.

GITTINS: You did?

COBURN: Yes, sir.

GITTINS: It was your own opinion; correct?

COBURN: Yes, sir.

GITTINS: And one of the ways to get that opinion across to your wife was to say, "about twenty minutes after—after about twenty minutes he sent the counterintelligence guys, which were right behind the car, just up the road and out of sight." That was one of the ways it makes it look like, supporting your theory that Lieutenant Pantano wanted to kill these guys. Isn't that true?

COBURN: I do not remember my state of mind when I wrote this letter, sir.

GITTINS: Tell us—tell the investigating officer why in a letter you were trying to send back to your wife to protect yourself, that you would tell her something happened that you knew did not happen. Please tell us that, sir.

COBURN: Okay. Again, I don't remember my state of mind when I wrote this letter. I don't remember the details of me writing the letter. I was writing the let-

ter quickly, details got mixed in with other statements. It was never—

GITTINS: What other statements—

COBURN: —never considered this letter to be part of a court
hearing.

GITTINS: You never thought when you wrote this letter that
you'd be sitting here in court, did you?

COBURN: It did not cross my mind at the time, no.

GITTINS: Were you still mad about the lieutenant firing you
from a squad leader position?

COBURN: I was never fired. I was moved from the position.

GITTINS: So it's your testimony that you were never fired? Is
that your testimony?

COBURN: Yes, sir.

GITTINS: And that perception was within the same two-
week period as your perception of Lieutenant
Pantano's shooting of two Iraqis; correct?

COBURN: Yes.

Camp Lejeune
2 February 2005

"Sir, I need you to be honest with me . . ."

It was a stupid thing to say to my appointed attorney, but I was trying to convey the awkward vulnerability of my position.

"Have you ever done a case like this before? One this high-
profile?" I knew the answer, but Phil was always one step ahead of me.

"We talked about civilian counsel earlier, and I've made a list of all
that I know." He slid a piece of paper across his desk.

I did some research over the next few hours and the name Charlie
Gittins came up over and over again. His aggressive style seemed like
the ideal complement to Phil's stealth approach. A perfect one-two
punch.

I called Charlie that night and we spoke during the recess of a
court-martial he was working in Quantico. He asked me a half-dozen
questions about the case before he agreed to defend me.

"Well," he said after a pause. "What kind of war chest do you
have?"

"Frankly, Mr. Gittins, the massive pay cut I took when I put the uniform back on has forced Jill and me to dig into our savings . . ."

"Well, I'll tell you, there are a lot of people out there that are going to want to help you, and we're gonna need it. One of my last clients, a former Top Gun pilot, had a lot of success raising money online . . ."

We're going to need it, he'd said. He was coming in.

I immediately thought of the grassroots campaigns of the 2004 election and how effectively the candidates had used the Internet. Charlie started listing our considerable expenses and the eventualities we had to be prepared for, not just in the lead-up to court-martial, but in the *worst* worst-case scenario of needing to appeal a conviction. Charlie had been a radar intercept officer on F-4 Phantoms, and he also knew that the time to prepare for combat was before the fight, not during it.

I was a little nervous about a high-profile guy like Charlie. Part of me felt that my innocence should be obvious. But I had thought that all along, and somehow the investigation only seemed to gather force as time went on. My other concern was the perception of guilt. Having a big-shot civilian attorney almost implied by default that you were in deep shit and you needed someone *really* skillful to get you off.

This was just another form of combat, and once again there were no good choices. I *was* in really big trouble, given the severity of the charges and the fact that none of my Marine attorneys could speak to the press. Their inability to tell my story publicly with the hearing almost three months away meant I would be unarmed tabloid fodder. In a post–Abu Ghraib world, I needed Charlie to ensure that I was not going to be defined by my enemies. Sun Tzu said that every battle is won or lost before it is ever fought. If the battle was to be defined, it would be defined by me.

Camp Lejeune
30 April 2005

After a short recess, Major Keane took the podium for the last time to deliver the government's closing argument. He turned to face the investigating officer.

"Sir, it has been a long week. We were both presented with an unenviable task. It [was] difficult to come into this investigation and present evidence of serious crimes committed by a fellow Marine officer. It's especially difficult because of the impressive record and admiration Lieutenant Pantano has compiled. Nevertheless, we were assigned this unpopular mission of presenting these disturbing facts about the actions of this lieutenant on April 15, 2004. You also have a morally challenging assignment. You must evaluate these troubling facts, using the statements, documents, testimony, and circumstantial evidence, using your own common sense."

Major Keane's tone matched his somber words. Now I could hear anger.

"NCOs truly are the backbone of our Marine Corps. Sergeant Coburn has endured a vicious smear campaign. Because Sergeant Coburn was an easy, vulnerable target, he was attacked, set up and exploited. Do not forget, though, that Sergeant Coburn has served this country and this Marine Corps for ten solid years. He deployed twice to the Middle East in support of Operation Iraqi Freedom. He too has been in harm's way, and he too is a brother Marine.

"You should not hold this attack against the accused. I doubt he had anything to do with it. But you should remember that Sergeant Coburn has spoken and maintained what happened on April 15, 2004, was wrong from the beginning. Yes, he spoke to the media and defended himself in the media. Who would not be tempted to do so in his shoes? It is ironic that the defense would find fault with that."

Keane looked toward the lens of the closed-circuit TV.

"Yes, he is a bit slow. No, he is not the model Marine. But he did see a serious crime and he testified about it. He, unlike the accused, has told a consistent account of what took place on April 15th. He is not proficient, he is not the smartest guy. And they were able to twist a lot of his words around and confuse him, the classic ploy when the facts are incriminating, attack the witnesses or attack a witness . . ."

I drifted back to the second day of the hearing as I struggled to understand why we were even here at all. Captain Bolling had been asking the battalion lawyer, Captain Schrantz, about how he first heard of my shoot.

BOLLING: What were the circumstances surrounding you learning about it?

SCHRANTZ: The battalion commander came up and ap-

proached me and said that the division SJ₄
[staff judge advocate] was on deck because of ₐ
potential officer case.

BOLLING: Who was the division SJA?

SCHRANTZ: Lieutenant Colonel Betz.

BOLLING: Was he part of a rapid investigation team appointed by General Mattis?

SCHRANTZ: That's what they were called. First Marine Division had a rapid incident assessment team that
would go out and investigate issues that were at
that time noteworthy and needed what they felt
was division oversight and oversight from the
general's primary staff. He came down as part of
what is called a RIAT [Reportable Incident Assessment Team].

BOLLING: Who was involved in that?

SCHRANTZ: For that particular instance, the only people I
know came were Lieutenant Colonel Betz and
Captain Gannon, the deputy.

BOLLING: Do you know who this rapid investigation team
interviewed?

SCHRANTZ: No, I don't.

BOLLING: Would it surprise you that the RIAT only interviewed Sergeant Coburn?

SCHRANTZ: Like I said, I don't know who they spoke to.

And here we were.

Major Keane continued his closing argument, and I listened more intently.

"One of the issues that has emerged was whether the accused's actions were reasonable in light of the perceived threat, taking into consideration the circumstances that existed at the time, leading up to the shooting of the two Iraqis.

"The accused in this case is not an ordinary lieutenant. He has prior experience as a Scout Sniper and several years working in the civilian sector. At the time the events unfolded in this case, he was thirty-three years old. This is perhaps one of the reasons that many of the Marines [who] have spoken on his behalf have indicated that his

and knowledge surpassed his peers.
the accused was articulate, and that he

uestion of what could have happened to
d decision maker to act so contrary to the
e supported him said? What is the explana-

he accused probably thought that if he said they
d not get reported. Who would care? They were
hey were insurgents and it will be forgotten. I will
other lieutenants will be jealous. My men will think
en he thought if he claimed self-defense it would get
were just Iraqi scum after all. The problem is that
the use of deadly force in self-defense must be reason-
l of the circumstances. The circumstances here are two
aqis in a previously strip-searched car, who could not possi-
threat.
world should know that Marines are the fiercest warriors on
net. Our enemies fear us for good reason. The world must also
that we fight with honor. Lieutenant Pantano has done many
ctful things. He has led a platoon in combat. War can bring out
best and worst in people. At times it absolutely brought out the
st in Second Lieutenant Pantano. On April 15th it brought out the
orst . . .
"After cutting through the haze and the smoke, in the end what we
have is that two prisoners were put on their knees and shot in the back.
The bottom line is that these facts in this case should be judged by
members of a court-martial. Your recommendation, should be to send
this case to a court-martial."

Wilmington, North Carolina
14 February 2005

"Happy Birthday, Mom. And Happy Valentine's Day! Did you and
Larry do anything fun?" After her divorce, my mother had found love
again, and she was happy as a schoolgirl. I was thrilled for her but worried about the bad impression all of this nonsense must have been
making among Larry's family and friends. If you knew me then you

knew the situation was crazy, hourly chaos, day, night, *middle* of the
night. But if you didn't . . . well, you didn't.

"Thank you, *Tesoro,*" my mother said, using my family nickname.
"You know I was busy yesterday with Anderson Cooper and Geraldo
and today was . . . was long. We taped for *CBS Evening News,* then
Dan Abrams, and finally Hannity and Colmes. Did you see that lawyer
on Abrams try and say you weren't even charged? I couldn't believe it!"

"Yeah, I TiVo'd it. That was stupid. Charlie held up the charge
sheet and made him look like an idiot. They're flailing. Forget about it.
What's on the plate tomorrow? Did you even get to eat today?"

"No. It's okay. Larry was going to take me out, but I had to cancel.
I'm having a sandwich now."

"Ma, it's not good to eat so late . . ."

"It's okay, Ilario. How are my grandsons?"

"They're great, Mom. They're . . . I'm sorry about your birthday.
I'm sorry about all of this, Mom. But we've gotta focus, what's on for tomorrow?"

"Mmmm. Let's look at my scroll here. You gonna write it down?"

"No, I just want to know . . ."

"Okay, let's see . . . 9:10 Tony Snow on Fox News Radio. 10:15
Kirby Wilber, KVI Seattle. 10:32 Rip Daniels, WJ2D. 2:30 Art Moore,
WorldNetDaily. 3:00 Bill Mazer, 1460 AM. 3:30 Sean Hannity, 770
AM. And 4:00 Joseph Farah, WorldNetDaily. Then Gittins is on Bill
O'Reilly at 8:00 p.m. and your friends Damon and J.R. are on Hannity
and Colmes at 9:00 P.M. Then I'm back on the radio at 9:30 P.M. with
Rusty Humphreys."

The DefendTheDefenders.org web site we'd created was amass-
ing a solid financial foundation—not only for my civilian legal needs,
but also for other veterans of the global war on terror.

"Home run, Mom. I really appreciate it . . . I think we're doing
something good, Mom. And we're making 'em nervous. They're realiz-
ing they've got no case."

"Whaddya mean?"

"Agents are swarming over the whole damn battalion. They're interviewing everyone. I'm hearing stories of guys getting interrogated
with three or four senior guys sweat'n 'em."

"They should have done that before they ruined your good name
and stole your career. That just makes me furious . . ." She had to
catch her breath.

"Well, hopefully people are seeing the consequences of rushing to judgment . . ."

"I know, Chickadee. I know how hard this is for you. But I also know that for the lives of your men, you'd do it all again."

"Yeah, I heard you say that on TV tonight. What, are we related or something?"

We both laughed a long time.

After hanging up the phone, I sat and went through articles on the case while TiVo'd broadcasts played in the background. I was a student of the media and I knew a little bit about how the news business worked. I was at the dinner when Marianne Pearl was honored by the Committee to Protect Journalists. I had teams in Pakistan and Afghanistan when her husband was butchered. I sat on couches with executive producers as we debated the merits of sending yet another documentary team down to Maryland and Virginia during the panic of the 2002 Washington sniper shooting spree. The decision had nothing to do with the good of the public. There was no *need* for another tragic story about a family's loved one lost. The market had long been saturated. Instead, it had to do with cash. Who would buy it and for how much?

I thought about my life and my love/hate relationship with the media. The business had fed me on more than one occasion, yet it fostered the hypersensitivity to the ugliness of combat that cripples our ability to wage war and protect our society. The 24/7 juggernaut of air time spawned the second-guessing games of pundits and analysts opining endlessly on "how it could have been done better . . ."

And yet without the help of the media in telling my story, I might not have been able to pay for my own defense. How did I reconcile the fact that I was a warrior proud to serve his country and yet the reason my story got so much attention was that my case embarrassed the establishment and the war?

The next morning, I got a frantic phone call from Chuck, another Marine bud from the Gulf. His mother had been surfing my story and found a web site with a number of bizarre and pranksterish digital images of my head inserted into different scenes. One was an electric chair. Another, more disturbing picture, was a jihadist in black robes with a white scarf hiding his face, holding a severed head. The image, no doubt taken from a hostage-slaying video, featured my face super-imposed upon that of the victim.

Above my head was the title: "HE DESERVED IT".

I was web-savvy enough to know how to search for the origin of the site's registration, and I was hoping the result would be a frat house in San Francisco or Massachusetts. I wasn't prepared for the result and I notified the authorities immediately:

Domain ID: D105727850-LROR
Created On: 14-Feb-2005 04:30:55 UTCLast
Updated On: 15-Feb-2005 04:30

Registrant Name: Muhammad Adil Khan
Registrant Street: Abdali Road
Registrant City: Multan
Registrant State/Province: xx
Registrant Postal Code: 00333
Registrant Country: PK
Registrant Phone: +1.0615159010
Registrant FAX: +1.0615159010
Tech Email: muhama.ata@gmail.com
Name Server: NS1.PGWARE.COM
Name Server: NS2.PGWARE.COM

Pakistan . . .

Okay. This had to be a joke. There was no way. But in the cool, un-emotional layers of my mind, I knew it was entirely possible that this was real. And the possibility was enough. We were dealing with a me-dieval vengeance-driven society. With my own eyes I had seen dozens of firefights over tribal disputes, and had been at the center of a few of them. Now I had the dubious honor of being the first and only name attributed to the actual killing of bad guys in the war on terror. Tommy Franks didn't pull any triggers in this war. Neither did Generals Abizaid, Casey, or Conway. Yes, they gave orders, but they had Special Forces security details and protection for their families. Certainly there had been hundreds if not thousands of heroes with Silver and Bronze Star medals for their valiant combat actions. The stark differ-ence was that their "alleged victims" were anonymous. My case had names, times, dates, and locations—all information that had been pre-viously unavailable to the enemy, but now created a ripe opportunity for a personal vendetta. The situation was further aggravated by Al-Jazeera running my story with a bogus picture of two blindfolded detainees and a caption suggesting that I had shot two bound and blindfolded men.

Even the Fallujah mosque shooter had been rightfully protected with anonymity. *Innocent until proven guilty.*

Not Lieutenant PANTANO, ILARIO.

Pantanos had survived blood feuds for hundreds of years, and we would survive for hundreds more. But this was wider than tribe versus tribe, and I had to accept that my family was now exposed to a host of new threats, from here at home and from overseas. Sadly, no one else in this process was thinking like the enemy. So Jill, Domenico, Pino, and I would have to protect ourselves. (Law enforcement officials would later warn us that individuals inside the U.S. were gathering biographical data on my mother, my wife, and me.)

Some folks thought I was "a disgrace to the uniform" and that as the "evil instrument" of an evil president, my family and I deserved whatever punishment lay ahead. And a few didn't mind telling us so.

> Subj:BURN IN HELL. DIE YOU FUCKING
>   MONSTER. MAY YOUR SLUT WIFE DIE ALSO
> Date: XXXXXXXX 9:31:29 AM
> From: dsmith1254@comcast.net
> To: ltpantano@aol.com

On February 17, Eileen Byrne, a radio host with WLS in the Chicago area, told my mother that "Ilario is America's son and you are no longer alone in the battle to clear his name." That afternoon she implored all of her listeners to hit the hostile site in Pakistan at the same time, and they did. Their synchronized visits overloaded the server and they kept hitting it until it crashed. Eileen wasn't the only one rallying her listeners.

The switchboard on Michael Savage's talk radio program was lit up for months with callers protesting my situation. Dr. Savage repeatedly invited my mother and attorney to give updates on the case, and on one such night, a U.S. congressman from the 3rd District in North Carolina was listening to the radio as he drove home. Walter Jones would later say that hearing the sincerity of my mother's staunch defense of her son caused him to launch an investigation of his own.

After Jones's staff spoke to attorneys on both sides, he was compelled to act. And I was amazed by his selflessness. Representative Jones introduced House Resolution 167 as a way of showing the support of the United States Congress for my actions in self-defense. If Walter Jones had bet wrong and I had been convicted, it would have been career suicide. I didn't even live in his district. Yet he was guided by his unwavering faith in the Lord, and I was inspired by his courage.

My situation had resonated with concerned citizens who offered their services, their money, and their time to help my defense and send a message of support to our troops. A plumber from Chesterfield, Missouri, wrote:

> I heard Mrs. Pantano on Michael Savage's show and want to help your son and others in the military who need legal assistance.
>
> Thanks for all you do to defend our country and support our troops.
>
> Thanks, Jim Finch

Jim had included a check for a thousand dollars.

A single one-dollar bill and a handwritten note came from an eight-year-old. A multiple-amputee Vietnam vet apologized that he couldn't give more because of his meager fixed income, but he wanted me to know that he prayed for me every day. Veterans of the Pacific campaigns sent crisp twenties and asked in shock if they would be prosecuted for "burning the Japs out of caves with flame throwers" or if they should have "waited longer to shoot down the kamikazes."

Concerned parents e-mailed me to ask if they should stop their children from enlisting. "Has the military gone mad?" they angrily demanded. The question nearly broke my heart and I'd shake my head at the monitor.

"Defending your country is an honor and a privilege," I told them. Their children's desire to serve should be supported at all costs.

"Don't be disheartened by my case . . ." I cautioned by e-mail and by letters. "I have faith that it will end well. But please remember the men and women that are there now. They need your support more than I do. A care package goes a long way. Believe me!"

From every chapter of my life, friends were reaching out in any way they could. From PS 124 to Horace Mann classmates. From Desert Storm to my sniper teammates. Chris, a floor trader at the NYMEX, rallied support from my colleagues on Wall Street. A waiter at my wedding reached out because he remembered the Marine Corps pin on my tuxedo and my toast just days after 9/11.

My fellow lieutenants from OCS and The Basic School sent in character letters by the dozen. Captain Barger, one of our TBS instructors, wrote on my behalf, she said, because of the outrage of her student lieutenants (my peers). Letters came from Iraq and Afghanistan and ships at sea. Glenn, a carpenter on the TV show *Lateline,* motivated me with the Spartan exhortation "Molon Labe." It was King Leonidas's fabled response to the advancing Persian army's demand that the Spartans lay down their weapons. "Molon Labe," King Leonidas replied. *Come and get them.*

Camp Lejeune
30 April 2005

Charlie Gittins strode to the podium after Keane was finished. This was the moment I had been anticipating.

" 'We had a good day. We killed two obvious insurgents.' That's the battalion operations officer for 2d Battalion, 2d Marines. That was his initial reaction on April 15th, 2004, when it was reported to him by Lieutenant Pantano that he had killed two Iraqi insurgents during an operation near Latafiyah.

"Lieutenant Pantano, his story, sir, if you think about the Marine Corps and him, he is a living embodiment of the Marine Corps Hymn. On the day that his nation was attacked by Osama bin Laden, Lieutenant Pantano shaved his head and said he was going to defend his country, and he did so . . . Lieutenant Pantano rejoins the Marine Corps, and as you heard, he didn't just go to The Basic School, didn't just go to OCS and get through, he excelled. He excelled in everything he did. He was the kind of lieutenant that if you tell him what to do, it gets done . . ."

Gittins was speaking with emotion now, his tone deep, persuasive.

"Sir, it says a lot about a Marine officer when his peers pick him to be the mess president in The Basic School. That wasn't an accident. That was his peers evaluating his judgment, evaluating his character.

They wanted Lieutenant Pantano to be their mess president. It wasn't an accident when his peers voted him to be the IOC class comman- dant. Again, his peers evaluated his credibility, professionalism, and they determined that he should be their leader.

"And then Lieutenant Pantano goes to 2d Battalion, 2d Marines. He reports in and he starts training his Marines. You heard about the evidence about how he's training his Marines. He goes over and above the call of duty . . .

"April 15th, 2004, Lieutenant Pantano was on a QRF mission. That mission ends up being a raid on a house, a suspected insurgent stronghold with a cache of weapons suspected to be there. Lieutenant Pantano does all the things a professional Marine officer is expected to do. He properly briefs the mission. He gives his men the five- paragraph order. They have a plan. They're executing the plan . . ."

Gittins reviewed my Marines' pursuit of the Iraqi insurgents flee- ing from the target house, our stopping their white sedan, and their subsequent detention.

"What's key here though is by the time the Iraqis are interrogated by the HIET team, Sergeant 'M' and Lance Corporal—or Corporal 'O' at the time, they have no idea—the HIET has no idea—they've got the Icom radios that there's been anything found in the house. That's the crucial fact Sergeant 'M' provides to you in this case. He would have interrogated these young men—the forty-year-old man and the eighteen-year-old in the vehicle—about what was in the house if he had known about it, but he did not know about it. Sergeant Coburn is entirely wrong in his testimony, whichever testimony you believe, whether it was he'd heard on the radio mortar aiming stake, mortar aiming stake and an AK-47, or mortar aiming stake, an AK-47, a box of wires and money, a flare gun, and propaganda. Whichever one of the versions he gave you believe, that did not happen until after Sergeant 'M' interrogated the two Iraqis. You know that because Sergeant 'M' told you it. He's a CI guy. He would have interrogated those guys on the information that had been pulled from the house. But he didn't do it because he didn't have that information.

"But notwithstanding that he didn't have the information about what was actually in the house, based on the demeanor that he ob- served as a professional counterintelligence human intelligence col- lector, he concluded that those guys were bad guys and they should be taken back for questioning—further questioning. So, there's more information, and that information is imparted to Lieutenant Pantano that they are going to go back. Then Lieutenant Pantano, after that's done, hears that there is contraband being found in the house . . . and that changes everything. Whatever happened to the vehicle the first time that the Navy corpsman investigated and looked at the car, there's now new information that suggests we need to go back and have a second look at it, and Lieutenant Pantano takes that upon himself while his platoon is still doing what they're doing to go conduct that search.

"You also remember that Sergeant 'M' said that the Iraqis were cuffed behind them for transport. They needed to have their cuffs cut anyway and put in front of them, so Lieutenant Pantano orders the cuffs cut. They've already been called out for an IED. He needs to get this done fast. The sun's coming down. This mission needs to be over with, and sir, how you know that is when you look—the government put in the significant events log for this day. . . . Look at the times, and you can see while Lieutenant Pantano and his team were actually doing this mission, they had a call about the IED, and that was the mission they went to next."

Gittins gestured toward the exhibits table where the printout of 2/2's significant events log was stacked among the other documents.

"It's all in the log and look in the log, it's clearly identified that these guys went from the takedown of this house—the raid on the house to an IED. The government put that in for you.

"While these two Iraqis are pulling the stuff out of the car again so that Lieutenant Pantano can himself look and see what's going on in this vehicle, they turn toward him in a hostile manner and he kills them. Within the Rules of Engagement, sir."

Gittins's voice was precise, coolly professional.

"Lieutenant Pantano has told this to virtually every person who has asked him, he told Gobles and Coburn at the time, 'They made a hostile action and I shot them.' He told his platoon sergeant, 'They made a hostile action. I shot them.' He went back and he told his operations officer, 'They made a hostile action and I shot them.' He told the colonel who took his statement, 'They turned toward me. I feared for my life. I killed them.' He told Stone Phillips he feared for his life and he explained how he felt the air being sucked out of his body when they turned toward him. The fact of the matter is that's exactly what happened. The Iraqis made an aggressive move toward him, and he shot them.

"The key to these charges, sir, it's not that these guys are dead and not that Lieutenant Pantano killed them. The killing had to be unlawful, that is, a lawful means without legal justification or excuse. It is a legal justification or excuse to kill someone if you have a reasonable fear for your own life, and under the ROE in this case, the ROE that was applicable in this case, all that had to happen is Lieutenant Pantano feel that he was threatened and he's standing there—he shouts according to HN Gobles, he shouts not once but twice, 'kuff,' 'stop,' and then the shooting starts. Coburn conveniently remembers none of that. But Coburn also testified that these individuals were on their knees."

Gittins paused, gathering energy.

"There's a couple of other factual discrepancies you need to at least think about—maybe not resolve, but you ought to bring them to the attention of the commanding general, because it's true, this is 'just an Article 32,' but you know, Congress created Article 32 for a reason. The Article 32 investigations 'stands as a bulwark against baseless charges.' The reason the Article 32 was enacted in the Uniform Code of Military Justice was to prevent people who shouldn't be tried from having to go on trial for their lives. It is a mechanism that the convening authority uses to determine whether or not a trial should be held. Your job, sir, is so crucial in this because the quality of your report is what tells the convening authority whether or not and how he should dispose of these charges. The more you tell the convening authority in your report, the more he has to go on to make a decision, a rational decision, because as we all know, he doesn't have to follow your recommendation. Your recommendation is advisory. So, to the extent that you feel one way or the other about this, it is critical—and I would—it is your duty—not just critical, it is your duty to give the convening authority as much information about your evaluation of credibility because credibility is important . . ."

Gittins carefully skirted sounding dogmatic.

"It is a fact that no one except Lieutenant Pantano saw what these Iraqis did before he started shooting." He continued, speaking with that well-modulated precision. "Neither HN Gobles nor Sergeant Coburn were actually looking at the two Iraqis near the car or at Lieutenant Pantano when the firing began. That is an uncontradicted fact. Lieutenant Pantano, an officer of impeccable integrity. He said the two Iraqis turned in an aggressive manner toward him. He felt threatened and he shot them. He did exactly what he was required to do under the circumstances . . .

" 'April wasn't so bad in Iraq.' His [Coburn's] testimony. 'Innocent Iraqis were going to be released.' Sir, we know that's absolutely, positively not true. Sergeant 'M' told you that. His perception—Sergeant Coburn's perception was so out of touch with reality that it's not worthy of belief. He believed he was doing a good job as a squad leader. How possibly could he have concluded that when you heard Captain Weston tell you that he repeatedly counseled Sergeant Coburn. He caught Coburn sleeping when he should be training, not once but twice. Sergeant Coburn just doesn't get it. He doesn't believe he's relieved as a squad leader and assigned to the radioman job because he was incompetent as a squad leader. He actually believes—his perception is that he was the most experienced guy on the radio and that was the place where he could help the platoon the most, not because he would have proved himself to be an incompetent squad leader that had put a squad in a kill box without providing security for them. He thought it was because he was such a great radio operator. The most senior sergeant in the platoon assigned to the lance corporal, PFC job, the new-guy job."

Now Gittins had allowed an edge of derision into his voice.

"What has to rank as the most unbelievable statement made by Sergeant Coburn, there is no circumstance in which he would shoot an unarmed Iraqi, none whatsoever. He would have to have a weapon. Sir, as a matter of common sense—and you can watch it on *Cops,* you can watch it on any show where they have the actual videos by police officers, police officers on a day-to-day basis are killed by people who have no weapons. In fact, the very first police officer to have been killed with his own weapon on his own video in his car was killed after two foreign speakers talked in a foreign language to be heard over the car—you could hear it over the—it's been on TV . . ."

American Legion Post 10
Wilmington
1 April 2005

Matt and his family had been helpful, watchful friends over Jill and Domenico while I was at war, and they didn't stop when my war came home. His mother, Sara, had given Jill a baby shower while I was gone, and now in my time of real need, she was firing off letters to the editor and calling any radio show that would hear her. Matt's cousin, Jenny, had smiled wide and proclaimed, "In times of crisis, Southern women fire the ovens and start baking."

And they did indeed. Even our new neighbors were stopping by with muffins and cheesecakes. I was humbled that Matt stepped up to take the role as my spokesperson to the local media, always standing proud in a Defend The Defenders T-shirt. He reached out to Mike Gregorio, commander of the local American Legion post, and Mike quickly enlisted his fellow Legionnaires to spread word of my case. The veterans held a monthly fish fry to fund their VA hospital visits and the care packages they sent to Iraq and Afghanistan. The previous fish fry, held in March 2005, had benefited a local Army National Guardsman, Sergeant Joey Bozik, who had lost both legs and an arm when the Humvee he was riding in was struck by an IED outside Baghdad. The Wilmington community had come out in force to raise money for this local hero. Mike convinced his fellow veterans to use the April 1 fish fry as a fundraiser for my defense.

None of the Legionnaires wanted to take a stand against their government or the military, they just wanted to ensure that one of their own was getting the best legal representation available. Mike, a cop for fourteen years, saw Defend The Defenders as a sort of Soldiers' Benevolent Association modeled loosely on the PBA, which helped police officers in communities around the country.

The law enforcement community was particularly sensitive to the issues of my case. In a letter to President Bush signed by directors of the Association for the Los Angeles Deputy Sheriffs, which represents approximately seven thousand sworn deputy sheriffs and district attorney investigators, these selfless members of the law enforcement community pledged their support of House Resolution 167. The letter was copied to all the members of the House and Senate, and called for the charges against me to be dismissed. Like Walter Jones before them, these tough cops were putting their neck on the line for me and for all the men and women in harm's way, and I was honored.

We pulled up to the back of the Legion hall, and Matt met me with two off-duty cops who had volunteered to look after Jill, Domenico, and Pino while I greeted well-wishers. Mike came out and gave me a big hug and started introducing me to folks. John was in the kitchen in a DTD shirt, shorts, and a white smock covered in all manner of fish guts and flour. "Hey, LT," he barked. "I want you to know that we're behind you. Semper Fi!" A former Marine, he had taken a bullet as a Connecticut state trooper that had left him partially paralyzed. He grabbed my hand with his good hand and I held it for a long moment.

"Semper Fi, brother," I replied as I hugged him.

John wasn't kidding; he and his family were behind me. His two daughters were taking tickets at the front door, and his wife was working the beverage line. The other men of the Legion and the ladies of the Women's Auxiliary put in a long day on my behalf. There were volunteers breading fish, others were frying. Some took tickets and others served cole slaw.

There was Lowell and Millie selling her wonderful desserts off of folding conference tables. Lowell had served on the USS *Tripoli* almost two of my lifetimes ago. Dave was retired from the Air Force and in his spare time he had woven me a cross-stitched picture of the Iwo Jima flag raising. Veterans in their eighties drove from as far away as Raleigh, over a hundred miles, to make donations. I was kissing babies one moment, shaking hands with my son's teachers and sharing tearful hugs with leather-clad Vietnam-Marine-vet bikers the next. That day they set a post record for the number of servings.

Congressman Jones arrived and embraced me warmly. Then he told me the details of the resolution he'd submitted to the House, HR167. I was completely overwhelmed by the turnout of support. The community had embraced my family, and Walter Jones had championed me like a son. I gave him a simple gray "USMC" T-shirt with black block letters and I told him why I loved it.

"Sir, this T-shirt is a simple gift, and it's a metaphor for the Corps. It might not be pretty, but it gets the job done every time."

"*What,* Mom?"

The irritated tone, probably the same as it had been twenty years ago when she asked to check my homework, and she was still as patient now as she was then. I could tell by her clipped excitement that this call was different from the calls earlier in the day, as we fine-tuned her interviews and travel arrangements. She was coming down soon for the hearing, but she wanted to come early to spend some time with her grandchildren before the real circus began. If the hearing went badly, I might be subjected to pretrial confinement, and Jill would need the help.

"Turn on C-SPAN right now. They're showing House speeches. Congressman Jones is on. Looks like you made an impression." *Click.*

I had to hang up. It made me sick to watch the news coverage live and as the nausea welled, I definitely couldn't be attached to a phone.

The "LIVE" graphic hovered above his bushy graying hair. The well of the House of Representatives was clearly visible behind him. A gentleman with a mild manner and a ferocious heart, he was obviously pained and emotional as he spoke.

". . . I continue Mona Charen's comments in her article 'Is the Marine Corps PC?' "

Jones lifted the page of the article and read. " 'A Marine Corps colleague asked how many guys do you know who would drop a hundred grand a year to go and sleep in fighting holes in the nasty mud and dust for what? Twenty-five grand a year? There are few and the rest of us owe them more than we can possibly express, which is why it is shocking to learn that Pantano may now be facing murder charges!'

"Mr. Speaker, that's why I'm on the floor. I want to read part of House Resolution 167, which I have introduced the day before we left for Easter . . . In his combat fitness report dated August 5th, 2004, nearly four months after the incident, Second Lieutenant Pantano's superior officers gave the following evaluation of his performance from March through July 2004. I'm just going to read a couple of these, Mr. Speaker:

" 'One: He is a Marine who leads from the front always and balances his aggressive style with true concern for the welfare of his Marines . . .'

"Mr. Speaker, this is the close of my resolution: '2nd Lt Pantano, United States Marine Corps, was defending the cause of Freedom, Democracy, and Liberty in his actions of April 15, 2004, that resulted in the deaths of two suspected Iraqi insurgents that subsequently have given rise to certain charges against him.'

"We need to stand behind our men and women who are in harm's way in Afghanistan and Iraq."

Camp Lejeune
30 April 2005

". . . What about the alternative scenario, sir?" Gittins continued.

"Lieutenant Pantano's standing in the—about three or four feet away from two Iraqis who were searching the vehicle, and the reason you have to stand relatively close while they're doing that is so you can see what they're doing, so that they can't do something that you—in front of them that you can't see. The alternative scenario, sir, Lieutenant Pantano is standing at the vehicle three or four feet away from these Iraqis."

Gittins's posture suggested combat alertness.

"They converse in Arabic. They decide they're going to take his weapon and they're going to rush him. Three or four feet, sir, that's two big giant steps, and Lieutenant Pantano—all one has to do is decide he's taking the weapon and the other one is taking Lieutenant Pantano. Lieutenant Pantano might get a shot off, but one of them is going to get to him. And if that had happened, that would truly be a crime. That would be truly a crime, to have a lieutenant of Marines killed by two Iraqis. We wouldn't be sitting around—in fact, I suspect that the battalions on this base—infantry battalions would be talking about how the lieutenant—the dumb lieutenant failed to kill these guys when he should have, that he waited too long, and gosh-darnit, it's a terrible thing, 'But you know, I wouldn't have done that. I would have killed those guys as soon as they made their first move.'

"That's the way Marines would be thinking. If Lieutenant Pantano had had his weapon taken from him and had been killed, we'd be talking about how the lieutenant failed to do what he should have done. He's in a lose-lose situation. He chose the choice that allowed him to be alive. That's the right choice. That's the right choice . . ."

Gittins's words seemed to echo. Major Winn listened hard.

"Government asked a bunch of questions about why, why, why. Lieutenant Pantano answered most of those questions. Why was the car searched again more thoroughly? Once you get that new information this stuff came from an arms cache, that's a reasonable thing to do, go back and look at the car again, and Lieutenant Pantano's a pretty aggressive guy . . .

"There was lots of reasons to re-search the car, not the least of which was, 'Where are the hidden compartments? How are they mov-

ing the stuff? Is there more still in the vehicle? Why did both search?'
Just look at the significant incident report, sir. There was a lot going on.
There's already an IED report that Lieutenant Pantano has to go to.
Sun's going down. They've been there awhile. Have them both pull the
stuff out. Perfectly reasonable under the circumstances, and it's a
commander's judgment. It's Lieutenant Pantano's judgment. He exer-
cised his judgment.

"You can say that his judgment is wrong, but that doesn't make it a
crime. You can say, 'He should have done it different,' but that doesn't
make it a crime, and it certainly doesn't make it murder. The earlier
search means nothing after the—after Lieutenant Pantano has more
information. That's the bottom line, sir."

Gittins wove more persuasive logic into his closing statement,
doubling back over ground already covered, refuting the prosecution's
arguments.

"Shot the Iraqis in the back. That's the government's theory of the
case."

Charlie Gittins pointed at the big photos on the easel. "Sir, that is
an exit wound. How do you know? Because you can see flesh and
bone. When I say that, I'm talking about exhibit 4(a), I believe. That is
an exit wound. It's a blowout in the back. It can only be from someone
being shot in the chest. How do you know that that's true, sir? It's so
simple it defies belief that the government even brings this up. An airplane crashes—when an airplane crashes, they have the instruments,
they leave marks. They call them witness marks. All the instruments
will be in the position where the airplane hits the ground. We have witness marks in this case. This guy slid down the door. His back slid
down the door. The only way he could be in that position with his back
against the doorjamb is to have been facing Lieutenant Pantano.

"He's shot—and if you look, he's actually turned—he's turned. The
way he's turned, it's inconsistent with what HN Gobles said happened.
His body is turned so that he is falling toward—away from the car.
How did he get that way? He turned toward Lieutenant Pantano as
Lieutenant Pantano said—Lieutenant Pantano put enough rounds in
his chest to blow out his back. And maybe he shot him—did he overkill
him? Maybe he did, but the first round is the only one that matters. We
don't know if the first round killed both of these guys. . . . The government wants you to recommend a trial by court-martial where there's no
evidence other than the lieutenant shot a lot of rounds after they were

down and what is clearly a blowout wound on the back, clearly so showing bone and muscle … .

"Iraq is a dangerous place April of 2004. Lieutenant Pantano had been in dangerous missions just a few days before. You have evidence chapter and verse about his outstanding character. He is not the kind of person who would kill without a reason. It just isn't accurate. And he had no reason. Sergeant Coburn's whole assumption about this case that permeates the letter is these were two innocent Iraqis who were going to be released. They weren't. They weren't. He's pissed off at the lieutenant—and we gave you Gillian's sworn statement where Coburn tells Gillian on the day of this mission, 'I hate the lieutenant, and I wish they'd take him out of here.' Well, he figured out a way to do it. He figured out a way to do it. He discredited the lieutenant, he discredited what the lieutenant has done. Maybe he believes it now, sir, but at the time he wrote the letter to his wife, he didn't report it. He didn't have the moral courage to report what he thought was a murder? He didn't have the moral courage over a month? In fact, he never did report it, sir. He never did report it. If he was truly—if he truly believed he had witnessed a murder, wouldn't he have reported it to somebody?"

The tension at the prosecution table seemed higher than I'd ever seen it.

"Sir," Gittins continued, speaking softly now, "what you have to remember is you can't import civilian standards into a combat situation. This isn't Chicago. This is Iraq, Indian country where bad guys do things like take you out and cut your head off, where they do things like shoot you in the head, behead you, cut off your limbs, set you on fire, and hang you from bridges, and that happened just a few days before this incident . . ."

No one in the room needed more details to picture the severed heads, the charred bodies hanging from those aquamarine steel bridge girders.

"The evidence you have, sir, shows that Lieutenant Pantano did go through the steps. He told these guys to stop twice. Gobles told you so under oath. Lieutenant Pantano told you so. It's in his statement. He told Stone Phillips about it. He's told ammo's cheap, sir. Empty the magazine. Ammo's cheap. Your life isn't."

Charlie Gittins breathed deeply, as if demonstrating the priceless value of life.

"The worst thing that could have happened to Lieutenant Pantano is that he was removed from his platoon. That was a punishment beyond words, because he was in combat with a platoon that loved him, that he loved, that he promised the families that he was going to bring their boys back. The best thing that could happen to Sergeant Coburn was that he got taken out of this platoon. That was the best possible thing that could happen to him."

Camp Lejeune
13 May 2005

Newly promoted Lieutenant Colonel Mark Winn submitted a sixteen-page report to 2nd Marine Division commander Major General Richard Huck, recommending that the charges be withdrawn.

Camp Lejeune
26 May 2005

Major General Huck dismissed all charges after reviewing Winn's report, as well as the findings of autopsies conducted on the exhumed remains of the two insurgents by the Armed Forces Institute of Pathology. The press release by the 2nd Marine Division announcing that I had been exonerated concluded:

"The best interests of 2nd Lt. Pantano and the government have been served by this process."

EPILOGUE

The day after the news of my exoneration I was called into the headquarters of the 2nd Marine Division. The white building was more
reminiscent of an antebellum mansion than a high-technology war-
fighting center. General Huck informed me by video link from Camp
Fallujah of his decision to dismiss all the charges. And he told me that
I would not be going back to 2/2. I was being transferred to my alma
mater, the 6th Marine Regiment, where I would pick up a platoon with
the 3rd Battalion that was preparing to go to Iraq. The battalion was
leaving for SASO training in California within the week and I needed
to start packing.

The chance to resume command of an infantry platoon was life-
affirming to a man whose professional identity was most proudly defined by his ability as a combat leader.

But I could not accept this tangible example that I had finally re-
gained the confidence of the Corps. So I felt deep sadness writing the
following letter:

1 June 2005

To: *Secretary of the Navy*
From: *Second Lieutenant Ilario Pantano /0302 USMC*
Via: *(1) Commanding Officer, 6th Marine Regiment*
    (2) Commanding General, 2d Marine Division, FMF
    (3) Commandant of the Marine Corps

Subj: *unconditional resignation of commission*
Ref: *(a) SECNAVINST 1920.6B*
    (b) MCO P1900.16E
    (c) DD Form 458 dtd 1 Feb 05
    (d) CG, 2d MarDiv ltr dtd 26 May 05

1. Pursuant to references (a) and (b), I respectfully request that the Secretary of the Navy accept the resignation of my commission as an officer in the United States Marine Corps. I understand that if my resignation is accepted that I will receive an Honorable characterization of service. I do not request to be tendered an appointment in the U.S. Marine Corps Reserve.

2. In reference (c), I was charged with offenses against the Uniform Code of Military Justice including, inter alia, premeditated murder. Following an Article 32 hearing, on 26–30 April 2005, the Commanding General, 2d Marine Division dismissed all charges against me, as reflected on reference (d). For the past year, my family and I have lived with the uncertainty of my future. I believe that the interests of my family and the Marine Corps would best be served by the acceptance of my unconditional resignation of my commission. I was meritoriously augmented as a result of my performance at the Basic School; my EAS, therefore, is "indefinite" and I serve at the pleasure of the President.

3. While I am satisfied that the charges against me had no merit and were dismissed as a result, a number of circumstances resulting from the process compel the conclusion that it is in both the Corps' and my interests that my resignation be granted:

    a. After I was charged, my photographs appeared frequently in the media. My name and likeness, and the allegations that I murdered "innocent Iraqis" all have been transmitted around the world and are available to Iraqi and third country national insurgents. If deployed back, I would represent a "high value target" to insurgents seeking to gain political, propaganda or military attention to their cause, while also attracting unnecessary additional danger to my Marines and myself in what is already an extremely dangerous place.

    b. As a result of my previous experience and the questioning of my judgment in a prior combat situation, my future presence in a combat unit would likely lead to *unwarranted scrutiny by both my superiors and subordinates of my actions in that already dangerous environment. Further, even if no actual additional scrutiny were applied, my Marines and I would have the specter that my decisions and actions would later be second-guessed, potentially leading to hesitation and unnecessary loss of life. I believe my presence in a combat unit under these circumstances would be detrimental to the morale and efficiency of the unit as well as present a palpable danger to the unit and its Marines.*

c. After I was charged with the murders of the two "innocent Iraqis," my family was subjected to threats to their lives over the Internet originating in Pakistan. As a result, at great personal expense, I was required to take extraordinary measures to ensure the security of my own home. I believe it would be unreasonable for me to be assigned away from my family while my family and I have been identified as targets of the enemies of the United States. Further, the emotional and psychological strain on my family for the year that the investigation was ongoing well exceeded the rigors of combat that I experienced. Continued military service as a result of this experience is not in my family's best interest, nor those of the Marine Corps, as my concerns about my family's safety are likely to weigh heavily on me any time I am separated from them.

4. Based upon the foregoing, I respectfully request that my unconditional resignation of my commission in the United States Marine Corps be accepted and that I not be tendered an appointment in the United States Marine Corps Reserve.

ILARIO PANTANO
2ndLt, USMC

Camp Lejeune
26 August 2005

On this date, I received my second Honorable Discharge from the United States Marine Corps.

GLOSSARY

ACF—Anti-Coalition Forces (sterile term abandoned by troops in favor of Muj, see below)

AK-47—7.62 mm, magazine-fed, Soviet-produced Iraqi assault rifle

ASR—Alternate Supply Route (multiple-lane highway)

AT-4—an antitank or antifortification shoulder-fired rocket

beehive round—an antipersonnel tank or artillery round that fires hundreds of sharp "flechettes"

BIAP—Baghdad International Airport

billet—assignment or job description

Bouncing Betty—pressure-sensitive antipersonnel land mine

C-130—four-engine cargo/troop transport plane

CAAT—Combined Anti-Armor Team, six to eight Humvees with heavy weapons

camelback—large water bladder carried on back (replaces canteens)

CAP—Combined Action Platoon (U.S. forces that train and fight beside Iraqi forces)

CI—counterintelligence

claymore—command-detonated antipersonnel mine

CO—commanding officer

COC—Combat Operations Center

cover—a Marine hat or helmet

deck—nautical (Marine) term for floor, ground

detcord—detonation cord, explosive compressed into a line to explode larger charges

Dragunov—7.62 mm, magazine-fed, Soviet sniper rifle with optical sight

EOD—Explosive Ordnance Disposal

fireside chat—informal briefing of troops in small settings or classrooms

Fitrep—Fitness Report, a regularly scheduled performance evaluation

flexi-cuff, flexcuffs—temporary plastic-strip handcuffs

FOB—Forward Operating Base, isolated outposts with minimal comforts and services

FRAGO—Fragmentary Order, a brief "who," "what," "when," "where" statement ("I got *fragged* with a mission.")

FX—field exercise

Hajji—derogatory (and often forbidden) military slang for Iraqi(s)

HESCO barrier—a collapsible blast-protection fortification, often filled with sand

HIET—Human Intelligence Exploitation Team

Humvee—High-mobility tactical vehicle, successor to the Jeep

Icom—small short-range tactical radio (walkie-talkie)

IED—improvised explosive device

ilum—illumination rounds, mortar or artillery, usually parachute flares

ING—Iraqi National Guard (formerly the Iraqi Civil Defense Corps)

IOC—Infantry Officer Course (Quantico, Va.)

IP—Iraqi National Police

KIA—Killed in Action

LAV-25—Light Armored Vehicle, armed with 25 mm automatic cannon

M-1A1—U.S. main battle tank

M-2—"Ma Deuce," .50 caliber heavy machine gun

M-240G—medium (7.62 mm) machine gun

M-4—collapsible-stock carbine version of the M-16

M-9—Beretta 9 mm semiautomatic pistol

M-14—7.62 mm magazine-fed assault rifle

M-16A4—5.56 mm magazine-fed assault rifle

M-203—breech-loaded, single-shot 40 mm grenade launcher attached to an M-16

M-249—see SAW below

M-40A1—7.62 mm bolt-action precision rifle with a 10 power scope

MEF—Marine Expeditionary Force (division augmented with aircraft and support assets)

MEU—Marine Expeditionary Unit

MK-19—40 mm automatic grenade launcher

MP—Military Police

MRE—Meals Ready to Eat (pouched field rations)

MRO—Marine Reported On (the subject of a fitness report)

MSPF—Maritime Special Purpose Force

MSR—Main Supply Route (multiple-lane highway)

Muj—generic military slang for insurgents that broadened from *mujahideen* (fighters of jihad) to include criminals, gangs, tribes, or anyone attacking Coalition forces

NCO—noncommissioned officer (corporal or sergeant)

NJP—nonjudicial punishment (forfeiture of pay, extra duty)

OCS—Officer Candidate School (Quantico, Va.)

OIF (I and II)—Operation Iraqi Freedom, 2003 to present

PES—Personnel Evaluation System

PK(M)—7.62 mm Soviet-design medium machine gun

QRF—Quick Reaction Force

RCT—Regimental Combat Team (three or more infantry battalions augmented with heavy assets such as tanks)

RIAT—Reportable Incident Assessment Team

ROE—Rules of Engagement

RPG—rocket-propelled grenade

RPK—7.62 mm Soviet-design squad automatic weapon variant of AK-47

5 S's and T—procedures for handling enemy detainees: Search, Segregate, Silence, Speed, Safeguard, and Tag

SASO—Security and Stability Operations

SAW—Squad Automatic Weapon, a light (5.56 mm) machine gun

SIGACT—Significant Action Events

SMAW—Shoulder-Launched Multipurpose Assault [rocket] Weapon

SMEAC—five-paragraph order (Situation, Mission, Execution, Administration and Logistics, Command and Control)

SNCO—staff noncommissioned officer (staff sergeant, gunnery sergeant, 1st sergeant, sergeant major)

SNO—Subject Named Officer

SOI—School of Infantry

SOP—Standard Operating Procedures

T-55, T-62—Soviet-built Iraqi main battle tanks

tac net—tactical radio network

TBS—The Basic School (Quantico, Va.)

TOW missile—Tube-Launched Optically Tracked Wire-Guided missile

tray rat(s)—tray rations: cooked, shelf-stable meals

up-armor—supplemental armor to protect troops in vehicles

utilities—Marine Corps combat/work fatigue uniforms

VBIED—vehicle-borne IED, a suicide car bomb

VCP—vehicle checkpoint

Warlords—2nd Battalion, 2nd Marine Regiment (2/2)

WIA—Wounded in Action

XO—executive officer (second in command)

Marine Corps infantry units (ascending size)

fire team: four riflemen (including one SAW-gunner)

squad: three fire teams

platoon: three squads and command group

company: three infantry platoons and a weapons platoon (total:150 men)

battalion: three rifle companies, weapons company, and H&S company (total: 800 men)

regiment: three or more battalions

division: three or more regiments

Marine Corps ranks (ascending order)

private (E-1)

private first class (E-2)

lance corporal (E-3)

corporal (E-4)

sergeant (E-5)

staff sergeant (E-6)

gunnery sergeant (E-7)

1st sergeant (E-8)

sergeant major (E-9)

warrant officer (CWO 1-4)
second lieutenant (0-1)
first lieutenant (0-2)
captain (0-3)
major (0-4)
lieutenant colonel (0-5)
colonel (0-6)
brigadier general (0-7)
major general (0-8)
lieutenant general (0-9)
general (0-10)

ACKNOWLEDGMENTS

When the time came to write this book, I asked the warrior I admire most, "What message do the American people need to hear from a boots-on-the-ground account?" Major Brian Neïl replied simply and without hesitation, as a commander should, "Let's start with Victory."

The countless Americans who supported Defend The Defenders and my family in our darkest hour understand the need for victory, and to you I am profoundly grateful.

The Warlords took the fight to the enemy from Tarawa to Fallujah. They fought while I was safely writing this book and others were sleeping peacefully in their beds. You are an instrument of our victory, and America owes you her thanks.

Lance Corporal Chris Johnson, Lance Corporals Mark Smith, Kettler, Jernigan, Simental, and all the wounded Warlords, thank you for your sacrifices so that others may live.

Staff Sergeant Jason Glew, diplomat and warrior, thank you for bringing our boys home when I no longer could.

The men of Easy 3: Corporal Aguirre, Lance Corporal Aladino, Lance Corporal Anderson, Corporal Andrado, Corporal Arjona, Lance Corporal Autie, Lance Corporal Baker, Corporal Braun, Lance Corporal Brown, Lance Corporal Chicas, Lance Corporal Cox, Lance Corporal Davis, Lance Corporal Dunham, Lance Corporal Fuentes, Corporal George, Lance Corporal Gillian, Doc Gobles, Lance Corporal Gueixeras, Lance Corporal Hurst, Lance Corporal Johnson C.,

Lance Corporal Johnson R., Corporal Magdaleno, Corporal Maloney, Lance Corporal Marion, Corporal Matchett, Corporal McPherson, Lance Corporal Perry, Lance Corporal Posada, Lance Corporal Sacchi, Lance Corporal Simonelli, Lance Corporal Sims, Lance Corporal Smith M., Lance Corporal Smith R., Corporal Stringham, Corporal Trent, Staff Sergeant Turner, Lance Corporal Williams, and of course, Sergeant "Stick" Word. You are my heroes and always will be.

And to all of your parents, whose faith in us never wavered, the greatest privilege of my life was being entrusted with your sons.

Captain "Big Cock" Weston, you kept us alive by pushing us hard. You kept me alive by never letting me feel forgotten.

Chaplain Eric Verhulst, thank you for ministering to our pain and for reminding us that our cause was just.

Lieutenant Colonel Kyser, Major Dixon, Lieutenant Colonel Detroux, and Major Warren for teaching us to "be the hunter not the hunted" and for having faith. Lieutenant Colonel West (Ret.), "for traveling through hell with a gasoline can" for your men. Colonel Morris (Ret.), for spreading the word, and Major Duncan (Ret.), for never letting the Corps forget where it came from.

The students and the instructors of OCC 182, TBS BOC 3-03, and IOC 1-04: you inspired me when I was among you, and you didn't leave me behind. Keep taking the fight to the enemy.

The "Head Hunters" of Scout Sniper Platoon (STA) 1/6: Gunny Howard, you've had my back since we were corporals; Gunny Crofts, thanks for putting a price on my head at SASO; Yoda and Loney, I read your posts out there and I know the rest of you had me under observation.

Hans, the Colonel, Chuck, Carlos, Liam, James, Deaton, Sergeant "O," and all the other misfits of 6th Marine TOW platoon: they say you can't pick your family, but we got lucky.

To the crew of the USS *Intrepid* Sea, Air & Space Museum, my second home: Scott, Donald, Larry and Maria, John, Jerry, Shirley, Doug, Seth, Kenny, Javier, Frank, Anthony, Rene, Felix, Jim, and of course Mr. Martinez.

John and Lynn, for being the first to jump into the breach, for remembering me on Veterans Day, and for introducing me to Tuck.

Haley, Michael, Ray, Jean, Lauren, Don, Lynn, Chris, June, Mike, Court, James, Faisal, Nancy, James, and Jake Dylan: for teaching me about the most important things in life.

My classmates at PS 124 and Horace Mann and to the teachers who took up arms to defend one of their own. Thanks to Alex, Jon, Chris, David, Clay, Justin, Gabe, Dan, Uncle David, and Noah for having faith in me. Hillary, as always, you went above and beyond, thank you.

Seth, thank you for serving your country with honor once, and after 9/11 putting the uniform back on to do it again in Sadr City.

Andy, Josh, Pam, and George, thank you for twenty years of love, friendship, and advice.

Steve Fishman, Rowan Scarborough, Kit Jarrell, Heidi Theiss, John Desantis, Roselee Papandrea, Brian Kates, Steve Cheng, Stone Phillips, and Dr. Michael Savage, thank you for trying to find the truth.

Sheriff Causey and the deputies of the New Hanover County Sheriff's Department, Officer Fey and the Wilmington Police Department, the Wilmington office of the FBI, and all of those in law enforcement who have kept our families safe while we are in the fight: thank you.

Darren, Andy, Byant, Eddie, Joe, Bob Jr., and Bob Sr., and the crew at Westside: thank you for burning a candle and looking out for my mom.

Matt, Sara, Tina, William, Jenny, Steve, Ian, Tim, Mike, Ellen, Amy, Ramsey, Joby, Lieutenant C., Kelly, Frank, Debbie, Libby, Chris, Sean, Ricci, Anthony, Hillary, Todd, Hillary, Jack, Boo, Ellen, Randy, Veronica, Jeff, Tony, Laney, Holly, Linnea, Lenny, Jolin, Avery, Mrs. Cook and Mrs. Spencer, Diane, and all the members of the Wilmington community who extended true Southern hospitality and made us feel like family during a very difficult time.

Harold, Charlie, Dave, George, John, and all the heroes at Post 10: thank you for your service to this country.

Congressman Walter B. Jones: you lead from the front. God bless you, sir.

Larry, Robert, Ellen, Larry, Marie, Jennifer, Richard, Connie, Furf, Nicole, Monique, Sadie, Linnet, Edwin, Yonald, Christina, Tim, Holly, Chris, Billie, Tiffany, Peggy, Zane, Gabrielle, Rita, Ian, Meghan, Greg, Katrina, HB, Norma, Darcy, Debbie, Randy, Italia, Angela, Maria, Mario, Angelo, Giovanni, Illenia, Norma, Debora, Cologero, Simone, Marco, and of course Uncle John, who by fighting and flying in Vietnam and every war since has been an example of heroism to us all.

Jeff, whose love, loyalty, and ferocity define "No better friend, no worse enemy." Billy, friend, gunfighter, and renaissance man. Damon, my advocate and my hawk. J.R., my consigliere, my partner, and my brother. I look forward to our next adventures.

Mel Berger, my super agent at William Morris: thank you for your expert counsel in bringing this project to fruition.

Kevin Smith, my editor extraordinaire, who guided us all through minefields with the help of copy editor Tom Pitoniak, Josh, Rod, and the crew at Pocket Books.

Louise Burke and Mary Matalin for having the guts to want to tell this story and for having the wisdom to tell it right. Thank you for your faith and support.

Oliver North and James Carville, thank you for being the men in the arena and doing the deeds that others can only talk about. *Semper Fidelis.*

Malcolm McConnell, my writing partner, whose pedigree as a meat-eater was exceeded only by his skill and patience as a master craftsman: thank you for your service to our country and for sharing your home and your family with me. We did it, Malcolm, we told the story that needed to be told and *this* lieutenant is grateful. Special thanks to your lovely wife, Carol, for her help and her service to our country and also to her beautiful mother, LaVerne.

Charlie Gittins and Phil Stackhouse, Brandon Bolling, and Courtney Trombly, you wrote this book as much as anybody, and without your tireless work and monstrous effort, the ending wouldn't have been as good. Thank you for retipping the scales and resetting the bar. I now have the dubious privilege of counting four fantastic defense attorneys as my friends. Thanks to Christine for shooting straight and keeping us on track and to Mr. Joshua for keeping us in the fight.

Howard, Ruth, Damon, Jeffrey, Susan, Gus, Jane, Warren, and Robert, your unwavering strength, love, and kindness kept our little boat afloat. Chris, Missy, Dotti, Claudia, and Jill #2, you stood with us as we jumped into the breach and supported our every move. Casey, thanks to you and your team at Firm Design for putting a face on DTD.

Lynda, you put your life on hold to stand up for me in ways that are truly amazing. Thank you for your unconditional love and support for all these years.

My beautiful wife, Jill, who has long endured ordeal after ordeal as her husband sought to do the right thing. Thank you, my love. Your support fuels me and your embrace protects me. Thank you for the precious gift of our two sons and for the boundless love that makes them so radiant. Thank you for your courage in the hard times behind us and in those yet to come. I know this wasn't what you bargained for, but don't worry, I have another great idea . . .

My sons, my two hearts, I had hoped and prayed that you would know none of this war, but that was not to be. I chose to fight because of love and to show you by example that there are things worth sacrificing for. To protect you, our family, and our country I would do it all again. All of it.

My father, whose gentle assurances I strive to live up to every day: you are my role model, my protector, and my friend. I can only hope to be a fraction of the father to my sons that you have been to me. Their Nonno is my greatest gift to them. *Ti voglio bene sempre.*

My mother, you have shown the world that there is no stronger force in nature than a mother's love for her child. I have had the special fortune of knowing that since the day I was born. Thank you for teaching me how to be an artist and a warrior, and making damn sure I was good at both.

And Mom, thank you for enduring all of my wars with the grace, courage, and dignity befitting the mother of a Marine.